NEW KING JAMES TOPICAL INDEX

OLD AND NEW TESTAMENTS

REVISED EDITION

INCLUDES TOPICAL CONCORDANCE

Terry R. Trammell, MTh.

WestBow Press books may be ordered through booksellers or by contacting:

WestBow Press
A Division of Thomas Nelson & Zondervan
1663 Liberty Drive
Bloomington, IN 47403
www.westbowpress.com
1 (866) 928-1240

ISBN: 978-1-4497-1944-9 (sc)
ISBN: 978-1-4497-4688-9 (e)

Library of Congress Control Number: 2011931402

Print information available on the last page.

WestBow Press rev. date: 05/31/2016

First

Covenant

(Old Testament)

How to Read & Use the Concordance

Example:

Aaron – **6**-1b8;1c;1c1,5-6; **9**-1a13;1b1; **10**-1b1; **11**-2b,2b1;3b2,3;3c2;3d3

In doing a search for a word, as in this example, I am using the name of "Aaron." Since we are looking for "Aaron," let's go to the concordance to see where we can find the name. The first place where "Aaron" is located in the Old Testament is **6**-1b8 as we can see above in the example. The bold number "**6**" is the page number in the Topical Index where "Aaron" is located. Now we look in Section "1", then Section "B" then in Number "8" to locate "Aaron." In the example below, I have underlined where "1b8" is located. So, we can see that the first place where "Aaron" is located in the Old Testament Topical Index is in Exodus 4:18—4:31. The second location of "Aaron" is Page 6, Section 1, Subsection c. Then again on Page 6, Section 1, then Section C, then in Numbers 1,5-6. In the example below, "Aaron" is located on Page **6.** In the example above, the bold numbers are ALL page numbers where "Aaron" is located in the Topical Index.

IMPORTANT: The semicolons separate the Sections. The Commas separate the Number locations and subsections. The bold numbers separate the page numbers.

EXODUS
(1:01—40:38)

1. **The Life & Times of Israel in Egypt** **(1:01—12:30)**

   A. Family of Israel Enslaved in Egypt **(1:01—1:22)**
   1. Suffering of Israel's Descendants (1:01—1:14)
   2. King of Egypt Commands Death of Hebrew Males (1:15—1:22)

   B. Moses Chosen by God to Lead Israel **(2:01—4:31)**
   1. The Birth of Moses (2:01—2:10)
   2. Moses Kills an Egyptian (2:11—2:15)
   3. Moses Flees to Midian (2:16—2:20)
   4. Moses Marries Zipporah (2:21—2:25)
   5. Moses Meets God at Mount Horeb (3:01—3:22)
   6. God Prepares Moses for Egypt (4:01—4:13)
   7. God Angered at Moses (4:14—4:17)
   8. Moses & Aaron Speak to Israelites in Egypt (4:18—4:31)

TABLE of CONTENTS

	BOOK of the BIBLE	SCRIPTURE TOPIC	PAGE #
I.	GENESIS	The Account of Creation	1
		Creation's Beginning	1
		The Life and Times of Adam & Eve	1
		Adam & Eve	1
		The Sons of Adam	1
		The Genealogy of Adam	1
		The Life & Times of Noah	1
		The Flooding of the Earth	1
		The Genealogy of the Sons of Noah	1
		Tower Called Babel Built in Shinar	1
		The Life & Times of Abraham	1
		Abram to Become a Great Nation	1
		Abram & Lot Separate	1
		Abram Promised a Son	2
		Judgment Comes to Sodom & Gomorrah	2
		The Birth and Near Sacrifice of Isaac	2
		Isaac Takes A Bride	2
		The Death of Abraham	2
		The Life & Times of Isaac	2
		The Genealogy of Isaac	2
		Isaac Deceives Abimelech	2
		Jacob Steals Esau's Blessing	2
		The Life & Times of Jacob	2
		Jacob's Genealogy Begins	2
		Jacob Returns to Canaan	3
		The Genealogy of Esau	3
		The Life & Times of Joseph	3
		Joseph's Days of Slavery	3
		The Story of Judah & Tamar	3
		Joseph Imprisoned	3
		Joseph Promoted Governor Over Egypt	3
		Joseph & Brothers Reunite in Egypt	3
		Israel & Family Move to Egypt	4
		Jacob & Joseph Die in Egypt	4
II.	EXODUS	The Life & Times of Israel in Egypt	4
		Family of Israel Enslaved in Egypt	4
		Moses Chosen by God to Lead Israel	4
		The *LORD* Sends Moses & Aaron to Pharaoh	4
		The Ten Plagues of Egypt	4
		The Passover	5
		Israel Departs Egypt After 430 Years; Journeys to Mount Sinai	5
		Departure from Egypt	5
		Escaping By Way of the Red Sea	5
		Israelites Dissatisfied	5
		The Israelites at Mount Sinai	5
		Israel Receives the Law of God	5
		The Tabernacle Instituted	6
		The Breaking of the Law	6
		The Construction of the Tabernacle	6
III.	LEVITICUS	The Way to Worship a Holy God	7
		Procedures for the Offering	7
		Requirements for the Priests	7

		Procedures for the People	7
		Procedures for the Altar	8
		Living A Life Pleasing to God	8
		Laws Concerning the Standards for the People	8
		Laws Concerning the Standards for the Priests	8
		Laws Concerning Festivals & Seasons	8
		Laws Concerning Being Obedient to God	8
IV.	NUMBERS	The Preparation of Israel at Mount Sinai	8
		Israel's First Census	8
		The Function of the Levites	8
		Sanctification of the People	9
		First Journey to the Promised Land	9
		Concerning the Promised Land	9
		Aaron & Miriam Develop Problems with Moses	9
		The Rebellion Against God	9
		God's Discipline Upon the People	9
		Miscellaneous Laws	9
		Rebellion Against Moses	9
		Obligations of the Levities	9
		The Next Generation	10
		Second Journey to the Promised Land	10
		The History of Balaam	10
		Israel's Second Census	10
		Procedures for Offerings	10
		Revenge on the Midianites	10
		Trans-Jordan Settled by the Two-and-a-Half Tribes	10
		Israel Camps on the Plains of Moab	10
		The Division of the Land of Canaan	11
V.	DEUTERONOMY	Moses Gives Inspirational Speech	11
		A Historical Review	11
		Rules for Godly Living	11
		Law Set Before the Children of Israel	11
		Review of the Ten Commandments	11
		The Command to Love The *LORD* Your God	11
		Regulations of Worship	11
		Regulations for Ruling	12
		Regulations for Human Relationships	12
		Consequences of Obedience & Disobedience	12
		Moses Calls for the Obedience from the Children of Israel	12
		God's Call to Obedience	12
		Moses Commissions Joshua to Replace Him	12
		Change in Leadership	12
VI.	JOSHUA	Israel Enters Canaan, the Promised Land	12
		Joshua Takes Charge	12
		Crossing the Jordan River	13
		Conquering the Land of Canaan	13
		Joshua Conquers the Central Part of Canaan	13
		Joshua & Israel's Conquest of Southern Canaan	13
		Joshua & Israel's Conquest of Northern Canaan	13
		Review of the Conquests of the Israelites	13
		The Dividing of Canaan, the Promised Land	13
		The *Twelve* Tribes Receive Their Inheritance	13
		Cities of Refuge Appointed	14
		Joshua's Farewell Address to the Trans-Jordan Tribes of Israel	14
		Joshua's Farewell Address to the Rulers of Israel	14

VII.	JUDGES	The Introduction of Israel's Disobedience	14
		Israel's Unfinished Job Concerning Canaan	14
		Disobedience & Defeat of Israel	14
		Israel Rescued by the Judges	14
		The First Period of Judges	14
		The Second Period of the Judges	14
		The Third Period of the Judges	14
		The Fourth Period of the Judges	14
		The Fifth Period of the Judges	15
		The Sixth Period of the Judges	15
		Israel's Apostasy During the Period of the Judges	15
		Micah & the Migration of the Danites	15
		The Benjamite War	15
VIII.	RUTH	The Unusual Relationship Between Ruth & Mother-in-Law Naomi	15
		Ruth's Loyalty to Naomi	15
		Ruth's Right to Glean Kinsman Field	16
		Naomi Generated Plan for Ruth	16
		Boaz Redeems & Marries Ruth	16
IX.	1st SAMUEL	Samuel, the Last Judge of Israel	16
		Samuel's Early Life & Calling	16
		The Ministry of Samuel	16
		Israel's War with the Philistines	16
		Israel Demands for Them a King	16
		Saul—Israel's First King	16
		The Rejection of Saul by The *LORD* for Disobedience	17
		David—Saul's Replacement	17
		David Chosen as King	17
		The Rise of David	17
		David Flees; Goes Into Exile	17
		David Seeks Refuge in Philistine Territory	17
X.	2nd SAMUEL	The Crowning of David Over the Kingdom	18
		David Crowned King	18
		David Crowned King Over All the Tribes of Israel	18
		David Victorious Over Many Nations Around Him	18
		David's Transgressions as King	18
		The Crimes of King David	18
		Upheaval in the House of David	18
		Absalom's Rebellion	18
		Upheaval in David's Kingdom	19
		David's Conclusion in the Kingdom	19
XI.	1st KINGS	The Kingdom United	19
		Solomon Replaces David, His Father as King	19
		The Wisdom of Solomon	19
		Solomon's Temple	20
		The Highs & Lows of Solomon's Reign	20
		Solomon's Demise	20
		The Kingdom Divided; Prophecy of Ahijah Comes to Pass	20
		Rehoboam Replaces Solomon, His Father as King	20
		Jeroboam Becomes King Over Israel	20
		Jeroboam's Judgment	20
		Chronicle of the Rulers in Judah & Israel	20
		The Ministry of Elijah, the Prophet of God	20
		The Reign of King Ahab	21

		The Reign of Jehoshaphat	21
		The Reign of Ahaziah	21
XII.	2nd KINGS	The Kingdom Divided	21
		The Reign of Ahaziah	21
		The Ministry of Elisha	21
		The Chronicles of the Kings of Israel & Judah	21
		The Deportation of Judah to Assyria	22
		The Surviving Kingdom of Judah	22
		The Kings of Judah	22
XIII.	1st CHRONICLES	The Genealogy from Adam to David	23
		Adam to Noah	23
		Noah to Abraham	23
		Abraham to Jacob (Israel)	23
		Jacob to David	23
		The Family of David	24
		The Genealogy of Israel (Jacob)	24
		Babylonian Exiles Return to Jerusalem	24
		David's Reign Over All Israel Lasts Forty Years	24
		David's Rise to the Throne	24
		The "Ark of the Covenant" Brought to Jerusalem	24
		The Wars of David	24
		Satan Moved Upon David to Take A Census of Israel	25
		David Makes Building Preparations for the Temple	25
XIV.	2nd CHRONICLES	Solomon's Reign Over All Israel Last Forty Years	25
		Solomon Begins His Reign Over Israel	25
		The Temple Solomon Built for the *LORD*	25
		The Temple Is Dedicated to The *LORD*	25
		Solomon's Popularity	25
		Kings of Judah Since the Death of Solomon to the Exile (931—597 B.C.)	26
		Rise of Rehoboam, Son of Solomon	26
		The Kings of Judah & Their Wickedness	26
XV.	EZRA	Return of the First Group of Exiles	27
		Zerubbabel Leads the First Group	27
		Construction of the Temple Undertaken	27
		Return of the Second Group of Exiles 80 Years Later (456 B.C.)	27
		Ezra Leads the Second Group	27
		The Reformations of Ezra at Jerusalem	28
XVI.	NEHEMIAH	Rebuilding the Walls of Jerusalem	28
		Nehemiah Returns to Jerusalem	28
		Beginning of the Rebuilding	28
		The Rebuilding Begins	28
		The Covenant Renewed	28
		The "Book of the Law" from Moses	28
		The Cities of Judah Repopulated	28
XVII.	ESTHER	The People of God in Dangerous Times	29
		King Ahasuerus Divorces Queen Vashti	29
		The Discovery of Esther	29
		Jews Threatened with Annihilation	29
		God Delivers His People from Annihilation	29
		Mordecai's Rise to Royalty	29

XVIII.	JOB	Job & His Troublesome Times	29
		The Testing of Job	29
		God Allows Satan to Attack Everything Except Job's Life	29
		Satan Commences His Attack Upon Job	29
		Job's Conversations with His Three Friends	30
		Round One of Conversations	30
		Round Two of Conversations	30
		Round Three of Conversations	30
		The Three Friends of Job Are Criticized	30
		Elihu Enters the Conversations	30
		Job Is Answered by God	30
		God Asks Job a Series of Questions	30
		The Final State of Job	31
		The Restoration of Job	31
XIX.	PSALMS	BOOK—1 (Psalm 1 – 41)	31
		BOOK—2 (Psalm 42 – 72)	32
		BOOK—3 (Psalm 73 – 89)	32
		BOOK—4 (Psalm 90 – 106)	33
		BOOK—5 (Psalm 107 – 150)	33
XX.	HEBREW ALPHABET		**33**
XXI.	PROVERBS	Fatherly Advice to the Younger Generation	35
		How to Gain Wisdom	35
		The Principles of Attaining Wisdom	35
		Difference Between Wisdom & Foolish Actions	35
		Practical Wisdom for Godly Living	35
		The Proverbs of Wisdom	35
		Wisdom for Leaders & Potential Leaders	36
		Wisdom Concerning Relationships	36
		Wisdom Concerning Actions	36
		Personal Words of Wisdom	36
XXII.	ECCLESIASTES	Solomon Speaks on His Life's Experiences	36
		The Uselessness of the Cycles of Life	36
		The Design of Life by The *LORD*	36
		Different Circumstances in Life	36
		Practical Wisdom of Solomon	37
XXIII.	SONG OF SOLOMON	The Relationship Between Solomon & the Shulammite Woman	37
		Day of the Wedding	37
		Courtship Memories	37
		Engagement Memories	37
		Shulammite Woman Has Troubling Dream	37
		The Bride's Beauty Praised	37
		The Tender Appeal of the Bride	37
		Love's Power	37
XXIV.	ISAIAH	Message of Divine Judgment	38
		Condemnation of the Children of Israel	38
		The Coming of the Messiah	38
		Judgment Against Heathen Nations	38
		The Future End-time Tribulation & The Kingdom	38
		The Devastation of the Earth	38
		The Condemnation of Israel & Judah	39
		Events During the Reign of King Hezekiah of Judah	39
		Message of Divine Comfort	39

		The Awesomeness of God	39
		Israel's Future Redeemer	39
		The Millennial Kingdom	40
		The Requirements for the Blessing	40
XXV.	JEREMIAH	The Judgment of God Upon Judah	40
		The *LORD* Calls Jeremiah to be a Prophet	40
		Jeremiah Prophesies Against Judah	40
		False Religion of Judah	40
		Judah Breaks Covenant with God	41
		Jeremiah Recommissioned	41
		Judah's Leaders Face Accusations from Jeremiah	41
		Judah Goes Into Captivity	41
		Hope of Resurrection of Judah Is Promised	41
		Restoration After Seventy Years of Tribulation	41
		Events "Before" the Destruction of Jerusalem	42
		Events "After" the Destruction of Jerusalem	42
		Jeremiah's Prophecies Against Other Nations	42
		Prophecies Against Other Nations	42
		Historical Events of the Fall of Jerusalem	43
XXVI.	LAMENTATIONS	Jerusalem Lies in Desolation	43
		Jerusalem Lies Bare of Any People	43
		How God Almighty Feels About Sin	43
		The Anger of the *LORD* Is Quenched	43
		Jeremiah Prays for Restoration of the People	43
XXVII.	EZEKIEL	Doom & Gloom Foreseen	43
		The Call & Commission of Ezekiel	43
		The Visions Given by God to Ezekiel	43
		Ezekiel's Commission to Judah	44
		Prophetic Visions Concerning Judah	44
		The Judgment & Punishment Is Absolute	44
		The Unfaithfulness of Israel	45
		The Rebellion of Israel	45
		Messages Against Foreign Nations	45
		Prophecies Against Other Nations	45
		Messages of the Hope for Israel	45
		The Restoration of Israel	45
		The War of Israel in the Latter Days	46
		A Glimpse of Israel in the Millennial Kingdom	46
		Vision of a New Temple	46
		The Temple—The *LORD*'s Dwelling Place	46
XXVIII.	DANIEL	Daniel's Life Under King Nebuchadnezzar	47
		The Life of Daniel, the Prophet of God	47
		The First Dream of King Nebuchadnezzar, King of Babylon	47
		King Nebuchadnezzar's Second Dream	47
		The Great Feast of King Belshazzar	48
		Daniel's Life Under King Darius	48
		The Plot Against Daniel	48
		The Visions of Daniel	48
		End-time Events Revealed to Daniel in Prophecies	48
		Prophecies Concerning the North & South Kings	48
XXIX.	HOSEA	The Faithful Husband & The Adulterous Wife	49
		Parallel Relationship Between Hosea's Wife Gomer & Israel	49
		The Faithful *LORD* & The Adulterous Israel	49

		The Case of the Adulterous Israel	49
		Israel's Restoration to the *LORD*	49
XXX.	JOEL	The Land That Was Laid Waste	49
		Introduction to Joel	49
		Characteristics of the Wasteland	49
XXXI.	AMOS	The Words of The *LORD* Spoken to Amos, the Prophet	50
		Introduction to Amos	50
		Prophecies of Judgment on the Neighbors of Israel	50
		The Judgment Messages of Amos, the Prophet	50
		Visions of Judgment	50
XXXII.	OBADIAH	The Destruction of Edom	50
		Edom's Destruction Is Coming	50
		Accusations Against Edom	50
		Restoration of Israel	50
XXXIII.	JONAH	The *LORD* Gives Jonah A Message	51
		Jonah Flees His Mission	51
		Jonah Fulfills His Mission	51
XXXIV.	MICAH	Prophecies of Judgment on Samaria & Judah	51
		The Introduction to Micah	51
		The Coming Judgment on the Two Capitals	51
		Judgment Upon the Leaders of Israel	51
		A Message of Accusation	51
XXXV.	NAHUM	The Introduction to Nahum, the Prophet	52
		The Majesty of the *LORD*	*52*
		The Character of the *LORD*	52
		The Judgment of the *LORD*	52
XXXVI.	HABAKKUK	Introduction to Habakkuk	52
		Conversation Between God & Habakkuk	52
		The Concerns of Habakkuk	52
		The Praises of Habakkuk	52
XXXVII.	ZEPHANIAH	Introduction to Zephaniah	52
		The Prophetic Judgments by Zephaniah	52
		The Day of The *LORD*'s Wrath	52
		The Day of the *LORD*'s Hope	53
XXXVIII.	HAGGAI	The *LORD* Gives Message To Haggai For Governor Zerubbabel & High Priest Jeshua	53
		The Calling for the Reconstruction of the Temple	53
		Encouragement to Complete the Temple	53
XXXIX.	ZECHARIAH	Encouraging Messages to Continue to Rebuild the Temple	53
		A Call to Repentance	53
		The Visions of Zechariah	53
		Encouraging Words of Zechariah	53
		Messages Concerning Israel's Future	53
		First Message: Israel Rejects Their Messiah	53
		Second Message: The Reign of the Coming Messiah	54

GENESIS
(1:01—50:26)

1. **The Account of Creation** **(1:01—2:03)**
   A. Creation's Beginning (1:01—2:03)

2. **The Life and Times of Adam & Eve** **(2:04—5:32)**
   A. Adam & Eve **(2:04—3:24)**
   1. Adam & Eve (2:04—2:07)
   2. Experiencing the Garden (2:08—2:25)
   3. The Downfall of Adam & Eve (3:01—3:24)

   B. The Sons of Adam **(4:01—4:26)**
   1. The Death of Abel by Cain (4:01—4:15)
   2. The Genealogy of Cain (4:16—4:24)
   3. Seth: Adam's New Son (4:25—4:26)

   C. The Genealogy of Adam **(5:01—5:32)**
   1. Adam's Children (5:01—5:32)

3. **The Life & Times of Noah** **(6:01—11:32)**
   A. The Flooding of the Earth **(6:01—8:22)**
   1. The Wickedness of Man & the Patience of God (6:01—6:12)
   2. Noah Builds an Ark (6:13—6:22)
   3. God's Judgment Upon Man by Flood (7:01—7:24)
   4. Noah & Family Saved Through Flood (8:01—8:19)
   5. God's Covenant with Man (8:20—8:22)

   B. The Genealogy of the Sons of Noah **(9:01—10:32)**
   1. The Rainbow—The Sign of the Covenant (9:01—9:17)
   2. The Sons of Noah (9:18—9:29)
   3. The Sons of Japheth (10:01—10:05)
   4. The Sons of Ham (10:06—10:07)
   5. The Sons of Cush (10:08—10:12)
   6. The Sons of Mizraim (10:13—10:14)
   7. The Sons of Canaan (10:15—10:20)
   8. The Sons of Shem (10:21—10:32)

   C. Tower Called Babel Built in Shinar **(11:01—11:32)**
   1. Tower Called Babel (11:01—11:09)
   2. The Genealogy of Shem (11:10—11:26)
   3. The Genealogy of Terah (11:27—11:32)

4. **The Life & Times of Abraham** **(12:01—25:18)**
   A. Abram to Become a Great Nation **(12:01—12:20)**
   1. God Makes Promises to Abram (12:01—12:09)
   2. Abram Dwells in Egypt (12:10—12:20)

   B. Abram & Lot Separate **(13:01—14:24)**
   1. Abram in the Land of Canaan (13:01—13:18)
   2. Lot Rescued by Abram (14:01—14:17)

3. Melchizedek Blesses Abram (14:18—14:24)

C. Abram Promised a Son **(15:01—17:27)**

1. The Covenant of God (15:01—15:21)
2. Trouble Comes to Canaan Through Hagar (16:01—16:16)
3. Abram Becomes Abraham by Circumcision (17:01—17:27)

D. Judgment Comes to Sodom & Gomorrah **(18:01—20:18)**

1. The Son of the Blessing (18:01—18:15)
2. Abraham Intercedes for Sodom (18:16—18:33)
3. The Carnality of Sodom (19:01—19:11)
4. The Destruction of Sodom & Gomorrah (19:12—19:29)
5. The Seduction of Lot (19:30—19:35)
6. The Sons of Lot by His Daughters (19:36—19:38)
7. Abimelech Deceived by Abraham (20:01—20:18)

E. The Birth and Near Sacrifice of Isaac **(21:01—23:20)**

1. The Birth of Isaac (21:01—21:07)
2. Abraham Casts Out Hagar & Ishmael (21:08—21:21)
3. Abraham's Treaty with Abimelech (21:22—21:34)
4. Abraham Tested for Obedience (22:01—22:19)
5. The Genealogy of Nahor (22:20—22:24)
6. Sarah Dies at 127 Years Old; Buried in Canaan (23:01—23:20)

F. Isaac Takes A Bride **(24:01—24:67)**

1. Rebekah Becomes Isaac's Bride (24:01—24:67)

G. The Death of Abraham **(25:01—25:18)**

1. Abraham Takes Keturah as His Bride (25:01—25:06)
2. Abraham Dies at Age of 175; Buried in Canaan (25:07—25:11)
3. The Genealogy of Ishmael (25:12—25:16)
4. Ishmael Dies at Age of 137 (25:17—25:18)

5. <u>The Life & Times of Isaac</u> **(25:19—28:09)**

A. The Genealogy of Isaac **(25:19—25:34)**

1. The Genealogy of Isaac (25:19—25:28)
2. Jacob Deceives Esau (25:29—25:34)

B. Isaac Deceives Abimelech **(26:01—26:35)**

1. Isaac Deceives Abimelech (26:01—26:35)

C. Jacob Steals Esau's Blessing **(27:01—28:09)**

1. Jacob Receives the Blessing (27:01—27:29)
2. Esau Receives No Blessing (27:30—27:40)
3. Jacob Flees to Haran (27:41—28:05)
4. Esau Takes a Bride Names Mahalath (28:06—28:09)

6. <u>The Life & Times of Jacob</u> **(28:10—36:43)**

A. Jacob's Genealogy Begins **(28:10—30:43)**

1. Jacob Makes Vow to God (28:10—28:22)
2. Jacob Meets Rachel (29:01—29:14)

3. Jacob Takes Leah As His Bride (29:15—29:27)
4. Jacob Takes Rachel As His Bride (29:28—29:30)
5. The Genealogy of Jacob (29:31—30:24)
6. Jacob's Prosperity (30:25—30:43)

B. Jacob Returns to Canaan **(31:01—35:29)**
1. Jacob Flees from Haran (31:01—31:21)
2. Jacob Pursued by Laban & His Sons (31:22—31:42)
3. The Covenant Made at Galeed (31:43—31:55)
4. Jacob Waits for Esau at Mahanaim (32:01—32:21)
5. Jacob Wrestles with God (32:22—32:32)
6. Jacob Meets Esau at Mahanaim (33:01—33:17)
7. Jacob Arrives in Shechem (33:18—33:20)
8. Shechem Defiles Dinah (34:01—34:24)
9. Sons of Jacob Revenge the Rape of Dinah (34:25—34:31)
10. God Tells Jacob to Return to Bethel (35:01—35:15)
11. Rachel Dies; Benjamin Born (35:16—35:22a)
12. The Twelve Sons of Jacob (35:22b—35:26)
13. Isaac Dies at Age 180 (35:27—35:29)

C. The Genealogy of Esau **(36:01—36:43)**
1. Esau's Lineage (36:01—36:14)
2. The Chiefs of the Sons of Esau, Now Edom (36:15—36:19)
3. The Sons of Seir, the Horite (36:20—36:30)
4. The Kings Who Reigned in Edom (36:31—36:39)
5. The Chiefs of Esau (36:40—36:43)

7. **<u>The Life & Times of Joseph</u>** **(37:01—50:26)**

A. Joseph's Days of Slavery **(37:01—37:36)**
1. Joseph's Prophetic Dream (37:01—37:11)
2. Joseph Goes Into Slavery for Twenty Shekels of Silver (37:12—37:36)

B. The Story of Judah & Tamar **(38:01—38:30)**
1. Tamar Seduces Judah (38:01—38:30)

C. Joseph Imprisoned **(39:01—40:23)**
1. Potiphar Buys Joseph as a Slave (39:01—39:23)
2. Joseph Interprets Butler & Baker's Dream (40:01—40:23)

D. Joseph Promoted Governor Over Egypt **(41:01—41:57)**
1. Joseph Interprets Pharaoh's Dream (41:01—41:36)
2. Joseph Promoted Second-in-Charge over Egypt (41:37—41:57)

E. Joseph & Brothers Reunite in Egypt **(42:01—45:28)**
1. Joseph's Ten Brothers Go to Egypt (42:01—42:24)
2. Ten Brothers Return to Jacob (42:25—42:38)
3. Benjamin Goes to Egypt with Brothers (43:01—43:34)
4. The Mystery of Joseph's Silver Cup (44:01—44:17)
5. Judah Pleads for Benjamin's Life (44:18—44:34)

6. Joseph's Identity Revealed (45:01—45:08)
7. The Brothers Return for Jacob in Canaan (45:09—45:28)

F. Israel & Family Move to Egypt **(46:01—47:26)**

1. Israel Travels to Egypt (46:01—46:27)
2. Israel Settles in the Land of Goshen at Age 130 (46:28—47:12)
3. Famine Comes to Egypt (47:13—47:26)

G. Jacob & Joseph Die in Egypt **(47:27—50:26)**

1. Joseph Makes a Promise to Jacob (47:27—47:31)
2. Jacob Blesses Ephraim & Manasseh (48:01—48:22)
3. Jacob Predicts Future over His Sons (49:01—49:28)
4. Jacob (Israel) Dies at Age 147; Buried with Abraham (49:29—49:33)
5. The Mourning over Jacob (50:01—50:14)
6. Joseph Forgives His Brothers (50:15—50:21)
7. Joseph Dies at Age 110 (50:22—50:26)

EXODUS
(1:01—40:38)

1. <u>**The Life & Times of Israel in Egypt**</u> **(1:01—12:30)**

A. Family of Israel Enslaved in Egypt **(1:01—1:22)**

1. Suffering of Israel's Descendants (1:01—1:14)
2. King of Egypt Commands Death of Hebrew Males (1:15—1:22)

B. Moses Chosen by God to Lead Israel **(2:01—4:31)**

1. The Birth of Moses (2:01—2:10)
2. Moses Kills an Egyptian (2:11—2:15)
3. Moses Flees to Midian (2:16—2:20)
4. Moses Marries Zipporah (2:21—2:25)
5. Moses Meets God at Mount Horeb (3:01—3:22)
6. God Prepares Moses for Egypt (4:01—4:13)
7. God Angered at Moses (4:14—4:17)
8. Moses & Aaron Speak to Israelites in Egypt (4:18—4:31)

C. The *LORD* Sends Moses & Aaron to Pharaoh **(5:01—7:13)**

1. Moses & Aaron's First Meeting (5:01—5:05)
2. No Straw for Bricks (5:06—5:21)
3. The *LORD*'s Promise of Deliverance (6:01—6:13)
4. The Descendants of Jacob, Called Israel (6:14—6:27)
5. Aaron—God's Prophet, Moses' Spokesperson (6:28—7:07)
6. Rod of Aaron Perform Miracles (7:08—7:13)

D. The Ten Plagues of Egypt **(7:14—11:10)**

1. First Plague: Water Becomes Blood (7:14—7:25)
2. Second Plague: Frogs Overtake the Land (8:01—8:15)
3. Third Plague: Dust Becomes Lice (8:16—8:19)
4. Fourth Plague: Swarms of Flies (8:20—8:32)

5. Fifth Plague: Livestock Stricken with Pestilence (9:01—9:07)
6. Sixth Plague: Boils Break Out Into Sores (9:08—9:12)
7. Seventh Plague: Fire Mingles with Hail (9:13—9:35)
8. Eighth Plague: East Wind Brings the Locust (10:01—10:20)
9. Ninth Plague: Three Days of Darkness (10:21—10:29)
10. Firstborn of Egyptians Declared to Die (11:01—11:10)

E. The Passover **(12:01—12:30)**

1. Passover Began on the 10th of Nisan (12:01—12:28)
2. Tenth Plague: Firstborn of Egyptian Struck (12:29—12:30)

2. <u>Israel Departs Egypt After 430 Years; Journeys to Mount Sinai</u> **(12:31—18:27)**

A. Departure from Egypt **(12:31—13:16)**

1. The Exodus (12:31—12:42)
2. Regulations for the Passover (12:43—12:51)
3. Consecration of the Firstborn (13:01—13:02)
4. Feast of Unleavened Bread (13:03—13:10)
5. The Regulations of the Firstborn (13:11—13:16)

B. Escaping By Way of the Red Sea **(13:17—15:21)**

1. Detour Through the Wilderness (13:17—13:22)
2. The *LORD* Parts the Red Sea (14:01—14:20)
3. The *LORD* Closes the Red Sea (14:21—14:31)
4. The Song of Deliverance (15:01—15:21)

C. Israelites Dissatisfied **(15:22—18:27)**

1. Complaints of Bitter Water (15:22—15:27)
2. Manna & Quail (16:01—16:36)
3. Moses Brings Forth Water from the Rock in Horeb (17:01—17:07)
4. Joshua Defeats the Amalekites (17:08—17:16)
5. Responsibility Divided (18:01—18:27)

3. <u>The Israelites at Mount Sinai</u> **(19:01—40:38)**

A. Israel Receives the Law of God **(19:01—24:18)**

1. Children of Israel at Mount Sinai (19:01—19:21)
2. Israel Receives the Ten Commandments (20:01—20:17)
3. Israelites Scared of God's Presence (20:18—20:21)
4. The Altar of Stone for the *LORD* (20:22—20:26)
5. Treatment of Slaves (21:01—21:11)
6. Law Concerning Personal Injury (21:12—21:27)
7. Law Concerning Animal Behavior (21:28—21:36)
8. Laws for Theft (22:01—22:04)
9. Property Damage Laws (22:05—22:06)
10. Laws Concerning Dishonesty (22:07—22:15)
11. Laws for Immorality (22:16—22:17)
12. Laws for Civil & Religious Obligations (22:18—22:31)
13. Equal Justice (23:01—23:09)
14. Sabbath & Feasts Laws (23:10—23:19)
15. The *LORD* Sends an Angel Before Israel (23:20—23:33)

16. Israel Ratifies the Covenant of the *LORD* (24:01—24:08)
17. The Glory of the *LORD* Revealed (24:09—24:18)

B. The Tabernacle Instituted **(25:01—31:18)**

1. Offerings for the Tabernacle (25:01—25:09)
2. Requirements for the Ark of the Testimony (25:10—25:16)
3. Requirements for the Mercy Seat (25:17—25:22)
4. Requirements for the Table of Showbread (25:23—25:30)
5. Requirements for the Golden Lampstand (25:31—25:40)
6. Curtains for the Tabernacle (26:01—26:14)
7. Boards for the Tabernacle (26:15—26:30)
8. Veils for the Tabernacle (26:31—26:37)
9. The Brazen Altar (27:01—27:08)
10. The Court of the Tabernacle (27:09—27:19)
11. The Oil for the Lamp (27:20—27:21)
12. Clothing for the Priests (28:01—28:04)
13. Requirements for the Ephod (28:05—28:08)
14. The Stones on the Shoulder Strap (28:09—28:14)
15. The Breastplate of Judgment (28:15—28:30)
16. The Remainder of the Garments to Be Made (28:31—28:43)
17. Instructions for the Consecration of the Priest (29:01—29:37)
18. The Daily Offerings (29:38—29:46)
19. Altar of Burning Incense (30:01—30:10)
20. The Atonement Money (30:11—30:16)
21. The Laver of Bronze (30:17—30:21)
22. The Holy Anointing Oil (30:22—30:33)
23. Making of the Incense (30:34—30:38)
24. The Builders of the Tabernacle (31:01—31:11)
25. The Sign of the Sabbath (31:12—31:18)

C. The Breaking of the Law **(32:01—34:35)**

1. Sins of the People with the Golden Calf (32:01—32:10)
2. Moses Intercedes with God for Israel (32:11—32:24)
3. Three Thousand Men Die Because of Rebellion (32:25—32:35)
4. Israel Departs Mount Sinai (33:01—33:06)
5. Moses Meets with the *LORD* (33:07—33:11)
6. The *LORD* Promises His Presence (33:12—33:23)
7. The Ten Commandments Remade (34:01—34:09)
8. The *LORD* Renews the Covenant (34:10—34:28)
9. Moses' Shining Face (34:29—34:35)

D. The Construction of the Tabernacle **(35:01—40:38)**

1. Rules for the Sabbath (35:01—35:03)
2. Instructions Concerning the Tabernacle (35:04—35:29)
3. God Names the Craftsmen (35:30—36:01)
4. The People Out Give Themselves (36:02—36:07)
5. The Tabernacle Curtains Are Made (36:08—36:19)
6. The Tabernacle Boards Are Made (36:20—36:34)
7. The Veil for the Tabernacle Is Made (36:35—36:38)
8. Ark of the Testimony Is Made (37:01—37:09)

9. Table for the Showbread Is Made (37:10—37:16)
10. The Golden Lampstand Is Made (37:17—37:24)
11. The Incense Altar Is Made (37:25—37:28)
12. Holy Anointing Oil Is Made (37:29—37:29)
13. The Bronze Altar Is Made (38:01—38:07)
14. The Bronze Laver Is Made (38:08—38:08)
15. The Court of the Tabernacle Is Made (38:09—38:20)
16. Materials Used in the Tabernacle (38:21—38:31)
17. Garments of the Ministry Made (39:01—39:01)
18. The Ephod Is Made (39:02—39:07)
19. The Breastplate Is Made (39:08—39:21)
20. The Remainder of the Garments Made (39:22—39:31)
21. Moses Inspects the Completed Work (39:32—39:43)
22. The Arrangement of the Tabernacle (40:01—40:16)
23. The Tabernacle Erected (40:17—40:33)
24. The *LORD* Fills the Tabernacle (40:34—40:38)

LEVITICUS
(1:01—27:34)

1. **The Way to Worship a Holy God** **(1:01—17:16)**

A. Procedures for the Offering **(1:01—7:38)**

1. Procedures for the Burnt Offering (1:01—1:17)
2. Procedures for the Grain Offering (2:01—2:16)
3. Procedures for the Peace Offering (3:01—3:17)
4. Procedure for the Sin Offering (4:01—4:35)
5. Procedures for the Trespass Offering (5:01—5:13)
6. Procedures for Restitution (5:14—6:07)
7. The Law Concerning Burnt Offerings (6:08—6:13)
8. The Law Concerning Grain Offerings (6:14—6:23)
9. The Law Concerning Sin Offerings (6:24—6:30)
10. The Law Concerning Trespass Offerings (7:01—7:10)
11. The Law Concerning Peace Offerings (7:11—7:21)
12. The Law Concerning Fat & Blood (7:22—7:27)
13. The Consecrated Portion for Aaron & His Sons (7:28—7:38)

B. Requirements for the Priests **(8:01—10:20)**

1. Aaron & Sons Ordained Into the Ministry (8:01—8:36)
2. The Beginning of the Priestly Ministry (9:01—9:24)
3. The Sacrilege Act of Nadab & Abihu (10:01—10:07)
4. Procedures for Priestly Conduct (10:08—10:20)

C. Procedures for the People **(11:01—15:33)**

1. Laws Concerning Consumption of Food (11:01—11:23)
2. Becoming Unclean (11:24—11:47)
3. Laws Concerning Purity After Childbirth (12:01—12:08)
4. Laws Concerning Purity of Leprosy (13:01—13:59)
5. The Law of the Leper After Cleansing (14:01—14:57)
6. Laws Concerning Bodily Discharge (15:01—15:33)

D. Procedures for the Altar **(16:01—17:16)**
1. Law of the Day of Atonement (16:01—16:04)
2. Preparations for the Day of Atonement (16:05—16:28)
3. Instructions for the Day of Atonement (16:29—16:34)
4. Laws Concerning Sacrificing (17:01—17:16)

2. **Living A Life Pleasing to God** **(18:01—27:34)**

A. Laws Concerning the Standards for the People **(18:01—20:27)**
1. Laws Concerning Sexual Relationships (18:01—18:30)
2. Laws Concerning Personal Conduct (19:01—19:37)
3. Punishments for Disobedience (20:01—20:27)

B. Laws Concerning the Standards for the Priests **(21:01—22:33)**
1. Standards of Conduct for Priests (21:01—22:16)
2. Laws Concerning Offerings (22:17—22:33)

C. Laws Concerning Festivals & Seasons **(23:01—25:55)**
1. Laws Concerning the Sabbath (23:01—23:03)
2. Laws Concerning Passover & Feast of Unleavened Bread (23:04—23:08)
3. Laws Concerning the Feast of Firstfruits (23:09—23:14)
4. Laws Concerning the Feasts of Weeks (23:15—23:22)
5. Laws Concerning the Feasts of Trumpets (23:23—23:25)
6. Laws Concerning the Day of Atonement (23:26—23:32)
7. Laws Concerning the Feast of Tabernacles (23:33—23:44)
8. Laws Concerning the Oil & the Bread (24:01—24:09)
9. Laws for Blasphemy (24:10—24:16)
10. Laws of Repercussion (24:17—24:23)
11. Laws Concerning the Sabbath Year (25:01—25:07)
12. Laws Concerning the Year of Jubilee (25:08—25:22)
13. Laws Concerning Redemption of Property (25:23—25:34)
14. Laws Concerning Redeeming the Poor & Enslaved (25:35—25:55)

D. Laws Concerning Being Obedient to God **(26:01—27:34)**
1. Blessings Received for Obedience (26:01—26:46)
2. Laws Concerning Vows to God (27:01—27:34)

NUMBERS
(1:01—36:13)

1. **The Preparation of Israel at Mount Sinai** **(1:01—10:10)**

A. Israel's First Census **(1:01—2:34)**
1. Counting of the Population (1:01—1:54)
2. Organization of the Tribes Determined (2:01—2:31)
3. Number of the Children of Israel = 603,550 (2:32—2:34)

B. The Function of the Levites **(3:01—4:49)**
1. The Records of Aaron & Moses (3:01—3:13)
2. Population of the Levites (3:14—3:39)

3. Dedication of the Levites to God (3:40—3:51)
4. Instructions for the Sons of Kohath (4:01—4:20)
5. Instructions for the Sons of Gershon (4:21—4:28)
6. Instructions for the Sons of Merari (4:29—4:33)
7. Census of the Levites = 8,580 (4:34—4:49)

C. Sanctification of the People **(5:01—10:10)**

1. Separation from Defilement (5:01—5:31)
2. Laws Concerning Taking a Nazirite Vow (6:01—6:27)
3. Concerning Offerings from the Leaders (7:01—7:89)
4. Consecrations of the Levites (8:01—8:26)
5. Observing the Annual Passover (9:01—9:14)
6. Being Led by God by Cloud & Fire (10:01—10:10)

2. First Journey to the Promised Land **(10:11—14:45)**

A. Concerning the Promised Land **(10:11—11:35)**

1. Israel Sets Out from the Wilderness of Sinai (10:11—10:36)
2. Children of Israel Begin to Murmur (11:01—11:15)
3. Elders Appointed (11:16—11:30)
4. The *LORD* Sends Quail from the Sea (11:31—11:35)

B. Aaron & Miriam Develop Problems with Moses **(12:01—12:16)**

1. Aaron & Miriam Complain Against Moses (12:01—12:08)
2. Miriam Becomes Leprous (12:09—12:16)

C. The Rebellion Against God **(13:01—14:45)**

1. The Report from the Twelve Spies (13:01—13:33)
2. Israel Afraid to Enter the Promise Land (14:01—14:25)
3. Death to the Complainers (14:26—14:38)
4. A Purpose Without Protection (14:39—14:45)

3. God's Discipline Upon the People **(15:01—21:35)**

A. Miscellaneous Laws **(15:01—15:41)**

1. Laws Concerning Offerings (15:01—15:21)
2. Unintentional Sins (15:22—15:29)
3. Presumptuous Sins (15:30—15:31)
4. Penalty for Sabbath Breakers (15:32—15:36)
5. Tassels (15:37—15:41)

B. Rebellion Against Moses **(16:01—17:13)**

1. Rebellion of Korah (16:01—16:40)
2. Complaints Against Moses & Aaron (16:41—16:50)
3. The Budding of Aaron's Rod (17:01—17:13)

C. Obligations of the Levities **(18:01—19:22)**

1. Bearing the Iniquity (18:01—18:07)
2. Aaron Given Charge Over the Offerings (18:08—18:20)
3. Supporting the Levites (18:21—18:32)
4. The Red Heifer Sacrifice (19:01—19:22)

D. The Next Generation **(20:01—21:35)**

1. Moses' Sin (20:01—20:13)
2. Rebellion Against Edom (20:14—20:22)
3. Aaron Dies; Son Eleazar Replaces Him (20:23—20:29)
4. Israel Defeats the Canaanites (21:01—21:03)
5. The Bronze Serpent (21:04—21:09)
6. Journey to Moab (21:10—21:20)
7. Israel Defeats the Kings of Sihon & Og (21:21—21:35)

4. <u>Second Journey to the Promised Land</u> **(22:01—36:13)**

A. The History of Balaam **(22:01—25:18)**

1. Balak Propositions Balaam (22:01—22:21)
2. A Donkey Talks as a Man (22:22—22:40)
3. Balaam Speaks His First Prophecy (22:41—23:12)
4. Balaam Speaks His Second Prophecy (23:13—23:26)
5. Balaam Speaks His Third Prophecy (23:27—24:14)
6. Balaam Speaks His Fourth Prophecy (24:15—25:25)
7. The Worship of Baal of Peor (25:01—25:18)

B. Israel's Second Census **(26:01—27:23)**

1. Tribes of Israel & Their Number = 601,730 (26:01—26:51)
2. Levites & Their Number = 23,000 (26:52—26:65)
3. The Laws of Inheritance (27:01—27:11)
4. Joshua's Appointment Over Israel (27:12—27:23)

C. Procedures for Offerings **(28:01—30:16)**

1. Daily Offerings (28:01—28:08)
2. Sabbath Offerings (28:09—28:10)
3. Monthly Offerings (28:11—28:15)
4. Passover Offerings (28:16—28:25)
5. Feast of Weeks Offerings (28:26—28:31)
6. Feast of Trumpets Offerings (29:01—29:06)
7. Day of Atonement Offerings (29:07—29:11)
8. Feast of Tabernacle Offerings (29:12—29:40)
9. The Law Concerning Vows (30:01—30:16)

D. Revenge on the Midianites **(31:01—31:54)**

1. Vengeance for the *LORD* on the Midianites (31:01—31:11)
2. Israel Returns with the Spoils of the Battle (31:12—31:24)
3. Plunder Divided Into Two Parts (31:25—31:54)

E. Trans-Jordan Settled by the Two-and-a-Half Tribes **(32:01—32:42)**

1. Tribes of Gad, Reuben & Half of Manasseh Settle the Trans-Jordan (32:01—32:42)

F. Israel Camps on the Plains of Moab **(33:01—33:56)**

1. Journey from Egypt to Moab Reviewed (33:01—33:49)
2. Instructions for Possessing Canaan (33:50—33:56)

G. The Division of the Land of Canaan **(34:01—36:13)**

1. The Boundaries of Canaan (34:01—34:15)
2. Eleazar and Joshua to Divide the Land (34:16—34:29)
3. Cities of the Levites (35:01—35:08)
4. The Avenger of Blood & the Cities of Refuge (35:09—35:28)
5. Statute of Judgment (35:29—35:34)
6. The Inheritance of Women (36:01—36:13)

DEUTERONOMY
(1:01—34:12)

1. Moses Gives Inspirational Speech (1:01—4:43)

A. A Historical Review **(1:01—4:43)**

1. The Command to Leave Sinai (1:01—1:08)
2. Moses Appoints Leaders (1:09—1:18)
3. Israel at Kadesh-Barnea (1:19—1:46)
4. Journey to the Transjordan (2:01—2:23)
5. The Conquest of the Transjordan (2:24—3:11)
6. Division of the Land of the Trans-Jordan (3:12—3:22)
7. Moses Is Forbidden to Enter the Promised Land (3:23—3:29)
8. Moses Urges Israel's Obedience (4:01—4:40)
9. Three "Cities of Refuge" East of the Jordan (4:41—4:43)

2. Rules for Godly Living (4:44—28:68)

A. Law Set Before the Children of Israel **(4:44—4:49)**

1. Law Set Before the Children of Israel (4:44—4:49)

B. Review of the Ten Commandments **(5:01—5:33)**

1. Review of the Ten Commandments (5:01—5:22)
2. The People Afraid of the Presence of God (5:23—5:33)

C. The Command to Love The *LORD* Your God **(6:01—11:32)**

1. The Greatest Commandment (6:01—6:09)
2. Be Careful to Obey the Commandments of God (6:10—6:25)
3. The Command to Drive Out the Nations (7:01—7:26)
4. Remember What The *LORD* Has Done (8:01—9:06)
5. The Golden Calf (9:07—9:29)
6. A New Pair of Ten Commandments (10:01—10:11)
7. The Call to Commitment to God (10:12—11:32)

D. Regulations of Worship **(12:01—16:17)**

1. Concerning the Central Sanctuary (12:01—12:32)
2. Punishments for False Prophets (13:01—13:18)
3. Commands Concerning Improper Foods (14:01—14:21)
4. Rules for Tithing (14:22—14:29)
5. Commands Concerning the Canceling of Debts (15:01—15:23)
6. Remember the Passover (16:01—16:08)
7. Remember the Feast of Weeks (16:09—16:12)
8. Remember the Feast of Tabernacles (16:13—16:17)

E. Regulations for Ruling **(16:18—20:20)**

1. Judges & Officers Appointed (16:18—17:13)
2. Appointment of Kings (17:14—17:20)
3. The Levites Have No Inheritance with Israel (18:01—18:08)
4. Law Concerning False Diviners (18:09—18:14)
5. Foretelling of the Messiah (18:15—18:19)
6. Law Concerning False Prophets (18:20—18:22)
7. Three "Cities of Refuge" for Manslayers (19:01—19:13)
8. Removal of Neighbor's Landmark Forbidden (19:14—19:14)
9. Law Concerning Witnesses (19:15—19:21)
10. Regulation Governing Warfare (20:01—20:20)

F. Regulations for Human Relationships **(21:01—26:19)**

1. Atonement for Manslaughter (21:01—21:09)
2. Marriage & Family Activities (21:10—21:22)
3. Various Rules & Regulations (21:22—22:12)
4. Laws Concerning Marriage Violations (22:13—22:30)
5. People Excluded from the Assembly (23:01—23:25)
6. Laws Concerning Divorce (24:01—25:19)
7. Regulations Concerning First Fruits (26:01—26:11)
8. Regulations Concerning Tithes (26:12—26:19)

G. Consequences of Obedience & Disobedience **(27:01—28:68)**

1. The Altar on Mount Ebal (27:01—27:10)
2. Curses from Mount Ebal (27:11—27:26)
3. Promise of Blessings for Obedience (28:01—28:14)
4. Promise for Curses for Disobedience (28:15—28:68)

3. <u>Moses Calls for the Obedience from the Children of Israel</u> **(29:01—30:20)**

A. God's Call to Obedience **(29:01—30:20)**

1. Moses Renews the Covenant Made In Moab (29:01—29:29)
2. A Call to Return to the *LORD* (30:01—30:10)
3. Life & Death Choice for the Israelites (30:11—30:20)

4. <u>Moses Commissions Joshua to Replace Him</u> **(31:01—34:12)**

A. Change in Leadership **(31:01—34:12)**

1. Joshua Becomes Israel's New Leader (31:01—31:08)
2. Public Reading of the Law Every Seven Years (31:09—31:13)
3. Israel's Disobedience Predicted (31:14—31:18)
4. The Song of Moses (31:19—32:47)
5. Moses to Die on Mount Nebo (32:48—32:52)
6. Moses' Final Blessings Upon the Children of Israel (33:01—33:29)
7. Moses Die at Age 120 on Mount Nebo in Moab (34:01—34:12)

<u>JOSHUA</u>

(1:01—24:33)

1. <u>Israel Enters Canaan, the Promised Land</u> **(1:01—5:15)**

A. Joshua Takes Charge **(1:01—2:24)**

1. The *LORD* Commissions Joshua (1:01—1:09)

2. Joshua Gives the Order to Cross (1:10—1:18)
3. Joshua Sends Out Two Spies; Rehab Hides Them (2:01—2:24)

B. Crossing the Jordan River **(3:01—5:15)**
1. Children of Israel Cross Into Canaan (3:01—3:17)
2. Stones of Commemoration (4:01—4:24)
3. The Next Generation Circumcised (5:01—5:12)
4. Joshua Meets the Captain of the *LORD*'s Host (5:13—5:15)

2. **<u>Conquering the Land of Canaan</u>** **(6:01—12:24)**

A. Joshua Conquers the Central Part of Canaan **(6:01—8:35)**
1. Jericho's Destruction by Joshua & the Israelites (6:01—6:27)
2. Israel Defeated at Ai (7:01—7:09)
3. Achan's Sin (7:10—7:26)
4. Israel Defeats Ai (8:01—8:29)
5. Covenant of the *LORD* Renewed at Ebal (8:30—8:35)

B. Joshua & Israel's Conquest of Southern Canaan **(9:01—10:43)**
1. The Gibeonites Deceive Israel (9:01—9:27)
2. Sun & Moon Stopped Over Gibeon (10:01—10:15)
3. Execution of the Five Amorite Kings (10:16—10:43)

C. Joshua & Israel's Conquest of Northern Canaan **(11:01—11:15)**
1. The Conquest of Northern Canaan (11:01—11:15)

D. Review of the Conquests of the Israelites **(11:16—12:24)**
1. Conquests by Moses & Joshua (11:16—12:24)

3. **<u>The Dividing of Canaan, the Promised Land</u>** **(13:01—24:33)**

A. The *<u>Twelve</u>* Tribes Receive Their Inheritance **(13:01—19:51)**
1. The *LORD*'s Instructions to Joshua (13:01—13:07)
2. Instructions for Division of Land East of the Jordan River (13:08—13:33)
   A. Reuben's Inheritance (13:15—13:23)
   B. Gad's Inheritance (13:24—13:28)
   C. East Manasseh's Inheritance (13:29—13:33)
3. The Land Divided West of the Jordan River (14:01—17:18)
   A. Instructions for the Land Division (14:01—14:06)
   B. Hebron—Caleb's Inheritance (14:06—14:15)
   C. Judah's Inheritance (15:01—15:12)
   D. Cities Occupied by Caleb (15:13—15:19)
   E. Cities Occupied by Judah (15:20—15:63)
   F. Inheritance of Ephraim & West Manasseh (16:01—16:04)
   G. Ephraim's Inheritance (16:05—16:10)
   H. West Tribe of Manasseh's Inheritance (17:01—17:18)
4. Allotments of the Remaining Land to be Divided (18:01—19:51)
   A. Instructions for the Land Division (18:01—18:10)
   B. Benjamin's Inheritance (18:11—18:28)
   C. Simeon's Inheritance (19:01—19:09)
   D. Zebulon's Inheritance (19:10—19:16)

E. Issachar's Inheritance (19:17—19:23)
F. Asher's Inheritance (19:24—19:31)
G. Naphtali's Inheritance (19:32—19:39)
H. Dan's Inheritance (19:40—19:48)
I. Joshua's Inheritance (19:49—19:51)

B. Cities of Refuge Appointed **(20:01—21:45)**
1. The Cities of Refuge (20:01—20:09)
2. The Cities of the Levities (21:01—21:42)
3. The *LORD*'s Promise Satisfied (21:43—21:45)

C. Joshua's Farewell Address to the Trans-Jordan Tribes of Israel **(22:01—22:34)**
1. Reuben, Gad, East Tribe of Manasseh Go Home (22:01—22:09)
2. The Trans-Jordan Tribes Erect Altar (22:10—22:34)

D. Joshua's Farewell Address to the Rulers of Israel **(23:01—24:33)**
1. Joshua's Address to the Rulers (23:01—23:28)
2. Joshua's Address to the People (24:01—24:28)
3. Joshua Dies at Age 110 (24:29—24:32)
4. Eleazar Dies; Age Unknown (24:33—24:33)

<u>JUDGES</u>
(1:01—21:25)

1. <u>The Introduction of Israel's Disobedience</u> **(1:01—3:06)**

A. Israel's Unfinished Job Concerning Canaan **(1:01—1:36)**
1. Conquering of Canaan Continues (1:01—1:36)

B. Disobedience & Defeat of Israel **(2:01—3:06)**
1. Disobedient Israel (2:01—3:06)

2. <u>Israel Rescued by the Judges</u> **(3:07—16:31)**

A. The First Period of Judges **(3:07—3:11)**
1. Oppressed by Mesopotamia; Delivered by Othniel (3:07—3:11)

B. The Second Period of the Judges **(3:12—3:31)**
1. Oppressed by Moab; Delivered by Ehud (3:12—3:30)
2. Oppressed by the Philistines; Delivered by Shamgar (3:31—3:31)

C. The Third Period of the Judges **(4:01—5:31)**
1. Oppressed by Canaan; Delivered by Deborah & Barak (4:01—4:24)
2. Song of Deborah, the Judge (5:01—5:31)

D. The Fourth Period of the Judges **(6:01—10:05)**
1. Israel Oppressed by the Midianites (6:01—6:10)
2. Gideon (Jerubbaal) Becomes Israel's Judge (6:11—6:27)
3. Altar of Baal Destroyed by Gideon (6:28—6:35)

4. Gideon's Fleece (6:36—6:40)
5. The Mighty Three-Hundred (7:01—7:25)
6. Gideon Conquers the Midianites (8:01—8:28)
7. The Death of Gideon (8:29—8:34)
8. The Tyranny of Abimelech (9:01—9:06)
9. The Parable of the Trees (9:07—9:21)
10. Abimelech's Destruction (9:22—9:57)
11. The Judgeship of Tola (10:01—10:02)
12. The Judgeship of Jair (10:03—10:05)

E. The Fifth Period of the Judges **(10:06—12:15)**

1. Oppressed by the Ammonites; Delivered by Jephthah (10:06—11:33)
2. Jephthah Exiled for Two Months (11:34—11:40)
3. Ephraim Angered at Jephthah (12:01—12:07)
4. The Judgeship of Ibzan (12:08—12:10)
5. The Judgeship of Elon (12:11—12:12)
6. The Judgeship of Abdon (12:13—12:15)

F. The Sixth Period of the Judges **(13:01—16:31)**

1. Oppressed by the Philistines; Delivered by Samson (13:01—13:25)
2. Samson Takes a Philistine Wife (14:01—14:20)
3. Samson's Mighty Exploits (15:01—15:20)
4. The Fall of Samson (16:01—16:22)
5. Samson Dies with the Philistines (16:23—16:31)

3. <u>Israel's Apostasy During the Period of the Judges</u> **(17:01—21:25)**

A. Micah & the Migration of the Danites **(17:01—18:31)**

1. Micah with His Private Priests (17:01—17:13)
2. The Migration of the Tribe of Dan to Laish (18:01—18:31)

B. The Benjamite War **(19:01—21:25)**

1. A Levite Takes a Concubine from Bethlehem (19:01—19:21)
2. The Hideous Crime of Gibeah (19:22—19:30)
3. Israel Makes War on Tribe of Benjamin (20:01—20:13)
4. The Execution of the War (20:14—20:48)
5. Benjamin Takes the Women of Jabesh Gilead as Wives (21:01—21:25)

<u>RUTH</u>
(1:01—4:22)

1. <u>The Unusual Relationship Between Ruth & Mother-in-Law Naomi</u> **(1:01—4:22)**

A. Ruth's Loyalty to Naomi **(1:01—1:22)**

1. Famine Hits Bethlehem; Elimelech Moves Family to Moab (1:01—1:05)
2. Ruth Goes to Moab with Naomi (1:06—1:18)
3. Naomi & Ruth Return to Bethlehem from Moab (1:19—1:22)

B. Ruth's Right to Glean Kinsman Field **(2:01—2:23)**

1. Ruth Gleans the Field of Boaz (2:01—2:03)
2. Ruth & Boaz Meet (2:04—2:07)
3. Ruth Protected by Boaz (2:08—2:13)
4. God Provides for Ruth Through Boaz (2:18—2:23)

C. Naomi Generated Plan for Ruth **(3:01—3:18)**

1. Suggestions to Ruth by Naomi (3:01—3:05)
2. Ruth Executes the Plan (3:06—3:09)
3. Agreed to by Boaz (3:10—3:18)

D. Boaz Redeems & Marries Ruth **(4:01—4:22)**

1. Ruth's Reward—A Husband (4:01—4:12)
2. Boaz & Ruth Have a Son Named Obed (4:13—4:17)
3. Ancestry from Perez to David (4:18—4:22)

1st SAMUEL
(1:01—31:13)

1. Samuel, the Last Judge of Israel **(1:01—7:17)**

A. Samuel's Early Life & Calling **(1:01—2:17)**

1. Hannah—Samuel's Mother (1:01—1:08)
2. Hannah's Earnest Prayer to God (1:09—1:18)
3. Birth & Consecration of Samuel (1:19—1:23)
4. Hannah's Sacrifice (1:24—1:28)
5. The Prophetic Song of Hannah (2:01—2:10)
6. Eli's Wicked Son's (2:11—2:17)

B. The Ministry of Samuel **(2:11—3:21)**

1. Hannah Blessed with Five More Children (2:11—2:21)
2. Corruption of Samuel's Household (2:22—2:26)
3. The *LORD* Calls Samuel to The Prophetic Ministry (3:01—3:21)

C. Israel's War with the Philistines **(4:01—7:17)**

1. Philistines Capture the Ark of the Covenant (4:01—4:11)
2. Eli Falls Dead at Age 98 (4:12—4:18)
3. Ichabod, Son of Phinehas Is Born (4:19—4:22)
4. Curse of the Ark on the Philistines (5:01—5:12)
5. Ark of the Covenant Restored to Israel (6:01—7:01)
6. Samuel Ministers Revival to Israel (7:02—7:17)

2. Israel Demands for Them a King **(8:01—15:35)**

A. Saul—Israel's First King **(8:01—12:25)**

1. Israel Rejects the Sons of Samuel as King (8:01—8:05)
2. Israel Rejects God as Their King (8:06—8:22)
3. Saul, a Benjamite—Israel's First King (9:01—9:27)
4. The Crowning of Saul as King (10:01—10:27)

5. Saul Defeats the Ammonites (11:01—11:15)
6. Saul's Farewell Address at Saul's Crowning (12:01—12:25)

B. The Rejection of Saul by The *LORD* for Disobedience **(13:01—15:35)**
1. The Sinful Sacrifice by Saul (13:01—13:23)
2. The Philistines Defeated (14:01—14:23)
3. Saul Makes a Rash Vow (14:24—14:52)
4. Saul's Partial Obedience (15:01—15:09)
5. The *LORD* Regrets Making Saul King (15:10—15:35)

3. <u>David—Saul's Replacement</u> **(16:01—31:13)**

A. David Chosen as King **(16:01—16:23)**
1. Samuel Anoints David (16:01—16:13)
2. Distressing Spirit from the *LORD* Troubles Saul (16:14—16:23)

B. The Rise of David **(17:01—18:30)**
1. David Defeats Goliath, the Giant (17:01—17:58)
2. David's Friendship with Jonathan, Saul's Son (18:01—18:04)
3. Saul's Displeasure with David (18:05—18:16)
4. David Marries King Saul's Daughter, Michal (18:17—18:30)

C. David Flees; Goes Into Exile **(19:01—26:25)**
1. King Saul Rejects David, Seeks His Life (19:01—19:10)
2. Michal Protects David, Her Husband (19:11—19:17)
3. The Prophet Samuel Protects David from King Saul (19:18—19:24)
4. King Saul's Son Jonathan Protects David (20:01—20:15)
5. Jonathan Makes a Covenant with David (20:16—20:42)
6. Ahimelech, the Priest, Protects David (21:01—21:05)
7. Achish, King of Gath, Protects David (21:06—21:15)
8. David Escapes to Cave of Adullam with 400 Men (22:01—22:05)
9. Saul Kills Ahimelech & Other Priests (22:06—22:23)
10. David Saves City of Keliah from the Philistines (23:01—23:13)
11. David in the Wilderness of Ziph (23:14—23:29)
12. David Spares King Saul's Life at Engedi (24:01—24:22)
13. The Prophet Samuel Dies (25:01—25:01)
14. David & Abigail, the Wife of Nabal (25:02—25:44)
15. David Spares King Saul's Life at Engedi Again (26:01—26:25)

D. David Seeks Refuge in Philistine Territory **(27:01—31:13)**
1. David Becomes a Philistine Servant (27:01—28:02)
2. King Saul Consults the Witch at Endor (28:03—28:25)
3. David Released by the Philistines; Returns to Philistia (29:01—29:11)
4. David Conquers the Amalekites (30:01—30:31)
5. The Philistines Defeat Israel; King Saul & Sons Killed (31:01—31:13)

2nd SAMUEL
(1:01—24:25)

1. **The Crowning of David Over the Kingdom** **(1:01—10:19)**

A. David Crowned King **(1:01—4:12)**

1. The Death of Saul Announced (1:01—1:10)
2. David's Reaction to Saul's Death (1:11—1:16)
3. Lamentation Over Saul & Jonathan (1:17—1:27)
4. David Anointed King Over Judah (2:01—2:07)
5. Ishbosheth Made King Over Israel (2:08—2:32)
6. Sons of David Born in Hebron (3:01—3:05)
7. Abner Deserts Ishbosheth & Joins David (3:06—3:21)
8. Joab Avenges His Brother's Death (3:22—3:30)
9. David Mourns the Death of Abner (4:01—4:12)

B. David Crowned King Over All the Tribes of Israel **(5:01—7:29)**

1. David Rules Over All of Israel (5:01—5:05)
2. David Conquers Jerusalem; Makes Jerusalem Capital (5:06—5:16)
3. David Conquers the Philistines at Baal Perazim (5:17—5:25)
4. The Ark of the Covenant Brought to Jerusalem (6:01—6:23)
5. David's Covenant with God Concerning the Kingdom (7:01—7:17)
6. David's Praise to God (7:18—7:29)

C. David Victorious Over Many Nations Around Him **(8:01—10:19)**

1. David Defeats Philistia, Moab, Zobah, Aram & Edom (8:01—8:18)
2. David Shows Mephibosheth Kindness (9:01—9:13)
3. David Defeats Ammon (10:01—10:19)

2. **David's Transgressions as King** **(11:01—24:25)**

A. The Crimes of King David **(11:01—12:31)**

1. David & Bathsheba's Adultery (11:01—11:13)
2. David Has Bathsheba's Husband Uriah Killed (11:14—11:27)
3. The *LORD* Sends Nathan to Expose David's Guilt (12:01—12:15)
4. David's First Son Taken In Judgment (12:16—12:23)
5. David Has a Second Son Named Solomon (12:24—12:25)
6. Joab Fights & Takes Rabbah of Ammon (12:26—12:31)

B. Upheaval in the House of David **(13:01—13:39)**

1. Amnon Rapes His Half-Sister Tamar (13:01—13:22)
2. Absalom Avenges Tamar's Rape; Has Amnon Killed (13:23—13:33)
3. Absalom Flees to Geshur (13:34—13:39)

C. Absalom's Rebellion **(14:01—18:33)**

1. Absalom Returns to David (14:01—14:24)
2. Absalom Forgiven (14:25—14:33)
3. Absalom's Revolt Against David (15:01—15:12)

4. Absalom Conquers & Takes Jerusalem (15:13—16:04)
5. David Goes to Bahurim; Cursed by Shimei (16:05—16:14)
6. Ahithophel's Wicked Advise to Absalom (16:15—17:04)
7. Hushai's Advise to Absalom (17:05—17:14)
8. Hushai Sends Message (17:15—17:23)
9. Absalom Conquered & Killed (17:24—18:18)
10. Absalom's Death Reaches David; David Mourns (18:18—18:33)

D. Upheaval in David's Kingdom **(19:01—20:26)**

1. Joab Rebukes David (19:01—19:08)
2. David Returns to Jerusalem (19:09—19:19a)
3. David Shows Mercy to Shimei (19:19b—19:23)
4. David Meets with Mephibosheth, Son of Saul (19:24—19:30)
5. David Shows Kindness to Barzillai (19:31—19:39)
6. Revolution Arises Within the Kingdom (19:40—20:26)

E. David's Conclusion in the Kingdom **(21:01—24:25)**

1. A Famine Hits the Land for Three Years (21:01—21:01)
2. Blood of the Gibeonites Avenged (21:02—21:10)
3. David Keeps Promise Made with Jonathan (21:11—21:14)
4. David & Servants Destroy the Philistine Giants (21:15—21:22)
5. The "Song of David" to the *LORD* (22:01—22:51)
6. The Last Words of David (23:01—23:07)
7. The Mighty Deeds of David's Men (23:08—23:39)
8. David Has a Census Performed From Dan to Beersheba (24:01—24:09)
9. David's Sin Costs Him Seventy-Thousand Lives (24:10—24:17)
10. David Buys Threshing Floor; Builds Altar to the *LORD* (24:18—24:25)

1st KINGS
(1:01—22:53)

1. **The Kingdom United** **(1:01—11:43)**

A. Solomon Replaces David, His Father as King **(1:01—3:01)**

1. The Struggle for the Crown (1:01—1:31)
2. Solomon Proclaimed King Over Israel & Judah (1:32—2:09)
3. Solomon Purges Kingdom; Executes Adonijah (2:10—2:25)
4. Abiathar Exiled; Joab Executed (2:26—2:35)
5. Solomon Has Shimei Executed (2:36—2:46)
6. Solomon Marries the Daughter of the Pharaoh of Egypt (3:01—3:01)

B. The Wisdom of Solomon **(3:02—4:34)**

1. Solomon Asks the *LORD* for Wisdom (3:02—3:15)
2. Solomon's Wisdom Displayed (3:16—3:28)
3. Solomon's Administration (4:01—4:28)
4. Solomon's Fame (4:29—4:34)

C. Solomon's Temple **(5:01—8:66)**

1. Solomon's Temple Preparations (5:01—5:18)
2. Construction of Solomon's Temple & Other Buildings (6:01—7:12)
3. Furnishings for Solomon's Temple (7:13—7:51)
4. Solomon's Temple Dedicated (8:01—8:66)

D. The Highs & Lows of Solomon's Reign **(9:01—10:29)**

1. Solomon's Relationship with the *LORD* (9:01—9:09)
2. Solomon's Relationship with Hiram (9:10—9:14)
3. Solomon's Relationship with His Servants (9:15—9:28)
4. Solomon Gets a Visit from the Queen of Sheba (10:01—10:13)
5. Solomon's Wealth (10:14—10:29)

E. Solomon's Demise **(11:01—11:43)**

1. Solomon's Polygamy & Idolatry (11:01—11:08)
2. The *LORD* Give's Solomon a Warning (11:09—11:13)
3. Many Enemies Rise Up Against Solomon (11:14—11:28)
4. Ahijah to Become King Over Ten Tribes of Israel (11:29—11:40)
5. The Passing of Solomon (11:41—11:43)

2. **The Kingdom Divided; Prophecy of Ahijah Comes to Pass** **(12:01—22:53)**

A. Rehoboam Replaces Solomon, His Father as King **(12:01—12:24)**

1. Northern Tribes Make a Request to Rehoboam (12:01—12:04)
2. Rehoboam Replies to Their Request (12:05—12:15)
3. Israel Revolts Against Rehoboam; Nation Splits (12:16—12:24)

B. Jeroboam Becomes King Over Israel **(12:25—13:34)**

1. Jeroboam's Idolatry (12:25—12:33)
2. Message from the "Man of God" from Judah (13:01—13:10)
3. "Man of God" Deceived & Killed by Lion (13:11—13:32)
4. Sin in the House of Jeroboam (13:33—13:34)

C. Jeroboam's Judgment **(14:01—14:20)**

1. Judgment Falls on House of Jeroboam (14:01—14:18)
2. Jeroboam Dies; Reigned 21 Years (14:19—14:20)

D. Chronicle of the Rulers in Judah & Israel **(14:21—16:34)**

1. Rehoboam's Reigned 17 Years in Judah (14:21—14:31)
2. Abijam Reigned 3 Years in Jerusalem (15:01—15:08)
3. Asa Reigned 41 Years in Jerusalem (15:09—15:24)
4. Nadab Reigned 2 Years Over Israel (15:25—15:32)
5. Baasha Reigned 24 Years in Israel (15:33—16:07)
6. Elah Reigned 2 Years in Tirzah of Israel (16:08—16:14)
7. Zimri Reigned 7 Days in Tirzah of Israel (16:15—16:20)
8. Omri Reigned 12 Years in Israel (16:21—16:28)
9. Ahab Reigned 22 Years in Samaria in Israel (16:29—16:34)

E. The Ministry of Elijah, the Prophet of God **(17:01—19:21)**

1. Elijah Predicts a Drought in the Land (17:01—17:24)

2. Elijah's Message to Ahab & the Prophets of Baal (18:01—18:19)
3. Victory at Mount Carmel for Elijah (18:20—18:40)
4. Rain Comes; Drought Ends (18:41—18:46)
5. Elijah Escapes to Mount Horeb (19:01—19:18)
6. Elijah Throws His Mantle Upon Elisha (19:19—19:21)

F. The Reign of King Ahab **(20:01—22:40)**
1. Ahab Defeats King Ben-Hadad of Syria (20:01—20:30)
2. Treaty Between Ahab & Ben-Hadad (20:31—20:34)
3. Ahab Condemned (20:25—20:43)
4. King Ahab Murders Naboth for His Vineyard (21:01—21:29)
5. The Final Battle of Ahab (22:01—22:40)

G. The Reign of Jehoshaphat **(22:41—22:50)**
1. Jehoshaphat Reigns Over Judah for 25 Years (22:41—22:50)

H. The Reign of Ahaziah **(22:51—22:53)**
1. Ahaziah Reigns Over Israel for 2 Years (22:51—22:53)

2nd KINGS
(1:01—25:30)

1. The Kingdom Divided **(1:01—17:41)**

A. The Reign of Ahaziah **(1:01—1:18)**
1. Judgment of God Falls Upon Ahaziah (1:01—1:18)

B. The Ministry of Elisha **(2:01—8:15)**
1. Elijah Is Translated to Heaven (2:01—2:11)
2. Elisha Begins His Ministry Unto the *LORD* (2:12—2:25)
3. Moab Rebels Against Israel (3:01—3:27)
4. The Miracle with the Jar of Oil (4:01—4:07)
5. The Miracle of Raising the Dead (4:08—4:37)
6. The Miracle of Purifying the Stew (4:38—4:41)
7. The Miracle of Feeding the One Hundred Men (4:42—4:44)
8. The Miracle of Healing Naaman's Leprosy (5:01—5:27)
9. The Miracle of the Floating Ax Head (6:01—6:07)
10. Elisha Successfully Opposes Syria (6:08—6:23)
11. Samaria Surrounded by Syria While in a Famine (6:24—7:02)
12. The Syrians Flee Samaria (7:03—7:20)
13. Restoration of the Shunammite Woman's Land (8:01—8:06)
14. Elisha Goes to Damascus; King Ben-Hadad Dies (8:06—8:15)

C. The Chronicles of the Kings of Israel & Judah **(8:16—17:02)**
1. Joram (Jehoram) Reigned 8 Years in Jerusalem (Judah) (8:16—8:24)
2. Ahaziah Reigned 1 Year in Jerusalem (Judah) (8:25—8:29)
3. Elisha Anoints Jehu King Over Israel (9:01—9:10)

4. Joram (Jehoram) Is Defeated by Jehu (9:11—9:26)
5. Jehu Defeats & Kills Ahaziah (9:27—9:29)
6. The Hideous Death of Jezebel (9:30—9:37)
7. Jehu Kills Ahab's Seventy Sons (10:01—10:11)
8. Jehu Kills Forty-two Brothers of Ahaziah at Beth Eked (10:12—10:17)
9. Jehu Destroys the Baal Worshipers (10:18—10:31)
10. Jehu Dies; Reigned in Israel 28 Years (10:32—10:36)
11. Athaliah Reigned in Judah 7 Years then Killed (11:01—11:17)
12. Jehoash (Joash) Reigned in Judah 40 Years (11:18—12:18)
13. Jehoash (Joash) Killed at the Landfill (12:19—12:21)
14. Jehoahaz Reigned in Israel 17 Years (13:01—13:09)
15. Jehoash, Son of Jehoahaz Reigned in Israel 16 Years (13:10—13:19)
16. Elisha Dies (13:20—13:21)
17. King Hazael of Aram Dies; His Son Ben-Hadad Becomes King (13:22—13:25)
18. Amaziah, Son of Joash Reigned in Judah 29 Years (14:01—14:22)
19. Jeroboam II Reigned in Israel 41 Years (14:23—14:29)
20. Azariah, Son of Amaziah Reigned in Judah 52 Years (15:01—15:07)
21. Zechariah, Son of Jeroboam II Reigned in Israel 6 Months (15:08—15:12)
22. Shallum, Son of Jabesh Reigned in Israel for 1 Month (15:13—15:16)
23. Menahem, Son of Gadi Reigned 10 Years in Israel (15:17—15:22)
24. Pekahiah, Son of Menahem Reigned in Israel 2 Years (15:23—15:26)
25. Pekah, Son of Remaliah Reigned in Israel 20 Years (15:27—15:31)
26. Jotham, Son of Uzziah Reigned in Judah 16 Years (15:32—15:38)
27. Ahaz, Son of Jotham Reigned in Judah 16 Years (16:01—16:20)
28. Hoshea, Son of Elah Reigned in Israel 9 Years (17:01—17:02)

D. The Deportation of Judah to Assyria **(17:03—17:41)**

1. King Hoshea & Israel Bound to Prison (17:03—17:06)
2. The Sins of the Sons of Israel (17:07—17:23)
3. Israel Resettled by Assyrians (17:24—17:41)

2. <u>The Surviving Kingdom of Judah</u> **(18:01—25:30)**

A. The Kings of Judah **(18:01—25:30)**

1. Hezekiah Reigned in Judah 29 Years (18:01—18:03)
2. Hezekiah's Accomplishments (18:04—18:16)
3. Hezekiah Delivered from Attacks of Sennacherib Attacks from Sennacherib (18:17—19:37)
4. Hezekiah's Illness & Recovery = Extended Life of 15 Years (20:01—20:11)
5. Hezekiah Foolish Before the Babylonians (20:12—20:19)

6. The Passing of King Hezekiah (20:20—20:21)
7. Manasseh Reigned in Judah 55 Years (21:01—21:18)
8. Ammon, Son of Manasseh Reigned in Judah 2 Years (21:19—21:26)
9. Josiah, Ammon's Son Reigned in Judah 31 Years (22:01—22:07)
10. The "Book of the Law" Found (22:08—22:20)
11. Josiah Renews the Covenant with the *LORD* (23:01—23:27)
12. Josiah Killed at the Battle in Megiddo (23:28—23:30)
13. Jehoahaz Reigned in Judah 3 Months (23:31—23:33)
14. Jehoiakim (Eliakim) Reigned in Judah 11 Years (23:34—23:37)
15. Judah Overtaken by King Nebuchadnezzar in 609 B.C. (24:01—24:07)
16. Jehoiachin Reigned in Jerusalem for 3 Months (24:08—24:16)
17. Zedekiah (Mattaniah) Reigned 11 Years (24:17—25:10)
18. Judah's Third Deportation (25:11—25:21)
19. Gedaliah Is Made Puppet Governor of Judah (25:22—25:26)
20. Jehoiachin Released from Prison in Babylon (25:27—25:30)

1st CHRONICLES
(1:01—29:30)

1. The Genealogy from Adam to David **(1:01—9:44)**

A. Adam to Noah **(1:01—1:04)**

1. Adam Lived 930 Years; Begets Seth (Gen.5:3-5)
2. Seth Lived 912 Years; Begets Enosh (Gen. 5:6-8)
3. Enosh Lived 905 Years; Begets Kenan (Gen. 5:9-11)
4. Kenan Lived 910 Years; Begets Mahalalel (Gen. 5:12-14)
5. Mahalalel Lived 895 Years; Begets Jared (Gen. 5:15-17)
6. Jared Lived 962 Years; Begets Enoch (Gen. 5:18-20)
7. Enoch Lived 365 Years; Begets Methuselah (Gen.5:21-24)
8. Methuselah Lived 965 Years; Begets Lamech (Gen. 5:25-27)
9. Lamech Lived 777 Years; Begets Noah (Gen. 5:28-31)
10. Noah Lived 950 Years; Begets Triplets—Shem, Ham & Japheth (Gen. 5:32)

B. Noah to Abraham **(1:05—1:27)**

1. The Genealogy of Japheth (1:05—1:07)
2. The Genealogy of Ham (1:08—1:16)
3. The Genealogy of Shem (Semites) (1:17—1:27)

C. Abraham to Jacob (Israel) **(1:28—1:54)**

1. Sons of Abraham (1:28—1:28)
2. The Genealogy of Ishmael (1:29—1:31)
3. The Genealogy of Keturah (1:32—1:33)
4. The Genealogy of Isaac (1:34—1:38)
5. The Genealogy of Esau (Edomites) (1:39—1:54)

D. Jacob to David **(2:01—2:55)**

1. The Sons of Jacob (Israel) (2:01—2:02)
2. The Genealogy of Judah (2:03—2:17)

3. The Genealogy of Hezron (2:18—2:55)

E. The Family of David **(3:01—3:24)**

1. The Sons of David (3:01—3:09)
2. The Sons of Solomon (3:09—3:16)
3. The Sons of Jeconiah (3:17—3:24)

F. The Genealogy of Israel (Jacob) **(4:01—8:40)**

1. The Sons of Judah (4:01—4:23)
2. The Sons of Simeon (4:24—4:43)
3. The Sons of Reuben (5:01—5:10)
4. The Sons of Gad (5:11—5:22)
5. The Sons of the East Tribe of Manasseh (5:23—5:26)
6. The Sons of Levi (6:01—6:81)
7. The Sons of Issachar (7:01—7:05)
8. The Sons of Benjamin (7:06—7:12)
9. The Sons of Naphtali (7:13—7:13)
10. The Sons of the West Tribe of Manasseh (7:14—7:19)
11. The Sons of Ephraim (7:20—7:29)
12. The Sons of Asher (7:30—7:40)
13. The Sons of Benjamin (8:01—8:28)
14. The Genealogy of King Saul, the Benjamite (8:29—8:40)

G. Babylonian Exiles Return to Jerusalem **(9:01—9:44)**

1. The Inhabitants of Jerusalem (9:01—9:13)
2. The Levites in Jerusalem (9:14—9:34)
3. The Family of King Saul, the Benjamite (9:35—9:44)

2. <u>David's Reign Over All Israel Lasts Forty Years</u> **(10:01—29:30)**

A. David's Rise to the Throne **(10:01—12:40)**

1. The Death of Saul & His Sons (10:01—10:14)
2. David Becomes King Over Israel (11:01—11:03)
3. David Captures Jerusalem (11:04—11:47)
4. David's Army Grows (12:01—12:40)

B. The "Ark of the Covenant" Brought to Jerusalem **(13:01—17:27)**

1. The Ark Enroute to Jerusalem (13:01—13:08)
2. The Death of Uzza (13:09—13:14)
3. David Flourishes at Jerusalem (14:01—14:07)
4. David & His Army Conquer the Philistines (14:08—14:17)
5. David Takes the "Ark of the Covenant" to Jerusalem (15:01—15:29)
6. The "Ark of God" Set in the Midst of the Tabernacle (16:01—16:06)
7. David's Celebration of the Ark (16:07—16:43)
8. The "Covenant of God" with David (17:01—17:27)

C. The Wars of David **(18:01—20:08)**

1. David's Battles & Conquests (18:01—20:08)

D. Satan Moved Upon David to Take A Census of Israel **(21:01—21:30)**

1. David Takes a Census of Israel (21:01—21:30)

E. David Makes Building Preparations for the Temple **(22:01—29:30)**

1. Preparations for Building the Temple Are Made (22:01—22:19)
2. Organization of the Levites (23:01—23:32)
3. The Twenty-four Groups of Levites (24:01—24:31)
4. The Musicians Are Assigned (25:01—25:31)
5. The Gatekeepers Are Assigned (26:01—26:19)
6. The Treasurers Are Assigned (26:20—26:28)
7. Officials & Judges Are Assigned (26:29—26:32)
8. The Military Ranks Are Assigned (27:01—27:34)
9. Solomon Chosen to Build the Temple (28:01—28:21)
10. Offerings for the Building of the Temple (29:01—29:09)
11. David Blesses the *LORD* Before All of the Assembly (29:10—29:20)
12. Solomon's Rise to the Throne (29:21—29:25)
13. David's Reign Comes to an End (29:26—29:30)

2nd CHRONICLES
(1:01—36:23)

1. Solomon's Reign Over All Israel Last Forty Years (1:01—9:31)

A. Solomon Begins His Reign Over Israel **(1:01—1:17)**

1. Solomon's Request for Wisdom from God (1:01—1:13)
2. Solomon's Wealth (1:14—1:17)

B. The Temple Solomon Built for the *LORD* **(2:01—4:21)**

1. Temple Preparations Are Made (2:01—2:18)
2. Temple Construction Begins (3:01—3:17)
3. Temple Furnishings for the Temple (4:01—4:21)

C. The Temple Is Dedicated to The *LORD* **(5:01—7:22)**

1. The "Ark of the Covenant" Brought into the Temple (5:01—5:14)
2. Solomon Speaks to the Tribes (6:01—6:42)
3. The Glory of God Fills the House (7:01—7:03)
4. Sacrifices to God & Dedication to the House (7:04—7:11)
5. Solomon Hears from God (7:12—7:22)

D. Solomon's Popularity **(8:01—9:31)**

1. Solomon's Cities (8:01—8:06)
2. Solomon's Forced Laborers (8:07—8:11)
3. Solomon's Burnt Offerings (8:12—8:13)
4. Solomon's Division of the Priests (8:14—8:16)
5. Solomon's "Men of the Sea" (8:17—8:18)
6. Solomon's Visit from the Queen of Sheba (9:01—9:12)
7. Solomon's Wealth (9:13—9:28)
8. Solomon's Death; Reigned Forty Years (9:29—9:31)

2. <u>Kings of Judah Since the Death of Solomon to the Exile (931—597 B.C.)</u> **(10:01—36:23)**

A. Rise of Rehoboam, Son of Solomon **(10:01—11:17)**

1. Ten Tribes of Israel Separate from Judah (10:01—10:19)
2. Rehoboam Obeys the *LORD* (11:01—11:04)
3. "Cities for Defense" Are Built in Judah (11:05—11:17)

B. The Kings of Judah & Their Wickedness **(11:18—36:23)**

1. Rehoboam Forsakes the *LORD* (11:18—12:12)
2. Rehoboam's Reign Ends; Resigned for Seventeen Years (12:13—12:16)
3. Abijah, Rehoboam's Son Reigns in Judah Three Years (13:01—13:22)
4. Asa, Son of Abijah Reigns in Judah Forty-one Years (14:01—14:08)
5. "Valley of Zephathah" War with Ethiopia (14:09—14:15)
6. King Asa of Judah Seek After the *LORD* (15:01—15:19)
7. King Baasha of Israel Makes War Against Judah (16:01—16:10)
8. King Asa Dies; Reigned Forty-one Years (16:11—16:14)
9. Jehoshaphat, Son of Asa Reigns in Judah Twenty-five Years (17:01—17:19)
10. Jehoshaphat's Association with King Ahab of Israel (18:01—19:03)
11. Reformations by King Jehoshaphat of Judah (19:04—19:11)
12. The *LORD* Destroys Ammon, Moab & Mount Seir (20:01—20:30)
13. Jehoshaphat's Reign Ends; Reigns Twenty-five Years (20:31—20:37)
14. Jehoram Reigns in Judah Eight Years (21:01—21:20)
15. Ahaziah Reigns in Judah One Year (22:01—22:09)
16. Athaliah Reigns in Judah Six Years (22:10—22:12)
17. Joash, Son of Ahaziah Reigns in Judah Forty Years (23:01—23:11)
18. Athaliah Slain by the Sword (23:12—23:15)
19. Jehoiada Makes Covenant with King & the People (23:16—23:21)
20. Joash Reigns Forty Years; Repairs Temple (24:01—24:14)
21. Jehoiada Dies at Age 130 (24:15—24:16)
22. Joash Forsakes the *LORD* (24:17—24:22)
23. Joash Killed in His Own Bed (24:23—24:27)
24. Amaziah, Son of Joash Reigns in Judah Twenty-nine Years (25:01—25:13)
25. Amaziah Forsakes the *LORD* (25:14—25:16)
26. Joash, King of Israel Defeats Amaziah (25:17—25:24)
27. Amaziah Killed in Lachish (25:25—25:28)
28. Uzziah, Son of Amaziah Reigns in Judah Fifty-two Years (26:01—26:15)
29. Uzziah Develops Proud Heart & Forsakes the *LORD* (26:16—26:23)
30. Jotham, Son of Uzziah Reigns in Judah Sixteen Years (27:01—27:09)
31. Ahaz, Son of Jotham Reigns in Judah Sixteen Years (28:01—28:04)

32. Judah Conquered by Israel & Syria (28:05—28:08)
33. Captives Returned to Judah (28:09—28:21)
34. Sacrificing to gods of Syria Became King Ahaz's Ruin (28:22—28:27)
35. Hezekiah, Son of Ahaz Reigns in Judah Twenty-nine Years (29:01—29:02)
36. King Hezekiah Cleanses the Temple of Idol Worship (29:03—29:19)
37. King Hezekiah Brings Revival to the Land (29:20—31:21)
38. Hezekiah Defeats the Assyrians (32:01—32:23)
39. The Last Days of King Hezekiah (32:24—32:33)
40. Manasseh Reigns in Judah Fifty-five Years (33:01—33:20)
41. Amon, Son of Manasseh's Reign & Death Two Years (33:21—33:25)
42. Josiah, Son of Amon Reigns in Judah Thirty-one Years (34:01—34:13)
43. Hilkiah, the Priest Finds the "Book of the Law" (34:14—34:28)
44. True Worship Restored (34:29—34:33)
45. King Josiah Celebrates the Passover in Jerusalem (35:01—35:19)
46. King Josiah Killed in Battle in the "Valley of Megiddo" (35:20—35:27)
47. Joahaz, Son of Josiah Reigns in Judah Three Months (36:01—36:04)
48. Jehoiakim Reigns in Judah Eleven Years (36:05—36:08)
49. Jehoiachin Reigns in Judah Three Months, Ten Days (36:09—36:10)
50. Zedekiah Reigns in Judah Eleven Years (36:11—36:21)
51. Decree of Cyrus, King of Persia (36:22—36:23)

EZRA
(1:01—10:44)

1. **Return of the First Group of Exiles** **(1:01—6:22)**
   A. Zerubbabel Leads the First Group **(1:01—2:70)**
   1. The Decree of Cyrus, King of Persia (1:01—1:11)
   2. A Census of the Returning Captives (2:01—2:70)

   B. Construction of the Temple Undertaken **(3:01—6:22)**
   1. The Sacrifices to the *LORD* Begin (3:01—3:06)
   2. Building of the Foundation Underway (3:07—3:13)
   3. Enemies of Judah Oppose the Rebuilding of the Temple (4:01—4:24)
   4. The Rebuilding Resumes (5:01—5:17)
   5. The Decree of Darius (6:01—6:12)
   6. The Completion of the Temple on 3 Adar (6:13—6:15)
   7. The Dedication of the Temple (6:16—6:18)
   8. The Passover Observed (6:19—6:22)

2. **Return of the Second Group of Exiles 80 Years Later (456 B.C.)** **(7:01—10:44)**
   A. Ezra Leads the Second Group **(7:01—8:36)**
   1. Ezra Arrives in Jerusalem (7:01—7:10)

2. The Decree from King Artaxerxes to Ezra (7:11—7:28)
3. The Genealogy Enrollment Who Returned with Ezra (8:01—8:36)

B. The Reformations of Ezra at Jerusalem **(9:01—10:44)**
1. Intermarriage with Pagans Condemned by Ezra (9:01—9:04)
2. Ezra's Confession to God (9:05—9:15)
3. People Confess the Improper Relationships with Pagans (10:01—10:17)
4. Judah Cleanses Themselves of Pagan Wives (10:18—10:44)

NEHEMIAH
(1:01—13:31)

1. Rebuilding the Walls of Jerusalem **(1:01—2:20)**

A. Nehemiah Returns to Jerusalem **(1:01—2:20)**
1. Nehemiah's Intercession (1:01—1:11)
2. Nehemiah's Request to King Artaxerxes (2:01—2:10)
3. Nehemiah Inspects the Walls (2:11—2:20)

2. Beginning of the Rebuilding **(3:01—7:73)**

A. The Rebuilding Begins **(3:01—7:73)**
1. The Rebuilding Begins (3:01—3:32)
2. Enemies Come Against the Rebuilding of the Wall (4:01—6:14)
   - A. By Insults (4:01—4:06)
   - B. By Plotting (4:07—4:23)
   - C. By Extortion (5:01—5:13)
   - D. Nehemiah's Generosity (5:14—5:19)
   - E. By Compromise (6:01—6:09)
   - F. By Treachery (6:10—6:14)
3. The Completion of the Wall (6:15—7:03)
4. People Registered by Genealogy (7:04—7:73)

3. The Covenant Renewed **(8:01—13:31)**

A. The "Book of the Law" from Moses **(8:01—10:39)**
1. Ezra Reads the "Book of the Law" (8:01—8:11)
2. The "Feast of Tabernacles" (8:12—8:18)
3. The People's Confession of Sins (9:01—9:38)
4. People Who Agreed with the Covenant (10:01—10:27)
5. Ordinances Made (10:28—10:39)

B. The Cities of Judah Repopulated **(11:01—13:31)**
1. Repopulating Jerusalem (11:01—11:36)
2. Priests & Levities Who Came with Zerubbabel (12:01—12:26)
3. The Wall of Jerusalem Dedicated (12:27—12:47)
4. Nehemiah's Reformations (13:01—13:31)

ESTHER
(1:01—10:03)

1. **The People of God in Dangerous Times** **(1:01—5:14)**

   A. King Ahasuerus Divorces Queen Vashti **(1:01—1:22)**
   1. The King Gives a Banquet (1:01—1:09)
   2. Queen Vashti Refuses to Obey King Ahasuerus's Request (1:10—1:18)
   3. Memucan Proposes Edict to King Ahasuerus (1:19—1:22)

   B. The Discovery of Esther **(2:01—2:23)**
   1. The King Seeks a New Queen (2:01—2:07)
   2. Hadassah (Esther) Was Brought to the Citadel of Susa (2:08—2:14)
   3. King Ahasuerus Makes Esther Queen (2:15—2:20)
   4. Mordecai's Discovers Plot to Kill the King (2:21—2:23)

   C. Jews Threatened with Annihilation **(3:01—5:14)**
   1. Haman's Plot Against Mordecai & the Jews (3:01—3:11)
   2. Jews to be Annihilated on 13 Adar (Yom Nicanor) (3:12—3:15)
   3. Mordecai Mourns Over Edict (4:01—4:14)
   4. Esther Agrees to Help the Jews (4:15—5:02)
   5. Esther Gives a Banquet for King Ahasuerus & Haman (5:03—5:08)
   6. Haman Plots to Kill Mordecai (5:09—5:14)

2. **God Delivers His People from Annihilation** **(6:01—10:03)**

   A. Mordecai's Rise to Royalty **(6:01—10:03)**
   1. Mordecai Honored by the King (6:01—6:14)
   2. Haman Hanged on His Own Gallows (7:01—7:10)
   3. Mordecai Becomes Second-in-Command (8:01—8:02)
   4. The Decree of King Ahasuerus (8:03—8:08)
   5. Queen Esther Saves the Jews from Annihilation (8:09—8:17)
   6. Israel Defeats Their Enemies on 13 Adar (Yom Nicanor) (9:01—9:19)
   7. The "Feast of Purim" Executed on 14 Adar (9:20—9:32)
   8. Mordecai's Fame (10:01—10:03)

JOB
(1:01—42:17)

1. **Job & His Troublesome Times** **(1:01—1:13)**

   A. The Testing of Job **(1:01—1:13)**
   1. Job's Life in Uz (1:01—1:05)
   2. Satan's Proposal to God (1:06—1:13)

2. **God Allows Satan to Attack Everything Except Job's Life** **(1:14—2:13)**

   A. Satan Commences His Attack Upon Job **(1:14—2:13)**
   1. Satan Attacks Job's Family & Possessions (1:14—1:22)

2. Job's Health Is Attacked (2:01—2:10)
3. Job's Three Comforting Friends (2:11—2:13)

3. **<u>Job's Conversations with His Three Friends</u>** **(3:01—31:40)**

A. Round One of Conversations **(3:01—14:22)**

1. Job Curses His Birth (3:01—3:26)
2. First Friend Reply: Eliphaz to Job
3. Job: Do Not Despise Chastening of the Almighty (5:01—5:27)
4. Job Replies to Eliphaz: My Righteousness Still Stands (6:01—6:30)
5. Job: No Comfort in My Suffering (7:01—7:21)
6. Second Friend Reply: Bildad to Job (8:01—8:22)
7. Job: I Am Blameless (9:01—9:35)
8. Job: Do Not Condemn Me (10:01—10:22)
9. Third Friend Reply: Zophar to Job (11:01—11:20)
10. Job's Reply to His Critical Friends (12:01—14:22)

B. Round Two of Conversations **(15:01—21:34)**

1. Eliphaz: Accuses Job of Being Foolish (15:01—15:35)
2. Job: Second Reply to Eliphaz (16:01—16:22)
3. Job: Prayer of Help (17:01—17:16)
4. Bildad: His Second Conversation with Job (18:01—18:21)
5. Job: His Trust Is in the *LORD* (19:01—19:29)
6. Zophar: Concerning the Wicked (20:01—20:29)
7. Job: His Reply to Zophar's Statement on the Wicked (21:01—21:34)

C. Round Three of Conversations **(22:01—31:40)**

1. Job: Accused of Being a Wicked Person by Eliphaz (22:01—22:30)
2. Job: Declares the Righteousness of God (23:01—23:17)
3. Job: Speaks Concerning the Violence Upon the Earth (24:01—24:25)
4. Bildad: Can a Man Be Righteous Before God? (25:01—25:06)
5. Job: The Moral Character of Man (26:01—26:14)
6. Job: Continues His Walk with God (27:01—27:23)
7. Job: His Opinion on Wisdom (28:01—31:40)

4. **<u>The Three Friends of Job Are Criticized</u>** **(32:01—37:24)**

A. Elihu Enters the Conversations **(32:01—37:24)**

1. Elihu: Opposes Job's Friend's Remarks to Him (32:01—32:22)
2. Job: Contradicted by Elihu (33:01—33:33)
3. Elihu: Declares the Justice of God (34:01—34:37)
4. Elihu: Self-Righteousness Condemned (35:01—35:16)
5. Elihu: Declares the Goodness of God (36:01—37:24)

5. **<u>Job Is Answered by God</u>** **(38:01—41:34)**

A. God Asks Job a Series of Questions **(38:01—41:34)**

1. Concerning God's Knowledge (38:01—40:02)
2. Job's Silence to God (40:03—40:05)
3. Concerning God's Power (40:06—41:34)

6. **The Final State of Job** **(42:01—42:17)**

A. The Restoration of Job **(42:01—42:10**

1. Job's Repentance (42:01—42:11)
2. Job's Restoration (42:12—42:15)
3. Job's Death at Age 140 (42:16—42:17)

PSALMS
(1:01—150:06)

1. **BOOK—1** **(1:01—41:13)**

Psalm 1—Praises God for His Justice (1:01—1:06)
Psalm 2—Ultimate Rule of God (2:01—2:12)
Psalm 3—Trusting God for Protection & Peace (3:01—3:08)
Psalm 4—Rejoicing in God's Protection & Peace (4:01—4:08)
Psalm 5—Secret of Close Relationship with God (5:01—5:12)
Psalm 6—Deliverance from Trouble (6:01—6:10)
Psalm 7—Request for Justice When Slandered (7:01—7:17)
Psalm 8—God Caring for His People (8:01—8:09)
Psalm 9—God Never Ignores Our Cries for Help (9:01—9:20)
Psalm 10—God's Awareness of Every Injustice (10:01—10:18)
Psalm 11—Stability in the Middle of Panic (11:01—11:07)
Psalm 12—Protection Against Manipulation (12:01—12:08)
Psalm 13—"Relief of Despair" Prayer (13:01—13:06)
Psalm 14—Denying God Is Foolish (14:01—14:07)
Psalm 15—Guidelines for Living a Blameless Life (15:01—15:05)
Psalm 16—Life Lived In Companionship with God (16:01—16:11)
Psalm 17—Justice for False Accusations & Persecution (17:01—17:15)
Psalm 18—Gratitude for Deliverance (18:01—18:50)
Psalm 19—God's Greatness (19:01—19:14)
Psalm 20—Victory in Battle Prayer (20:01—20:09)
Psalm 21—Praising God After the Victory of the Battle (21:01—21:13)
Psalm 22—From Great Suffering to Great Joy (22:01—22:31)
Psalm 23—Prayer of Safety (23:01—23:06)
Psalm 24—God's Authority (24:01—24:10)
Psalm 25—Prayer for Defense & Guidance (25:01—25:22)
Psalm 26—Declaring Loyalty to God (26:01—26:12)
Psalm 27—Prayer for Help & Hope (27:01—27:14)
Psalm 28—Prayer When Surrounded by Trouble (28:01—28:09)
Psalm 29—Peace & Strength to Weather Storms of Life (29:01—29:11)
Psalm 30—Celebration of God's Deliverance (30:01—30:12)
Psalm 31—Trust in the *LORD* (31:01—31:24)
Psalm 32—Thankful for God's Goodness (32:01—32:11)
Psalm 33—Rejoicing in the *LORD* (33:01—33:22)
Psalm 34—God Hears & Acts on Those Who Love Him (34:01—34:22)
Psalm 35—Prayer for Being Treated Unjustly (35:01—35:28)
Psalm 36—Concerning the Transgression of the Wicked (36:01—36:12)
Psalm 37—Stand Fast in the *LORD* (37:01—37:40)
Psalm 38—Sorrow for Sin (38:01—38:22)
Psalm 39—Appeal for the Mercy of God (39:01—39:13)

Psalm 40—Waiting Patiently on God (40:01—40:17)
Psalm 41—Prayer for Mercy When You Feel Abandoned (41:01—41:13)

2. **BOOK—2** **(42:01—72:20)**

Psalm 42—Thirty for God (42:01—42:11)
Psalm 43—Hope in Discouragement (43:01—43:05)
Psalm 44—Plea for Victory in Weariness (44:01—44:26)
Psalm 45—Praising the *LORD* (45:01—45:17)
Psalm 46—God Provides Refuge, Security & Peace (46:01—46:11)
Psalm 47—Recognizing the *LORDSHIP* of God (47:01—47:09)
Psalm 48—God's Presence is Our Joy, Security & Salvation (48:01—48:14)
Psalm 49—Trusting in Worldly Possessions Is Useless (49:01—49:20)
Psalm 50—God Seeks Sincerity of Heart (50:01—50:23)
Psalm 51—Prayer for Mercy, Forgiveness & Cleansing (51:01—51:19)
Psalm 52—God Judges Evildoers (52:01—52:09)
Psalm 53—The Fool Says "There Is No God" (53:01—53:06)
Psalm 54—Prayer for Help (54:01—54:07)
Psalm 55—Prayer When Hurt by a Friend (55:01—55:23)
Psalm 56—Prayer in the Midst of Fear (56:01—56:13)
Psalm 57—Prayer for God's Help in Times of Trouble (57:01—57:11)
Psalm 58—Prayer for the Justice of God (58:01—58:11)
Psalm 59—Prayer & Praise for God's Help (59:01—59:17)
Psalm 60—Trust in God (60:01—60:12)
Psalm 61—Prayer for Security & Assurance (61:01—61:08)
Psalm 62—Trust in the *LORD* with All of Your Heart (62:01—62:12)
Psalm 63—Desiring God's Presence, Provision & Protection (63:01—63:11)
Psalm 64—Prayer When People Conspire Against You (64:01—64:10)
Psalm 65—Thankfulness for God's Bounty (65:01—65:13)
Psalm 66—God, Our Heavenly Father Answers Prayers (66:01—66:20)
Psalm 67—Joy in Spreading the Good News About God (67:01—67:07)
Psalm 68—Remembering the Power & Glory of God (68:01—68:35)
Psalm 69—Prayer of Distress (69:01—69:36)
Psalm 70—Urgent Prayer for "HELP" (70:01—70:05)
Psalm 71—God's Faithfulness (71:01—71:24)
Psalm 72—The Righteousness & Justice of God (72:01—72:20)

3. **BOOK—3** **(73:01—89:52)**

Psalm 73—Trusting God for the Future (73:01—73:28)
Psalm 74—Prayer for Help to Defend the Causes of God (74:01—74:23)
Psalm 75—Prayer of Thankfulness to God (75:01—75:10)
Psalm 76—Prayer for God to Punish the Evildoers (76:01—76:12)
Psalm 77—Comfort Through the Hard Times (77:01—77:20)
Psalm 78—Lessons for the Past (78:01—78:72)
Psalm 79—Cry Out to God in Times of Injustice & Disaster (79:01—79:13)
Psalm 80—Prayer for Revival & Restoration (80:01—80:19)
Psalm 81—Celebrate God's Goodness (81:01—81:16)
Psalm 82—Judgment of God (82:01—82:08)

Psalm 83—Combatting the Enemies of God	(83:01—83:18)
Psalm 84—The Presence of God	(84:01—84:12)
Psalm 85—From Reverence to Restoration	(85:01—85:13)
Psalm 86—Trusting God in Times of Deep Trouble	(86:01—86:17)
Psalm 87—City of God	(87:01—87:07)
Psalm 88—God Understands Our Deepest Misery	(88:01—88:18)
Psalm 89—The Mercy of God	(89:01—89:52)

4. **BOOK—4** **(90:01—106:48)**

Psalm 90—The Mercies of God	(90:01—90:17)
Psalm 91—Prayer for Safety & Protection	(91:01—91:16)
Psalm 92—Psalm of Thanksgiving	(92:01—92:15)
Psalm 93—The Nature of God	(93:01—93:05)
Psalm 94—The Wicked Will Not Prevail	(94:01—94:23)
Psalm 95—Invitation to Worship God	(95:01—95:11)
Psalm 96—Psalm on How to Praise Our God	(96:01—96:13)
Psalm 97—Our God Is Righteous & Just	(97:01—97:12)
Psalm 98—Psalm of Joy & Victory	(98:01—98:09)
Psalm 99—Praise for God's Fairness & Holiness	(99:01—99:09)
Psalm 100—Psalm of Thanksgiving	(100:01—100:05)
Psalm 101—Prayer for Help to Walk Blameless	(101:01—101:08)
Psalm 102—Prayer for Distress	(102:01—102:28)
Psalm 103—God's Love for Us	(103:01—103:22)
Psalm 104—Our Appreciation Toward God's Goodness	(104:01—104:35)
Psalm 105—Remembering the Miracles of God	(105:01—105:45)
Psalm 106—The Patience of God	(106:01—106:48)

5. **BOOK—5** **(107:01—150:06)**

Psalm 107—Our Thankfulness Toward God	(107:01—107:43)
Psalm 108—Victory in the Strength of God	(108:01—108:13)
Psalm 109—Righteous Indignation for Liars & Slanderers	(109:01—109:31)
Psalm 110—The Credentials of the Messiah	(110:01—110:07)
Psalm 111—Everything God Does Is Good	(111:01—111:10)
Psalm 112—Faith in God	(112:01—112:10)
Psalm 113—God's Endless Love & Care for the Needy	(113:01—113:09)
Psalm 114—Celebrate the Great Work of God in Our Lives	(114:01—114:08)
Psalm 115—Put God First	(115:01—115:18)
Psalm 116—Praise God for Your Salvation	(116:01—116:19)
Psalm 117—Another Reason to Praise God	(117:01—117:02)
Psalm 118—Confidence in God's Eternal Love	(118:01—118:29)
Psalm 119—Stay True to God & His Word	(119:01—119:176)

HEBREW ALPHABET

Name of Letter	Numerical Value	Passage in Psalms
1. Aleph	1	(119:01—119:08)
2. Beth	2	(119:09—119:16)
3. Gimel	3	(119:17—119:24)

4. Daleth	4	(119:25—119:32)
5. He	5	(119:33—119:40)
6. Waw	6	(119:41—119:48)
7. Zayin	7	(119:49—119:56)
8. Heth	8	(119:57—119:64)
9. Teth	9	(119:65—119:72)
10. Yŏd	10	(119:73—119:80)
11. Kaph	20	(119:81—119:88)
12. Lamed	30	(119:89—119:96)
13. Mem	40	(119:97—119:104)
14. Nun	50	(119:105—119:112)
15. Samek	60	(119:113—119:120)
16. Ayin	70	(119:121—119:128)
17. Pé	80	(119:129—119:136)
18. Tsadde	90	(119:137—119:144)
19. Qoph	100	(119:145—119:152)
20. Resh	200	(119:153—119:160)
21. Shin	300	(119:161—119:168)
22. Tau	400	(119:169—119:176)

Psalm 120—Prayer for Deliverance from False Accusers (120:01—120:07)
Psalm 121—Prayer for Help (121:01—121:08)
Psalm 122—Getting Into the Presence of God (122:01—122:09)
Psalm 123—God's Mercy (123:01—123:04)
Psalm 124—The Protection from the *LORD* (124:01—124:08)
Psalm 125—God Is Our Protector (125:01—125:05)
Psalm 126—God's Power Releases Us from Sin (126:01—126:06)
Psalm 127—Life Without God Is Senseless (127:01—127:05)
Psalm 128—The Marriage Prayer (128:01—128:06)
Psalm 129—God Brings Us Through the Tough Times (129:01—129:08)
Psalm 130—Assurance of the *LORD*'s Forgiveness (130:01—130:08)
Psalm 131—Trust & Contentment (131:01—131:03)
Psalm 132—Honor God (132:01—132:18)
Psalm 133—Joy of Harmonious Relationships (133:01—133:03)
Psalm 134—Worship God & Experience His Blessings (134:01—134:03)
Psalm 135—A Psalm of Praise (135:01—135:21)
Psalm 136—God's Love Never Ends (136:01—136:26)
Psalm 137—Sorrow Makes It Difficult to be Joyful (137:01—137:09)
Psalm 138—Thanksgiving for Answered Prayers (138:01—138:08)
Psalm 139—God Knows Us & Is With Us (139:01—139:24)
Psalm 140—Prayer for Protection of Slander or Threats (140:01—140:13)
Psalm 141—Prayer for Help When Facing Temptations (141:01—141:10)
Psalm 142—Prayer When Overwhelmed & Desperate (142:01—142:07)
Psalm 143—Prayer in the Midst of Hopelessness & Depression (143:01—143:12)
Psalm 144—Rejoicing in God in Prosperity or Adversity (144:01—144:15)

Psalm 145—Everyone Joining Together Worshiping God (145:01—145:21)
Psalm 146—Help of Man vs. Help of God (146:01—146:10)
Psalm 147—God's Greatest Joy—Our True Worship of Him (147:01—147:20)
Psalm 148—Let All Creation Praise the *LORD* (148:01—148:14)
Psalm 149—A Psalm of Victory (149:01—149:09)
Psalm 150—A Closing Hymn of Praise (150:01—150:06)

PROVERBS
(1:01—31:31)

1. **Fatherly Advice to the Younger Generation** **(1:01—9:18)**

A. How to Gain Wisdom **(1:01—1:07)**

1. The Beginning of Knowledge (1:01—1:07)

B. The Principles of Attaining Wisdom **(1:08—7:27)**

1. Avoid Evil Influences (1:08—1:19)
2. Do Not Reject Wise Council (1:20—1:33)
3. Wisdom Will Deliver You from Immoral Women (2:01—2:22)
4. Wisdom for the Young (3:01—3:04)
5. Trust the *LORD* with All of Your Heart (3:05—3:12)
6. Values of Wisdom (3:13—3:20)
7. Sound Wisdom & Discretion (3:21—3:35)
8. God's Wisdom Equals Long Life (4:01—4:13)
9. Avoid the Path of the Wicked (4:14—4:19)
10. Keep Your Heart Pure (4:20—4:27)
11. Warning Against Adultery (5:01—5:23)
12. Beware of Becoming a Co-Signer (6:01—6:05)
13. Avoid Laziness (6:06—6:15)
14. Abominable Things of God (6:16—6:19)
15. Beware of Flattering Lips from an Adulteress (6:20—6:35)
16. Avoid the Clever Adulteress (7:01—7:27)

C. Difference Between Wisdom & Foolish Actions **(8:01—9:18)**

1. The Qualities of Wisdom (8:01—8:21)
2. Wisdom's Origin (8:22—8:31)
3. The Man of Wisdom (8:32—8:36)
4. The Foolishness of the Woman (9:01—9:18)

2. **Practical Wisdom for Godly Living** **(10:01—24:34)**

A. The Proverbs of Wisdom **(10:01—24:34)**

1. Difference Between the Lives of the Righteous & the Wicked (10:01—15:33)
2. Proverbs That Encourages Godly Living (16:01—22:16)
3. Words of the Wise (22:17—23:35)
4. Wisdom Concerning Various People (24:01—24:34)

3. **Wisdom for Leaders & Potential Leaders** (25:01—31:31)

A. Wisdom Concerning Relationships **(25:01—26:28)**

1. Concerning Relationships with Kings (25:01—25:07)
2. Concerning Relationships with Neighbors (25:08—25:20)
3. Concerning Relationships with Enemies (25:21—25:24)
4. Concerning Relationship with Yourself (25:25—26:02)
5. Concerning Relationships with Foolish People (26:03—26:12)
6. Concerning Relationships with Lazy People (26:13—26:16)
7. Concerning Relationships with Gossipers (26:17—26:28)

B. Wisdom Concerning Actions **(27:01—29:27)**

1. Concerning Life (27:01—27:27)
2. Concerning Law (28:01—28:10)
3. Concerning Wealth (28:11—28:28)
4. Concerning Stubbornness (29:01—29:27)

C. Personal Words of Wisdom **(30:01—31:31)**

1. The Words of Agur (Hebrew means "gathered") (30:01—30:33)
2. The Words of Lemuel (31:01—31:09)
   (Hebrew means "God is with me.")
3. The Virtuous (31:10—31:31)

ECCLESIASTES
(1:01—12:14)

1. **Solomon Speaks on His Life's Experiences** (1:01—12:14)

A. The Uselessness of the Cycles of Life **(1:01—2:26)**

1. The Tedious Cycle of Life (1:01—1:11)
2. The Uselessness of Human Wisdom (1:12—1:17)
3. The Uselessness of Pleasure (2:01—2:07)
4. The Uselessness of Wealth (2:08—2:11)
5. The End of the Wise & the Folly (2:12—2:23)
6. Be Content with God's Blessings (2:24—2:26)

B. The Design of Life by The *LORD* **(3:01—3:22)**

1. There Is a Time for Everything (3:01—3:08)
2. The Task Which God Has Given (3:09—3:11)
3. The Gifts of God (3:12—3:15)
4. Future Judgment (3:16—3:22)

C. Different Circumstances in Life **(4:01—6:12)**

1. Concerning the Oppressed (4:01—4:03)
2. Concerning Working (4:04—4:08)
3. Concerning Friendships (4:09—4:12)
4. Concerning Success (4:13—4:16)
5. Concerning Vows (Pledges) to God (5:01—5:07)
6. Concerning Riches (5:08—6:12)

D. Practical Wisdom of Solomon **(7:01—12:14)**

1. Counsel Concerning Wisdom & Foolishness (7:01—7:14)
2. Advantages & Limitations of Wisdom (7:15—8:01)
3. Submitting to Earthly Authority (8:02—8:09)
4. Death Must Come (8:10—8:14)
5. Summary of Solomon's Discoveries (8:15—9:12)
6. More Proverbs Concerning Wisdom & Folly (9:13—10:21)
7. The Value of Persevering (11:01—11:08)
8. Remember God in Your Youth (11:09—12:08)
9. Final Words (12:09—12:14)

SONG OF SOLOMON
(1:01—8:14)

1. The Relationship Between Solomon & the Shulammite Woman **(1:01—8:14)**

A. Day of the Wedding **(1:01—2:07)**

1. The Activities of This Day (1:01—2:07)

B. Courtship Memories **(2:08—3:05)**

1. Shulammite Woman Reflects on Courtship with Solomon (2:08—2:16)
2. Do Not Awaken Love Too Soon (3:01—3:05)

C. Engagement Memories **(3:06—5:01)**

1. Solomon Returns in His Royalty (3:06—3:11)
2. Solomon Expresses His Love & Admiration (4:01—4:07)
3. Solomon Proposes; Shulammite Woman Accepts Marriage Proposal (4:08—5:01)

D. Shulammite Woman Has Troubling Dream **(5:02—6:03)**

1. The Marriage Separation (5:02—5:08)
2. Shulammite's Love & Admiration for Solomon (5:09—6:03)

E. The Bride's Beauty Praised **(6:04—7:09)**

1. Solomon Praises His Beloved's Beauty (6:04—6:09)
2. Solomon Sleeps with His Beloved (6:10—6:13)
3. The Marriage Relationship Intensifies (7:01—7:09)

F. The Tender Appeal of the Bride **(7:10—8:05)**

1. Bride Takes Initiative to Lovemaking (7:10—7:13)
2. Bride's Desire to Show Husband Affection Publicly (8:01—8:03)
3. Don't Awaken Love Too Soon (8:04—8:05)

G. Love's Power **(8:06—8:14)**

1. Description of the Power of Love [(8:06—8:07)]
2. The Girl's Moral State as a Young Woman (8:08—8:10)
3. The Bride Shares All with Solomon (8:11—8:12)
4. Solomon & Bride's Devotion (8:13—8:14)

ISAIAH
(1:01—66:24)

1. **Message of Divine Judgment** **(1:01—23:18)**

A. Condemnation of the Children of Israel **(1:01—6:13)**

1. Judah's Wicked Lifestyle (1:01—1:20)
2. Jerusalem Plays the Harlot (1:21—1:23)
3. Restoration Promised (1:24—1:31)
4. The Glory of the Future House of God (2:01—2:04)
5. The Day of the *LORD* (2:05—2:22)
6. Judgment Befalls Judah & Jerusalem (3:01—4:01)
7. Mount Zion Renewed (4:02—4:06)
8. The Parable of the Vineyard (5:01—5:30)
9. The Calling of Isaiah to be a Prophet (6:01—6:13)

B. The Coming of the Messiah **(7:01—12:06)**

1. Isaiah Sent to Meet King Ahaz of Judah (7:01—7:09)
2. The Sign of Immanuel (7:10—7:25)
3. The Fall of Israel & Syria to Assyria (8:01—8:10)
4. Fear God & Revere His Word (8:11—8:22)
5. The Sign of the Messiah (9:01—9:07)
6. Samaria's Judgment (9:08—10:04)
7. Assyria Judged; Israel Returns Home (10:05—10:34)
8. The Branch of Jesse (11:01—11:16)
9. A Hymn of Praise (12:01—12:06)

C. Judgment Against Heathen Nations **(13:01—23:18)**

1. Judgment Against Babylon (13:01—13:22)
2. The *LORD* Has Compassion (14:01—14:02)
3. The Fall of Nebuchadnezzar (14:03—14:11)
4. The Fall of Lucifer (14:12—14:23)
5. Judgment Against Assyria (14:24—14:27)
6. Judgment Against Philistia (14:28—14:32)
7. Judgment Against Moab (15:01—16:14)
8. Judgment Against Syria & Israel (17:01—17:14)
9. Judgment Against Ethiopia (18:01—18:07)
10. Judgment Against Egypt (19:01—19:15)
11. Future Blessings for Egypt, Assyria & Israel (19:16—19:25)
12. Isaiah's Sign Against Egypt & Ethiopia (20:01—20:06)
13. Judgment Against Babylon (21:01—21:10)
14. Judgment Against Edom (21:11—21:12)
15. Judgment Against Arabia (21:13—21:17)
16. Judgment Against Jerusalem (22:01—22:25)
17. Judgment Against Tyre (23:01—23:18)

2. **The Future End-time Tribulation & The Kingdom** **(24:01—39:08)**

A. The Devastation of the Earth **(24:01—27:13)**

1. The Coming Judgment Upon the Earth (24:01—24:23)
2. Victories in the Kingdom Age (25:01—25:12)
3. A Song of Praise (26:01—26:21)
4. The Restoration of Israel (27:01—27:13)

B. The Condemnation of Israel & Judah **(28:01—35:10)**

1. Woe to Samaria of Ephraim (28:01—28:15)
2. A Stone for Foundation in Zion (28:16—28:22)
3. Listen & Hear the Words of God (28:23—28:29)
4. Woe to Jerusalem for Her Hypocrisy (29:01—29:24)
5. Woe to Jerusalem for Trusting in Egypt (30:01—30:26)
6. Judgment on Assyria (30:27—30:33)
7. The Foolishness of Not Trusting God (31:01—31:09)
8. A King Will Reign in Righteousness (32:01—32:20)
9. Destruction of Assyria (33:01—33:09)
10. Coming Judgment Upon Zion (33:10—33:24)
11. Judgment on the Nations (35:01—35:10)

C. Events During the Reign of King Hezekiah of Judah **(36:01—39:08)**

1. King Sennacherib of Egypt Boasts Against the *LORD* (36:01—36:22)
2. Deliverance from Sennacherib's Attack Assured (37:01—37:07)
3. Assyria Threatens Judah (37:08—37:20)
4. God's Reply to Hezekiah's Prayer (37:21—37:35)
5. Judah Triumphs Over Assyria (37:36—37:38)
6. King Hezekiah's Life Extended (38:01—38:22)
7. King Hezekiah's Stupidity (39:01—39:08)

3. <u>Message of Divine Comfort</u> **(40:01—66:24)**

A. The Awesomeness of God **(40:01—48:22)**

1. Concerning Israel's Release from Babylonian Captivity (40:01—40:11)
2. Concerning God's Creation (40:12—40:31)
3. Concerning God's Help to His People (41:01—41:20)
4. Concerning the Uselessness of Idols (41:21—41:29)
5. Concerning God Providing His Servant, the *LORD* (42:01—42:20)
6. Concerning Israel's Stubborn Disobedience (42:21—42:25)
7. Concerning Israel's Restoration (43:01—43:28)
8. Concerning God's Blessing on Israel (44:01—44:05)
9. There Is No Other God but Yahweh (44:06—44:08)
10. Concerning Idolatry (44:09—44:20)
11. Israel Not Forgotten; Will Be Restored (44:21—44:28)
12. Concerning Cyrus, God's Instrument (45:01—45:25)
13. Dead Idols (46:01—46:13)
14. Concerning the Humiliation of Babylon (47:01—47:15)
15. Concerning Judah's Release from the Babylonians (48:01—48:22)

B. Israel's Future Redeemer **(49:01—59:21)**

1. God's Servant, the Messiah (49:01—49:26)
2. God's Servant, the Hope of Israel (50:01—50:11)
3. The *LORD* Comforts the Faithful Remnant (51:01—51:23)
4. Jerusalem Redeemed by the *LORD* (52:01—52:12)
5. The Suffering Servant of God, the Messiah (52:13—53:12)
6. Salvation for the Gentiles (54:01—54:17)

7. An Invitation to Salvation in God's Servant, the Messiah (55:01—55:13)
8. Salvation for the Gentiles (56:01—56:08)
9. Rebuke for the Blind Watchmen (56:09—56:12)
10. Israel's Useless Idolatry (57:01—57:13)
11. The Healing for the Backslider (57:14—57:21)
12. Fasting That Pleases God (58:01—58:14)
13. Dealing with Sin (59:01—59:08)
14. Confessed Sin (59:09—59:15)
15. Blotting Out Sin (59:16—59:21)

C. The Millennial Kingdom **(60:01—62:12)**

1. The Blessing of the Gentiles Toward Zion (60:01—60:22)
2. The Good News of Salvation (61:01—61:11)
3. The Restoration of Israel (62:01—62:12)

D. The Requirements for the Blessing **(63:01—66:24)**

1. The Judgment of the Enemies of God (63:01—63:06)
2. God's Mercy Remembered (63:07—63:14)
3. A Prayer of Repentance (63:15—64:12)
4. God's Judgment Is Righteous (65:01—65:16)
5. The Characteristics of the Millennial Kingdom (65:17—65:25)
6. Worship—True & False (66:01—66:13)
7. The Indignation of God (66:14—66:24)

JEREMIAH
(1:01—52:34)

1. **The Judgment of God Upon Judah** **(1:01—29:32)**

A. The *LORD* Calls Jeremiah to be a Prophet **(1:01—1:19)**

1. The Calling of Jeremiah (1:01—1:10)
2. Jeremiah's Confirmation (1:11—1:19)

B. Jeremiah Prophesies Against Judah **(2:01—6:30)**

1. The Case of God Against the Sins of Judah (2:01—2:37)
2. Disgraceful Israel (3:01—3:05)
3. Israel Called to Repent (3:06—4:04)
4. Judgment Predicted Against Judah (4:05—4:31)
5. The Justice of the Judgment of God Upon Judah (5:01—5:31)
6. Destruction Arriving from the North (Babylon) (6:01—6:30)

C. False Religion of Judah **(7:01—10:25)**

1. Trusting in Deceptive Words (7:01—7:27)
2. Judah's Repulsive Religion Judged (7:28—8:03)
3. The Danger of False Teaching (8:04—8:17)
4. Jeremiah Mourns for Judah (8:18—9:16)
5. Judah Mourns in Judgment (9:17—9:26)
6. The Foolishness of Idolatry (10:01—10:16)
7. Judah's Captivity Is Coming (10:17—10:25)

D. Judah Breaks Covenant with God **(11:01—15:09)**

1. The Evidence Against Judah (11:01—11:17)
2. Schemes to Kill Jeremiah (11:18—11:23)
3. Jeremiah's Question to the *LORD* (12:01—12:04)
4. The *LORD*'s Reply to Jeremiah (12:05—12:17)
5. Significance of the Linen Sash (13:01—13:11)
6. Significance of the Wine Bottles (13:12—13:14)
7. Warning Against Pride & Arrogance (13:15—13:27)
8. Drought Lays Hold of Judah (14:01—14:06)
9. Jeremiah Intercedes for Judah (14:07—14:22)
10. The *LORD* Will Not Relent (15:01—15:09)

E. Jeremiah Recommissioned **(15:10—20:18)**

1. Jeremiah's Sorrow (15:10—15:18)
2. Jeremiah's Restoration (15:19—15:21)
3. God Puts Restrictions on Jeremiah's Life (16:01—16:13)
4. Restoration of Israel Promised by the *LORD* (16:14—16:21)
5. The Sins of Judah (17:01—17:13)
6. Jeremiah Prays for Vindication (17:14—17:18)
7. Hallow the Sabbath Day (17:19—17:27)
8. The Parable of the Potter (18:01—18:11)
9. The Warning of God Rejected (18:12—18:17)
10. Another Conspiracy Against Jeremiah (18:18—18:23)
11. The Sign of the Broken Flask (Jar) (19:01—19:15)
12. Jeremiah Is Persecuted by Pashhur (20:01—20:06)
13. Jeremiah Complains Concerning His Lot (20:07—20:18)

F. Judah's Leaders Face Accusations from Jeremiah **(21:01—23:40)**

1. Jeremiah's Message to Zedekiah: "Jerusalem Doomed!" (21:01—21:10)
2. Jeremiah's Message to the King of Judah (21:11—22:10)
3. The Message to the Sons of Josiah (22:11—22:30)
   A. To Jehoahaz (Shallum) (22:11—17)
   B. To Jehoiakim (22:18—23)
   C. To Jehoiachin (Coniah) (22:24—30)
4. The Message Concerning the Messiah (23:01—23:08)
5. The False Prophets (23:09—23:40)

G. Judah Goes Into Captivity **(24:01—29:32)**

1. The Parable of the Figs in a Basket (24:01—24:10)
2. Captivity to Last Seventy Years (605—536 B.C.) (25:01—25:11)
3. Jeremiah Protected from Death by Ahikam (26:01—26:24)
4. Sign of the Yoke (27:01—27:22)
5. False Prophecy from Hananiah, Son of Azur (28:01—28:14)
6. Doom of Hananiah, the False Prophet (28:15—28:17)
7. Jeremiah's Letters to the Jews in Captivity in Babylon (29:01—29:32)

2. <u>**Hope of Resurrection of Judah Is Promised**</u> **(30:01—45:05)**

A. Restoration After Seventy Years of Tribulation **(30:01—33:26)**

1. Israel & Judah to Be Restored (30:01—30:24)

2. Restoration of Israel Concerning the Northern Kingdom (31:01—31:22)
3. Restoration of Israel Concerning the Southern Kingdom (31:23—31:26)
4. A New Covenant for All of Israel (31:27—31:40)
5. Jeremiah Buys a Field (587/586 B.C.) (32:01—32:25)
6. Israel's Return to Jerusalem Assured (32:26—32:44)
7. The Promise of Restoration Reassured (33:01—33:13)
8. The Davidic Covenant Reaffirmed (33:14—33:26)

B. Events "Before" the Destruction of Jerusalem **(34:01—39:18)**

1. Jeremiah's Message to King Zedekiah (34:01—34:07)
2. King Zedekiah's Message to the People: "Release the Slaves" (34:08—34:10)
3. People Reversed Decision on Slavery (34:11—34:11)
4. Cities of Judah— "Desolation Without Inhabitation" (34:12—34:22)
5. Jeremiah's Message to the Rechabites (35:01—35:19)
6. Baruch, Jeremiah's Scribe Reads Scroll in the Temple (36:01—36:10)
7. Baruch, Jeremiah's Scribe Reads Scroll in Secretary's Room (36:11—36:19)
8. Jehoiakim, Son of King Josiah Burns Jeremiah's Scroll (36:20—36:26)
9. Jeremiah Commanded to Rewrite the Scroll (36:27—36:32)
10. King Zedekiah's Useless Hopes (37:01—37:10)
11. Jeremiah Thrown Into Prison (37:11—37:21)
12. Jeremiah Lifted from the Dungeon (38:01—38:13)
13. King Zedekiah Meets Secretly with Jeremiah for Advice (38:14—38:28)
14. The Fall of Jerusalem (39:01—39:10)
15. Nebuzaradan, Babylonian Captain Sets Jeremiah Free (39:11—39:18)

C. Events "After" the Destruction of Jerusalem **(40:01—45:05)**

1. Jeremiah Released in Ramah; Sent to Gedaliah (40:01—40:16)
2. The Revolt Against Gedaliah (41:01—41:18)
3. Migration to Egypt Forbidden (42:01—42:22)
4. Jeremiah Taken to Egypt; Ministers to the Jews There (43:01—43:13)
5. Jews to be Punished in Egypt for Their Idolatry (44:01—45:05)

3. <u>**Jeremiah's Prophecies Against Other Nations**</u> **(46:01—52:34)**

A. Prophecies Against Other Nations **(46:01—51:64)**

1. Prophecies Concerning Egypt (46:01—46:26)
2. God Will Save Israel (46:27—46:28)
3. Prophecies Concerning Philistia (47:01—47:07)
4. Prophecies Concerning Moab (48:01—48:47)
5. Prophecies Concerning Ammon (49:01—49:06)
6. Prophecies Concerning Edom (49:07—49:22)
7. Prophecies Concerning Damascus (49:23—49:27)
8. Prophecies Concerning Kedar & Hazar (49:28—49:33)

9. Prophecies Concerning Elam (49:34—49:39)
10. Prophecies Concerning Babylon & Babylonia (50:01—50:46)
11. Babylon's Total Desolation (51:01—51:64)

B. Historical Events of the Fall of Jerusalem (52:01—52:34)
1. A Review of the Fall of Jerusalem (52:01—52:11)
2. The Temple & the City of Jerusalem Plundered & Blundered (52:12—52:23)
3. Jerusalem Taken Into Captivity a Third Time (581 B.C.) (52:24—52:30)
4. Jehoiachin Released from Prison (562 B.C.) (52:31—52:34)

LAMENTATIONS
(1:01—5:22)

1. <u>**Jerusalem Lies in Desolation**</u> **(1:01—5:22)**

A. Jerusalem Lies Bare of Any People (1:01—1:22)
1. Jeremiah Mourns for Jerusalem (1:01—1:17)
2. The *LORD* is Righteous (1:18—1:22)

B. How God Almighty Feels About Sin (2:01—3:66)
1. The Anger of God Against the Sin of Jerusalem (2:01—2:10)
2. Jeremiah's Weeping & Mourning Continues (2:11—2:22)
3. Jeremiah's Anger (3:01—3:18)
4. Jeremiah's Hope in the *LORD* (3:19—3:38)
5. Jeremiah's Suffering (3:39—3:54)
6. Jeremiah's Prayer to the *LORD* (3:55—3:66)

C. The Anger of the *LORD* Is Quenched (4:01—4:22)
1. The Decline of Jerusalem (4:01—4:12)
2. The Cause of Jerusalem's Decline (4:13—4:20)
3. Jerusalem's Future Hope (4:21—4:22)

D. Jeremiah Prays for Restoration of the People (5:01—5:22)
1. The People Cry Out to the *LORD* (5:01—5:22)

EZEKIEL
(1:01—48:35)

1. <u>**Doom & Gloom Foreseen**</u> **(1:01—19:14)**

A. The Call & Commission of Ezekiel (1:01—1:03)
1. The Hand of the *LORD* Upon Ezekiel (1:01—1:03)

B. The Visions Given by God to Ezekiel (1:04—1:28)
1. Vision of the Four Living Creatures (1:04—1:14)
2. Vision of the Four Wheels (1:15—1:21)
3. Vision of the Glowing Firmament (1:22—1:28)

C. Ezekiel's Commission to Judah **(2:01—3:27)**

1. God Sends Ezekiel to a Stubborn & Rebellious Israel (2:01—3:15)
2. Ezekiel is Made a Watchman for Israel (3:16—3:27)

D. Prophetic Visions Concerning Judah **(4:01—11:25)**

1. Symbolism Using the Clay Tablet (Brick) (4:01—4:03)
2. Israel's Duration of Captivity (390 Years) (4:04—4:05)
3. Judah's Duration of Captivity (40 Years) (4:06—4:08)
4. Symbolism Using the Bread (4:09—4:17)
5. Symbolism of Ezekiel Using a Sword Shaving His Head (5:01—5:17)
6. Judah's Idolatry Calls Down God's Judgment (6:01—6:14)
7. The Complete Destruction of Judah (7:01—7:27)
8. Vision of Wickedness in the Temple (8:01—8:18)
9. Vision of the Wicked Being Slaughtered (9:01—9:11)
10. Vision of the Burning City (10:01—10:22)
11. Vision of the Wicked Leaders (11:01—11:13)
12. Promise of Restoration (11:14—11:25)

E. The Judgment & Punishment Is Absolute **(12:01—19:14)**

1. The Sign of Judah Going Into Captivity (12:01—12:16)
2. The Sign of Eating in Fear (12:17—12:28)
3. Warning to False Prophets (13:01—13:16)
4. Warning to False Prophetesses (13:17—13:23)
5. Warning Against Idolatry (14:01—14:11)
6. Warning Against Unfaithfulness (14:12—14:23)
7. Parable of the Fruitless Vine (15:01—15:08)
8. Jerusalem—The Unfaithful Wife (16:01—16:07)
9. Israel Becoming the *LORD*'s Bride (16:08—16:14)
10. Israel Becoming the Unfaithful Wife (16:15—16:34)
11. The Punishment for Israel's Unfaithfulness (16:35—16:52)
12. The Restoration of the Captives of Sodom & Samaria (16:53—16:59)
13. Israel's Everlasting Covenant with God (16:60—16:63)
14. The Parable of the Eagle & the Vine (17:01—17:10)
15. Explanation of the "Parable of the Eagle & the Vine" (17:11—17:21)
16. Israel Exalted At Last (17:22—17:24)
17. The Proverb Proven Wrong (18:01—18:32)
    - A. The *LORD* Cancels the Proverb (18:01—04)
    - B. Rebellion Bears It's Own Responsibility (18:05—13)
    - C. Individual Accountability (18:14—20)
    - D. Repentance Brings Forgiveness (18:21—23)
    - E. Iniquity Brings Judgment (18:24—29)
    - F. Repentance Needed (18:30—32)
18. Lamentation for the Princes of Israel (19:01—19:14)
    - A. Request for a Funeral Song (19:01—02)
    - B. Refers to Jehoahaz Taken to Prison (609 B.C.) (19:03—04)
    - C. Refers to Jehoiachin Taken to Prison (587 B.C.) (19:05—09)

D. Nebuchadnezzar Conquers Israel (586 B.C.) (19:10—14)

2. <u>The Unfaithfulness of Israel</u> **(20:01—24:27)**

A. The Rebellion of Israel **(20:01—24:27)**

1. Unfaithfulness of Israel (20:01—20:32)
   - A. Leaders of Israel Request a Message from the *LORD* (20:01—04)
   - B. Israel in Egypt (20:05—09)
   - C. Israel on Their Way to Kadesh-Barnea (20:10—17)
   - D. Israel in the Wilderness (20:18—26)
   - E. Israel Arrives Into Canaan (20:27—29)
   - F. Israel in Ezekiel's Time (20:29—32)
2. Israel's Future Restoration (20:33—20:44)
3. Forest Fire in the Negev (20:45—20:49)
4. God's Sword—The Avenging Babylonian Army (21:01—21:32)
5. The Sins of Jerusalem (22:01—22:16)
6. House of Israel in the Furnace (22:17—22:22)
7. The Wicked Leaders (22:23—22:31)
8. Parable of the Two Harlot Sisters (23:01—23:49)
   - A. Who They Are (23:01—04)
   - B. What They Did (23:05—21)
   - C. Their Judgment (23:22—49)
9. Parable of the Boiling Pot (24:01—24:14)
10. Ezekiel's Wife Taken by God (24:15—24:27)

3. <u>Messages Against Foreign Nations</u> **(25:01—32:32)**

A. Prophecies Against Other Nations **(25:01—32:32)**

1. Concerning Ammon (25:01—25:07)
2. Concerning Moab (25:08—25:11)
3. Concerning Edom (25:12—25:14)
4. Concerning Philistia (25:15—25:17)
5. Concerning Tyre (26:01—28:19)
   - A. The Judgment (26:01—21)
   - B. The Lamentation (27:01—36)
   - C. Prophecy Against the King of Tyre (28:01—10)
   - D. Lamentation for the King of Tyre (28:11—19)
6. Concerning Sidon (28:20—28:24)
7. Concerning Egypt (29:01—32:32)
   - A. The Judgment (29:01—16)
   - B. The Plundering of Egypt (29:17—21)
   - C. Lamentation of Egypt (30:01—19)
   - D. Prophecy Against Pharaoh of Egypt (30:20—26)
   - E. Egypt—Pride Was Their Destruction (31:01—18)
   - F. Lamentation for Pharaoh & Egypt (32:01—16)
   - G. Egypt & Neighbors Consigned to the Pit (32:17—32)

4. <u>Messages of the Hope for Israel</u> **(33:01—39:29)**

A. The Restoration of Israel **(33:01—37:28)**

1. Ezekiel—Israel's Watchman (33:01—33:09)
2. God's Judgment Is Fair & Just (33:10—33:20)
3. The Demise of Jerusalem (33:21—33:22)

- 4. The Sins of Israel's Guilt (33:23—33:29)
- 5. The Exiles Heard But No Heed (33:30—33:33)
- 6. The Shepherds of Israel (34:01—34:31)
  - A. The False Shepherds of Israel (34:01—10)
  - B. God—The True Shepherd (34:11—31)
- 7. Israel Reborn (35:01—37:28)
  - A. Judgment on Mount Seir (35:01—15)
  - B. Israel's Covenant (36:01—38)
  - C. The Parable of the Dry Bones (37:01—14)
  - D. Reuniting of Israel As One Nation (37:15—28)

B. The War of Israel in the Latter Days **(38:01—39:29)**

- 1. The Invasion of Israel by the Nation of Magog (Russia) (38:01—38:16)
- 2. Judgment on Gog of Magog (38:17—38:23)
- 3. The Armies of Gog of Magog Destroyed (39:01—39:10)
- 4. The Burial of Gog in Israel (39:11—39:17)
- 5. The Great Supper of God (39:18—39:20)
- 6. Israel Is Restored to Her Land (39:20—39:29)

5. <u>A Glimpse of Israel in the Millennial Kingdom</u> **(40:01—48:35)**

A. Vision of a New Temple **(40:01—42:20)**

- 1. God Speaks to Ezekiel Concerning the Temple (40:01—40:04)
- 2. The Temple (40:05—42:20)
  - A. The Temple Wall (40:05—05)
  - B. The Eastern Gate (40:06—16)
  - C. The Outer Court (40:17—19)
  - D The Northern Gate (40:20—23)
  - E. The Southern Gate (40:24—27)
  - F. The Inner Court (40:28—37)
    - 1. The South Gate (40:28—31)
    - 2. The East Gate (40:32—34)
    - 3. The North Gate (40:35—37)
  - G. The Place for Sacrifices (40:38—43)
  - H. Chambers for Singers & Priests (40:44—46)
  - I. The Measurement of the Court (40:47—47)
  - J. The Temple Porch (40:48—49)
  - K. The Sanctuary Measurements (41:01—04)
  - L. The Side Chambers on the Wall (41:05—11)
  - M. The Building at Its Western End (41:12—12)
  - N. Dimensions & Design of the Temple Area (41:13—26)
  - O. The Chambers for the Priests (42:01—20)

B. The Temple—The *LORD*'s Dwelling Place **(43:01—48:35)**

- 1. The Glory of the *LORD* Returns (43:01—43:06)
- 2. The Temple Must Be Holy (43:07—43:12)
- 3. The Altar (43:13—43:27)
  - A. Measurements of the Altar (43:13—17)
  - B. Procedures for Consecration (43:18—27)
- 4. The Prince in the East Gate (44:01—44:03)

5. People Allowed in the Temple (44:04—44:09)
6. Laws Governing the Priests (44:10—44:31)
7. The Holy District of the *LORD* (45:01—45:06)
8. Land Allotted to the Princes (45:07—45:08)
9. Laws Concerning the Prince (45:09—45:17)
10. Offerings & the Holy Days (45:18—46:15)
    A. At Feasts (45:18—25)
    B. At Sabbaths & New Moons (46:01—15)
11. The Rules & Regulations for the Prince (46:16—46:18)
12. Preparations for the Offerings (46:19—46:24)
13. The River of Living Water Flowing Eastward from the Temple (47:01—47:12)
14. The Boundaries of the Nation of Israel (47:13—47:23)
15. The Dividing of the Land (48:01—48:29)
16. The Names of the Gates of the City (48:30—48:35)

DANIEL
(1:01—12:13)

1. **Daniel's Life Under King Nebuchadnezzar** **(1:01—5:31)**

A. The Life of Daniel, the Prophet of God **(1:01—1:21)**
1. Daniel Departed to Babylon (1:01—1:07)
2. Daniel's Faithfulness to God in Babylon (1:08—1:16)
3. Daniel's Reputation in Babylon (1:17—1:21)

B. The First Dream of King Nebuchadnezzar, King of Babylon **(2:01—3:30)**
1. Nebuchadnezzar Doesn't Reveal His Dream (2:01—2:03)
2. Nebuchadnezzar Addresses Astrologers Concerning Dream (2:04—2:16)
3. God Reveals Dream to Daniel (2:17—2:23)
4. Daniel Explains the Dream to King Nebuchadnezzar (2:24—2:36)
5. Daniel Interprets the Dream to King Nebuchadnezzar (2:37—2:45)
6. Daniel & Friends Were Promoted (2:46—2:49)
7. Nebuchadnezzar Has Image of Gold Erected (3:01—3:07)
8. Daniel's Friends Refuse to Worship the Image (3:08—3:12)
9. Faith in the Furnace (3:13—3:18)
10. Daniel's Friends Protected in the Fiery Furnace (3:19—3:23)
11. A Fourth Person Noticed in the Fire (3:24—3:25)
12. Nebuchadnezzar Releases Daniel & Friends; Gives Praises to God (3:26—3:30)

C. King Nebuchadnezzar's Second Dream **(4:01—4:36)**
1. Nebuchadnezzar's Public Decree (4:01—4:03)
2. Nebuchadnezzar's Second Dream (4:04—4:18)
3. Daniel's Interpretation of Second Dream (4:19—4:27)
4. The Fulfillment of the Second Dream (4:28—4:33)
5. Nebuchadnezzar Is Restored (4:34—4:36)

D. The Great Feast of King Belshazzar **(5:01—5:31)**

1. Temple Vessels Are Defiled (5:01—5:04)
2. Handwriting on the Wall by God (5:05—5:09)
3. The Queen Mother Proclaims Daniel Can Explain Handwriting (5:10—5:12)
4. Daniel Explains Handwriting on Wall (5:13—5:24)
5. Interpretation of Dream (5:25—5:31)

2. <u>**Daniel's Life Under King Darius**</u> **(6:01—12:13)**

A. The Plot Against Daniel **(6:01—6:28)**

1. Daniel's Promotion (6:01—6:03)
2. The Plot Against Daniel (6:04—6:09)
3. Daniel's Prayer (6:10—6:11)
4. The Prosecution of Daniel (6:12—6:15)
5. Daniel Cast Into Den of Lions (6:16—6:24)
6. The Decree of King Darius Concerning God (6:25—6:28)

B. The Visions of Daniel **(7:01—8:27)**

1. Vision of the Four Beasts (7:01—7:08)
2. Vision of the Ancient of Days (7:09—7:14)
3. Interpretation of the Four Beasts (7:15—7:22)
4. Interpretation of the Fourth Beast (7:23—7:28)
5. Vision of a Ram (8:01—8:04)
6. Vision of the Male Goat (8:05—8:08)
7. Vision of the Horn (8:09—8:12)
8. Length of the Vision (8:13—8:14)
9. Gabriel Explains the Vision (8:15—8:19)
10. Explanation of the Vision of the Ram (8:20—8:20)
11. Explanation of the Male Goat (8:21—8:22)
12. Explanation of the Little Horn Rising (8:23—8:26)
13. Daniel Couldn't Understand Vision (8:27—8:27)

C. End-time Events Revealed to Daniel in Prophecies **(9:01—10:21)**

1. Daniel Reviews Jeremiah's Prophecy (9:01—9:03)
2. Daniel Intercedes for His People to God (9:04—9:19)
3. Gabriel Explains Seventy-year Prophecy by Jeremiah to Daniel (9:20—9:27)
   - A. Gabriel Appears to Daniel (9:20—23)
   - B. Seventy Times Seven (490 yrs) Prophecy Explained to Daniel (9:24—27)
4. Daniel's Vision of a Glorious Messenger (10:01—10:09)
5. The Glorious Hand Touches Daniel (10:10—10:17)
6. Strength from the Glorious Messenger (10:18—10:21)

D. Prophecies Concerning the North & South Kings **(11:01—12:13)**

1. Concerning Persia (11:01—11:02)
2. Concerning Greece (11:03—11:04)
3. Concerning Egypt & Aram (Syria) (11:05—11:20)
4. Antiochus Epiphanes (11:21—11:35)
5. The End-time Antichrist (11:36—11:45)
6. Concerning Israel (12:01—12:13)

HOSEA
(1:01—14:09)

1. **The Faithful Husband & The Adulterous Wife** **(1:01—3:05)**
   A. Parallel Relationship Between Hosea's Wife Gomer & Israel **(1:01—3:05)**
      1. The Unfaithfulness of Gomer, Hosea's Wife (1:01—1:09)
      2. The Future Restoration of Israel (1:10—2:01)
      3. The Punishment for the Unfaithful Wife (2:02—2:13)
      4. The Restoration of Israel & Gomer (2:14—2:23)
      5. Israel Returns to God (3:01—3:05)

2. **The Faithful *LORD* & The Adulterous Israel** **(4:01—14:09)**
   A. The Case of the Adulterous Israel **(4:01—10:15)**
      1. The Indictment Against Israel (4:01—4:10)
      2. Purpose of Indictment (4:11—4:19)
      3. The Verdict Against Israel Is In (5:01—5:15)
      4. Israel Pleas for Mercy (6:01—6:03)
      5. The *LORD*'s Reply (6:04—6:11)
      6. The Crimes of Israel (7:01—7:16)
      7. The Apostasy of Israel (8:01—8:14)
      8. The Judgment Against Israel to Come (9:01—9:17)
      9. The Verdict Is Captivity (10:01—10:15)

   B. Israel's Restoration to the *LORD* **(11:01—14:09)**
      1. The Love of God for Israel (11:01—11:12)
      2. Israel's Continuing Sin (12:01—12:14)
      3. The Relentless Judgment Upon Israel (13:01—13:16)
      4. Israel Finally Restored (14:01—14:09)

JOEL
(1:01—3:21)

1. **The Land That Was Laid Waste** **(1:01—3:21)**
   A. Introduction to Joel **(1:01—1:01)**

   B. Characteristics of the Wasteland **(1:02—3:21)**
      1. Locusts—The Cause of the Wasteland (1:02—1:12)
      2. Mourning—The Reaction to the Land Laid Waste (1:13—1:20)
      3. The Day of the *LORD* (2:01—2:11)
      4. A Call to Personal Repentance (2:12—2:14)
      5. A Call to National Repentance (2:15—2:17)
      6. God's Outpouring of Forgiveness (2:18—2:27)
      7. The Promise of Israel's Future Deliverance (2:28—2:32)
      8. God's Judgment on the Gentiles (3:01—3:15)
      9. Restoration of Judah (3:16—3:21)

AMOS
(1:01—9:15)

1. **The Words of The *LORD* Spoken to Amos, the Prophet** **(1:01—2:16)**

A. Introduction to Amos **(1:01—1:02)**

B. Prophecies of Judgment on the Neighbors of Israel **(1:03—2:16)**

1. Judgment on Damascus (1:03—1:05)
2. Judgment on Gaza (1:06—1:08)
3. Judgment on Tyre (1:09—1:10)
4. Judgment on Edom (1:11—1:12)
5. Judgment on Ammon (1:13—1:15)
6. Judgment on Moab (2:01—2:03)
7. Judgment on Judah (2:04—2:05)
8. Judgment on Israel (2:06—2:16)

C. The Judgment Messages of Amos, the Prophet **(3:01—6:14)**

1. The Present Judgment of Israel (3:01—3:15)
2. Israel's Depravity (4:01—4:13)
3. The Future Judgment of Israel (5:01—6:14)
   - A. A Lamentation for Israel (5:01—17)
   - B. The First Woe of Judgment to Come (5:18—27)
   - C. The Second Woe of Judgment to Come (6:01—02)
   - D. The Third Woe of Judgment to Come (6:03—14)

D. Visions of Judgment **(7:01—9:15)**

1. The Locusts (7:01—7:03)
2. The Fire (7:04—7:06)
3. The Plumb Line (7:07—7:09)
4. Amaziah's Opposition (7:10—7:17)
5. The Summer Fruit (8:01—8:14)
6. Destruction of Israel (9:01—9:10)
7. Restoration of Israel (9:11—9:15)

OBADIAH
(1:01—2:21)

2. **The Destruction of Edom** **(1:01—2:21)**

A. Edom's Destruction Is Coming **(1:01—1:09)**

1. Destruction Is Certain (1:01—1:04)
2. Destruction Is Total (1:05—1:09)

B. Accusations Against Edom **(1:10—1:14)**

1. Violence Against Brother (1:10—1:10)
2. Opposition to His Brother (1:11—1:14)

C. Restoration of Israel **(2:01—2:21)**

1. Israel's Final Triumph (2:01—2:21)

JONAH
(1:01—4:11)

1. **The *LORD* Gives Jonah A Message** **(1:01—1:01)**

A. Jonah Flees His Mission **(1:01—2:10)**

1. Jonah Disobeys the *LORD* (1:01—1:03)
2. The Great Storm in the Mediterranean Sea (1:04—1:09)
3. Jonah Blamed for the Sailor's Problems at Sea (1:10—1:16)
4. Jonah's Prayer (1:17—2:09)
5. Jonah Delivered from the Fish (2:10—2:10)

B. Jonah Fulfills His Mission **(3:01—4:11)**

1. Jonah Preaches at Nineveh (3:01—3:04)
2. The People at Nineveh Believed God (3:05—3:10)
3. Jonah's Complaint to God (4:01—4:03)
4. God's Kindness to Jonah (4:04—4:11)

MICAH
(1:01—7:20)

1. **Prophecies of Judgment on Samaria & Judah** **(1:01—7:20)**

A. The Introduction to Micah **(1:01—1:01)**

B. The Coming Judgment on the Two Capitals **(1:02—2:13)**

1. Judgment Upon Samaria (1:02—1:07)
2. Judgment Upon Judah (1:08—1:09)
3. The Route of the Invading Army (1:10—1:15)
4. Future Judgment of God Upon the Children of Judah (1:16—1:16)
5. Cause of the Judgment = Woe to Evildoers (2:01—2:05)
6. False Prophets (2:06—2:11)
7. The Hope of Future Restoration (2:12—2:13)

C. Judgment Upon the Leaders of Israel **(3:01—5:15)**

1. Trial of the Leaders (3:01—3:04)
2. Trial of the False Prophets (3:05—3:08)
3. The Judgment Upon Jerusalem (3:09—3:12)
4. The Promise of the Coming Kingdom (4:01—4:05)
5. Jerusalem's Future Captivity (4:06—5:01)
6. The Coming Messiah (5:02—5:15)
   A. The Messiah's First Coming (5:02—03)
   B. The Messiah's Second Coming (5:04—15)

D. A Message of Accusation **(6:01—7:20)**

1. The *LORD*'s First Accusation (6:01—6:05)
2. Israel's First Reply to the *LORD* (6:06—6:08)
3. The Second Accusation from the *LORD* (6:09—6:16)
4. Israel's Second Reply to the *LORD* (7:01—7:10)
5. Comfort & Forgiveness for Israel (7:11—7:20)

NAHUM
(1:01—3:19)

1. **The Introduction to Nahum, the Prophet** **(1:01—1:01)**

2. **The Majesty of the *LORD*** **(1:02—3:19)**
   A. The Character of the *LORD* **(1:02—1:14)**
      1. The Attributes of the *LORD* (1:02—1:08)
      2. The Anger of the *LORD* (1:09—1:14)

   B. The Judgment of the *LORD* **(1:15—3:19)**
      1. Judgment Proclaimed on Nineveh (1:15—1:15)
      2. Judgment Predicted on Nineveh (2:01—2:02)
      3. The Description of the Judgment (2:03—2:13)
      4. The Woe of Nineveh (3:01—3:19)

HABAKKUK
(1:01—3:19)

1. **Introduction to Habakkuk** **(1:01—1:01)**

2. **Conversation Between God & Habakkuk** **(1:02—3:19)**
   A. The Concerns of Habakkuk **(1:02—2:20)**
      1. Habakkuk's First Concern (1:02—1:04)
      2. The *LORD*'s First Reply (1:05—1:11)
      3. Habakkuk's Second Concern (1:12—2:01)
      4. The *LORD*'s Second Reply (2:02—2:04)
      5. Woe to the Wicked (2:05—2:20)

   B. The Praises of Habakkuk **(3:01—3:19)**
      1. Habakkuk's Prayer (3:01—3:02)
      2. Praise for the Glory of God (3:03—3:04)
      3. Praise for the Power of God (3:05—3:16)
      4. Habakkuk's Joy (3:17—3:19)

ZEPHANIAH
(1:01—3:20)

1. **Introduction to Zephaniah** **(1:01—1:01)**

2. **The Prophetic Judgments by Zephaniah** **(1:01—1:01)**
   A. The Day of The *LORD*'s Wrath **(1:02—3:07)**
      1. Judgment Upon the Whole Earth (1:02—3:07)
         A. Judgment Upon Judah (1:02—2:03)
         B. Judgment Upon Gaza (2:04—07)
         C. Judgment Upon Moab (2:08—11)
         D. Judgment Upon Ethiopia (2:12—12)
         E. Judgment Upon Assyria (2:13—15)
         F. Judgment Upon Jerusalem (3:01—07)

B. The Day of the *LORD*'s Hope **(3:08—3:20)**
1. A Faithful Remnant (3:08—3:13)
2. The Promise of Restoration (3:14—3:20)

HAGGAI
(1:01—2:23)

1. <u>**The *LORD* Gives Message To Haggai For Governor Zerubbabel & High Priest Jeshua**</u> **(1:01—1:01)**

A. The Calling for the Reconstruction of the Temple **(1:01—1:15)**
1. The Building Command Goes Forth (1:01—1:11)
2. The Obedience of the People (1:12—1:15)

B. Encouragement to Complete the Temple **(2:01—2:23)**
1. The Coming Glory of God's House (2:01—2:09)
2. A Call to Cleanness (2:10—2:19)
3. God Chooses Zerubbabel as a Signet (God's Authority) (2:20—2:23)

ZECHARIAH
(1:01—14:21)

1. <u>**Encouraging Messages to Continue to Rebuild the Temple**</u> **(1:01—8:23)**

A. A Call to Repentance **(1:01—1:06)**

B. The Visions of Zechariah **(1:07—6:08)**
1. Vision of the Horses (1:07—1:11)
2. The *LORD* Will Comfort Zion (1:12—1:17)
3. Vision of the Four Horns & Four Craftsmen (1:18—1:21)
4. Vision of Man with Measuring Line (2:01—2:13)
5. Vision of the High Priest (3:01—3:10)
6. Vision of the Golden Lampstand (4:01—4:14)
7. Vision of the Flying Scroll (5:01—5:04)
8. Vision of the Woman in a Basket (5:05—5:11)
9. Vision of the Four Chariots (6:01—6:08)

C. Encouraging Words of Zechariah **(6:09—8:23)**
1. The Crowning of Joshua (6:09—6:15)
2. Obedience Better Than Fasting (7:01—7:07)
3. Disobedience Resulted In Captivity (7:08—7:14)
4. The Future of Jerusalem (8:01—8:23)

2. <u>**Messages Concerning Israel's Future**</u> **(9:01—14:21)**

A. First Message: Israel Rejects Their Messiah **(9:01—11:17)**
1. Judgment on the Enemies of Israel (9:01—9:08)
2. The Coming Messiah (9:09—9:17)
   A. The Messiah's First Coming Contrasted (9:09—09)
   B. The Messiah's Second Coming Contrasted (9:10—17)
3. Restoration of All of Israel (10:01—10:12)
4. Israel's Desolation (11:01—11:03)

5. Prophecy of the Two Shepherds (11:04—11:17)
   A. The Sheep Reject Their Shepherd (11:04—14)
   B. The Sheep Given to an Evil Shepherd (11:15—17)

B. Second Message: The Reign of the Coming Messiah (12:01—14:21)
1. The Coming Deliverance of Judah (12:01—13:09)
   A. Physical Deliverance (12:01—09)
   B. Spiritual Deliverance (12:10—13:06)
   C. The Shepherd Savior (13:07—13:09)
2. The Second Coming of the *LORD* (14:01—14:15)
3. The Kingdom of the *LORD* (14:16—14:21)

MALACHI
(1:01—4:06)

3. **God's Enduring Love for Israel** **(1:01—1:05)**

A. His Love Made Known **(1:01—1:05)**
1. Jacob Loved (1:01—1:02)
2. Esau Hated (1:03—1:05)

4. **God's Anger Against Israel** **(1:06—4:06)**

A. The Sins of the Priests **(1:06—2:09)**
1. Polluted Offerings by the Priests (1:06—1:14)
2. Unfaithful Priests (2:01—2:09)

B. The Sins of the People **(2:10—3:15)**
1. Intermarriage to Daughters of a Foreign god (2:10—2:12)
2. Divorce (2:13—2:16)
3. Irreverence Towards the *LORD* (2:17—2:17)
4. The Coming Messenger Will Judge (3:01—3:05)
5. Israelites Robbing God (3:06—3:12)
6. Presumptuous Attitudes (3:13—3:15)

C. The Faithful Few **(3:16—4:06)**
1. A Book of Remembrance (3:16—3:18)
2. The Great Day of the *LORD* (4:01—4:06)

How to Read & Use the Concordance

Example:

Aaron – **6**-1b8;1c;1c1,5-6; **9**-1a13;1b1; **10**-1b1; **11**-2b,2b1;3b2,3;3c2;3d3

In doing a search for a word, as in this example, I am using the name of "Aaron." Since we are looking for "Aaron," let's go to the concordance to see where we can find the name. The first place where "Aaron" is located in the Old Testament is **6**-1b8 as we can see above in the example. The bold number "**6**" is the page number in the Topical Index where "Aaron" is located. Now we look in Section "1", then Section "B" then in Number "8" to locate "Aaron." In the example below, I have underlined where "1b8" is located. So, we can see that the first place where "Aaron" is located in the Old Testament Topical Index is in Exodus 4:18—4:31. The second location of "Aaron" is Page 6, Section 1, Subsection c. Then again on Page 6, Section 1, then Section C, then in Numbers 1,5-6. In the example below, "Aaron" is located on Page **6.** In the example above, the bold numbers are ALL page numbers where "Aaron" is located in the Topical Index.

IMPORTANT: The semicolons separate the Sections. The Commas separate the Number locations and subsections. The bold numbers separate the page numbers.

EXODUS
(1:01—40:38)

1. **The Life & Times of Israel in Egypt** **(1:01—12:30)**
   - **A. Family of Israel Enslaved in Egypt** **(1:01—1:22)**
     - 1. Suffering of Israel's Descendants (1:01—1:14)
     - 2. King of Egypt Commands Death of Hebrew Males (1:15—1:22)
   - **B. Moses Chosen by God to Lead Israel** **(2:01—4:31)**
     - 1. The Birth of Moses (2:01—2:10)
     - 2. Moses Kills an Egyptian (2:11—2:15)
     - 3. Moses Flees to Midian (2:16—2:20)
     - 4. Moses Marries Zipporah (2:21—2:25)
     - 5. Moses Meets God at Mount Horeb (3:01—3:22)
     - 6. God Prepares Moses for Egypt (4:01—4:13)
     - 7. God Angered at Moses (4:14—4:17)
     - 8. Moses & Aaron Speak to Israelites in Egypt (4:18—4:31)

A

Aaron – **6**-1b8;1c;1c1,5-6; **9**-1a13;1b1; **10**-1b1; **11**-2b,2b1;3b2,3;3c2;3d3
Aarons Rod – **11**-3b3
Abandoned – **34**-P41
Abdon – **16**-2e6
Abel – **3**-2b1
Abiathar – **21**-1a4
Abigail – **19**-3c14
Abihu – **9**-1b3
Abijah – **28**-2b3-4
Abijam – **22**-2d2
Abimelech – **4**-4d7;4e3;5b1; **16**-2d8,10
Abner – **19**-1a7; **20**-1a9
Abominable – **38**-1b14
Abraham – **4**-4c3;4d2,7;4e2-4;4g,4g1-2; **6**-7g4; **25**-1b;1c,1c1
Abram – **3**-4a,4a1-2;4b,4b1-2; **4**-4b3;4c,4c3
Absalom – **20**-2b2-3;2c,2c1-4,6-7,9-10
Absolute – **47**-1e
Accepts – **40**-1c3
Accomplishments – **24**-2a2
Account – **3**-#1
Accountability – **48**-1e17c
Accusation(s) – **33**-P17; **44**-1f; **54**-1b; **55**-1d,1d3
Accused – **32**-3c1
Accusers – **36**-P120
Achan – **14**-2a3
Achish – **19**-3c7
Activities – **13**-2f2; **39**-1a1
Actions – **38**-3b
Acts – **34**-P34
Adam – **3**-2b,2b3;2c; **25**-#1;1a,1a1
Adam & Eve – **3**-#2;2a,2a1,3
Address – **15**-3c,d;3d1,2; **18**-2a6
Addresses – **51**-1b2
Administration – **21**-1b3
Admiration – **40**-1c2;1d2
Adonijah – **21**-1a3
Adullam – **19**-3c8
Adulteress – **38**-1b15,16
Adulterous – **52**-#1;#2;2a
Adultery – **20**-2a1; **37**-1b11
Advantages – **39**-1d2
Adversity – **37**-P144
Advice – **37**-#1; **45**-2b13
Advise – **20**-2c6-7
Affection – **40**-1f2
Afraid – **11**-2c2; **13**-2b2
After – **33**-P21; **45**-2c
Against – **11**-2b1;2c;3b2;3d2; **20**-2c3; **22**-1e3;2a3; **23**-1b3; **28**-2b7; **30**-2a2; **31**-1c1; **33**-P12; **34**-P64; **37**-1b11; **41**-1c,1c1;1c5-10,12-17; **42**-2c1; **43**-1b,1b1,4; **44**-1d1,7;1e10; **45**-2c2,#3;3a; **46**-1b1 **47**-1e5,6; **48**-#3;3a;3a5c; **49**-3a7d; **51**-2a,2a2; **52**-2a1,3; **53**-2a8; **54**-1b,1b1; **58**-#2
Age – **41**-2a2
Agreed – **17**-1c3; **30**-3a4
Agree(s) – **31**-1c4
Agur – **38**-3c1
Ahab – **22**-2d9;2e2; **23**-2f,2f1-5; **24**-1c7
Ahaz – **24**-1c27; **29**-2b34-35; **41**-1b1
Ahaziah – **23**-2h,2h1;1a,1a1;1c2; **24**-1c5,8; **28**-2b15,17
Ahijah – **22**-1e4;#2
Ahikam – **44**-1g3
Ahimelech – **19**-3c6,9
Ahithophel – **20**-2c6
Ai – **14**-2a2,4
Aleph – **36**-#1
All of Your Heart – **34**-P62
Allotment(s) – **15**-3a4
Allotted – **50**-5b8
Allowed – **50**-5b5
Allow(s) – **31**-#2
Almighty – **32**-3a3
Altar – **7**-3a4; **8**-3b9,19;3d11,13; **9**-1d; **14**-2g1; **15**-3c2; **16**-2d3; **21**-2e10; **50**-5b3,5b3a
Altar of Stone – **7**-3a4
Amalekites – **7**-2c4; **19**-3d4
Amaziah – **24**-1c20; **28**-2b24-28; **54**-1d4
Ammon – **20**-1c3;2a6,8;2b12; **46**-3a5; [illegible]
Ammonites – **16**-2e1; **18**-2a5
Amnon – **20**-2b1-2; **48**-3a1
Amon – **29**-2b41-42
Amorite(s) – **14**-2b3
Amos – Pg**53**; #1;1a; **54**-1c
Ancestry – **17**-1d3
Ancient of Days – **51**-2b2
Angel – **7**-3a15
Angered – **6**-1b7; **16**-2e3
Anger(s) – **46**-1b1,3;1c; **56**-2a2; **58**-#2
Anger of God – **46**-1b1
Anger of the *Lord* – **46**-1c; **56**-2a2
Annihilated – **31**-1c2
Annihilation – **31**-1c,#2;2a5
Announced – **19**-1a1
Annual – **10**-1c5
Anointed – **19**-1a4
Anoint(s) – **18**-3a1; **24**-1c3
Anointing – **8**-3b22
Anointing Oil – **8**-3d12
Another – **36**-P117; **44**-1e10
Answered – **37**-P138
Answer(s) – **34**-P66
Antichrist – **52**-1d5
Antiochus Epiphanes – **52**-1d4
Appeal – **34**-P39; **40**-1f
Appears – **52**-1c3a
Appointed – **11**-2a3; **13**-2e1; **15**-3b
Appoint(s) – **12**-1a2
Appointment(s) – **12**-4b4;2e2
Apostasy – **16**-#3; **53**-2a7
Appreciation – **35**-P104
Arabia – **41**-1c15
Aram – **20**-1c1; **52**-1d3
Area – **50**-5a2n

Arises – **21**-2d6
Ark – **3**-3a2; **18**-1c4-5; **26**-2b,2b1,5-7; **27**-1c1
Ark of the Covenant – **18**-1c1,5; **20**-1b4; **26**-2b,2b5; **27**-1c1
Ark of God – **26**-2b6
Ark of the Testimony – **7**-3b2; **8**-3d8
Armies – **49**-4b3
Army – **26**-2a4;2b4; **48**-2a4; **55**-1b3
Arrangement – **9**-3d22
Arrives – **5**-6b7; **29**-2a1; **48**-2a1e
Arriving – **43**-1b6
Arrogance – **44**-1d7
Asa – **22**-2d3; **28**-2b4,6,8-9
Asher – **15**-3a4f; **26**-1f12
Assembly – **13**-2f5; **27**-2e11
Assigned – **27**-2e4-8
Association – **28**-2b10
Assurance – **34**-P61; **37**-P130
Assured – **42**-2c2; **45**-2a6
Assyria – **24**-1d; **41**-1b3,7;1c5,11; **42**-2b6,9;2c3,5; **56**-2a1e
Assyrian(s) – **24**-1d3; **29**-2b38
Astrologers – **51**-1b2
At Last – **47**-1e16
Athaliah – **28**-2b16,18
Atonement – **8**-3b20; **9**-1c2-3; **10**-2c6; **13**-2f1
Attacked – **32**-2a2
Attack(s) – **24**-2a3; **31**-Job#2;2a; **42**-2c2
Attaining – **37**-1b
Attitudes – **58**-2b6
Attributes – **56**-2a1
Authority – **33**-P24; **39**-1d3; **57**-1b3
Avenger of Blood – **12**-4g4
Avenged – **21**-2e2
Avenge(s) – **20**-1a8;2b2
Avenging – **48**-2a4
Avoid – **37**-1b1,9; **38**-1b13,16
Awaken – **40**-1b2;1f3
Awareness – **33**-P10
Awesomeness – **42**-3a
Ax Head – **23**-1b9
Ayin – **36**-#16
Azariah – **24**-1c20
Azur – **45**-1g5

B

Baal – **12**-4a7; **16**-2d3; **22**-2e2; **24**-1c9
Baasha – **22**-2d5
Baal Perazim – **20**-1b3
Babel – **3**-3c,3c1
Babylon – **25**-2a20; **41**-1c1,12; **42**-3a14; **43**-1b6; **45**-1g7; **46**-3a10-11; **50**-1a1-3; **51**-1b
Babylonia – **46**-3a10
Babylonian(s) – **24**-2a5; **26**-1g; **42**-3a1,15; **45**-2b15; **48**-2a4
Babylonian Captivity – **42**-3a1
Backslider – **43**-3b11
Bahurim – **20**-2c5
Baker – **5**-7c2
Balaam – **11**-4a,4a1,3,4; **12**-4a5-6
Balak – **11**-4a1
Banquet – **31**-1a1;1c5
Barak – **16**-2c1
Bare – **46**-1a
Baruch – **45**-2b6-7
Barzillai – **21**-2d5
Basket – **57**-1b8
Bathsheba – **20**-2a1-2
Battle(s) – **12**-4d2; **23**-2f5; **25**-2a12; **26**-2c1; **29**-2b46; **33**-P20,21
Bears – **47**-1e17b
Bearing – **11**-3c1
Beast – **51**-2b1,3,4
Beauty – **40**-1e,1e1
Became – **29**-2b34
Become(s) – **6**-1d1,3; **11**-2b2; **14**-4a1; **16**-2d2; **19**-3d1; **22**-1a4;2b; **26**-2a2; **31**-2a3
Becoming – **9**-1c2; **38**-1b12; **47**-1e9-10
Bed – **28**-2b23
Beersheba – **21**-2e8
Before – **7**-3a15; **27**-2e11; **32**-3c4
Behavior – **7**-3a7
Being – **32**-3c1; **47**-1d9
Befalls – **40**-1a6
Before – **45**-2b
Began – **7**-1e1
Begets – **25**-1a1-10
Begin(s) – **11**-2a2; **23**-1b2; **27**-1b2; **29**-1b1; **30**-2a,2a1
Beginning – **9**-1b2; **37**-1a1
Believed – **55**-1b2
Beloved – **40**-1e1-2
Ben-Hadad – **23**-2f1-2
Benjamin – **5**-6b11;7e3,5; **15**-3a4b; **16**-3b3,5; **26**-1f8,13
Benjamite – **16**-3b; **18**-2a3; **26**-1g3
Běth (Pronounced: bait) – **36**-#2
Beth Eked – **24**-1c8
Bethel – **5**-6b10
Bethlehem – **16**-3b1,3,5; **17**-1a1,3
Better – **57**-1c2
Between – **52**-1a; **56**-#2
Beware – **38**-1b12,15
Bildad – **32**-3a6;3b4;3c4
Birth – **6**-1b1; **18**-1a3; **32**-3a1
Bitter Water – **7**-2c1
Blamed – **54**-1a3
Blameless – **32**-3a7; **33**-P15; **35**-P101
Blasphemy – **10**-2c9
Bless(s) – **4**-4b3; **6**-7g2; **27**-2e11
Blessing(s) – **4**-4d1;5c1-2; **14**-2g3;4a6; **37**-134; **39**-1a6; **41**-1c11; **42**-3a8; **43**-3c1;3d
Blessing, Son of the – **4**-4d1
Blind Watchmen – **42**-3b9
Blood – **6**-1d1; **9**-1a12; **12**-4g4; **21**-2e2
Blotting Out – **43**-3b15
Blundered – **46**-3b2
Boards – **8**-3d6
Boasts – **42**-2c1

Boaz – **17**-1b1-4;1c3;1d,1d2
Bodily Discharge – **9**-1c6
Boiling Pot – **48**-2a9
Boils – **6**-1d6
Bones – **49**-4a7c
Book 1 – **33**
Book 2 – **34**
Book 3 – **35**
Book 4 – **35**
Book 5 – **35-36**
Book of Remembrance – **58**-2c1
Book of the Law – **24**-2a10; **29**-2b43; **30**-3a,3a1
Born – **5**-6b11; **18**-1c3; **19**-1a6
Bottles – **44**-1d6
Bound – **24**-1d1
Boundaries – **12**-4g1; **50**-5b14
Bounty – **34**-P65
Branch – **41**-1b8
Brazen Altar – **8**-3b9
Bread – **47**-1d4
Break(s) – **6**-1d6; **44**-1d
Breaker(s) – **11**-3a4
Breaking – **8**-3c
Breastplate – **8**-3b15; **9**-3d19
Brick(s) – **6**-1c2; **47**-1d1
Bride – **4**-4f1;4g1;5c4; **5**-6a3-4; **40**-1e;1f,1f1-2;1g3-4; **47**-1e9
Brings – **37**-P129; **48**-1e17d-e
Broken Flask – **44**-1e11
Bronze – **8**-3b22
Bronze Altar – **8**-3d13
Bronze Laver – **8**-3d14
Bronze Serpent – **11**-3d5
Brother(s) – **5**-7e,7e1-3,7; **6**-7g6; **20**-1a8; **24**-1c8; **54**-1b1-2
Brought – **20**-1b4; **26**-2b; **27**-1c1; **31**-1b2
Budding – **11**-3b3
Build(s) – **3**-3a2; **21**-2e10; **27**-2e9
Builder(s) – **8**-3b24
Building(s) – **21**-1c2; **27**-2e,2e1,10; **29**-1b2; **30**-#2; **50**-5a2m; **57**-1a1
Built – **3**-3c; **27**-1b; **28**-2a3
Burial – **49**-4b4
Burns – **45**-2b8
Burning – **8**-3b19; **47**-1d10
Burnt Offering(s) – **9**-1a1,7; **27**-1d3
Butler – **5**-7c2
Buys – **21**-2e10; **45**-2a5

C

Cain – **3**-2b1-2
Caleb – **15**-3a3b,d
Calf – **8**-3c1; **13**-2c5
Call(s) – **14**-#3;3a,3a2; **18**-1b3; **43**-1a; **46**-1a; **47**-1d6; **53**-1b4,5; **57**-1b2; Zech.1a
Called – **13**-2c7; **43**-1b3
Calling – **18**-1a; **40**-1a8; **43**-1a1; **57**-1a
Came – **30**-3b2
Camp(s) – **12**-4f
Canaan (Person) – **3**-3b7
Canaan (Place) – **3**-4b1; **4**-4c2;4e6;4g2; **5**-6b;7e7; **12**-4f2;4g4g1; **14**-#1;1b1;#2;2a;2b; **15**-2c,2c1;#3; **16**-2c1; **48**-2a1e
Canaanites – **11**-3d4
Cancels – **47**-1e17a
Canceling – **13**-2d5
Capital – **20**-1b2
Captain – **14**-1b4; **45**-2b15
Captives – **29**-2b33,1a2; **47**-1e12
Captivity – **42**-3a1; **44**-1c7;1g,1g2; **45**-1g7; **46**-3b3; **47**-1d2,3;1e1; **53**-2a9; **55**-1c5; **57**-1c3
Capture(s) – **18**-1c1; **26**-2a3
Careful – **13**-2c2
Care – **36**-P113
Caring – **33**-P8
Carnality – **4**-4d3
Case – **43**-1b1; **52**-2a
Case of God – **43**-1b1
Cast – **4**-4e2; **51**-2a5
Cast Out – **4**-4e2
Cause – **46**-1c2; **53**-1b1; **55**-1b5
Causes of God – **35**-P74
Cave – **19**-3c8
Cave of Adullam – **19**-3c8
Celebrate(s) – **29**-2b45; **35**-P81; **36**-P114
Celebration – **26**-2b7; **34**-P30
Census – **21**-2e8; **29**-1a2
Central Part – **14**-2a
Central Sanctuary – **13**-2d1
Certain – **54**-1a1
Chambers – **50**-5a2h,o
Change – **14**-4a
Characteristics – **43**-3d5; **53**-1b
Charge – **5**-7d2; **11**-3c2; **14**-1a
Chastening – **32**-3a3
Census – **10**-1a;1b7; **12**-4b; **26**-2d,2d1
Character – **32**-3c5; **56**-2a
Childbirth – **9**-1c3
Children – **18**-1b1
Children of Israel – **10**-1a3; **11**-2a2; **13**-2a,2a1; **14**-#3;4a6;1b1; **40**-1a
Children of Judah – **55**-1b4
Chief(s) – **5**-6c2,5
Choice – **14**-3a3
Chooses – **57**-1b3
Chosen – **6**-1b; **18**-3a; **27**-2e9
Chronicles (1st) – Pg**25**
Chronicles (2nd) – Pg**27**
Chronicle(s) – **22**-2d; **23**-1c
Circumcised – **14**-1b3
Circumcision – **4**-4c3
Circumstance(s) – **39**-1c
Citadel of Susa – **31**-1b2
City(ies) – **12**-4g3,4; **15**-3a3d-e;3b,3b1-2; **19**-3c10; **27**-1d1; **28**-2a3; **30**-3b; **45**-2b4; **46**-3b2; **47**-1d10; **50**-5b16;
Cities for Defense – **28**-2a3
City of God – **35**-P87

Cities of Refuge – **12**-4g4; **13**-1a9;2e7; **15**-3b,3b1
Civil – **7**-3a12
Clay Tablet – **47**-1d1
Cleanness – **57**-1b2
Cleanses – **29**-2b36; **30**-2b4
Cleansing – **9**-1c5; **34**-P51
Clever – **38**-1b16
Close Relationship – **33**-P5
Closing – **37**-P150
Clothing – **8**-3b12
Cloud & Fire – **10**-1c6
Co-Signer – **38**-1b12
Combating – **35**-P83
Come(s) – **4**-4c2;4d; **6**-7f3; **23**-2e4; **27**-2e13; **30**-2a2; **39**-1d4; **53**-2a8; **54**-1c3b-d
Coming – **54**-1a; **55**-1c4,6;1c6a-b; **57**-1b1; **58**-2a2;1a2a-b;2b,2b1-2; Mal.2b4
Comfort(s) – **32**-3a5; **35**-P77; **42**-#3;3b3; **55**-1d5; **57**-1b2
Comforting – **32**-2a3
Coming – **41**-1b;2a1; **42**-2b10; **44**-1c7; **55**-1b
Commanded – **45**-2b9
Command(s) – **6**-1a2; **12**-1a1; **13**-2c,2c3;2d3,5; **31**-2a3
Commandment(s) – **7**-3a2; **13**-2b,2b1;2c1,2,6
Commence(s) – **31**-2a
Commemoration – **14**-1b2
Commission(s) – **14**-#4;1a1; **46**-1a
Commitment – **13**-2c7
Companionship – **33**-P16; **41**-1c2
Complain(s) – **11**-2b1; **44**-1e13
Complainer(s) –**11**-2c3
Complaint(s) – **7**-2c1; **11**-3b2; **55**-1b3
Complete – **47**-1d7; **57**-1b
Completed – **9**-3d21
Completion – **29**-1b6; **30**-2a3
Compromise – **30**-2a2e
Concerning – **7**-6-7,10; **8**-3d2; **9**-1c1,3,4,6;1d4;2a,2a1-2; **10**-2b,2b2;2c1-8,11-14;2d,2d2;1c2,3; **11**-2a, 3a1; **12**-4c9; **13**-2d1,3,5;2e4,6,9;2f4,6; **14**-2f7-8; **20**-1b5; **32**-3b6;3c3; **34**-P36; **38**-2a4;3a,3a1-7; 3b,3b1-4; **39**-1c1-6;1d1,6; **42**-3a1-8,10,11,14,15; **44**-1e13;1f4; **45**-2a2-3;3a1,3,4; **46**-3a5-10; **47**-1c;1d; **48**-3a1-6; **49**-3a7;5a1; **50**-5b9; **51**-1b2;2a6; **52**-1d,1d1-3,6; **57**-#2
Concern(s) – **56**-2a,2a1,3
Conclusion – **21**-2e
Concubine – **16**-3b1
Condemned – **23**-2f3; **30**-Ezra2b1; **32**-4a4
Condemn(s) – **32**-3a8
Condemnation – **40**-1a; **41**-2b
Conduct(s) – **9**-1b4;2a2; **10**-2b1
Confessed – **43**-3b14
Confess – **30**-Ezra2b3
Confession – **30**-2b2;3a3
Confidence – **36**-P118
Confirmation – **43**-1a2
Coniah – **44**-1f3c
Conquer(s) – **14**-2a; **16**-2d6; **19**-3d4; **20**-1b2-3;2c4; **26**-2b4
Conquered – **20**-2c9; **28**-2b32
Conquering – **14**-#2
Conquest(s) – **12**-1a5; **14**-2b; **15**-2c;2d,2d1; **26**-2c1
Consecrated – **9**-1a13
Consecration – **7**-2a3; **8**-3b17; **10**-1c4; **18**-1a3; **50**-5b3b
Consequences – **14**-2g
Consigned – **49**-3a7g
Conspiracy – **44**-1e10
Conspire – **34**-P64
Construction – **8**-3d; **21**-1c2; **27**-1b2; **29**-1b
Consults – **19**-3d2
Consumption – **9**-1c1
Content (Feelings) – **39**-1a6
Contentment – **37**-P131
Continue(s) – **32**-3c6; **46**-1b2; **57**-#1
Continuing – **53**-2b2
Contradicted – **32**-4a2
Contrasted – **58**-2a2a-b
Conversation(s) – **32**-#3;3a;3b,3b4;3c;4a; **56**-#2
Corruption – **18**-1b2
Cost(s) – **21**-2e9
Couldn't – **52**-1b13
Council – **37**-1b2
Counsel – **39**-1d1
Counting – **10**-1a1
Court – **8**-3b10;3d15; **49**-5a2c,f; **50**-5a2i
Court of the Tabernacle – **8**-3b10;3d15
Courtship – **40**-1b,1b1
Covenant – **3**-3a5;3b1; **4**-4c1; **5**-6b3; **7**-3a16; **8**-3c8; **14**-3a1;2a5; **18**-1c1,5; **19**-3c5; **20**-1b5; **25**-2a11; **26**-2b8; **27**-1c1; **28**-2b19; **30**-3a4; **44**-1d; **45**-2a4,8; **47**-1e13; **49**-4a7b
Covenant of God – **26**-2b8
Craftsmen – **8**-3d3
Creation – **3**-#1; **37**-P148; **42**-3a2
Creatures – **47**-1b1
Credentials – **36**-P110
Cries – **33**-P9
Crime(s) – **16**-3b2; **20**-2a; **52**-2a6
Critical – **32**-3a10
Criticized – **32**-#4
Cross – **14**-1a2;1b1
Crossing – **14**-1b
Crowned – **19**-1a; **20**-1b
Crown – **21**-1a1
Crowning – **18**-2a4,6; **19**-#1; **57**-1c1
Cry Out – **35**-P79
Cursed – **20**-2c5
Curse(s) – **14**-2g2,4; **18**-1c4; **32**-3a1
Curtains – **8**-3b6;3d5
Cush – **3**-3b5
Cycle(s) – **39**-1a,1a1
Cyrus – **29**-2b51;1a1; **42**-3a12

D

Daily – **8**-3b18; **12**-4c1
Daleth – **36**-#4
Damage – **7**-3a9
Damascus – **23**-1b14; **46**-3a7; **53**-1b1

Dan – **15**-3a4h; **16**-3a2; **21**-2e8
Danger – **43**-1c3
Dangerous Times – **31**-#1
Daniel – Pg**50**; #1;1a,1a1-3; **51**-1b3-6,8,10,12;1c3;1d3-4;#2;2a,2a1-5;2b; **52**-1b13;1c,1c1-5
Danites – **16**-3a
Darius – **29**-1b5
Darkness – **6**-1d9
Daughter(s) – **19**-3b4; **21**-1a6; **58**-2b1
David – **17**-1d3; **18**-#3,3a,3a1; **19**-3b,3b1-4;3c,3c1-8-12,14-15;3d,3d1,3-4;1a,1a2,4,6-7; 2nd Samuel 1a,1a2,1a4,6-7; **20**-1a9;1b,1b1-3,5-6;1c,1c1-3;#2;2a,2a1-5; **20**-2b;2c1,3,5,10;2d,2d1-5, **21**-2e,2e3-4,6-10; 1stKings1a; **25**-1e,1e1; **26**-1e,1e1;2a,2a2-4;2b3-5,7-8;2c,2c1; **27**-2d,2d1; 2e,2e11,13
Davidic – **45**-2a8
Day of Atonement – **9**-1d2-3; **10**-2c6; **12**-4c7
Day of the *LORD* – **40**-1a5; **53**-1b3; **56**-Zep.2a; **57**-2b
Day(s) – **6**-1d9; **22**-2d7; **29**-2b39,49; **39**-1a,1a1; **44**-1e7; **49**-4b; **50**-5b10; **51**-2b2; **53**-1b3
Dead – **18**-1c2; **23**-1b5; **42**-3a13
Dealing – **43**-3b13
Death – **3**-2b1; **4**-4g; **6**-1a2; **11**-2c3; **14**-3a3; **16**-2d7; **19**-1a1-2; **20**-1a8-9,2c10; **24**-1c6; **26**-2a1,2b2; **28**-1d8,#2; **29**-2b41; **39**-1d4; **44**-1g3
Deborah – **16**-2c1-2
Debts – **13**-2d5
Deceived – **4**-4d7; **22**-2b3
Deceive(s) – **4**-5a2;5b1; **14**-2b1
Deceptive Words – **43**-1c1
Decision – **45**-2b3
Declared – **6**-1d10
Declare(s) – **32**-3c2;4a3,5
Declaring – **33**-P26
Decline – **46**-1c1-2
Decree – **29**-2b51;1a1;1b5;2a2; **31**-2a4; **51**-1c1;2a6
Dedicated – **21**-1c4; **27**-1c; **30**-3b3
Dedication – **10**-1b3; **27**-1c4; **29**-1b7
Deeds – **21**-2e7
Deep – **35**-P86
Deepest – **35**-P88
Defeated – **14**-2a2; **18**-2b2; **24**-1c4
Defeat(s) – **7**-2c4; **11**-3d4,7; **14**-2a4; **18**-2a5 **19**-3b1;3d5; **20**-1c1,3; **23**-2f1; **24**-1c5; **28**-2b26; **29**-2b38; **31**-2a6
Defend – **35**-P74
Defense – **28**-2a3; **33**-P25
Defiled – **51**-1d1
Defile(s) – **5**-6b8
Defilement – **10**-1c1
Delivered – **16**-2a1;2b1-2;2c1; **17**-2f1; **24**-2a3; **54**-1a5
Deliver(s) – **31**-#2; **37**-1b3
Deliverance – **6**-1c3; **7**-2b4; **33**-P6,18; **34**-P30; **36**-P120; **42**-2c2; **53**-1b7; **58**-2b1,2b1a-b
Demand(s) – **18**-#2
Demise – **22**-1e; **49**-4a3
Den of Lions – **51**-2a5
Denying – **33**-P14
Departed – **50**-1a1
Depart(s) – **7**-#2; **8**-3c4
Departure – **7**-2a
Deportation – **24**-1d; **25**-2a18
Depravity – **54**-1c2
Depression – **37**-P143
Descendant(s) – **6**-1a1;1c4
Description – **40**-1g1; **56**-2b3
Deserts – **19**-1a7
Design – **39**-1b; **50**-5a2n
Desire – **40**-1f2
Desiring – **34**-P63
"Desolation Without Inhabitation" – **45**-2b4
Desolation – **45**-2b4; **46**-3a11;#1; **58**-2a4
Despair – **33**-P13
Desperate – **37**-P142
Despise – **32**-3a3
Destroyed – **16**-2d3; **49**-4b3
Destroy(s) – **21**-2e4; **24**-1c9; **28**-2b12
Destruction – **4**-4d4; **14**-2a1; **16**-2d10; **42**-2b9; **43**-1b6; **45**-2b;2c; **47**-1d7; **49**-3a7e; **54**-1d6;#1;1a,1a1-2
Determined – **10**-1a2
Detour – **7**-2b1
Deuteronomy – Pg**12**
Devastation – **41**-2a
Develop(s) – **11**-2b; **28**-2b29
Devotion – **40**-1g4
Dies – **5**-6b11,13; **6**-7g,7g4,7;1d10; **8**-3c3; **11**-3d3; **14**-4a5; **15**-3d3-4; **17**-2f5; **19**-3c13; **22**-2c2; **23**-1b14; **28**-2b8,21
Difference – **38**-1c;2a1
Different – **39**-1c
Difficult – **37**-P137
Dimensions – **50**-5a2n
Dinah – **5**-6b8-9
Disaster – **35**-P79
Discipline – **11**-#3
Discouragement – **34**-P43
Discovers – **31**-1b4
Discovery(ies) – **31**-1b; **39**-1d5
Discretion – **37**-1b7
Disgraceful – **43**-1b2
Dishonesty – **7**-3a10
Disobedience – **9**-2a3; **14**-2g,2g4; **18**-2b; **42**-3a6; **57**-1c3
Disobeys – **54**-1a1
Displayed – **21**-1b2
Displeasure – **19**-3b3
Dissatisfied – **7**-2c
Distress – **34**-P69; **35**-P102
Distressing – **19**-3a2
District – **50**-5b7
Divided – **7**-2c5; **12**-4d3; **15**-3a3-4; **22**-#2; **23**-#1
Divide(s) – **12**-4g2
Dividing – **15**-#3; **50**-5b15
Divine – **40**-#1; **42**-#3
Diviners – **13**-2e4
Division – **12**-4g; **13**-1a6; **15**-3a2,3a3a,3a4a; **27**-1d4
Divorce(s) – **13**-2f6; **31**-1a; **58**-2b2
Donkey – **11**-4a2
Don't – **40**-1f3

Doom – **45**-1g6; **46**-#1
Doomed – **44**-1f1
Doesn't – **51**-1b1
Downfall – **3**-2a3
Dream – **5**-7a1;7c2;7d1; **40**-1d; **51**-1b,1b1-5;1c,1c2-4;1d5
Drive – **13**-2c3
Drive Out – **13**-2c3
Drought – **22**-2e1,4; **44**-1d8
Dry Bones – **49**-4a7c
Dungeon – **45**-2b12
Duration – **47**-1d2-3
During – **42**-2c
Dust – **6**-1d3
Dwelling – **50**-5b

E

Early Life – **18**-1a
Earnest Prayer – **18**-1a2
Earth – **32**-3c3; **41**-2a,2a1; **56**-2a1
Earthly – **39**-1d3
East – **6**-1d8; **13**-1a9; **15**-3a2,3a2c
Eastward – **50**-5b13
East Gate – **49**-5a2f2; **50**-5b4
Eastern Gate – **49**-5a2b
East Manasseh – **15**-3a2c;3c1; **26**-1f5
East Wind – **6**-1d8
Ebal – **14**-2a5
Eating – **47**-1e2
Ecclesiastes – Pg**39**
Edict – **31**-1a3;1c3
Edom (Esau) – **5**-6c2,4; **11**-3d2; **20**-1c1; **41**-1c14; **46**-3a6; **48**-3a3; **53**-1b4;#1;1a;1b
Edomites – **25**-1c5
Egypt – **3**-4a2; **5**-7d,7d2;7e,7e1,3; **6**-f1,3;7g;1a,1a2;1b6,8; **7**-2a; **12**-4f1; **21**-1a6; **41**-1c10-12;2b5; **42**-2c1; **45**-2c35;3a1; **48**-2a1b; **49**-3a7;3a7b-g; **52**-1d3
Egyptian(s) – **6**-1b2;1d10; **7**-1e2
Ehud – **16**-2b1
Eight Years – **23**-1c1; **28**-2b14
Elah – **22**-2d6; **24**-1c28
Elam – **46**-3a9
Eleazar – **11**-3d3; **12**-4g2; **15**-3d4
Elder(s) – **11**-2a3
Eleven Years – **25**-2a14,17; **29**-2b48,50
Eli – **18**-1a6;1c2
Eliakim – **25**-2a14
Elihu – **32**-4a,4a1-5
Elijah – **22**-2e,2e1-2; **23**-2e3,4-5;1b,1b1-2,10,14
Elimelech – **17**-1a1
Eliphaz – **32**-3a2,4;3b1-2; **32**-3c1
Elisha – **23**-1b2,10,14; **24**-1c3,16
Elon – **16**-2e5
Encouragement – **57**-1b
Encourages – **38**-2a2
Encouraging – **57**-#1;1c
End(s) – **23**-2e4; **27**-2e13; **28**-2b2,13; **37**-P136; **50**-5a2m
Endless – **36**-P113
End-time – **41**-#2; **52**-1c;1d5
Enduring – **58**-#1
Enemies – **22**-1e3; **29**-1b3; **30**-2a2; **31**-2a6; **35**-P83; **38**-3a3; **43**-3d1; **57**-2a1
Engagement – **40**-1c
Engedi – **19**-3c12,15
Enoch – **25**-1a6-7
Enosh – **25**-1a2-3
Enrollment – **29**-2a3
Enroute – **26**-2b1
Enslaved – **6**-1a; **10**-2c14
Enter(s) – **11**-2c2; **13**-1a7; **14**-#1; **32**-4a
Ephod – **8**-3b13;3d18
Ephraim – **6**-7g2; **15**-3a3f-g; **16**-2e3; **26**-1f11; **41**-2b1
Equal Justice – **7**-3a13
Equals – **37**-1b8
Erected – **9**-3d23; **51**-1b7
Erect(s) – **15**-3c2
Esau (Edom) – **4**-5a2;5c4; **5**-6b4,6;6c1,2,5; **58**-1a2
Escaping – **7**-2b
Escapes – **19**-3c8; **23**-2e5
Esther – Pg**31; 31**-1b,1b2-3;1c4-5
Eternal – **36**-P118
Ethiopia – **28**-2b5; **41**-1c9,12; **56**-2a1d
Events – **42**-2c; **45**-2b;2c; **46**-3b; **52**-1c
Everlasting – **47**-1e13
Every – **33**-P10
Everyone – **37**-P145
Everything – **31**-#2; **36**-P111; **39**-1b1
Evidence – **44**-1d1
Evil – **37**-1b1
Evil Shepherd – **58**-2a5b
Evildoers – **34**-P52; **35**-P76 **55**-1b5
Exalted – **47**-1e16
Except – **31**-#2
Excluded – **13**-2f5
Executed – **21**-1a4-5; **31**-2a7
Execute(s) – **17**-1c2; **21**-1a3
Execution – **15**-2b3; **16**-3b4
Exiled – **16**-2e2; **21**-1a4
Exile(s) – **19**-3c; **28**-#2; **29**-#1,#2; **26**-1g; **49**-4a5
Exodus – Pg**6**; **7**-2a1
Experience(s) – **37**-P134; **39**-#1
Experiencing – **3**-2a2
Explanation – **47**-1e15; **52**-1b10-12
Explained – **52**-1c3b;1c3b
Explain(s) – **51**-1b4;1d3,4; **52**-1b9;1c3
Exploit(s) – **16**-2f3
Expose – **20**-2a3
Expresses – **40**-1c2
Extended – **24**-2a4; **42**-2c6
Extortion – **30**-2a2c
Ezekiel – Pg**46**; **46**-46-1a,1a1; **47**-1b;1c1-2;1d5; **48**-2a1f; **49**-4a1;5a1
Ezra – Pg**29; 29**-2a,2a1-3; **30**-2b,2b1-2;3a1

F

Face – **8**-3c9; **44**-1f
Facing – **37**-P141

Fair – **49**-4a2
Fairness – **35**-P99
Faith – **36**-P112; **51**-1b9
Faithful – **52**-#1;#2; **57**-2b1; **58**-2c
Faithfulness – **35**-P71; **42**-3b3; **50**-1a2
Fall(s) – **16**-2f4; **18**-1c2; **41**-1b3;1c3-4; **45**-2b14; **46**-3b,3b1
False – **13**-2d2;2e4,6; **33**-P17; **43**-1c,1c3,; **45**-1g5-6; **49**-4a6a
False Accusers – **36**-P120
False Diviners – **13**-2e4
False Prophet(s) – **13**-2d2;2e6; **44**-1f5; **45**-1g6; **47**-1e3; **55**-1b6;1c2
False Prophetesses – **47**-1e4
False Religion – **43**-1c
False Teaching – **43**-1c3
Fame – **21**-1b4; **31**-2a8
Family – **6**-1a; **13**-2f2; **17**-1a1; **26**-1e;1g3; **32**-2a1
Famine – **6**-7f3; **21**-2e1; **23**-1b11
Farewell – **15**-3c-d; **18**-2a6
Farewell Address – **15**-3c-d; **18**-2a6
Fasting – **43**-3b12; **57**-1c2
Father – **21**-1a; **22**-2a; **34**-P66
Fatherly – **37**-#1
Fear – **34**-P56; **41**-1b4; **47**-1e2
Fear God – **41**-1b4
Feast(s) – **7**-3a14; **50**-5b10a; **51**-1d
Feasts of Firstfruits – **10**-2c3
Feast of Purim – **31**-2a7
Feasts of Tabernacles – **10**-2c7; **12**-4c8; **13**-2d8; **30**-3a2
Feasts of Trumpets – **10**-2c5; **12**-4c6
Feast of Unleavened Bread – **10**-2c1
Feasts of Weeks – **10**-2c4; **12**-4c5; **13**-2d7
Feeding – **23**-1b7
Feel(s) – **34**-P41; **46**-1b
Festival(s) – **10**-2c
Few – **58**-2c
Field – **17**-1b,1b1; **45**-2a5
Fiery – **51**-1b10
Fifteen – **24**-2a4
Fifth – **6**-1d5
Fifth Period – **16**-2e
Fifty-two – **24**-1c20
Fifty-five – **24**-2a7; **29**-2b40
Fifty-eight – **28**-2b28
Fights – **20**-2a6
Fill(s) – **9**-3d24; **27**-1c3
Final – **14**-4a6; **23**-2f5; **39**-1d9; **54**-1c1
Finally – **53**-2b4
Finds – **29**-2b43
Fire – **6**-1d7; **10**-1c6; **48**-2a3; **51**-1b11; **54**-1d2
Firmament – **47**-1b3
First – **6**-1d1; **10**-1a; **11**-#2;4a3; **16**-2a; **18**-2a3; **29**-1a; **32**-3a2; **36**-P115; **51**-1b; **54**-1c3b; **56**-2a1-2; **57**-2a
First Coming – **55**-1c6a;1d1-2; **58**-2a2a
First Period – **16**-2a
First Son – **20**-2a4
First Woe – **54**-1c3b
Firstborn – **6**-1d10; **7**-1e2;2a3,5
Firstfruits – **10**-2c3; **14**-2f7
Fish – **54**-1a5
Five – **15**-2b3; **18**-1b1
Flask – **44**-1e11
Flattering Lips – **38**-1b15
Flee(s) – **4**-5c3; **5**-6b1; **6**-1b3; **19**-3c; **20**-2b3; **23**-1b12; **54**-1a
Fleece – **16**-2d4
Flies – **6**-1d4
Floating – **23**-1b9
Flood(s) – **3**-3a4
Flooding – **3**-3a
Flourishes – **26**-2b3
Flowing – **50**-5b13
Flying Scroll – **57**-1b7
Folly – **39**-1a5;1d6
Fool – **34**-P53
Foolish – **24**-2a5; **32**-3b1; **33**-P14; **38**-1c;3a5
Foolishness – **38**-1c4; **39**-1d1; **42**-2b7; **43**-1c6
Foolish Actions – **38**-1c
Foolish People – **38**-3a5
Food(s) – **13**-2d3
Forbidden – **13**-1a7;2e8; **45**-2c3
Forced Laborers – **27**-1d2
Foreign – **48**-#3
Foreign god – **58**-2b1
Foreseen – **46**-#1
Forest Fire – **48**-2a3
Foretelling – **13**-2e5
Forgive(s) – **6**-7g6
Forgiven – **20**-2c2
Forgiveness – **34**-P51; **37**-P130; **48**-1e17d; **53**-1b6; **55**-1d5
Forgotten – **42**-3a11
Forsakes – **28**-2b1,22,25,29
Forth – **57**-1a1
Forty Years – **26**-#2; **27**-#1; **28**-1d8;2b17,20
Forty-one – **22**-2d3; **24**-1c19; **28**-2b4,8
Forty-two – **24**-1c8
Found – **24**-2a10
Foundation – **29**-1b2; **41**-2b2
Four – **47**-1b1,2; **51**-2b1,3
Four Beasts – **51**-2b1,3
Four Chariots – **57**-1b3; Zech.1b9
Four Craftsmen – **57**-1b3
Four Horns – **57**-1b3
Four Living Creatures – **47**-1b1
Fourth – **6**-1d4;4a6; **16**-2d; **51**-1b11;2b4
Four-hundred – **19**-3c8
Fourth Period – **16**-2d
Free – **45**-2b15
Friends – **32**-2a3;#3;3a2,6,9;#4;4a1; **34**-P55; **51**-1b7,8,10,12
Friendship(s) – **19**-3b2; **39**-1c3
Frogs – **6**-1d2
Fruit – **54**-1d5
Fulfillment – **51**-1c4
Fulfills – **55**-1b
Function – **10**-1b

Funeral Song – **48**-1e18a
Furnace – **48**-2a6; **51**-1b9-10
Furnishings – **21**-1c3; **27**-1b3
Future – **6**-7g3; **35**-P73; **39**-1b4; **40**-1a4; **41**-1c11;#2; **42**-3b; **46**-1c3; **52**-1a2; **53**-1b7; **54**-1c3; **55**-1b4;1c5; **57**-1c4;#2
Future Blessings – **41**-1c11
Future Restoration – **48**-2a2; **55**-1b7

G

Gabriel – **52**-1b9;1c3;1c3a; **52**-1c3,1c3a
Gad – **12**-4e1; **15**-3a2b;3c1; **26**-1f4
Gadi – **24**-1c23
Gain – **37**-1a
Galeed – **5**-6b3
Gallows – **31**-2a2
Garment(s) – **8**-3b16;3d17; **9**-3d20
Gate(s) – **49**-5a2b,d,e;5a2f1-2; **50**-5a2f3;5b4,16
Gatekeepers – **27**-2e5
Gath – **19**-3c7
Gathered – **38**-3c1
Gaza – **53**-1b2; **57**-2a1b
Gedaliah – **25**-2a19; **45**-2c1-2
Genealogy – **29**-2a3; **30**-2a4
Genealogy of – Adam – **3**-2c
Adam to David – **25**-#1
Cain – **3**-2b2
Esau – **5**-6c; **25**-1c5
Ham – **25**-1b2
Hezron – **25**-1d3
Isaac – **4**-5a1; **25**-1c4
Ishmael – **4**-4g3; **25**-1c2
Jacob – **4**-6a; **5**-6a5; **26**-1f
Japheth – **25**-1b1
Judah – **25**-1d2
Keturah – **25**-1c3
Nahor – **4**-4e5
Saul – **26**-1f14
Shem – **3**-3c2; **25**-1b3
Sons of Noah – **3**-3b2
Terah – **3**-3c3
Generated – **17**-1c
Generation – **11**-3d; **14**-1b3; **37**-#1
Generosity – **30**-2a2d
Genesis – Pg**3**
Gentiles – **42**-3b6,8; **43**-3c1; **53**-1b8
Gershon – **10**-1b5
Geshur – **20**-2b3
Giant(s) – **19**-3b1; **21**-2e4
Gibeah – **16**-3b2
Gibeon – **14**-2b2
Gibeonites – **14**-2b1; **21**-2e2
Gideon – **16**-2d2-4,6-7
Gifts – **39**-1b3
Gimel – **36**-#3
Girl – **40**-1g2
Give(s) – **8**-3d4; **12**-#1; **14**-1a2; **22**-1e2; **31**-1a1;1c5; **31**-1c5; **51**-1b12; **54**-#1; **57**-#1
Given – **11**-3c2; **39**-1b2; **47**-1b; **58**-2a5b
Glean(s) – **17**-1b,1b1
Glimpse – **49**-#5
Gloom – **46**-#1
Glorious Hand – **52**-1c5
Glorious Messenger – **52**-1c4,6
Glory – **7**-3a17; **27**-1c3; **40**-1a4; **50**-5b1
Glory of God – **27**-1c3; **34**-P68; **56**-2b2; **57**-1b1
Glory of the *LORD* – **7**-3a17; **50**-5b1
Glowing – **47**-1b3
Goat – **51**-2b6
God Almighty – **46**-1b
God – **3**-3a1,3,5;4a1; **6**-1b,1b5-7;1c5; **7**-3a3; **8**-3c2;3d3; **9**-#1;#2; **10**-2d,2d2;1b3;1c6; **11**-2c;#3; **13**-2b2;2c,2c2,7;3a; **14**-3a; **17**-1b4; **18**-1a2;2a2; **20**-1b5-6; **22**-2b2-3;2e; **23**-1a1; **26**-2b6,8; **27**-1a1;1c3-5; **30**-2b2; **31**-#1;#2; **32**-3c2,4,6;4a3,5; **33**-P1-5,8-10,14,16,19,21,24,26; **34**-P30,32,34,39-40,42,46-48,50,53,57-60,63,65-68; **35**-P71-76,79,81-84,86-90,93,95-97,99,103-108; **36**-111-119,123-126; **37**-P127,129,132,134,136,139,144,146,147;1b8; **38**-1b14; **39**-1a6; 1b2-3;1c5; **40**-1a4; **41**-1b4;2b3; **42**-2b7;2c4;3a,3a2,3,5,8,12;3b1,2,5,7; **43**-3b12;3d1,2,4,7;#1;1b1 1b5; **44**-1d;1e3,9; **45**-3a2; **46**-1b,1b1; **47**-1b;1c1;1d6;1e13; **48**-2a4,10; **49**-4a2,4a6b;4b5;5a1; **50**-1a,1a2; **51**-1b3,12;1d2;2a6; **52**-1c2;1a5; **53**-2b1;1b6,8; **55**-1b2-4;1b4; **56**-#2;2b2-3; **57**-1b1,3; **58**-#1;#2;2b5
God's Blessings – **39**-1a6
God's Sword – **48**-2a4
Godly Living – **13**-#2; **38**-#2;2a2
god(s) – **29**-2b34; **58**-2b1
Gog – **49**-4b2-4
Gog of Magog – **49**-4b2-3
Gold – **51**-1b7
Golden Calf – **8**-3c1; **13**-2c5
Golden Lampstand – **7**-3b5; **8**-3d10; **57**-1b6
Goliath – **19**-3b1
Gomer – **52**-1a;1a1,4
Gomorrah – **4**-4d,4d4
Good – **36**-P111
Goodness – **32**-4a5; **34**-P32; **35**-P81,104
Good News – **34**-P67; **43**-3c2
Goshen – **6**-7f2
Gossipers – **38**-3a7
Governing – **13**-2e10; **50**-5b6
Governor – **5**-7d; **25**-2a19; **57**-#1
Grain Offering – **9**-1a2,8
Gratitude – **33**-P18
Great – **33**-P22; **36**-P114; **49**-4b5; **51**-1d; **54**-1a2; **58**-2c2
Greatest – **13**-2c1; **33**-P19; **37**-P147
Great Day of the *LORD* – **58**-2c2
Great Joy – **33**-P22
Great Storm – **54**-1a2
Great Suffering – **33**-P22
Great Supper of God – **49**-4b5
Great Work of God – **36**-P114
Greece – **52**-1d2

Group(s) – **27**-2e3; **29**-1a;2a
Grows – **26**-2a4
Guidance – **33**-P25
Guidelines – **33**-P15
Guilt – **20**-2a3; **49**-4a4

H

Habakkuk – Pg**56; 56**-#1;#2;2a,2a1,3;2b,2b1,4
Hadassah – **31**-1b2
Hagar – **4**-4c2;4e2
Haggai – Pg**57**; **57**-#1
Hail – **6**-1d7
Half-Sister – **20**-2b1
Hallow – **44**-1e7
Ham – **3**-3b4; **25**-1a10;1b2
Haman – **31**-1c1,5-6;2a2
Hananiah – **45**-1g5-6
Hand of the LORD – **46**-1a1
Handwriting – **51**-1d2-4
Hanged – **31**-2a2
Hannah – **18**-1a1-2,4-5;1b1
Haran – **4**-5c3; **5**-6b1
Hard Times – **35**-P77
Harlot – **40**-1a2; **48**-2a8
Harmonious Relationships – **37**-P133
Hazar – **46**-3a8
Hĕ (Pronounced: hay) – **36**-#5
Head – **47**-1d5
Healing – **23**-1b8; **43**-3b11
Health – **32**-2a2
Hear(s) – **27**-1c5; **34**-P34; **41**-2b3
Heard – **49**-4a5
Heart – **28**-2b29; **34**-P50,62; **37**-1b5,10
Heathen – **41**-1c
Heaven – **23**-1b1
Heavenly Father – **34**-P66
Hebrew – **6**-1a2
Hebron – **15**-3a3b; **19**-1a6
Heed – **49**-4a5
Help – **31**-1c4; **32**-3b3; **33**-P9,27; **34**-P54,57,59,70; **35**-P74,101; **36**-P121; **37**-P141,146; **42**-3a3
Her (Jerusalem) – **41**-2b4; **49**-4b6
Heth – **36**-#8
Hezekiah – **24**-2a1-6; **29**-2b35-39; **42**-2c4
Hide(s) – **14**-1a3
Hideous – **16**-3b2; **24**-1c6
High Priest – **57**-#1; Zech.1b5
Highs & Lows – **22**-1d
Hilkiah – **29**-2b43
Him (Trinity Related) – **37**-P147
Hiram – **22**-1d2
His (God Related) – **31**-2a2; **36**-P119,134; **42**-3a5; **58**-1a
His (Non-God Related) – **40**-1c1-2;1e1-2; **44**-1e13; **47**-1d5; **51**-1b1; **52**-1c2; **54**-1a; **55**-1b
His (God's) Own – **31**-2a2
His (God's) Word – **36**-P119; **41**-1b4
History – **11**-4a
Historical – **12**-1a; **46**-3b
Hold – **44**-1d8
Holiness – **35**-P99
Holy – **8**-3b22;3d12; **9**-#1; **50**-5b2,7,10
Home – **15**-3c1; **41**-1b7
Honor God – **37**-P132
Honored – **31**-2a1
Hope(s) – **33**-P27; **34**-P43; **42**-3b2; **45**-#2;2b10; **46**-1b4;1c3; **49**-#4; **55**-1b7; **57**-2b
Hopelessness – **37**-P143
Horeb – **7**-2c3; **23**-2e5
Horite – **5**-6c3
Horn – **51**-2b7; **52**-1b12
Horse – **57**-1b1
Hosea – Pg**52**; **52**-1a,1a1
Hoshea – **24**-1c28;1d1
Host(s) – **14**-1b4
House – **20**-2b; **22**-2b4;2c1; **27**-1c3-4; **48**-2a6; **57**-1b1
House of God – **40**-1a
Household – **18**-1b2
Human Relationships – **13**-2f
Human Wisdom – **39**-1a2
Humiliation – **42**-3a14
Hurt – **34**-P55
Husband – **17**-1d1; **19**-3c2; **20**-2a2; **40**-1f2; **52**-#1
Hushai – **20**-2c7-8
Hymn – **37**-P150; **41**-1b9
Hypocrisy – **41**-2b4

I

Ibzan – **16**-2e4
Ichabod – **18**-1c3
Identity – **5**-7e6
Idols – **42**-3a4,13
Idol Worship – **29**-2b36
Idolatry – **22**-1e1;2b1; **42**-3a10; **43**-3b10;1c6; **45**-2c5; **47**-1d6;1e5
Ignores – **33**-P9
Illness – **24**-2a4
Image – **51**-1b7-8
Image of Gold – **51**-1b7
Immanuel – **41**-1b2
Immoral – **37**-1b3
Immorality – **7**-3a11
Imprisoned – **5**-7c
Improper – **13**-2d3; **30**-2b3
Incense – **8**-3b19,23
Incense Altar – **8**-3d11
Indictment – **52**-2a1-2
Indignation – **35**-P109; **43**-3d7
Individual – **48**-1e17c
Influences – **37**-1b1
Inhabitation – **45**-2b4
Inhabitants – **26**-1g1
Inheritance – **12**-4b3;4g6;2e3; **15**-3a,3a2a-c;3a3b-c;3a3f-h,3a4b-i
Iniquity – **11**-3c1; **48**-1e17e
Initiative – **40**-1f1
Injury – **7**-3a6

Injustice – **33**-P10; **35**-P79
Inner Court – **49**-5a2f
Inspect(s) – **9**-3d21; **30**-1a3
Inspirational – **12**-#1
Instituted – **7**-3b
Instruction(s) – **8**-3b17;3d2; **9**-1d3; **10**-1b4-6; **12**-4f2; **15**-3a1,3a3a,3a4a
Instrument – **42**-3a12
Insults – **30**-2a2a
Intensifies – **40**-1e3
Intercedes – **4**-4d2; **8**-3c2; **44**-1d9; **52**-1c2
Intercession – **30**-1a1
Intermarriage – **30**-2b1; **58**-2b1
Interpret(s) – **5**-7c2;7d1; **51**-1b5
Interpretation – **51**-1c3;1d5;2b3-4
Introduction – **53**-1a; Amos1a; **55**-1a; **56**-#1;#1
Invading – **55**-1b3
Invasion – **49**-4b1
Invitation – **35**-P95; **42**-3b7
Irreverence – **58**-2b3
Isaac – **4**-4e1;4f,4f1;5a1;5b1
Isaiah – Pg**40**;1a9; **41**-1b1,12
Ishbosheth – **19**-1a5,7
Ishmael – **4**-4e2
Israel (Person) – **6**-7f,7f1-2;1a,1a1;1b;1c4; **7**-#2;3a,3a1-2,15-16; **11**-2a2; **25**-1c;1d1
Israel's (Nation) – **8**-3c2,4; **10**-#1;1a,1a3; **11**-2a1;2c2;3d4,7; **12**-4b,4b1,4;4d2;1a3; **13**-1a8;2a,2a1;2e3; **14**-#3;4a1,3,6;#1;1b1;2a2,4 ;2b,2b1; **15**-2c;3c,d; **16**-#2;2d1,2; **18**-#1;1c,1c5-6;#2;2a,2a1-3; **19**-3d5;1a5; **20**-1b,1b1; **21**-1a2; **22**-1e4;2a3;2b;2d,2d4-9; **23**-1b3;1c; **24**-1c3,10,14-15,19, 21-25,28;1d1-3; **26**-2a2; **27**-2d,2d1;1a; **28**-2a1;2b7,10,26,32; **31**-2a6; **40**-1a; **41**-1b3,7,8,11 **41**-2a4;2b; **42**-3a1,6-8,11;3b,3b2; **43**-3b10;3c3;1b2,3; **44**-1e4; **45**-2a1-4,6;3a2; **47**-1c1-2;1d2; 1e9-11,13,16; **48**-1e18,1e18d; **48**-#2;2a,2a1a-f,2a2,6; **49**-#4;4a,4a1,4,6,4a6 a,4a7,4a7b,d; 4b,4b1,4,6;#5; **50**-5b14; **52**-1d6 ;1a,1a2,4,5;#2;2a,2a1,3,4,6; **53**-2a7-8;2b,2b1-4;1b7; Amos1b,1b8; **54**-1c1-3; **55**-1c;1d2,4,5; **57**-#2;2a,2a1; **58**-2a3-4; Mal.#1;#2
Israelites – **6**-1b8; **7**-2c;#3;3a3; **14**-3a3;2a1; **15**-2d; **58**-2b5
Issachar – **15**-3a4e; **26**-1f7

J

Jabesh – **24**-1c22
Jabesh Gilead – **16**-3b5
Jacob – **4**-5a2;5c1,3,6a,6a1-2; **5**-6a3-6;6b1-2,4-7,9-10,12;7e2,7; **6**-7g,7g1-5;1c4; **25**-1c;1d,1d1; **58**-1a1
Jair – **16**-2d12
Japheth – **3**-3b3; **25**-1a10;1b1
Jared – **25**-1a5-6
Jar of Oil – **23**-1b4;1c1
Jeconiah – **26**-1e3
Jehoahaz – **25**-2a13; **48**-1e18b
Jehoahaz (Shallum) – **44**-1f3a
Jehoiachin – **25**-2a16,20; **29**-2b49
Jehoiachin (Coniah) – **44**-1f3c; **46**-3b4; **48**-1e18c
Jehoiada – **28**-2b19,21
Jehoiakim – **25**-2a14; **29**-2b48; **44**-1f3b; **45**-2b8
Jehoram – **28**-2b14
Jehoshaphat – **23**-2g,2g1; **28**-P9-11,13-14
Jephthah – **16**-2e1-3
Jehu – **24**-1c3-5,7-10
Jeremiah – Pg**43**; **43**-1a,1a1,2;1b;1c4; **44**-1d2-4,9;1e,1e1-3,6,10,12,13;1f,1f1-2;1g3; **45**-1g7;2a5;2b1,5-9, 11-13,15;2c1,4;#3; **46**-1a1;1b2-6;1d; **52**-1c1,3
Jericho – **14**-2a1
Jeroboam I – **22**-2b,2b1,4;1c,1c1-2
Jeroboam II – **24**-1c19,21
Jerubbaal – **16**-2d2
Jerusalem – **20**-1b2,4;2c4; **21**-2d2; **22**-2d2-3; **23**-1c1-2; **25**-2a16; **26**-1g,1g1-2;2a3;2b,2b1,3,5; **29**-2b45; 2a1; **30**-2b;#1;1a;3b1,3; **40**-1a2,6; **41**-1c16;2b4-5; **42**-3b4; **44**-1f1; **45**-2a6;2b,2b14;2c; **46**-3b, 3b1-3;#1;1a,1a1;1b1;1c1-3; **47**-1e8; **48**-2a5; **49**-4a3; **55**-1c3,5; **55**-2a1f; **57**-1c4
Jeshua – **57**-#1
Jesse – **41**-1b8
Jew(s) – **31**-1c,1c1,4;2a5; **45**-1g7;2c4-5
Jezebel – **24**-1c6
Joab – **20**-1a8;2a6;2d1; **21**-1a4
Joahaz – **29**-2b47
Joel – Pg**53; 53**-1a
Joash – **28**-2b17,20,22-24,26
Job – Pg**31; 31**-#1;1a,1a1;#2;2a; **32**-2a1-3;#3;3a1-10;3b1-5,7;3c1-3,5-7;#4;4a1-2
Joins – **19**-1a7
Joining – **37**-P145
Jonah – Pg**54**; **54**-#1;1a,1a1,3-5; **55**-1b;1b1,3
Jonathan – **19**-3b2;3c4-5;1a3; **21**-2e3
Joram – **23**-1c1; **24**-1c4
Jordan – **13**-1a9
Jordan River – **14**-1b; **15**-3a2-3
Joseph – **5**-7a,7a1-2;7c,7c2;7d,7d1-2;7e,7e1,6; **6**-7g,7g1,6-7
Joshua – **7**-2c4; **12**-4b4;4g2; **14**-#4;4a1;1a,1a1-3;1b4;2a,2a1;2b; **15**-2c;2d1;3a1,3a4i;3c-d;3d1-3; **57**-1c1
Josiah – **24**-2a9; **25**-2a11-12; **29**-2b42,45-46; **44**-1f3; **45**-2b8
Jotham – **24**-1c26-27; **28**-2b30-31
Journey(s) – **7**-#2; **10**-#2; **11**-3d6;#4; **12**-4f1;1a4
Joy – **33**-P22; **34**-P48,67; **35**-P98; **37**-P133,147; **56**-2b4
Joyful – **37**-P137,147
Judah (Person) – **5**-7b;7b1; **15**-3a3c,e
Judah (Place) – **19**-1a4; **21**-1a2; **22**-2b2;2d1; **23**-2g1;1c;1c1-2; **24**-1c18,20,26-27;1d;#2;2a;2a1,7-9;1d; #2;2a;2a1,7-9; **25**-2a13-15,18-19; **26**-1f1; **28**-#2;2a1,3;2b;2b3-4,6,9,11,14-17,24,28,30-32; **29**-2b33,35,40,42,47-50;1b3; **30**-2b4;3b; **40**-1a1,6; **41**-1b1;2b; **42**-2c;2c3,5; **42**-3a15; **43**-#1;1b; 1b1,4,5;1c;1c2,4,5; **44**-1c7;1d;1d1,8,9;1e5;1f, 1f2;1g; **45**-#2;2a1;2b4; **47**-1c;1d;1d3,6,7;1e1; **53**-1b9;1b7; **55**-#1;1b2,4; **56**-2a1a; **58**-2b1

Judged – **41**-1b7; **43**-1c2
Judge(s) – **13**-2e1, Pg**16**; **16**-#2;2a;2b;2c,2c2;2d,2d2;2e; **17**-2f;#3; **18**-#1; **27**-2e7; **34**-P52; **58**-2b4
Judgment – **3**-3a3; **4**-4d; **8**-3b15; **12**-4g5; **20**-2a4; **22**-2c,2c1; **23**-1a1; **35**-P82; **39**-1b4; **40**-#1;1a6; **41**-1b6;1c,1c1;1c5-10,12-17;2a1; **42**-2b6,10-11; **43**-3d1,4;#1;1b4-5;1c5; **47**-1d6;1e; **48**-1e17e 2a8c;3a5a; **49**-3a7a;4a2,4a7a;4b2; **53**-2a8;2b3;1b8;1b,1b1-8; **54**-1c;1c1,3;1c3b-d;1d; **55**-#1;1b, 1b1,2,4,5;1c,1c3; **56**-2b;2b1-3; Zep.#2;2a1;2a1a-f; **57**-2a1
Judgment of God – **23**-1a1; **35**-P82; **43**-1b5; **55**-1b4
Judgeship – **16**-2d11-12,2e4-6
Just – **35**-P97; **49**-4a2
Justice – **7**-3a13; **33**-P1,7,17; **43**-1b5
Justice of God – **32**-4a3; **34**-P58; **35**-P72;

K

Kadesh-Barnea – **12**-1a3; **48**-2a1c
Kaph – **36**-#11
Kedar – **46**-3a8
Keliah – **19**-3c10
Kenan – **25**-1a3-4
Keturah – **4**-4g1
Killed – **19**-3d5; **20**-2a2;2b2;2c9; **22**-2b3; **24**-1c11,13; **25**-2a12; **28**-2b23,27; **29**-2b46
Kill(s) – **6**-1b2; **19**-3c9; **24**-1c5,7-8; **31**-1b4;1c6; **44**-1d2
Kindness – **20**-1c2;2d5; **55**-1b4
King Ahab – **23**-2f,2f4; **28**-2b10
King Ahasuerus – **31**-1a;1a2-3;1b3;1c5;2a4
King Ahaz – **29**-2b34; **41**-1b1
King Artaxerxes – **29**-2a2; **30**-1a2
King Asa – **28**-2b6,8
King Baasha – **28**-2b7
King Belshazzar – **51**-1d
King Ben-Hadad – **23**-2f1;1b14
King Darius – **51**-#2;2a6
King Hezekiah – **29**-2b36-37,39; **42**-2c,2c6,7
King Jehoshaphat – **28**-2b11
King Josiah – **29**-2b45-46; **45**-2b8
King Nebuchadnezzar – **25**-2a15; **50**-#1; **51**-1b;1b4-5;1c
King Sennacherib – **42**-2c1,2,6,7
King Zedekiah – **45**-2b1,2,10,13
King(s) – **5**-6c4; **6**-1a2; **11**-3d7; **13**-2e2; **15**-2b3; **18**-#2;2a,2a1-4;2b5;3a; **19**-3b4;3c1,3,4,12,15;3d2,5, 1a;1a4-5; **20**-1b;2a; **21**-1a,1a2; **22**-1e4;2a;2b; **23**-1b14;1c; **24**-1c3,17;1d1;2a,2a6; **26**-1f14; 1g3;2a2; **28**-#2;2b;2b6-8,10-11;2b19,26; **29**-2b51;1a1;2a2; **31**-1a1;1b1,4;2a1; **41**-1b1; **42**-2b8; 2c;2c1,6,7; **44**-1f2; **48**-5a5c-d; **51**-1d;#2;2a6; **52**-1d
Kingdom – **19**-#1; **20**-1b5, **21**-2d,2d6;2e; **21**-#1;1a3; **22**-#2; **23**-#1; **24**-#2; **38**-3a1; **41**-#2;2a2; **43**-3c;3d5 **45**-2a2-3; **49**-#5; **55**-1c4; **58**-2b3
Kingdom Age – **41**-2a2
Kings (1st) – Pg**21**
Kings (2nd) – Pg**23**
Kinsman – **17**-1b
Knowledge – **37**-1a1
Known – **58**-1a
Knows – **37**-P139
Kohath – **10**-1b4
Korah – **11**-3b1

L

Laban – **5**-6b2
Laborers – **27**-1d2
Lachish – **28**-2b27
Laid – **53**-#1;1b2
Laish – **16**-3a2
Lamech – **25**-1a8-9
Laměd – **36**-#12
Lamentation – **19**-1a3; **48**-1e18;3a5b,d; **49**-3a7c,f; **54**-1c3a
Lamentations – Pg**46**
Lamp – **8**-3b11
Lampstand – **7**-3b5; **8**-3d10
Land – **5**-7f2; **6**-1d2; **11**-#2;2a;2c2;#4; **12**-4g,4g2; **13**-1a6-7; **14**-#1;#2; **15**-#3;3a2;#3;3a2-3;3a3a, 3a4,3a4a; **21**-2e1; **22**-2e1; **23**-1b13; **29**-2b37; **49**-4b6; **50**-5b8,15; **53**-#1;1b2
Landmark – **13**-2e8
Last – **17**-#1; **21**-2e6; **29**-2b39; **44**-1g2; **47**-1e16
Last Days – **29**-2b39
Last Words of David – **21**-2e6
Latter Days – **49**-4b
Laver – **8**-3b21;3d14
Law(s) – **7**-3a6-12,14; **8**-3c; **9**-1c1,3-6;1d1,4; **10**-2b,2b2;2c1-14;2d,2d2;1c2; **11**-3a,3a1; **12**-4b3;4c9; **13**-2a,2a1;2e4,6,9;2f4,6; **14**-4a2; **38**-3b2; **50**-5b6,9
Lays – **44**-1d8
Laziness – **38**-1b13
Lazy People – **38**-3a6
Lead(s) – **6**-1b; **29**-1a;2a
Leader(s) – **10**-1c3; **12**-1a2; **14**-4a1; **38**-#3; **44**-1f; **47**-1d11; **48**-2a1a;2a7; **55**-1c,1c1
Leadership – **14**-4a
Leah – **5**-6a3
Leave – **12**-1a1
Led – **10**-1c6
Lemuel – **38**-3c2
Length – **52**-1b8
Leper – **9**-1c5
Leprous – **11**-2b2
Leprosy – **9**-1c4; **23**-1b8
Lessons – **35**-P78
Letters – **45**-1g7
Levi – **26**-1f6
Levites – **10**-1b;1b2,3,7;1c4; **11**-3c,3c3; **12**-4b2;4g3-4;2e3; **15**-3b2; **16**-3b1; **26**-1g2; **27**-2e2-3; **30**-3b2
Leviticus – Pg**9**
Lice – **6**-1d3
Lies (Down) – **46**-#1;1a
Life – **14**-3a3; **18**-1a; **19**-3c1,12,15; **24**-2a4; **31**-1a1;#2; **33**-P15; **34**-P29; **37**-P127;1b8; **38**-3b1; **39**-#1;1a,

1a1;1b;1c; **42**-2c6; **44**-1e3; **50**-#1;1a; **51**-#2
Lifestyle – **40**-1a1
Life & Times of Abraham – **3**-**#4**
Adam & Eve – **3**-**#2**
Isaac – **4**-4e;#5
Israel – **6**-**#1**
Jacob – **4**-**#6**
Joseph – **5**-#7
Noah – **3**-**#3**
Lifted – **45**-2b12
Limitations – **39**-1d2
Linen Sash – **44**-1d5
Lion – **22**-2b3
Listen & Hear – **41**-2b3
Little Horn – **52**-1b12
Lived – **25**-1a1-10; **33**-P16
Live(s) – **21**-2e9; **36**-P114; **38**-2a1
Livestock – **6**-1d5
Living – **13**-#2; **33**-P15-16; **38**-2a2; **47**-1b1
Living Water – **50**-5b13
Locust(s) – **6**-1d8; **53**-1b1; **54**-1d1
Long Life – **37**-1b8
LORD – **6**-1c,1c3; **7**-2b2-3;3a4,15-17; **8**-3c5,6,8; **11**-2a4; **12**-4d1; **13**-2c,2c4; **14**-3a2;1a1;1b4;2a5; **15**-3a1;3b3; **18**-1b3;2b,2b5; **19**-3a2; **20**-2a3; **21**-2e5,10;1b1; **22**-1d1;1e2; **23**-1b2; **25**-2a11 **27**-2e11;1b;1c; **28**-2a2;2b1,6,12; **29**-1b1; **32**-3b5; **34**-P31,33,37,45; **36**-P124; **37**-P130,148;1b5 **39**-1b; **40**-1a5; **41**-1c2; **42**-2c1;3a5;3b3-4; **43**-1a; **44**-1d3,4,10;1e4; **46**-1a2;1b4,6;1c;1d1; **47**-1e9,1e17a; **48**-2a1a; **50**-5b;5b1,7; **52**-#2;2a5; **53**-2b;1b3;#1; **54**-#1;1a1; **55**-1d1-4; **56**-#2; 2a;2a1-2;2b; Hab.2a2,4; **57**-#1; Zech.1b2; **58**-2b2-3; Mal.2b3;2c2
LORDSHIP – **34**-P47
Lot (Person) – **3**-4b2
Lot (Life) – **44**-1e13
Lot, Sons of – **4**-4d6
Love – **13**-2c; **34**-P34; **35**-P103; **36**-P113,118; **37**-P136; **40**-1b2;1c2;1d2;1f3;1g,1g1; **53**-2b1; **58**-#1;1a
Loved – **58**-1a1
Love of God – **53**-2b1
Lovemaking – **40**-1f1
Loyalty – **17**-1a; **33**-P26
Lucifer (Satan) – **41**-1c4

M

Made – **8**-3b16;3d5-15,17-18; **9**-3d19-20; **14**-3a1; **19**-1a5; **21**-2e3; **25**-2a19; **27**-2e1;1b1; **30**-3a5; **47**-1c2; **58**-1a
Magog – **49**-4b1-3
Mahalalel – **25**-1a4-5
Mahalath – **4**-5c4
Mahanaim – **5**-6b4
Majesty of the *LORD* – **56**-#2
Make(s) – **16**-3b3; **18**-2b3; **19**-3c5; **22**-2a1; **27**-2e; **28**-2b7,19; **31**-1b3; **37**-P137
Making – **8**-3b23; **18**-2b5
Malachi – Pg**58**
Male Goat – **51**-2b6; **52**-1b11
Man – **11**-4a2; **32**-3c4; **37**-P146; **57**-1b4
Man of God – **22**-2b2-3; **38**-1c3
Man of Wisdom – **38**-1c3
Manasseh – **6**-7g2; **12**-4e1; **15**-3a3f,h; **24**-2a7-8; **29**-2b40-41
Manipulation – **33**-P12
Manna – **7**-2c2
Manslaughter – **13**-2f1
Manslayers – **13**-2e7
Mantle – **23**-2e6
Marriage – **13**-2f2,4; **21**-1a6; **37**-P128; **40**-1c3;1d1;1e3
Marry(ies) – **6**-1b4; **17**-1d; **19**-3b4 Mattaniah – **25**-2a17
Measurement(s) – **50**-5a2i,k;5b3a
Measuring Line – **57**-1b4
Medianites – **12**-4d,4d1
Mediterranean Sea – **54**-1a2
Meet(s) – **5**-6b6; **6**-1b5; **8**-3c5; **14**-1b4; **17**-1b2; **21**-2d4; **41**-1b1; **45**-2b13
Meeting – **6**-1c1
Megiddo – **25**-2a12; **29**-2b46
Melchizedek – **4**-4b3
Mem – **36**-#13
Memories – **40**-1b;1c
Memucan – **31**-1a3
Men – **8**-3c3; **23**-1b7
Men of the Sea – **28**-1d5
Menahem – **24**-1c23-24
Mephibosheth – **20**-1c2; **21**-2d4
Merari – **10**-1b6
Mercy – **21**-2d3; **34**-P39,41,51; **35**-P89; **36**-P123; **43**-3d2; **52**-2a4
Mercies – **35**-P90
Mercy Seat – **7**-3b3
Mesopotamia – **16**-2a1
Message(s) – **20**-2c8; **22**-2b2;2e2; **40**-#1; **42**-#3; **44**-1f1-4; **45**-2b1,2,5; **48**-2a1a;#3; **49**-#4; **54**-1c;#1; **55**-1d; **57**-Hag.#1; Zech.#1;1c;#2;2a
Messenger – **52**-1c4,6; **58**-2b4
Messiah – **13**-2e5; **36**-P110; **41**-1b,1b5; **42**-3b1,5,7; **44**-1f4; **55**-1c6;1c6a-b; **58**-2a2,2a2a-b;2b
Methuselah – **25**-1a7-8
Micah – **16**-3a,3a1; Pg**55; 55**-1a
Michal – **19**-3b4;3c2
Middle – **33**-P11
Midian – **6**-1b3
Midianites – **16**-2d1,6
Midst – **26**-2b6; **34**-P55; **37**-P143
Mighty – **16**-2d5;2f3
Migration – **16**-3a,3a2; **45**-2c3
Military – **27**-2e8
Millennial Kingdom – **43**-3c;3d5; **49**-#5
Mingle(s)(ed) – **6**-1d7
Ministers – **18**-1c6; **45**-2c4
Ministry – **8**-3d17; **9**-1b1-2; **18**-1b,1b3; **22**-2e; **23**-1b,1b2
Miracle(s) – **6**-1c6; **23**-1b4-9; **35**-P105
Mighty Deeds of David's Men – **21**-2e7
Miriam – **11**-2b,2b1-2
Miscellaneous – **11**-3a

Misery – **35**-P88
Mission – **54**-1a; **55**-1b
Mizraim – **3**-3b6
Moab – **11**-3d6; **12**-4f; **14**-3a1;4a7; **16**-2b1; **17**-1a1-3; **20**-1c1; **23**-1b3; **28**-2b12; **41**-1c7; **45**-3a4; **48**-3a2; **53**-1b6; **56**-2a1c
Money – **8**-3b20
Month(s) – **24**-1c22; **25**-2a13,16
Monthly – **12**-4c3
Moons – **50**-5b10b
Moral – **32**-3c5; **40**-1g2
Moral Character – **32**-3c5
Mordecai – **31**-1b4;1c1,3,6;2a;2a1,3,8;2a8
Moses – **6**-1b;1b1-8;1c;1c1,5; **7**-2c3; **8**-3c2,5,9; **9**-3d21; **10**-1b1; **11**-2b,2b1;3b,3b2;3d1; **12**-#1;1a2; **13**-1a7-8; **14**-#3;3a1;#4;4a4-7; **15**-2d1; **30**-3a
Mother – **18**-1a1; **51**-1d3
Mount Carmel – **23**-2e3
Mount Ebal – **14**-2g1-2
Mount Horeb – **6**-1b5; **23**-2e5
Mount Nebo – **14**-4a5,7
Mount Seir – **28**-2b12; **49**-4a7a
Mount Sinai – **7**-#2;#3;3a1; **8**-3c4; **10**-#1
Mount Zion – **40**-1a7
Mourns – **20**-1a9;2c10; **31**-1c3; **43**-1c4-5; **46**-1a1
Mourning – **6**-7g5; **46**-1b2; **53**-1b2
Moved – **27**-2d
Move(s) – **6**-7F; **17**-1a1;
Murders – **23**-2f4
Murmur – **11**-2a2
Musicians – **27**-2e4
Must Be – **50**-5b2
Mystery – **5**-7e4

N

Naaman – **23**-1b8
Nabal – **19**-3c14
Naboth – **23**-2f4
Nadab – **9**-1b3; **22**-2d4
Nahum – Pg**55**; **55**-#1
Named – **17**-1d2
Name(s) – **8**-3d3; **50**-5b16
Naomi – **17**-#1;1a;1a1-2;1c,1c1
Naphtali – **15**-3a4g; **26**-1f9
Nathan – **20**-2a3
Nation(s) – **13**-2c3; **20**-1c; **22**-2a3; **41**-1c; **42**-2b11; **45**-#3;3a; **48**-#3;3a; **49**-4a7d;4b1; **50**-5b14
National Repentance – **53**-1b5
Nature of God – **35**-P93
Nazirite – **10**-1c2
Nebuchadnezzar – **25**-2a15; **41**-1c3; **48**-1e18d; **51**-1b;1b1,2,4,5,7,12;1c;1c1,2,5
Nebuzaradan – **45**-2b15
Needed – **48**-1e17f
Needy – **36**-P113
Negev – **48**-2a3
Nehemiah – Pg**30; 30**-1a;1a1-3;2a2d;3b4
Neighbor(s) – **13**-2e8; **38**-3a2; **49**-3a7g; **53**-1b
Never – **33**-P9; **37**-P136
New – **31**-1b1; **45**-2a4; **49**-5a
New Moons – **50**-5b10b
News – **34**-P67; **43**-3c2
Next Generation – **14**-1b3
Nine – **24**-1c28
Nineveh – **55**-1b1-2; **56**-2b1,2,4
Ninth – **6**-1d9
Noah – **3**-#3;3a2,4;3b2; **25**-1a;1a9-10;1b
North – **43**-1b6; **52**-1d
North & South – **52**-1d
North Gate – **50**-5a2f3
Northern – **15**-2c,2c1; **22**-2a1; **45**-2a2; **49**-5a2d
Northern Gate – **49**-5a2d
Noticed – **51**-1b11
Number(s) – Pg**10**; **12**-4b1-2
Nun (Pronounced: noon) – **36**-#14

O

Obadiah – Pg**54**
Obed – **17**-1d2
Obedience – **10**-2d1; **13**-1a8; **14**-2g,2g3;#3;3a; **18**-2b4; **57**-1a2; Zech.1c2
Obedient to God – **10**-2d
Obey(s) – **13**-2c2; **28**-2a2; **31**-1a2
Obligation(s) – **7**-3a12; **11**-3c
Observed – **29**-1b8
Observing – **10**-1c5
Occupied – **15**-3a3d-e
Offering(s) – **7**-3b1; **8**-3b18; **9**-1a;1a1-5,7-11; **10**-2b2;1c3; **11**-3a1;3c2; **12**-4c,4c1-8; **27**-2e10;1d3; **50**-5b10,12; **58**-2a1
Officers – **13**-2e1
Officials – **27**-2e7
Og – **11**-3d7
Oil – **8**-3b11,22;3d12
Oil & the Bread – **10**-2c8
Omri – **22**-2d8
One-hundred – **23**-1b7
One – **23**-1c2; **24**-1c22; **28**-2b15; **49**-4a7d
Opinion – **32**-3c7
Oppose(s) – **23**-1b10; **29**-1b3; **32**-4a1
Opposition – **54**-1d4
Oppressed – **16**-2a1; 2b1-2; 2c; 2d1; 2e1; **17**-2f1; **39**-1c1
Ordained – **9**-1b1
Order – **14**-1a2
Ordinances – **30**-3a5
Organization – **10**-1a2; **27**-2e2
Origin – **38**-1c2
Othniel – **16**-2a1
Outer Court – **49**-5a2c
Outpouring – **53**-1b6
Overtake (en) – **6**-1d2; **25**-2a15
Overwhelmed – **37**-P142
Own – **47**-1e17b

P

Pagans – **30-**2b1;2b3-4
Panic – **33-**P11
Parts – **12-**4d3
Parable of the Boiling Pot – **48-**2a9
Parable of the Dry Bones – **49-**4a7c
Parable of the Eagle & the Vine – **47-**1e14,15
Parable of the Figs in a Basket – **44-**1g1
Parable of the Fruitless Vine – **47-**1e7
Parable of the Potter – **44-**1e8
Parable of the Trees – **16-**2d9
Parable of the Two Harlot Sisters – **48-**2a8
Parable of the Vineyard – **40-**1a8
Parallel – **52-**1a
Partial – **18-**2b4
Pashhur – **44-**1e12
Pass – **22-**#2
Passing – **22-**1e5; **24-**2a6
Passover – **7-**1e;1e1;2a2; **10-**2c2;1c5; **12-**4c4; **13-**2d6; **29-**2b45;1b8
Past – **35-**P78
Path – **37-**1b9
Patience – **3-**3a1; **35-**P106
Patiently – **34-**P40
Pe (Pay) – **36-**#17
Peace – **33-**P3-4; **34-**P29,46
Peace Offering – **9-**1a3,11
Pekah – **24-**1c25
Pekahiah – **24-**1c24
Penalty – **11-**3a4
People – **8-**3c1;3d4; **9-**1c;2a; **10-**1c; **11-**#3; **13-**2b1;2f5; **15-**3d2; **28-**2b19; **30-**2b3;2a4;3a3-4; **31-**#1,#2; **33-**P8; **34-**P64; **38-**2a4;3a5-6; **42-**3a3; **45-**2b2-3; **46-**1a;1d,1d1; **50-**5b5; **52-**1c2; **55-**1b2; **57-**1a2 **58-**2b
Peor – **12-**4a7
Perez – **17-**1d3
Performed – **21-**2e8
Perform – **6-**1c6;
Period – **16-**2a;2b;2c;2d;2e;2f,#3
Persecuted – **44-**1e12
Persecution – **33-**P17
Persevering – **39-**1d7
Persia – **29-**2b51;1a1; **52-**1d1
Person – **32-**3c1; **51-**1b11
Personal – **7-**3a6; **9-**2a2; **38-**3c; **53-**1b4
Personal Conduct – **9-**2a2
Personal Injury – **7-**3a6
Personal Repentance – **53-**1b4
Personal Words – **38-**3c
Pestilence – **6-**1d5
Pharaoh – **5-**7d1; **6-**1c; **21-**1a6; **49-**3a7d,f
Philistia – **19-**3d3; **20-**1c1; **41-**1c6; **45-**3a3; **48-**3a4
Philistine(s) – **16-**2b2;2f1,2,5; **18-**1c;1c1,4;2b2; **19-**3c10;3d,3d1,3,5; **20-**1b3; **21-**2e4; **26-**2b4
Phinehas – **18-**1c3
Physical – **58-**2b1a
Pit – **49-**3a7g
Place – **50-**5a2g;5b
Plains of Moab – **12-**4f
Plague(s) – **6-**1d;1d1-9; **7-**1e2
Plan – **17-**1c,1c2
Plays – **40-**1a2
Plea(s) – **34-**P44; **52-**2a4
Plead(s) – **5-**7e5
Pleases – **43-**3b12
Pleasing – **9-**#2
Pleasure – **39-**1a3
Pledges – **39-**1c5
Plot(s) – **31-**1b4;1c1,6; **51-**2a,2a2
Plotting – **30-**2a2b
Plumb Line – **54-**1d3
Plunder – **12-**4d3
Plundered – **46-**3b2
Plundering – **49-**3a7b
Polluted – **58-**2a1
Polygamy – **22-**1e1
Poor & Enslaved – **10-**2c14
Popularity – **27-**1d
Population – **10-**1a1;1b2
Porch – **50-**5a2j
Portion – **9-**1a13
Possessing – **12-**4f2
Possessions – **32-**2a1; **34-**P49
Potential – **38-**#3
Potiphar – **5-**7c1
Pot – **48-**2a9
Potter – **44-**1e8
Power – **34-**P68; **36-**P126; **40-**1g,1g1; **56-**2b3
Practical Wisdom – **38-**#2; **39-**1d
Praised – **40-**1e
Praise(s) – **20-**1b6; **33-**P1; **34-**P59; **35-**P96,99; **36-**P116,117; **37-**P135,148,150; **41-**1b9;2a3; **56-**2b;2b3-4
Praising – **33-**P21; **34-**P45
Prayer(s) – **18-**1a2; **32-**3b3; **33-**P13,20,23,25,27-28; **34-**P35,41,51,54-59,61,64,66,69-70; **35-**P91,101,102; **36-**P120,121; **37-**P128,138,140-143; **42-**2c4; **43-**3d3; **46-**1b6; **51-**2a3; **54-**1a4; **56-**2b1
Prays – **44-**1e6; **46-**1d
Preaches – **55-**1b1
Preparations – **50-**5b12
Predicted – **14-**4a3; **43-**1b4; **56-**2b2
Predict(s) – **6-**7g3; **22-**2e1
Prepare(s) – **6-**1b6
Preparation(s) – **10-**#1;1c1; **27-**2e,2e1;1b1
Presence – **7-**3a3; **8-**3c6; **34-**P48,63
Presence of God – **13-**2b2; **34-**P63; **35-**P84; **36-**P122
Present – **54-**1c1
Presumptuous – **11-**3a3; **58-**2b6
Prevail – **35-**P94
Pride – **44-**1d7; **49-**3a7e
Priest(s) – **8-**3b12,17; **9-**1b; **10-**2b,2b1; **16-**3a1; **19-**3c6,9; **27-**1d4; **29-**2b43; **30-**3b2; **50-**5a2h,o;5b6; **58-**2a;2a1-2
Priestly – **9-**1b2,4

Prince(s) – **48**-1e18; **50**-5b4,8,9,11;
Prison – **24**-1d1; **25**-2a20; **45**-2b11; **46**-3b4; **48**-1e18b-c
Private – **16**-3a1
Problem(s) – **11**-2b; **54**-1a3
Procedure(s) – **9**-1a;1a1-6;1b4;1c;1d; **12**-4c; **50**-5b3b
Proclaimed – **21**-1a2; **56**-2b1
Proclaims – **51**-1d3
Promise(s) – **6**-7g1;1c3; **8**-3c6; **14**-2g3-4; **15**-#3;3b3; **45**-2a7; **47**-1d12; **53**-1b7; **55**-1c4; **57**-2b2
Promised – **4**-4c; **40**-1a3; **44**-1e4; **45**-#2
Promised Land – **11**-#2;2a;2c2;#4; **13**-1a7; **14**-#1; **15**-#3
Promoted – **5**-7d,7d2; **51**-1b6
Promotion – **51**-2a1
Property – **7**-3a9; **10**-2c13
Prophesies – **43**-1b; **45**-#3;3a;3a1,3,4; **46**-3a5-10; **48**-3a; **52**-1c;1d; **53**-1b; **55**-#1
Prophecy – **11**-4a3-4; **22**-#2; **45**-1g5; **48**-3a5c; **49**-3a7d; **52**-1c1,3;1c3b; **58**-2a5
Prophet(s) – **6**-1c5; **13**-2d2;2e6; **19**-3c3,13; **22**-2e,2e2; **40**-1a9; **43**-1a; **44**-1f5; **53**-#1; **54**-1c; **55**-#1
Prophet of God – **22**-2e; **50**-1a
Prophet Samuel – **19**-3c3;3c13
Prophetic – **5**-7a1; **18**-1a5;1b3; **47**-1c;1d; **56**-Zep.#2
Proposal – **31**-1a2; **40**-1c3
Proposes – **31**-1a3; **40**-1c3
Propositions – **11**-4a1
Prosecution – **51**-2a4
Prosperity – **5**-6a6; **37**-P144
Protected – **17**-1b3; **44**-1g3; **51**-1b10
Protect(s) –**19**-3c2-4,6-7
Protection – **11**-2c4; **33**-P3-4,12; **34**-P63; **35**-P91; **36**-P124; **37**-P140
Protector – **36**-P125
Proud Heart – **28**-2b29
Proven – **47**-1e17
Proverbs – Pg**37; 38**-2a,2a2; **39**-1d6; **47**-1e17;1e17a
Provide(s) – **17**-1b4; **34**-P46
Providing – **42**-3a5
Provisions – **34**-P63
Psalm(s) – Pg**33; 35**-P92,96,98,100; **37**-P135,149
Publicly – **40**-1f2
Public – **14**-4a2; **51**-1c1
Public Reading – **14**-4a2
Punish – **35**-P76
Punished – **45**-2c5
Punishment(s) – **9**-2a3; **13**-2d2; **47**-1e,1e11; **52**-1a3
Puppet Governor – **25**-2a19
Pure – **37**-1b10
Purges – **21**-1a3
Purifying – **23**-1b6
Purity – **9**-1c3-4
Purpose – **11**-2c4; **52**-2a2
Pursued – **5**-6b2

Q

Qoph – **36**-#19
Quail – **7**-2c2; **11**-2a4
Quality – **38**-1c1
Queen – **22**-1d4; **28**-1d6; **31**-1a,1a2;1b1,3;2a5; **51**-1d
Queen Esther – **31**-2a5
Queen Mother – **51**-1d3
Queen of Sheba – **22**-1d4; **28**-1d6
Queen Vashti – **31**-1a,1a2
Quenched – **46**-1c
Question – **44**-1d3

R

Rabbah – **20**-2a6
Rachel – **4**-6a2; **5**-6a4;6b11
Rahab – **14**-1a3
Rain – **23**-2e4
Rainbow – **3**-3b1
Raising – **23**-1b5
Ram – **51**-2b5; **52**-1b10
Ramah – **45**-2c1
Ranks – **27**-2e8
Rape(s) – **5**-6b9; **20**-2b1-2
Rash – **18**-2b3
Ratify(s) – **7**-3a16
Reaches – **20**-2c10
Reaction – **19**-1a2; **53**-1b2
Reading – **14**-4a2
Reads – **30**-3a1; **45**-2b6-7
Reaffirmed – **45**-2a8
Reason – **36**-P117
Reassured – **45**-2a7
Rebekah – **4**-4f1
Rebellion – **8**-3c3; **11**-2c;3b,3b1;3d2; **20**-2c; **47**-1e17b; **48**-2a
Rebellious – **47**-1c1
Rebels – **23**-1b3
Reborn – **49**-4a7
Rebuild – **57**-#1
Rebuilding – **29**-1b3-4; **30**-#1;#2;2a,2a2
Rebuke(s) – **21**-2d1; **42**-3b9
Received – **10**-2d1
Receive(s) – **7**-3a2; **15**-3a
Rechabites – **45**-2b5
Recognize – **34**-P47
Recommissioned – **44**-1e
Reconstruction – **57**-1a
Record(s) – **10**-1b1
Recovery – **24**-2a4
Red Heifer – **11**-3c4
Red Sea – **7**-2b;2b2-3
Redeemed – **42**-3b4
Redeem(s) – **17**-1d
Redeemer – **42**-3b
Redeeming – **10**-2c14
Redemption of Property – **10**-2c13
Refers – **48**-1e18b-c
Reflects – **40**-1b1
Reformations – **28**-2b11; **30**-2b;3b4
Refuge – **12**-4g4; **13**-1a9;2e7; **15**-3b,3b1; **19**-3d; **34**-P46
Refuse(s) – **31**-1a2; **51**-1b8
Registered – **30**-2a4

Regret(s) – **18**-2b5
Regulation(s) – **7**-2a2,5; **13**-2d;2e;2e10;2f,2f3; **14**-2f7-8; **50**-5b11
Rehoboam – **22**-2a;2a1-3;2d1; **28**-2a,2a2;2b1-3
Reigned – **5**-6c4; **22**-2c2;2d1-9; **23**-1c1-2; **24**-1c10-12,14-15,18-28;2a1,7-9; **25**-2a13-14,16-17; **28**-1d8; 2b8
Reign(s) – **22**-1d, **23**-2f;2g,2g1;2h,2h1; **26**-#2; **27**-2e13;1a; **28**-2b2-4,9,13-17,20,24,28,30-31; **29**-2b35,
40-41,47-50; **42**-2b8;2c; **58**-2b
Rejected – **44**-1e9;
Reject(s) – **18**-2a1-2; **19**-3c1; **37**-1b2; **57**-2a; **58**-2a5a
Rejection – **18**-2b
Rejoicing – **33**-P4; **34**-P33; **37**-P144
Relationship(s) – **9**-2a1; **13**-2f; **17**-#1; **22**-1d1-3; **30**-2b3; **33**-P5; **37**-P133; **38**-3a; **39**-#1; **40**-1e3; **52**-1a
Released – **19**-3d3; **25**-2a20; **45**-2c1; **46**-3b4
Release(s) – **36**-P126; **42**-3a1; **42**-3a15; **45**-2b2; **51**-1b12
"Release the Slaves" – **45**-2b2
Relent – **44**-1d10
Relentless – **53**-2b3
Relief – **33**-P13
Religion – **43**-1c,1c2
Religious – **7**-3a12
Remade – **8**-3c7
Remainder – **8**-3b16; **9**-3d20
Remaining – **15**-3a4
Remaliah – **24**-1c25
Remarks – **32**-4a1
Remembered – **43**-3d2
Remember – **13**-2c4;2d6-8; **39**-1d8
Remembrance – **58**-2c1
Remembering – **34**-P68; **35**-P105
Remnant – **42**-3b3; **57**-2b1
Removal – **13**-2e8
Renewed – **14**-2a5; **30**-#3; **40**-1a7
Renew(s) – **8**-3c8; **14**-3a1; **25**-2a11
Repairs – **28**-2b20
Repent – **43**-1b3
Repentance – **43**-3d3; **48**-1e17d,f; **53**-1b4-5; **57**-1a
Repercussion – **10**-2c10
Replace(s) – **11**-3d3; **14**-#4; **21**-1a; **22**-2a
Replacement – **18**-#3
Replies – **22**-2a2; **32**-3a4
Reply – **32**-3a2,6,9-10;3b2,7; **42**-2c4; **44**-1d4; **52**-2a5; **55**-1d2,4; **56**-2a2,4
Repopulated – **30**-3b
Repopulating – **30**-3b1
Report – **11**-2c1
Repulsive – **43**-1c2
Reputation – **50**-1a3
Request – **22**-2a1-2; **27**-1a1; **30**-1a2; **31**-1a2; **33**-P7; **48**-1e18a;2a1a
Requirement(s) – **7**-3b2-5; **8**-3b13; **9**-1b; **43**-3d
Rescued – **3**-4b2; **16**-#2
Resettled – **24**-1d3
Resh – **36**-#20
Responsibility – **7**-2c5; **47**-1e17b
Restoration – **23**-1b13; **35**-P80,85; **40**-1a3; **41**-2a4; **42**-3a7; **43**-3c3; **44**-1e2,4; **45**-2a;2a2,3,7; **46**-1d; **47**-1d12;1e12; **48**-2a2; **49**-4a; **52**-1a2,4; **53**-2b;1b9; **54**-1d7;1c; **57**-2b2; **58**-2a3
Restored – **18**-1c5; **29**-2b44; **42**-3a11; **45**-2a1; **49**-4b6; **51**-1c5; **53**-2b4
Restitution – **9**-1a6
Restrictions – **44**-1e3
Resurrection – **45**-#2
Resulted – **57**-1c3
Resumes – **29**-1b4
Returned – **29**-2b33;2a3
Return(s) – **5**-6b;6b10;7e2,7; **12**-4d2; **14**-3a2; **17**-1a3; **19**-3d3; **20**-2c1; **21**-2d2; **26**-1g; **29**-#1;#2; **30**-1a; **40**-1c1; **41**-1b7; **45**-2a6; **50**-5b1; **52**-1a5
Returning – **29**-1a2
Reuben – **12**-4e1; **15**-3a2a;3c1; **26**-1f3
Reunite – **5**-7e
Reunited – **49**-4a7
Revealed – **5**-7e6; **7**-3a17; **52**-1c
Reveal(s) – **51**-1b1,3
Revenge(s) – **5**-6b9; **12**-4d
Revere – **41**-1b4
Reverence – **35**-P85
Reversed – **45**-2b3
Reviewed – **12**-4f1
Review(s) – **12**-1a; **13**-2b,2b1; **15**-2d; **46**-3b1; **52**-1c1
Revival – **18**-1c6; **29**-2b37; **35**-P80
Revolt(s) – **20**-2c3; **22**-2a3; **45**-2c2
Revolution – **21**-2d6
Reward – **17**-1d1
Rewrite – **45**-2b9
Riches – **39**-1c6
Right (Choice) – **17**-1b
Righteous – **32**-3c4;4a4; **35**-P97,109; **43**-3d4; **46**-1a2
Righteousness – **32**-3a4; **32**-3c2; **35**-P72; **38**-2a1; **42**-2b8
Righteousness Indignation – **35**-P109
Rise – **19**-3b; **22**-1e3; **26**-2a; **27**-2e12; **28**-2a; **31**-2a
River – **14**-1b; **15**-3a2-3; **50**-5b13
Robbing – **58**-2b5
Rock – **7**-2c3
Rod – **6**-1c6; **11**-3b3
Room – **45**-2b7
Round One – **32**-3a
Round Two – **32**-3b
Round Three – **32**-3c
Route – **55**-1b3
Royalty – **31**-2a; **40**-1c1
Ruin – **29**-2b34
Rule(s)(Noun) – **8**-3d1; **13**-#2;2d4;2f3; **33**-P2; **50**-5b11
Rule(s) (Verb) – **20**-1b1
Rulers – **15**-3d,3d1; **22**-2d
Ruling – **13**-2e
Russia – **49**-4b1
Ruth – Pg**17; 17**-#1;1a;1a2-3;1b;1b1-4;1c;1c1-2;1d;1d1-2

S

Sabbath(s) – **7**-3a14; **8**-3b25;3d1; **10**-2c1,11; **11**-3a4; **12**-4c2; **44**-1e7; **50**-5b10b
Sabbath Day – **44**-1e7
Sabbath Year – **10**-2c11
Sacrifice(s) – **11**-3c4; **18**-1a4;2b1; **27**-1c4; **29**-1b1; **50**-5a2g
Sacrificing – **9**-1d4; **29**-2b34
Sacrilege Act – **9**-1b3
Safety – **33**-P23; **35**-P91
Sailors – **54**-1a3
Salvation – **34**-P48; **36**-P116; **42**-3b6-8; **43**-3c2
Samaria – **22**-2d9; **23**-1b11-12; **41**-1b6;2b1; **47**-1e12; **55**-#1;1b1
Samek – **36**-#15
Samson – **16**-2f1-5
Samuel (1st) – Pg**18**; #1;1a;1a1,3;1b;1b2-3;1c6;2a1;3a1; **19**-3c3,13
Samuel (2nd) – Pg**19**
Sanctification – **10**-1c
Sanctuary – **13**-2d1; **50**-5a2k
Sash – **44**-1d5
Satan – **27**-2d; **31**-1a2;#2;2a; **32**-2a1
Satisfied – **15**-3b3
Saul – **18**-2a;2a3-6;2b;2b1,3-5;#3; **19**-3a2;3b2-4;3c1,3-4,9,12,15;3d2,5;1a1-3; **21**-2d4; **26**-2a1
Saved – **3**-3a4;
Save(s) – **19**-3c10; **31**-2a5; **45**-3a2
Savior – **58**-2b1c
Scared – **7**-3a3
Schemes – **44**-1d2
Scribe – **45**-2b6-7
Scroll – **45**-2b6-9
Sea – **11**-2a4; **28**-1d5; **54**-1a2-3
Season(s) – **10**-2c
Second – **5**-7d2; **6**-1d2; **11**-#4;4a4; **12**-4b; **16**-2b; **29**-2a; **32**-3a6;3b2,4; **51**-1c;1c2-4; **54**-1c3c; **55**-1d3-4; **56**-2a3-4; **58**-2a2b;2b,2b1
Second Coming – **55**-1c6b; **58**-2a2b;2b2
Second-In-Command – **31**-2a3
Second Period – **16**-2b
Second Son – **20**-2a5
Second Woe – **54**-1c3c
Secret – **33**-P5
Secretly – **45**-2b13
Secretary – **45**-2b7
Security – **34**-P46,48,61
Seduce(s) – **5**-7b1
Seduction – **4**-4d5
Seek(s) – **19**-3c1;3d; **28**-2b6; **31**-1b1; **34**-P50
Seir – **5**-6c3; **28**-2b12
Self-Righteousness – **32**-4a4
Semites – **25**-1b3
Send(s) – **6**-1c; **7**-3a15; **11**-2a4; **14**-1a3; **20**-2a3;2c8; **47**-1c1
Sent – **41**-1b1; **45**-2c1
Sennacherib – **24**-2a3
Senseless – **37**-P127
Separate – **28**-2a1
Separation – **10**-1c1; **40**-1d1
Serpent – **11**-3d5
Servant(s) – **19**-3d1; **21**-2e4; **22**-1d3; **42**-3a5;3b1,2,5,7
Set(s) – **13**-2a1; **26**-2b6; **45**-2b15
Seth – **3**-2b3; **25**-1a1-2
Settled – **12**-4e
Settle(s) – **12**-4e1
Seven – **14**-4a2; **22**-2d7
Seventeen – **22**-2d1; **28**-2b2
Seventh – **6**-1d7
Seventy – **24**-1c7
Seventy-thousand – **21**-2e9
Seventy Times Seven – **52**-1c3b
Seventy Year(s) – **44**-1g2; **45**-2a; **52**-1c3
Sexual Relationships – **9**-2a1
Shallum – **24**-1c22; **44**-1f3a
Shamgar – **16**-2b2
Shares – **40**-1g3
Shaving – **47**-1d5
Shechem – **5**-6b7-8
Shem – **3**-3b8; **25**-1a10;1b3
Sheep – **58**-2a5a-b
Shepherds – **49**-4a6;4a6a-b; **58**-2a5;2a5a-b;2b1c
Shimei – **20**-2c5; **21**-2d3;1a5
Shin – **36**-#21
Shining – **8**-3c9
Shoulder – **8**-3b14
Show(s) – **20**-1c2; **21**-2d3,5; **40**-1f2
Showbread – **7**-3b4; **8**-3d9
Shulammite – **39**-#1; **40**-1b1;1c3;1d,1d2
Shunammite – **23**-1b13
Side Chambers – **50**-5a2L
Sidon – **48**-3a6
Sign – **3**-3b1; **8**-3b25; **41**-1b2,5,12; **44**-1g4; **47**-1e1-2
Signet – **57**-1b3
Significance – **44**-1d5-6
Sihon – **11**-3d7
Silver – **5**-7a2;7e4
Singers – **50**-5a2h
Simeon – **15**-3a4c; **26**-1f2
Sin(s) – **8**-3c1; **11**-3a2-3;3d1; **14**-2a3; **21**-2e9; **22**-2b4; **24**-1d2; **30**-3a3; **34**-P38; **36**-P126; **43**-3b13-15; **43**--1b1; **44**-1e5; **46**-1b,1b1; **48**-2a5; **49**-4a4; **53**-2b2; **58**-2a;2b
Sincerity – **34**-P50
Sinful – **18**-2b1
Sin Offering – **9**-1a4,9
Sinai – **8**-3c4; **11**-2a1; **12**-1a1
Sisters – **48**-2a8
Six – **24**-1c21; **28**-2b16
Six Months – **24**-1c21
Six Years – **28**-2b16
Sixteen – **24**-1c26-27; **28**-2b30-31
Sixth – **6**-1d6; **16**-2f
Sixth Period – **16**-2f
Slain – **28**-2b18
Slandered – **33**-P7;

Slander – **37**-P140
Slanderers – **35**-P109
Slaughtered – **47**-1d9
Slave(s) – **5**-7c1; **7**-3a5; **45**-2b2
Slavery – **5**-7a;7a2; **45**-2b3
Sleeps – **40**-1e2
Sodom – **4**-4d;4d2-4; **47**-1e12
Solomon – **20**-2a5; **21**-1a;1a2-3,4-5;1b;1b1-4;1c;1c1-4; **22**-1d;1d1-4;1e;1e1-3,5;1d;1d1-5;1e;1e1-3,5, **22**-2a; **26**-1e2; **27**-2e9,12;1a;1a1-2;1b;1c2,5;1d;1d1-5; **28**-1d5-8;#2;2a; **39**-#1;1d,1d5; Pg**39** **39**-#1; **40**-1b1;1c1-3;1d2;1e1-2;1g3-4 Son(s) – **3**-2b3; **5**-6b2,9;6c2-3; **6**-7g3; **9**-1a13;1b1; **10**-1b4-6; **11**-3d3; **17**-1d2; **18**-1a6;1c3;2a1;3b2;3c4; **19**-3d5;1a6; **21**-2d4; **24**-1c7,15,17-18,20-28;1d2,8,9; **25**-1c1;1d1; **26**-1e1-3;1f1-13;2a1; **28**-2a, 2b3-4,9; **29**-2b47; **44**-1f3; **45**-1g5;2b8
Son of the Blessing – **4**-4d1
Song – **7**-2b4; **18**-1a5; **21**-2e5; **41**-2a3; **48**-1e18a
Song of David – **21**-2e5
Song of Moses – **14**-4a4
Song of Praise – **41**-2a3
Song of Solomon – Pg**39**
Soon – **40**-1b2;1f3
Sores – **6**-1d6
Sorrow – **34**-P38; **37**-P137; **44**-1e1
Sound Wisdom – **37**-1b7
South – **52**-1d
Southern – **14**-2b; **45**-2a3
Southern Canaan – **14**-2b
South Gate – **49**-5a2f1
Southern Gate – **49**-5a2e
Spare(s) – **19**-3c12
Speak(s) – **6**-1b8; **11**-4a3-4; **12**-4a5-6; **27**-1c2; **32**-3c3; **39**-#1; **49**-5a1
Speech – **12**-#1
Spies – **11**-2c1; **14**-1a3
Spirit (Evil) – **19**-3a2
Spiritual – **58**-2b1b
Splits – **22**-2a3
Spoils – **12**-4d2
Spoken – **53**-#1
Spokesperson – **6**-1c5
Stability – **33**-P11
Standard(s) – **9**-2a; **10**-2b,2b1
Stand(s) – **32**-3a4
Stand Fast – **34**-P37
State – **40**-1g2
Statement – **32**-3b7
Statute – **12**-4g5
Stay True – **36**-P119
Steal(s) – **4**-5c
Stew – **23**-1b6
Stone(s) – **7**-3a4; **8**-3b14; **41**-2b2
Stones of Commemoration – **14**-1b2
Stopped – **14**-2b2
Storm(s) – **33**-P29; **54**-1a2
Strap – **8**-3b14
Straw – **6**-1c2
Strength – **34**-P29; **35**-P108; **52**-1c6
Stricken – **6**-1d5
Struck – **7**-1e2
Struggle – **21**-1a1
Stubborn – **42**-3a6; **47**-1c1
Stubbornness – **38**-3b4
Stupidity – **42**-2c7
Submitting – **39**-1d3
Success – **39**-1c4
Successfully – **23**-1b10
Suffering – **6**-1a1; **32**-3a5; **33**-P22; **42**-3b5; **46**-1b5
Suggestion(s) – **17**-1c1
Summary – **39**-1d5
Summer – **54**-1d5
Sun & Moon – **14**-2b2
Supporting – **11**-3c3
Surrounded – **23**-1b11; **33**-P28
Surviving – **24**-#2
Susa – **31**-1b2
Swarm(s) – **6**-1d4
Sword – **28**-2b18; **47**-1d5
Symbolism – **47**-1d1,4-5
Syria – **23**-2f1;1b10-12; **28**-2b32; **29**-2b34; **41**-1b3;1c8; **52**-1d3

T

Table of Showbread – **7**-3b4; **8**-3d9
Tablet – **47**-1d1
Tabernacle(s) – **7**-3b,3b1; **8**-3b6-8,10,24;3d;3d2,5-7,15,16; **9**-3d22-24; **10**-2c7; **26**-2b6
Taken – **20**-2a4; **45**-2c4; **46**-3b3; **48**-1e18b-c;2a10
Take(s) – **14**-1a; **16**-2f2;3b1,5; **20**-2a6;2c4; **26**-2b5; **27**-2d,2d1; **40**-1f1
Taking – **10**-1c2
Tamar (Judah) – **5**-7b,7b1
Tamar (King David) – **20**-2b1-2
Task – **39**-1b2
Tassels – **11**-3a5
Talk(s) – **11**-4a2
Tau – **36**-#22
Teaching – **43**-1c3
Tedious – **39**-1a1
Temple – **21**-1c;1c1-4; **27**-2e;2e1,9-10;1b;1b1-3;1c,1c1; **28**-2b20; **29**-2b36;1b,3,6-7; **45**-2b6; **46**-3b2; **47**-1d8; **49**-5a;5a1,2;5a2a; **50**-5a2j,n;5b;5b2,5,13; **51**-1d1; **57**-1a;1b; Zech.#1
Temptations – **37**-P141
Ten – **5**-7e1-2; **6**-1d; **7**-3a2; **24**-1c23
Ten Commandments – **7**-3a2; **8**-3c7; **13**-2b,2b1;2c6
Ten Days – **29**-2b49
Ten Tribes – **22**-1e4; **28**-2a1
Tender – **40**-1f
Tenth – **7**-1e2
Territory – **19**-3d
Tested – **4**-4e4
Testing – **31**-1a
Testimony – **8**-3d8

Teth – **36**-#9
Thankful – **34**-P32
Thankfulness – **34**-P65; **35**-P75,107
Thanksgiving – **35**-P92,100; **37**-P138
Theft – **7**-3a8
Their Destruction – **49**-3a7e
Their Judgment – **48**-2a8c
Their Messiah – **57**-2a
Their Way – **48**-2a1c
Themselves – **8**-3d4; **30**-2b4
"There Is No God" – **34**-P53
"There Is No Other God but Yahweh" – **42**-3a9
Third – **6**-1d3; **12**-4a5; **16**-2c; **25**-2a18; **32**-3a9; **46**-3b3; **54**-1c3d
Third Woe – **54**-1c3d
Thirsty – **34**-P42
Thirty-one – **24**-2a9; **29**-2b42
Third Period – **16**-2c
Threats – **37**-P140
Threatened – **31**-1c
Threatens – **42**-2c3
Three – **6**-1d9; **13**-1a9;2e7; **28**-2b3; **32**-2a3;#3;3c;#4
Three Months – **25**-2a13,16; **29**-2b47,49
Three Years – **22**-2d2; **28**-2b3
Three-hundred – **16**-2d5
Three-thousand – **8**-3c3
Throne – **26**-2a; **27**-2e12
Through – **3**-3a4; **4**-4c2; **7**-2b1; **17**-1b4; **35**-P77; **37**-P129
Thrown – **45**-2b11
Throws – **23**-2e6
Three Years – **21**-2e1
Threshing Floor – **21**-2e10
Time(s) – **31**-#1; **34**-P57; **35**-P77,79,86; **37**-P129; **39**-1b1; **46**-3b3; **48**-2a1f
Tirzah – **22**-2d6-7
Tithe(s) – **14**-2f8
Tithing – **13**-2d4
Together – **37**-P145
Tola – **16**-2d11
Total – **46**-3a11; **54**-1a2
Touches – **52**-1c5
Tough Times – **37**-P129
Toward(s) – **35**-P104,107; **43**-3c1; **58**-2b3
Tower – **3**-3c,3c1
Transgression(s) – **20**-#2; **34**-P36
Transjordan – **12**-4e,4e1; 1a4-5; **13**-1a6; **15**-3c,3c2
Translated – **23**-1b1
Treachery – **30**-2a2f
Treasurers – **27**-2e6
Treatment – **7**-3a5
Treated – **34**-P35
Treaty – **4**-4e3; **23**-2f2
Trespass Offering – **9**-1a5,10
Trial – **55**-1c1-2
Tribe(s) – **10**-1a2; **12**-4b1;4e,4e1; **15**-3a;3a3h;3c;3c1-2; **16**-3a2; **20**-1b; **22**-1e4;2a1; **26**-1f5,10; **27**-1c2; **28**-2a1
Tribulation – **41**-#2; **45**-2a
Triplets – **25**-1a10
Triumph(s) – **42**-2c5; **54**-1c1
Trouble(s) – **4**-4c2; **19**-3a2; **33**-P6,28; **34**-P57; **35**-P86
Troubling – **40**-1d
Troublesome – **31**-#1
True – **29**-2b44; **37**-P147; **43**-3d6; **49**-4a6b
True & False – **43**-3d6
Trumpets – **10**-2c5
Trust – **32**-3b5; **34**-P31,60,62; **37**-1b5
Trust In God – **34**-P60
Trust in the *LORD* – **34**-P62; **37**-1b5
Trusting – **33**-P3; **34**-P49; **35**-P73,86; **41**-2b5; **42**-2b7; **43**-1c1
Tsadde – **36**-#18
Twelve – **11**-2c1; **15**-3a; **22**-2d8
Twelve Spies – **11**-2c1
Twelve Tribes – **15**-3a
Twenty – **5**-7a2; **24**-1c25
Twenty-one – **22**-2c2
Twenty-two – **22**-2d9
Twenty-four – **22**-2d5; **27**-2e3
Twenty-five – **23**-2g1; **28**-2b9,13
Twenty-nine – **24**-1c18;2a1; **28**-2b24; **29**-2b35
Two – **12**-4d3; **22**-2d4; **23**-2h1; **24**-1c24; **29**-2b41; **32**-3b; **48**-2a8 **55**-1b
Two Capitals – **55**-1b
Two Months – **16**-2e2
Two Shepherds – **58**-2a5
Two Spies – **14**-1a3
Two-and-a-Half – **12**-4e
Tyranny – **16**-2d8
Tyre – **41**-1c17; **48**-3a5;3a5c-d; **53**-1b3

U

Ultimate – **33**-P2
Unclean – **9**-1c2
Understand – **52**-1b13
Undertaken – **29**-1b
Unfaithful – **47**-1e8,10; **52**-1a3; **58**-2a2
Unfaithfulness – **47**-1e6,11; **48**-#2;2a1; **52**-1a1
Unintentional – **11**-3a2
United – **21**-#1
Unjustly – **34**-P35
Upheaval – **20**-2b; **21**-2d
Urge(s) – **13**-1a8
Urgent – **34**-P70
Uriah – **20**-2a2
Using – **47**-1d1,4,5
Useless – **34**-P49; **43**-3b10; **45**-2b10
Uselessness – **39**-1a;1a2-4; **42**-3a4
Uz – **31**-1a1
Uzza – **26**-2b2
Uzziah – **24**-1c26; **28**-2b28-30

V

Valley of Megiddo – **29**-2b46
Valley of Zephathah – **28**-2b5
Value(s) – **37**-1b6; **39**-1d7

Various – **13**-2f3; **38**-2a4
Veil(s) – **8**-3b8;3d7
Vengeance – **12**-4d1
Verdict – **52**-2a5; **53**-2a9
Vessels – **51**-1d1
Victory – **23**-2e3; **33**-P20,21; **34**-P44; **35**-P98,108; **37**-P149
Victories – **41**-2a2
Victorious – **20**-1c
Vindication – **44**-1e6
Vineyard – **23**-2f4; **40**-1a8
Violation(s) – **13**-2f4
Violence – **32**-3c3; **54**-1b1
Virtuous – **38**-3c3
Vision(s) – **47**-1b;1b1-3;1c;1d;1d8-11; **49**-5a; **51**-2b;2b1,2,5-7; **52**-1b8-10;1c4; **54**-1d; **57**-1b;1b1,3-9
Vision of a Ram – **51**-2b5; **52**-1b10
Vision of Ancient of Days – **51**-2b2
Vision of Four Beasts – **51**-2b1
Vision of Man with Measuring Line – **57**-1b4
Vision of the Flying Scroll – **57**-1b7
Vision of the Four Chariots – **57**-1b9
Vision of the Four Horns & Four Craftsmen – **57**-1b3
Vision of the Golden Lampstand – **57**-1b6
Vision of the Horn – **51**-2b7
Vision of the High Priest – **57**-1b5
Vision of the Horses – **57**-1b1
Vision of the Male Goat – **51**-2b6; **52**-1b11
Vision of the Woman in a Basket – **57**-1b8
Visit – **22**-1d4; **28**-1d6
Vow(s)(Pledge) – **10**-2d2;1c2; **12**-4c9; **18**-2b3; **39**-1c

W

Wait(s) – **5**-6b4
Waiting – **34**-P40
Walk – **32**-3c6; **35**-P101
Wall(s) – **30**-#1;1a3;2a2,3;3b3; **49**-5a2a; **50**-5a2L; **51**-1d2,4
War(s) – **16**-3b;3b3-4; **18**-1c; **26**-2c; **28**-2b5,7; **49**-4b
Warfare – **13**-2e10
Warning – **22**-1e2; **37**-1b11; **44**-1d7;1e9; **47**-1e3-6
Waste – **53**-#1;1b2
Wasteland – **53**-1b,1b1
Watchman – **47**-1c2; **49**-4a1
Watchmen – **42**-3b9
Water – **6**-1d1; **7**-2c1,3; **50**-5b13
Waw – **36**-#6
Way – **48**-2a1c
Wealth – **22**-1d5; **27**-1a2; **28**-1d7; **38**-3b3; **39**-1a4
Weariness – **34**-P44
Weather – **34**-P29
Wedding – **39**-#1
Weeks – **10**-2c4
Weeping – **46**-1b2
West – **15**-3a3;3a3f,h
Western – **50**-5a2m
West Manasseh – **15**-3a3f,h; **26**-1f10
What They Did – **48**-2a8b
Wheels – **47**-1b2
Who They Are – **48**-2a8a
Whole – **56**-2a1
Wicked – **18**-1a6; **20**-2c6; **32**-3b6-7;3c1; **34**-P36; **35**-P94; **37**-1b9; **38**-2a1; **40**-1a1; **47**-1d9,11; **48**-2a7; **56**-2a5
Wickedness – **3**-3a1; **28**-2b; **47**-1d8
Wife – **16**-2f2; **19**-3c14; **47**-1e8,10; **48**-2a10; **52**-#1;1a;1a1,3,4
Wilderness – **7**-2b1; **48**-2a1d
Wilderness of Sinai – **11**-2a1
Wind – **6**-1d8
Wine Bottles – **44**-1d6
Wilderness of Ziph – **19**-3c11
Wisdom – **21**-1b;1b1-2; **27**-1a1; **32**-3c7; **37**-1a;1b;1b3,4,6-8; **38**-1c;1c1-3;#2;2a;2a4;#3;3a-c; **39**-1a2;1d; 1d1,2,6
Wise – **37**-1b2; **38**-2a3; **39**-1a5
Wisdom & Folly – **39**-1d6
Wise & the Folly – **39**-1a5
Witch at Endor – **19**-3d2
Without – **11**-2c4; **37**-P127; **45**-2b4
Witnesses – **13**-2e9
Wives – **16**-3b5; **30**-2b4
Woe – **41**-2b1,4,5; **54**-1c3b-d; **55**-1b5; **56**-2b4; Hab.2a5
Woman – **23**-1b13; **38**-1c4; **39**-#1; **40**-1b1;1c3;1d;1g2
Woman in a Basket – **57**-1b8
Women – **12**-4g6; **16**-3b5; **37**-1b3
Word(s) – **21**-2e6; **36**-P119; **38**-2a3;3c;3c1-2; **39**-1d9; **43**-1c1; **53**-#1; **57**-1c
Words of God – **41**-2b3
Work – **36**-P114
Working – **39**-1c2
Worldly – **34**-P49
Worship – **9**-#1; **12**-4a7; **13**-2d; **29**-2b36,44; **35**-P95; **37**-P134,147; **43**-3d6; **51**-1b8
Worshipers – **25**-1c9
Worship God – **37**-P134,145
Worshiping – **37**-P145
Wrath – **56**-Zeph.2a
Wrestles – **5**-6b5
Wrong – **47**-1e17

X

Y

Yahweh – **42**-3a9
Year(s) – **7**-#2; **10**-2c11,12; **14**-4a2; **21**-2e1; **22**-2d1-6,8-9; **23**-2g1;2h1; **24**-1c10-12,14-15,18-20,23-28; **44**-1g2;2a1,4,7-9; **25**-2a14,17;1a1-10; **28**-2b2-4,8-9,13-14; **29**-2b35,40-42,48,50;#2; **45**-2a
Year of Jubilee – **10**-2c12
Yod – **36**-#10
Yoke – **44**-1g4
Young – **37**-1b4; **40**-1g2
Younger Generation – **37**-#1
Your – **36**-P116; **37**-1b10; **39**-1d8
Yourself – **38**-3a4

Youth – **39**-1d8

Z

Zayin – **36**-#7
Zebulon – **15**-3a4d
Zechariah – **24**-1c21; Pg**57; 57**-1b;1c
Zedekiah – **25**-2a17; **29**-2b50; **44**-1f1; **45**-2b1,2,10,13
Zephaniah – Pg**56; 56**-#1;#2
Zephathah – **28**-2b5
Zerubbabel – **30**-3b2; **57**-#1
Zimri – **22**-2d7
Zion – **40**-1a7; **41**-2b2; **42**-2b10; **43**-3c1; **57**-1b2
Ziph – **19**-3c11
Zipporah – **6**-1b4
Zobah – **20**-1c1
Zophar – **32**-3a9;3b6-7

PERSON	DEATH AGE	LOCATION	SCRIPTURE REF.
Abraham	175	4-4g2	Genesis 25:06 – 25:11
Adam	930	25-1a1	Genesis 5:3 – 5:5
Eli	98	18-1c2	1st Samuel 4:12 – 4:18
Enoch	365	25-1a7	Genesis 5:21 – 5:24
Enosh	905	25-1a3	Genesis 5:9 – 5:11
Isaac	180	5-6b13	Genesis 35:27 – 35:29
Ishmael	137	4-4g4	Genesis 25:17 – 25:18
Jacob (Israel)	147	6-7g4	Genesis 49:29 – 49:33
Jared	962	25-1a6	Genesis 5:18 – 5:20
Jehoiada	130	28-2b21	2nd Chronicles 24:15 – 24:16
Joseph	110	6-7g7	Genesis 50:22 – 50:26
Joshua	110	15-3d3	Joshua 24:29 – 24:32
Kenan	910	25-1a4	Genesis 5:12 – 5:14
Lamech	777	25-1a9	Genesis 5:28 – 5:31
Mahalalel	895	25-1a5	Genesis 5:15 – 5:17
Methuselah	965	25-1a8	Genesis 5:25 – 5:27
Moses	120	14-4a7	Deut. 34:01 – 34:12
Noah	950	25-1a10	Genesis 5:32 – 5:32
Sarah	127	4-4e6	Genesis 23:01 – 23:20
Seth	912	25-1a2	Genesis 5:6 – 5:8

DATES

3 Adar – **29**-1b6
13 Adar (Yom Nicanor) – **31**-1c2, 2a6
14 Adar (Feast of Purim) – **31**-2a7
10th of Nisan – **7**-1e1

NUMBERS & YEARS

2nd-in-Charge – **5**-7d2
3 Days of Darkness – **6**-1d9
3 Year Famine – **21**-2e1
10 Plagues of Egypt – **6**-1d
12 Sons of Jacob – **5**-6b12
12 Spies – **11**-2c1
20 Shekels of Silver – **5**-7a2
40 Years – **47**-1d3
80 Years Later—Return of Second Group of Exiles – **29**-#2
130 – Israel Settles in Land of Goshen – **6**-7f3
300 Mighty Men – **16**-2d5
365 Years – **25**-1a7
390 Years – **47**-1d2
400 Men, David Escapes With to Cave of Adullam – **19**-3c8
430 Years - Journeys to Mt Sinai After Departing Egypt – **7**-#2
490 Years – **52**-1c3b
456 B.C. – **29**-#2
562 B.C. – **46**-3b4
581 B.C. – **46**-3b3
586 B.C. – **48**-1e18d
587/586 B.C. – **45**-2a5
587 B.C. – **48**-1e18c
605—536 B.C. – **44**-1g2
609 B.C. – **25**-2a15; **48**-1e18b
777 Years – **25**-1a9
895 Years – **25**-1a5
905 Years – **25**-1a3
910 Years – **25**-1a4
912 Years – **25**-1a2
930 Years – **25**-1a1
931—597 B.C. – **28**-#2
950 Years – **25**-1a10

962 Years – **25**-1a6
965 Years – **25**-1a8
3,000 Men Die – **8**-3c3
8,580 = First Levite Census – **10**-1b7
23,000 = Second Levite Census – **12**- 4b2
70,000 Lives, David's Sin Costs – **21**-2e9
603,550 = First Israel Census – **10**-1a3
601,730 = Second Israel Census – **12**-4b1

THE WORKS of GOD/LORD

GOD – Angered at Moses – **6**-1b7
Being Led by Cloud & Fire by – **11**-1c6
Call to Commitment to – **13**-2c7
Call to Obedience – **14**-3a
Commandments of – **13**-2c2
Covenant of to Abram – **4**-4c1
Covenant with Man – **3**-3a5
David's Covenant with – **20**-1b5
Faithfulness – **35**-P71
Glory of – **27**-1c3
Goodness of – **32**-4a5
Hannah's Earnest Prayer to – **18**-1a2
Help in Times of Trouble – **34**-P57
Israel Receives the Ten Commandments – **7**-3a
Israel Receives the Law of – **7**-3a
Israel Rejects Him as King – **18**-2a2
Jacob Makes Vow to – **5**-6a1
Jacob Wrestles with – **5**-6b5
Judgment by Flood – **3**-3a3
Judgment Falls Upon Ahaziah – **23**-1a1
Judgment of – **35**-P82
Justice of – **32**-4a3
Leads Israel by Cloud & Fire – **11**-1c6
Mercy of God – **35**-P89
Moses Intercedes for Israel – **8**-3c2
Moses Meets at Mt Horeb – **6**-1b5
Names the Craftsmen of the Tabernacle – **8**-3d3
Patience of – **3**-3a1
Presence of – **13**-2b2
Righteousness & Justice of – **35**-P72
Tells Jacob to Return to Bethel – **5**-6b10

LORD – Calls Samuel to a Prophetic Ministry – **18**-1b3
Closes the Red Sea – **7**-2b3
Command to Love – **13**-2c
Commissions Joshua – **15**-1a1
Distressing Spirit Troubles Saul – **19**-3a2
Fills the Tabernacle – **9**-3d24
Gifts of (Manna & Quail) – **7**-2c2
Glory of the – **7**-3a17
His Covenant Renewed at Ebal – **15**-2a5
His Glory Revealed – **8**-3a17
His Instructions to Joshua – **15**-3a1
His Promise Satisfied – **16**-3b3
Joshua Meets Captain of His Host – **15**-1b4
Moses Meets with Him – **8**-3c5
Parts the Red Sea – **7**-2b2
Promise of Deliverance – **6**-1c3
Promises His Presence to Israel – **8**-3c6
Promise Satisfied – **16**-3b3
Regrets Making Saul King – **19**-2b5
Rejected Saul for Disobedience – **19**-2b
Renews the Covenant After Moses Broke the Stones – **8**-3c8
Sends an Angel Before Israel – **8**-3a15
Sends Moses & Aaron to Pharaoh – **6**-1c
Sends Nathan to Expose David's Guilt – **20**-2a3
Sends Saul Distressing Spirit – **19**-3a2
Send Quail from the Sea – **11**-2a4
Vengeance on Midian – **12**-4d1

Second

Covenant

(New Testament)

How to Read & Use the Concordance

Example:

Aaron – **6**-1b8;1c;1c1,5-6; **9**-1a13;1b1; **10**-1b1; **11**-2b,2b1;3b2,3;3c2;3d3

In doing a search for a word, as in this example, I am using the name of "Aaron." Since we are looking for "Aaron," let's go to the concordance to see where we can find the name. The first place where "Aaron" is located in the Old Testament is **6**-1b8 as we can see above in the example. The bold number "**6**" is the page number in the Topical Index where "Aaron" is located. Now we look in Section "1", then Section "B" then in Number "8" to locate "Aaron." In the example below, I have underlined where "1b8" is located. So, we can see that the first place where "Aaron" is located in the Old Testament Topical Index is in Exodus 4:18—4:31. The second location of "Aaron" is Page 6, Section 1, Subsection c. Then again on Page 6, Section 1, then Section C, then in Numbers 1,5-6. In the example below, "Aaron" is located on Page **6.** In the example above, the bold numbers are ALL page numbers where "Aaron" is located in the Topical Index.

IMPORTANT: The semicolons separate the Sections. The Commas separate the Number locations and subsections. The bold numbers separate the page numbers.

EXODUS
(1:01—40:38)

1. **The Life & Times of Israel in Egypt** **(1:01—12:30)**

A. Family of Israel Enslaved in Egypt **(1:01—1:22)**

1. Suffering of Israel's Descendants (1:01—1:14)
2. King of Egypt Commands Death of Hebrew Males (1:15—1:22)

B. Moses Chosen by God to Lead Israel **(2:01—4:31)**

1. The Birth of Moses (2:01—2:10)
2. Moses Kills an Egyptian (2:11—2:15)
3. Moses Flees to Midian (2:16—2:20)
4. Moses Marries Zipporah (2:21—2:25)
5. Moses Meets God at Mount Horeb (3:01—3:22)
6. God Prepares Moses for Egypt (4:01—4:13)
7. God Angered at Moses (4:14—4:17)
8. Moses & Aaron Speak to Israelites in Egypt (4:18—4:31)

TABLE of CONTENTS

	BOOK of the BIBLE	SCRIPTURE TOPIC	PAGE #
I.	MATTHEW	Jesus Christ, the King—His Genealogy & His Birth	1
		Birth of the King	1
		Jesus Christ, the King—His Ministry Begins	1
		Jesus' Preaching Ministry Begins in Galilee	1
		Jesus Preaches His "Sermon on the Mount"	1
		Principles for Kingdom Living	1
		Practices for Kingdom Living	2
		Proof of Kingdom Living	2
		Jesus Christ, the King—Proof of His Authority	2
		The Power of Jesus Christ	2
		The Anointed Teaching Concerning Christ's Kingdom **(11:01—12:50)**	2
		The Parables of Jesus Christ	2
		Jesus Christ, the King—Different Reactions to His Ministry	3
		Jesus' Ministry Comes Under Fire	3
		Mighty Works of Jesus Christ	3
		Jesus Rejected by Religious Leaders	3
		Revelations of the Teachings of Jesus Christ	3
		Presentation of King Jesus	3
		King Jesus Publicly Presented to Jerusalem	3
		More Parables By Jesus	4
		Conflict Between Jesus & the Religious Leaders	4
		End-Time Messages from the Mount of Olives	4
		Jesus' Messages Concerning the End-Times	4
		The Last Week of the Life of Jesus Christ, Our *LORD*	4
		Resurrection of Jesus Christ & the Great Commission	5
II.	MARK		
		Jesus Christ, the Servant—His Birth & Preparation for Ministry	5
		Preparation of the Servant	5
		Jesus Christ, the Servant—His Ministry & Message	5
		His Ministry Begins in Galilee	5
		More Parables of Jesus	5
		The Sovereign Power of Jesus	5
		The Precepts of Jesus	6
		Jesus Christ, the King—His Sacrifice	6
		Jesus, the Servant Presents Himself	6
		Jesus Christ, the King—His Success at the Cross	7
		His Success at the Cross	7
III.	LUKE		
		Jesus Christ, the Savior—His Birth & Preparation for Ministry	7
		Luke's Purpose in Writing His Gospel Account	7
		Events Leading Up to the Birth of Jesus Christ	7
		Events Leading Up to Ministry of Jesus Christ	8
		Jesus Christ, the Savior—His Ministry	8
		Galilee—Where Jesus Begins	8
		Jesus' Power & Authority Presented	8
		Jesus Instructs the Pharisees	9
		Jesus Christ, the Savior—His Ministry Expands	9
		Disciples Chosen; Beatitudes Given	9
		Principles of Kingdom Living	9
		The Ministry of Jesus Christ in Galilee	9
		Jesus Christ, the Savior—His Rejection	10
		Jesus' Ministry on Journey to Jerusalem	10

		Instructions In Light of Rejection of Jesus Christ	11
		Jesus Christ, the Savior—His Death, Burial & Resurrection	12
		Passion Week—His Last Week Alive	12
IV.	JOHN		
		Jesus Christ, the Son of God—His Birth & Preparation	14
		Jesus Prepares for His Ministry	14
		Jesus Christ, the Son of God—His Presentation to the World	14
		John, the Baptist Presents Yeshua, the Messiah	14
		John, the Baptist Presents His Disciples to Jesus	14
		Jesus' Presentation at Cana in Galilee	14
		Jesus Christ, the Son of God—His Message & Ministry	14
		The People's Belief & Unbelief	14
		Opposition to Jesus' Ministry in Galilee	15
		Opposition to Jesus' Ministry in Jerusalem	16
		Jesus Christ, the Son of God His Death & Resurrection	16
		Jesus Prepares His Disciples	16
		The Death of Jesus Christ, the Son of God	17
		The Resurrection of Jesus Christ, the Son of God	17
V.	ACTS		
		The Ministry of Peter, Apostle of Jesus Christ	18
		The Beginning of the Church	18
		The Progression of the Church	18
		The Church Expands to Samaria & to Gaza	18
		Followers of Jesus Christ Scatter to the Countryside	18
		King Herod's Persecution of the Church in Antioch	19
		The Ministry of Paul, an Apostle of Jesus Christ	19
		Paul's First Missionary Journey (A.D. 48—49)	19
		The Council at Jerusalem	19
		Paul's Second Missionary Journey (A.D. 50—52)	20
		Paul's Third Missionary Journey (A.D. 53—57)	20
		The Power of the Word	20
		Paul's Journey to Rome	20
VI.	ROMANS		
		Introduction to Romans	21
		Sinfulness of Man	21
		The Condemnation of Sin	21
		The Sinfulness of the Gentiles	21
		The Sinfulness of the Jews	21
		Justification Imputed Through Jesus Christ	21
		The Revelation of Righteousness	21
		The Illustration of Righteousness	21
		The Benefits of Righteousness	21
		Sanctification Imparted Through Jesus Christ	21
		The Principles of Sanctification	21
		The Practice of Sanctification	22
		The Power of Sanctification	22
		The Vindication of Our Righteousness	22
		Israel's Past, Present & Future	22
		The Application of Our Righteousness	22
		Our Responsibilities As Christians	22
		Paul's Final Greetings and Personal Notes	22
		Benediction of Paul	22
VII.	1st CORINTHIANS		
		Church Problems Addressed by Paul	23
		Expressions from Paul	23
		Divisions Within the Church	23
		Divisions—The Fact	23
		Divisions—The Cause	23

Divisions—The Consequences 23
The Example of Paul 23
Disorder in the Church 23
Immorality Within the Church 23
Questions Addressed from the Corinthian Church 23
Instructions on Christian Marriage 23
Instructions on Christian Freedom 23
Instructions on Public Worship 23
Instructions on the Resurrection 24
Instructions on Personal Matters 24

VIII. 2nd CORINTHIANS

Paul's Second Missionary Journey to Corinth 24
Paul Explains Himself 24
Paul Explains His Change of Plans 24
Constructive Criticism Necessary 24
The Ministry of Paul, an Apostle of Jesus Christ 24
Paul Defends His Ministry 24
Marks of the Ministry 25
Paul Defends the Collection 25
Paul Defends His Authority 25

IX. GALATIANS

Introduction to Galatians 25
Authenticity of the Gospel 25
Paul Defends "Justification By Faith" 25
Authenticity of the Gospel 25
Superiority of the Gospel 25
Freedom of the Gospel 26

X. EPHESIANS

Greetings from Paul, the Apostle 26
Greetings from Paul to the Church of Ephesus 26
The Position of the Believers in Christ 26
Unity in Christ 26
The Practice of the Believers in Christ 26
In the Body of Christ 26
In Our Personal Life 26
In Our Home Life 27
The Whole Armor of God 27
Final Exhortations 27

XI. PHILIPPIANS

Introduction and Greetings 27
Greetings from Paul 27
Paul's Present Circumstances 27
Joy in Suffering 27
Joy in Serving 27
Joy in Believing 27
Joy in Giving 27
Final Exhortations 28

XII. COLOSSIANS

Introduction to the Colossians 28
Greetings from Paul 28
The Preeminence of Christ in the Church 28
Supremacy of Christ 28
Our Freedom in Christ 28
What Christians Should Do 28
Character of the New Man 28
Christian Graces 28
Final Exhortations 28
Final Greetings 28

XIII.	1st THESSALONIANS	Introduction to 1st Thessalonians	28
		Greetings from Paul, Silvanus and Timothy	28
		Paul's Commendation of the Thessalonians	28
		The Thessalonians Faithfulness to the *LORD*	28
		Paul's Concern for the Thessalonians	29
		Their Tribulations	29
		Timothy Visits the Thessalonians	29
		Thessalonians Receive Instructions from Paul	29
		Watchfulness for the *LORD*	29
XIV.	2nd THESSALONIANS	Introduction to 2nd Thessalonians	29
		Greetings from Paul, Silvanus & Timothy	29
		Encouragement in Persecution	29
		The Bright Hope of the Return of the *LORD*	29
		The Day of the *LORD*	*29*
		Explanation of the Day of the *LORD*	29
		Living in the Light of Christ's Return	30
XV.	1st TIMOTHY	Introduction to 1st Timothy	30
		Paul's Greeting to Timothy	30
		Precepts Concerning Doctrine	30
		Paul's Exhortations Concerning Doctrine	30
		Paul's Exhortations to the Church	30
		Paul's Exhortations to Leaders	30
		Paul's Exhortations in Church Discipline	30
		Paul's Exhortations in Other Duties	30
XVI.	2nd TIMOTHY	Introduction to 2nd Timothy	30
		Greetings from Paul to Timothy	30
		Paul Charges Timothy to Persevere in the Present	31
		Foundations of Christian Service	31
		Characteristics of a Faithful Minister	31
		Paul Charges Timothy to Persevere in the Future	31
		Difficult Times for Christian Service	31
		Paul's Valedictory	31
XVII.	TITUS	Introduction to Titus	31
		Greetings from Paul to Titus	31
		Elders in the Church	31
		Leadership in the Church	31
		Operation of the Church	31
		Right Living in the Church	31
		Right Living in Society	31
XVIII.	PHILEMON	Introduction to Philemon	32
		Greetings from Paul and Timothy	32
		Praise for Philemon	32
		Paul's Appreciation of Philemon	32
		Paul's Plea to Philemon	32
		Paul's Appeal for Onesimus	32
XIX.	HEBREWS	The Superiority of the Person of Jesus Christ	32
		Christ Is Greater Than the Angels	32
		Christ Is Greater Than Moses	33
		The Superiority of the Work of Jesus Christ	33
		Christ Is Greater Than Old Testament Priesthood	33
		The Superiority of Faith by the Christian	34

		Full Assurance of Faith	34
		The Endurance of Faith	35
XX.	**JAMES**	Introduction to James	36
		Greetings from James to the Jewish Christians	36
		The Test of Faith	36
		Genuine Religion	36
		Genuine Faith	36
		The Victory of Faith	36
XXI.	**1st PETER**	Introduction to 1st Peter	37
		Greetings from Peter to the Elect Pilgrims	37
		The Believer's Salvation in Jesus Christ	37
		God's Great Blessings	37
		The Believer's Sanctification in Jesus Christ	37
		The Submission of the Believer	37
		Conduct in the Midst of Living Before the World	38
XXII.	**2nd PETER**	Introduction to 2nd Peter	38
		Greetings from Peter to the Faithful	38
		The Development of Faith	38
		Guidance for Growing Christians	38
		Dangers to Growing Christians	38
		Hope for Growing Christians	39
XXIII.	**1st JOHN**	Conditions for Fellowship	40
		God Is Light	40
		Characteristics of Fellowship	40
		God Is Love	40
		God Is Life	40
XXIV.	**2nd JOHN**	Introduction to 2nd John	41
		Greetings to the Elect Lady—The Church	41
		Abiding in the Commandments of God	41
		Walking in the Love of God	41
		Abiding Not With Deceivers	41
		Watch Out For False Teachers	41
		John's Final Words	41
		John's Farewell Message	41
XXV.	**3rd JOHN**	Introduction to 3rd John	41
		Greeting to Gaius	41
		The Influence of Gaius	41
		Living by the Standards of the Gospel	41
		Diotrephes and Demetrius	41
		Diotrephes	41
		Demetrius	41
		John's Final Words	41
		John's Farewell Message	41
XXVI.	**JUDE**	Introduction to Jude	41
		Jude's Greeting to the Called	41
		The Danger of False Teachers	41
		The Exposure of the False Teachers	41
		Defense Against False Teachers	42
		Jude's Doxology	42

XXVII. REVELATION

Introduction to Revelation 42
Introduction and Benediction 42
The Things Which You Have Seen 42
The Vision of the Son of Man 42
The Things Which Are Being Seen 43
Letters to the Seven Churches 43
The Things Which Are to be Seen After This 45
Message for the Seven Churches 45
The Opening of the Seven Seals 45
The Seven Trumpets of Judgment 46
Observing of the Great Tribulation 46
The Seven Bowls of Judgment 49
Seizing the Final Victory 49
The Second Coming of Jesus Christ 50
The Beginning of the Millennium 50
All Things Made New 51
Parables of Jesus Christ in the Four Gospels 53

1. Parables Concerning The Teachings of Jesus 53
    A. Parable Concerning Humility 53
    B. Parable Concerning The Kingdom of God 53
    C. Parables Concerning Neighbors 53
    D. Parables Concerning Prayer 53
    E. Parables Concerning Obedience & Service 53
    F. Parables Concerning Wealth 53
2. Parables Concerning The Goodness of God 54
    A. Parables Concerning God's Love 54
    B. Parables Concerning Thankfulness 54
3. Parables Concerning The Future of The Coming Judgments 54
    A. The Return of the LORD 54
4. Parables Concerning the Values of God 54
    A. The Values of God 54

Topical Concordance for the New Testament 55

MATTHEW
(1:01—28-20)

1. **Jesus Christ, the King—His Genealogy & His Birth** **(1:01—4:11)**

A. Birth of the King **(1:01—4:11)**

1. Genealogy of Christ, the King (1:01—1:17)
2. Announcement of the Coming Christ (1:18—1:25)
3. Kings of the East Visit the Christ Child (2:01—2:12)
4. Jesus & Family Flee to Egypt (2:13—2:18)
5. Jesus & Family Return to Nazareth (2:19—2:23)
6. John the Baptist Preaches in Judean Wilderness (3:01—3:12)
7. Jesus Baptized by John the Baptist (3:13—3:17)
8. The Temptations of Jesus by Satan (4:01—4:11)
   A. Jesus Led Into Wilderness by Holy Spirit (4:01—01)
   B. Jesus Fasted Forty Days & Forty Nights (4:02—02)
   C. Satan Dares Jesus to Make Bread (4:03—04)
   D. Satan Dares God to Rescue Jesus (4:05—07)
   E. Satan Desires Worship from Jesus (4:08—11)

2. **Jesus Christ, the King—His Ministry Begins** **(4:12—7:29)**

A. Jesus' Preaching Ministry Begins in Galilee **(4:12—4:25)**

1. Jesus Begins His Ministry (4:12—4:17)
2. Jesus Chooses Four Fishermen in Galilee (4:18—4:22)
3. Jesus Travels Throughout Galilee (4:23—4:25)

B. Jesus Preaches His "Sermon on the Mount" **(5:01—5:16)**

1. Jesus Gives the Beatitudes (Blessings) (5:01—5:12)
   A. The Poor in Spirit (5:03)
   B. Those Who Mourn (5:04)
   C. The Meek (5:05)
   D. Who Hunger & Thirst for Righteousness (5:06)
   E. The Merciful (5:07)
   F. The Pure in Heart (5:08)
   G. The Peace Makers (5:09)
   H. Those Persecuted for Righteousness Sake (5:10)
   I. When People Revile & Persecute You (5:11)
   J. Rejoice & Be Exceedingly Glad (5:12)
2. Jesus Teaches Who Is the "Salt & the Light" (5:13—5:16)

C. Principles for Kingdom Living **(5:17—5:48)**

1. Laws of Moses (5:17—5:20)
2. Law of Anger & Murder (5:21—5:22)
3. Law of Reconciliation (5:23—5:26)
4. Law of Lust & Adultery (5:27—5:30)
5. Law of Divorce (5:31—5:32)
6. Law of Vows & Oaths (5:33—5:37)
7. Law of Retaliation (5:38—5:42)
8. Law of Love (5:43—5:48)

D. Practices for Kingdom Living **(6:01—7:12)**

1. Concerning Giving to the Needy (6:01—6:04)
2. Concerning Prayer (6:05—6:15)
3. Concerning Fasting (6:16—6:18)
4. Concerning Money (6:19—6:24)
5. Concerning Worrying (6:25—6:34)
6. Concerning Judging Others (7:01—7:05)
7. Concerning Being Prudent (Good Judgment) (7:06—7:06)
8. Concerning Prayer (7:07—7:11)
9. Law of Reciprocation (7:12—7:12)

E. Proof of Kingdom Living **(7:13—7:29)**

1. Concerning Going to Heaven (7:13—7:14)
2. Concerning Fruitful Lives (7:15—7:20)
3. Concerning Obedience to God's Word (7:21—7:29)

3. <u>Jesus Christ, the King—Proof of His Authority</u> **(8:01—13:52)**

A. The Power of Jesus Christ **(8:01—10:42)**

1. Power Over Uncleanness (8:01—8:04)
2. Power Over Distance in Faith (8:05—8:13)
3. Power Over Diseases (8:14—8:17)
4. Power Over Discipleship (8:18—8:22)
5. Power Over Nature (9:01—9:08)
6. Power Over Demonic Forces (9:09—9:13)
7. Paralyzed Man Forgiven & Healed (9:14—9:17)
8. Tax Collector Forgiven (9:18—9:26)
9. Concerning Fasting (9:27—9:34)
10. Power Over Death (9:35—9:35)
11. Power Over Blindness & Deafness (9:36—9:38)
12. Jesus' Anointing on the Disciples Sent Out (10:01—10:42)

B. The Anointed Teaching Concerning Christ's Kingdom **(11:01—12:50)**

1. John the Baptist's Doubt Concerning Jesus (11:01—11:19)
2. Jesus Promises Rest for the Soul (11:20—11:30)
3. Controversies Concerning the Sabbath (12:01—12:14)
   A. Disciples Pick Wheat on the Sabbath (12:01—08)
   B. Jesus Heals Man's Hand on the Sabbath (12:09—14)
4. Large Crowds Follow Jesus (12:15—12:21)
5. Jesus Accused of Being Under Satan's Power (12:22—12:37)
6. Religious Leaders Asks Jesus for Miracle (12:38—12:45)
7. Jesus Describes His Authentic Family (12:46—12:50)

C. The Parables of Jesus Christ **(13:01—13:52)**

1. Parable of the Four Soils (13:01—13:09)
2. Parable of the Four Soils Defined (13:10—13:23)
3. Parable of the Wheat & the Tares (13:24—13:30)
4. Parable of the Mustard Seed (13:31—13:32)
5. Parable of the Leaven (13:33—13:35)
6. Parable of the Wheat & Tares Defined (13:36—13:43)
7. Parable of the Hidden Treasure (13:44—13:44)

8. Parable of the Expensive Pearl (13:45—13:46)
9. Parable of the Dragnet (Fishing Net) (13:47—13:52)

4. **<u>Jesus Christ, the King—Different Reactions to His Ministry</u>** **(13:53—20:33)**

A. Jesus' Ministry Comes Under Fire **(13:53—14:12)**

1. Citizens of Nazareth Reject Teachings of Jesus (13:53—13:58)
2. John the Baptist Beheaded by Herod for a Dance (14:01—14:12)

B. Mighty Works of Jesus Christ **(14:13—15:39)**

1. Jesus Feeds Five Thousand Miraculously (14:13—14:21)
2. Jesus Walks on Sea of Galilee (14:22—14:33)
3. Jesus Heals All Who Touched Him (14:34—14:36)
4. Jesus Teaches on Inner Purity (15:01—15:20)
5. Woman's Daughter Delivered from Demon by Jesus (15:21—15:28)
6. Healing Marveled by the People (15:29—15:31)
7. Jesus Feeds Four Thousand Miraculously (15:32—15:39)

C. Jesus Rejected by Religious Leaders **(16:01—16:12)**

1. Religious Leaders Asks for Heavenly Sign (16:01—16:04)
2. Jesus Warns Against False Teaching (16:05—16:12)

D. Revelations of the Teachings of Jesus Christ **(16:13—20:33)**

1. Peter Proclaims Jesus as the Messiah (16:13—16:20)
2. First Prediction Concerning Death of Jesus (16:21—16:26)
3. Revelation of Christ's Second Coming (16:27—16:28)
4. The Transfiguration of Jesus on Mountain (17:01—17:13)
5. Demon-Possessed Boy Delivered by Jesus (17:14—17:21)
6. Second Prediction Concerning Death of Jesus (17:22—17:23)
7. Coin Found in Mouth of Fish to Pay Tax (17:24—17:27)
8. Jesus Teaches About Humility (18:01—18:06)
9. Warning Concerning Temptations (18:07—18:14)
10. Warning Concerning Looking Down on People (18:15—18:20)
11. Warning Concerning Forgiving Fellow Believers (18:21—18:35)
12. Teaching Concerning Marriage & Divorce (19:01—19:12)
13. Jesus Said, "Do Not Hinder the Children" (19:13—19:15)
14. Teaching Concerning Wealth (19:16—19:30)
    A. Jesus Speaks to Rich Young Ruler (19:16—27)
    B. Jesus Teaches on Rewards for Serving Him (19:18—30)
15. Parable of the Vineyard Workers (20:01—20:16)
16. Third Prediction Concerning Death of Jesus (20:17—20:19)
17. True Worship=Serving Others (20:20—20:28)
18. Blind Beggars Healed by Jesus (20:29—20:33)

5. **<u>Presentation of King Jesus</u>** **(21:01—23:39)**

A. King Jesus Publicly Presented to Jerusalem **(21:01—21:27)**

1. Jesus' Triumphal Entry Into Jerusalem (21:01—21:11)
2. Jesus Cleanses the Temple Again (21:12—21:17)
3. Jesus Curses Fig Tree (21:18—21:22)
4. Religious Leaders Challenges Jesus' Authority (21:23—21:27)

B. More Parables By Jesus **(21:28—22:14)**

1. Parable of the Two Sons (21:28—21:32)
2. Parable of the Wicked Farmers (21:33—21:46)
3. Parable of the Wedding Feasts (22:01—22:14)

C. Conflict Between Jesus & the Religious Leaders **(22:15—23:39)**

1. Jesus Answers Questions About Taxes (22:15—22:22)
2. Jesus Answers Questions About the Resurrection (22:23—22:33)
3. Jesus Answers Questions About Greatest Commandment (22:34—22:40)
4. Jesus' Question Couldn't Be Answered by Religious Leaders (22:41—22:46)
5. Jesus Warns People Concerning Religious Leaders (23:01—23:12)
6. Jesus Condemns Religious Leaders (23:13—23:36)
7. Jesus Again Grieves Over Jerusalem (23:37—23:39)

6. <u>End-Time Messages from the Mount of Olives</u> **(24:01—28:20)**

A. Jesus' Messages Concerning the End-Times **(24:01—25:46)**

1. Message Concerning Destruction of Future Temple (24:01—24:02)
2. Signs of the End of this Age of Dispensation (24:03—24:28)
3. Sign of the *LORD*'s Return (24:29—24:31)
4. Parable of Fig Tree (24:32—24:35)
5. Jesus' Followers Commanded to be Watchful of His Return (24:36—24:51)
6. Parable of Ten Virgins (25:01—25:13)
7. Parable of Loaned Money (25:14—25:30)
8. End-time Judgment of the Unbelievers (25:31—25:46)

B. The Last Week of the Life of Jesus Christ, Our *LORD* **(26:01—27:66)**

1. The Plot to Kill Jesus, the Messiah (26:01—26:05)
2. Mary of Bethany Anoints Jesus' Head with Perfumed Oil (26:06—26:13)
3. Judas Betrays Jesus (26:14—26:16)
4. Disciples Prepare for Passover (26:17—26:19)
5. The Last Supper (26:20—26:30)
6. Jesus Predicts Peter's Denial Again (26:31—26:35)
7. Jesus Agonizes in the Garden of Gethsemane (26:36—26:46)
8. The Betrayal & Arrest of Jesus (26:47—26:56)
9. Jesus Questioned by High Priest Caiaphas (26:57—26:68)
10. Peter Denies Jesus Three Times (26:69—26:75)
11. The Sanhedrin Condemns Jesus (27:01—27:02)
12. Judas Hangs Himself (27:03—27:10)
13. Jesus Stands Trial Before Pilate (27:11—27:14)
14. Jesus Handed Over to be Crucified (27:15—27:26)
15. Jesus Mocked by Roman Soldiers (27:27—27:31)
16. Jesus Led Away to be Crucified (27:32—27:34)
17. Jesus Nailed to the Cross (27:35—27:37)
18. Two Criminals Crucified with Jesus (27:38—27:40)

19. Jesus Mocked by Religious Leaders (27:41—27:44)
20. Jesus Dies on the Cross (27:45—27:50)
21. Disasters in Jerusalem After Jesus Dies (27:51—27:56)
22. Jesus' Buried in Borrowed Tomb (27:57—27:61)
23. Roman Guards Posted at Tomb of Jesus (27:62—27:66)

C. Resurrection of Jesus Christ & the Great Commission (28:01—28:20)

1. Jesus Rises from the Dead (28:01—28:07)
2. Jesus Appears to the Women (28:08—28:10)
3. Religious Leaders Bribe the Guards to Lie (28:11—28:15)
4. The Great Commission (28:16—28:20)

<u>MARK</u>
(1:01—16:20)

1. <u>Jesus Christ, the Servant—His Birth & Preparation for Ministry</u> (1:01—1:13)

A. Preparation of the Servant (1:01—1:13)

1. John, the Baptist Prepares the Way for the Messiah (1:01—1:08)
2. Jesus Baptized by John, the Baptist (1:09—1:11)
3. Jesus Tempted by Satan in the Wilderness (1:12—1:13)

2. <u>Jesus Christ, the Servant—His Ministry & Message</u> (1:14—10:52)

A. His Ministry Begins in Galilee (1:14—3:35)

1. His Preaching Begins (1:14—1:15)
2. Jesus Calls His First Four Disciples (1:16—1:20)
3. Jesus Demonstrates His Authority Over Demons (1:21—1:28)
4. Jesus Demonstrates His Authority Over Diseases (1:29—1:39)
5. Jesus Heals Man of Leprosy (1:40—1:45)
6. Paralyzed Man Healed (2:01—2:12)
7. Jesus Eats at Matthew's House with Sinners (2:13—2:17)
8. Jesus Expresses Authority Over Religiosity (2:18—3:06)
   A. Concerning Fasting (2:18—22)
   B. Picking Wheat on the Sabbath (2:23—28)
   C. Healing on the Sabbath (3:01—06)
9. Jesus' Authority Over Demons (3:07—3:12)
10. Jesus Selects His Twelve Disciples (3:13—3:19)
11. Jesus' Authority Over Condemnation (3:20—3:30)
12. Jesus' Definition of His True Family (3:31—3:35)

B. More Parables of Jesus (4:01—4:34)

1. Parable of the Four Soils (4:01—4:25)
2. Parable of the Wheat & the Tares (4:26—4:29)
3. Parable of the Mustard Seed (4:30—4:34)

C. The Sovereign Power of Jesus (4:35—9:01)

1. Jesus Calms Storm on the Lake (4:35—4:41)
2. Jesus Drives Demons from Man Into Herd of Pigs (5:01—5:20)
3. Jesus' Power Over Sickness & Death (5:21—5:43)

4. Jesus Rejected by Kinsmen in Nazareth (6:01—6:06a)
5. Jesus Sends Out His Twelve Disciples (6:06b—6:13)
6. John the Baptist Killed for a Dance (6:14—6:29)
7. Jesus Miraculously Feeds Five Thousand People (6:30—6:44)
8. Jesus Walks on Water (6:45—6:52)
9. All Who Touched Jesus Were Healed (6:53—6:56)
10. Jesus Taught on Inward Purity (7:01—7:23)
    A. Jewish Rituals (7:01—05)
    B. Hypocrisy (7:06—07)
    C. Idolatry (7:08—13)
    D. Foods Don't Defile a Person (7:14—19)
    E. Thought-Life Defiles a Person (7:20—23)
11. Jesus Delivers a Girl of a Demon (7:24—7:30)
12. Jesus Heals a Deaf Man (7:31—7:37)
13. Jesus Miraculously Feeds Four Thousand People (8:01—8:10)
14. Religious Leaders Ask Jesus for a Sign from Heaven (8:11—8:13)
15. Jesus Warned People Concerning Wrong Teaching (8:14—8:21)
16. Jesus Heals a Blind Man (8:22—8:26)
17. Peter Declares Jesus Is the Messiah (8:27—8:30)
18. First Time That Jesus Prophesied His Death (8:31—8:32)
19. Jesus Rebukes Peter; Satan Spoke Through Him (8:33—8:33)
20. True Follower of Jesus Christ (8:34—9:01)

D. The Precepts of Jesus (9:02—10:52)

1. Jesus Transfigured on a Mountaintop (9:02—9:13)
2. Demon-Possessed Boy Delivered & Healed (9:14—9:29)
3. Second Time That Jesus Prophesied His Death (9:30—9:32)
4. Jesus Prepares His Disciples (9:33—10:45)
    A. The Attitude of His Disciples (9:33—41)
    B. Warning About Temptation (9:42—50)
    C. Marriage & Divorce (10:01—12)
    D. Children & the Kingdom of God (10:13—16)
    E. Concerning Wealth (10:17—31)
    F. Third Time Jesus Prophesied His Death (10:32—34)
    G. Servanthood (10:35—45)
5. Jesus Heals Blind Beggar Bartimaeus (10:46—10:52)

3. Jesus Christ, the King—His Sacrifice (11:01—15:47)

A. Jesus, the Servant Presents Himself (11:01—15:47)

1. Sunday—His Activities (11:01—11:11)
    A. His Triumphal Entry Into Jerusalem (11:01—11)
2. Monday—His Activities (11:12—11:19)
    A. Fig Tree Cursed (11:12—14)
    B. The Temple Cleansed (11:15—19)
3. Tuesday—His Teachings (11:20—13:37)
    A. Concerning Faith (11:20—26)
    B. Concerning His Authority (11:27—33)
    C. Concerning Israel's Leaders (12:01—12)
    D. Concerning Taxes (12:13—17)
    E. Concerning the Resurrection (12:18—27)

F. Concerning the Great Commission (12:28—34)
G. Concerning His *LORD*ship (12:35—37)
H. Concerning Pride (12:38—40)
I. Concerning Giving (12:41—44)
J. Concerning the Future (13:01—37)
1. Disciples Questions (13:01—04)
2. The Seven-Year Tribulation (13:05—23)
3. His Second Coming (13:24—27)
4. Parable of the Fig Tree (13:28—31)
5. Exhortation to be Alert (13:32—37)

4. Wednesday—Activities of Other People (14:01—14:11)
A. Religious Leaders Plot (14:01—02)
B. Mary of Bethany Anoints Jesus Head (14:03—09)
C. Judas Plans to Betray Jesus (14:10—11)

5. Thursday—Activities—Passover to Arrest (14:12—14:52)
A. Passover Prepared (14:12—16)
B. Passover Celebrated (14:17—21)
C. *LORD*'s Supper Instituted (14:22—25)
D. Jesus Predicts Peter to Deny Him (14:26—31)
E. Prayer & Agonizing in Gethsemane (14:32—42)
F. Jesus Arrested in Gethsemane (14:43—52)

6. Friday—Trials & Crucifixion (14:53—15:47)
A. Trial Before the Sanhedrin (14:53—65)
B. Peter Denies Jesus (14:66—72)
C. Trial Before Pilate (15:01—15)
D. Jesus Beaten & Abused by Soldiers (15:16—20)
E. Crucifixion of Jesus Christ (15:21—32)
F. Death of Jesus Christ (15:33—41)
G. Burial of Jesus Christ (15:42—47)

4. Jesus Christ, the King—His Success at the Cross (16:01—16:20)

A. His Success at the Cross (16:01—16:20)

7. Sunday—His Resurrection (16:01—16:20)
A. Resurrection of Jesus from the Dead (16:01—08)
B. Appearances of Jesus Last Forty Days (16:09—18)
C. Jesus' Ascension Into Heaven (16:19—20)

LUKE
(1:01—24:53)

1. Jesus Christ, the Savior—His Birth & Preparation for Ministry (1:01—4:13)

A. Luke's Purpose in Writing His Gospel Account (1:01—1:04)

B. Events Leading Up to the Birth of Jesus Christ (1:05—2:20)

1. Birth of John, the Baptist Foretold to Zechariah (1:05—1:25)
A. The Barrenness of Elizabeth (1:05—07)
B. Angel Gabriel Visits Zechariah (1:08—12)
C. Elizabeth Bears a Son—John the Baptist (1:13—13)
D. John Prepares the Way of the *LORD* (1:14—20)
E. Zechariah Becomes Mute (1:21—25)

2. The Birth of Christ Foretold (1:26—1:38)
   A. Angel Gabriel Visits Mary, the Virgin (1:26—28)
   B. Mary to Have a Child Named Jesus (1:29—34)
   C. The Holy Spirit to Come Upon Mary (1:35—38)
3. Mary Visits Elizabeth in Judea (1:39—1:56)
   A. Mary Travels to Hills of Judea; Visits Elizabeth (1:39—40)
   B. Elizabeth Filled with the Holy Spirit (1:41—41)
   C. Mother of the *LORD* Visits Elizabeth (1:42—45)
   D. Mary Gives Praise to the *LORD* (1:46—56)
4. Birth of John, the Baptist (1:57—1:80)
   A. John Is Born (1:57—58)
   B. John's Circumcision Ceremony (1:59—66)
   C. Zechariah Filled with the Holy Spirit (1:67—67)
   D. Zechariah Prophecies Over John (1:68—79)
   E. John Lives in Wilderness Before Ministry (1:80—80)
5. Jesus Christ Is Born In Bethlehem (2:01—2:20)
   A. Census Is Decreed (2:01—05)
   B. Jesus Is Born (2:06—07)
   C. Angel of the *LORD* Visits Shepherds (2:08—15)
   D. Jesus Visited by Shepherds (2:16—20)

C. Events Leading Up to Ministry of Jesus Christ (2:21—4:13)

1. Jesus Is Presented to the Temple (2:21—2:40)
   A. Jesus' Circumcision & Purification Ceremony (2:21—24)
   B. The Song of Simeon (2:25—35)
   C. Anna, a Prophet in Temple Praising God (2:36—38)
   D. Jesus Returns to Nazareth (2:39—40)
2. Jesus at Age 12 Speaks to Religious Leaders (2:41—2:52)
   A. Jesus Left Behind at the Temple (2:41—45)
   B. Jesus Speaks to Religious Leaders in Temple (2:46—50)
   C. Jesus Returns to Nazareth with His Mother (2:51—52)
3. John, the Baptist Prepares the Way for Jesus (3:01—3:18)
4. John Imprisoned by King Herod Antipas (3:19—3:20)
5. Jesus Baptized in the Jordan River by John (3:21—3:22)
6. Genealogy from Jesus Back to Adam (3:23—3:38)
7. Jesus Is Lead to Wilderness to be Tempted by Satan (4:01—4:13)

2. <u>Jesus Christ, the Savior—His Ministry</u> (4:14—6:11)

A. Galilee—Where Jesus Begins (4:14—4:30)

1. His Preaching in Galilee (4:14—4:15)
2. Jesus Rejected in Hometown of Nazareth (4:16—4:30)
   A. Jesus Reads the Scroll from Isaiah (4:16—20)
   B. Jesus Says "Today, Scripture Has Been Fulfilled" (4:21—22)
   C. Jesus' Remarks Angered the People (4:23—28)
   D. The Angry Mob Tried to Kill Jesus (4:29—30)

B. Jesus' Power & Authority Presented (4:31—5:32)

1. His Power Over Demons (4:31—4:37)

A. Demon-Possessed Man Speaks Out to Jesus (4:31—37)

2. Jesus Heals Simon Peter's Mother-in-Law & Others (4:38—4:41)
3. Jesus Preaches Throughout Judea (4:42—4:44)
4. The First Disciples Are Called (5:01—5:11)
   - A. Jesus Goes Fishing with Simon (5:01—07)
   - B. Simon, James & John Forsake All for Jesus (5:08—11)
5. Jesus Heals Man of Advanced Leprosy (5:12—5:16)
6. Jesus Heals Paralyzed Man on Sleeping Mat (5:17—5:26)
7. Jesus Eats Supper with Levi, the Tax Collector (5:27—5:32)

C. Jesus Instructs the Pharisees **(5:33—6:11)**

1. Pharisees Ask Jesus About Fasting (5:33—5:35)
2. Parable of the Wineskins (5:36—5:39)
3. Disciples Pick Wheat on the Sabbath (6:01—6:05)
4. Jesus Heals Man on the Sabbath (6:06—6:11)

3. <u>Jesus Christ, the Savior—His Ministry Expands</u> (6:12—9:50)

A. Disciples Chosen; Beatitudes Given **(6:12—6:26)**

1. Jesus Selects the Twelve (6:12—6:16)
2. Jesus Gives His "Sermon on the Mound" (6:17—6:26)
   - A. Blessed Are Those Who Are Poor (6:20)
   - B. Blessed Are Those Who Hunger (6:21a)
   - C. Blessed Are Those Who Weep (6:21b)
   - D. Blessed Are the Hated, Mocked & Cursed (6:22)
   - E. Reward Is Waiting on You in Heaven (6:23)
   - F. Woe to the Rich; Consolation Already Received (6:24)
   - G. Woe to the Prosperous; Hunger Awaits You (6:25a)
   - H. Woe to the Careless Laughter; Turns to Sorrow (6:25b)
   - I. Woe to You Who Receive Open Praise (6:26)

B. Principles of Kingdom Living **(6:27—6:49)**

2. Jesus Teaches Concerning Kingdom Living (6:27—6:49)
   - A. Love Your Enemies (6:27—36)
   - B. Don't Judge, Don't Criticize—Instead Forgive (6:37—38)
   - C. Blind Leading the Blind (6:39—42)
   - D. Good Fruit vs. Bad Fruit (6:43—45)
   - E. Life's Foundations (6:46—49)

C. The Ministry of Jesus Christ in Galilee **(7:01—9:50)**

1. Jesus Heals Roman Centurion (7:01—7:10)
2. Widow's Son Raised from the Dead (7:11—7:17)
3. Jesus Eases Doubt of John, the Baptist (7:18—7:35)
4. Jesus' Feet Anointed by Immoral Woman (7:36—7:50)
5. Healed Women Finance Jesus' Ministry (8:01—8:03)
6. Parable of the Four Soils (8:04—8:08)
7. Parable of Four Soils Explained (8:09—8:18)
8. True Family of Jesus Defined (8:19—8:21)

9. Jesus Calms the Stormy Sea of Galilee (8:22—8:25)
10. Jesus Encounters Demon-Possessed Man (8:26—8:39)
  A. Jesus, Disciples Arrive in Land of Gadarenes (8:26—26)
  B. Jesus Confronts Demon-Possessed Man (8:27—29)
  C. Man Filled with a Legion (6,000) of Demons (8:30—31)
  D. Legion of Demons Enter Herd of Pigs (8:32—33)
  E. Demon-Possessed Man Delivered (8:34—37a)
  F. Jesus Leaves Land of the Gadarenes (8:37b—39)
11. Jesus' Power Over Woman's Sickness (8:40—8:48)
12. Jairus' Daughter Raised from the Dead (8:49—8:56)
13. Jesus Sends Out His Twelve Disciples (9:01—9:06)
14. King Herod Antipas Has John, the Baptist Killed (9:07—9:09)
15. Jesus Miraculously Feeds Five Thousand People (9:10—9:17)
16. Peter Proclaims Jesus as the Messiah (9:18—9:20)
17. Jesus Predicts His Death for First Time (9:21—9:22)
18. The Cost of Being a Disciple of Jesus (9:23—9:26)
19. The Transfiguration on the Mountain (9:27—9:36)
20. Demon-Possessed Boy Delivered by Jesus (9:37—9:42)
21. Jesus Predicts His Death a Second Time (9:43—9:45)
22. The Least Would Be the Greatest (9:46—9:48)
23. Anyone Who Is Not Against You Is For You, Says Jesus (9:49—9:50)

4. <u>Jesus Christ, the Savior—His Rejection</u> (9:51—19:27)

A. Jesus' Ministry on Journey to Jerusalem (9:51—11:54)

1. Samaritans Reject Jesus (9:51—9:56)
2. True Cost of Discipleship (9:57—9:62)
3. Jesus Chooses Seventy-two Other Disciples (10:01—10:16)
4. The Seventy-two Disciples Return to Jesus (10:17—10:24)
5. Parable of the Good Samaritan (10:25—10:37)
6. Attitude Difference Between Mary & Martha (10:38—10:42)
7. Jesus Teaches on Prayer (11:01—11:13)
  A. The *LORD's* Prayer (11:01—04)
  B. Parable of the Friend (11:05—08)
  C. Ask, Seek & Knock (11:09—10)
  D. The Good Father (11:11—13)
8. Jesus Cast Out Mute Spirit (11:14—11:14)
9. Religious Leaders Reject Jesus (11:15—11:28)
  A. Jesus Accused of Being Possessed by Satan (11:15—16)
  B. Kingdom Divided Is Doomed (11:17—28)
10. Warning Against Unbelief (11:29—11:32)
  A. Sign of Jonah (11:29—30)
  B. Sign of the Queen of Sheba (11:31—31)
  C. Sign of the People of Nineveh (11:32—32)
11. Parable of the Lighted Lamp (11:33—11:36)
12. Jesus Rejects Religious Leaders (11:37—11:54)
  A. Jesus Dines at Home of a Pharisee (11:37—38)
  B. Jesus Exposes Hypocritical Ways of Pharisees (11:39—54)
    1. The Heart Purity of the Pharisees (11:39—41)
    2. The Compassion of the Pharisees (11:42—42)
    3. Proudness of the Pharisees Exposed (11:43—45)
    4. Pharisee's Religiosity Exposed (11:46—49)

5. Responsible for Prophet's Death (11:50—51)
6. Pharisees Hide "Key to Knowledge" (11:52—52)
7. Religious Leaders Furious (11:53—54)

B. Instructions In Light of Rejection of Jesus Christ **(12:01—19:27)**

1. Jesus Warns Against Hypocrisy (12:01—12:12)
2. Jesus Warns Against Covetousness (12:13—12:21)
3. Jesus Warns Against Worry (12:22—12:34)
4. Jesus Gives Warning Concerning His Return (12:35—12:48)
    - A. Wedding Feast Example (12:35—38)
    - B. Homeowner Example (12:39—41)
    - C. Parable of the Faithful & Unfaithful Servant (12:42—47)
    - D. To Much Is Given, Much Is Required (12:48—48)
5. Warning Concerning the Coming Division (12:49—12:53)
6. Warning Concerning the Coming Future Crisis (12:54—12:59)
    - A. Discerning the Signs of the Times (12:54—56)
    - B. Deciding Right & Wrong (12:57—59)
7. Jesus Calls People to Repent (13:01—13:09)
    - A. Repent or Perish (13:01—05)
    - B. Parable of the Fig Tree (13:06—09)
8. The Healing of the Crippled Woman (13:10—13:17)
    - A. Jesus Glorified (13:10—13)
    - B. Jesus Criticized (13:14—17)
9. What Is the Kingdom of God Like (13:18—13:21)
    - A. A Mustard Seed (13:18—19)
    - B. Yeast for Bread (13:20—21)
10. Jesus Teaches How People Are Saved (13:22—13:30)
11. Jesus Mourns Over Jerusalem (13:31—13:35)
    - A. Jesus Refers to King Herod as a Fox (13:31—33)
    - B. Jerusalem "City Who Kills the Prophets" (13:34—35)
12. Pharisees Are Given Instructions (14:01—14:24)
    - A. Jesus Heals Man on the Sabbath (14:01—06)
    - B. Parable of the Guest (14:07—14)
    - C. Parable of the Great Feast (14:15—24)
13. Cost of Being a Disciple (14:26—14:35)
14. Parable of the Lost Sheep (15:01—15:07)
15. Parable of the Lost Coin (15:08—15:09)
    - A. Crown of Rejoicing (15:10—10)
16. Parable of the Lost Son (15:11—15:31)
17. Parable of the Shrewd Manager (16:01—16:18)
18. Parable of the Rich Man & the Beggar (16:19—16:31)
19. Forgiveness & Faith (17:01—17:10)
    - A. Woe to the Tempter (17:01—02)
    - B. If Sinner Repents, Forgive Him (17:03—04)
    - C. Mustard Seed Faith (17:05—06)
    - D. Obedience Is Our Duty (17:07—10)
20. Lesson on Gratitude (Ten Lepers Healed) (17:11—17:19)
21. Jesus Teaches Concerning His Second Coming (17:20—17:37)
    - A. No Visible Signs (17:20—21)
    - B. False Christ & His False Comings (17:22—25)
    - C. As in the Days of Noah (17:26—27)

- D. As in the Days of Lot (17:28—37)
- 22. Jesus Teaches on Persistent Prayer (18:01—18:14)
  - A. Parable of the Persistent Widow (18:01—05)
  - B. Lesson from the Evil Judge (18:06—08)
  - C. Parable of the Praying Pharisee & Tax Collector (18:09—14)
- 23. Jesus Blesses the Little Children (18:15—18:17)
- 24. Jesus Teaches on Sacrifice (18:18—18:30)
  - A. Lesson from the Rich Young Ruler (18:18—27)
  - B. Rewards for Sacrificing for God's Kingdom (18:28—30)
- 25. Jesus Predicts His Death a Third Time (18:31—18:34)
- 26. Blind Beggar Healed on Road to Jericho (18:35—18:43)
- 27. Salvation Comes to Zacchaeus's (Notorious Sinner) Home (19:01—19:10)
- 28. Parable of King with Ten Servants (19:11—19:27)
  - A. The Unwanted King (19:11—14)
  - B. The Account of the Ten Servants (19:15—27)
    - 1. First Servant—Ten-Fold Return (19:15—17)
    - 2. Second Servant—Five-Fold Return (19:18—19)
    - 3. Third Servant—No Gain, Hid Money (19:20—25)
    - 4. Faithfulness vs. Unfaithfulness (19:26—26)
    - 5. Enemies of the King Executed (19:27—27)

5. Jesus Christ, the Savior—His Death, Burial & Resurrection (19:28—24:53)

A. Passion Week—His Last Week Alive (19:28—24:53)

- 1. Sunday—His Triumphal Entry (19:28—19:44)
  - A. Jesus Enters Jerusalem on a Donkey (19:28—44)
    - 1. Two Disciples Go Retrieve Donkey (19:28—35)
    - 2. Followers Wave Palm Branches (19:36—37)
    - 3. People Shout Praises to God (19:38—38)
    - 4. Pharisees Try to Rebuke People (19:39—40)
    - 5. Jewish Leaders Rejected Salvation (19:41—44)
- 2. Monday—His Temple Work (19:45—19:48)
  - A. Temple Cleared Again by Jesus (19:45—48)
- 3. Tuesday—His Ministry Work (20:01—21:38)
  - A. Jesus' Authority Questioned (20:01—08)
  - B. Parable of the Wicked Farmers (20:09—19)
  - C. Jesus Questioned About Paying Taxes (20:20—26)
  - D. Jesus Questioned About the Resurrection (20:27—40)
  - E. Religious Leaders Questioned (20:41—47)
  - F. Jesus Teaches About the Widow's Mite (21:01—04)
  - G. Jesus' Discourse on the Mount of Olives (21:05—38)
    - 1. The Sign of Jesus' Return (21:05—07)
    - 2. False Christs to Come (21:08—08)
    - 3. Disasters to Come (21:09—11)
    - 4. Great Persecution to Come (21:12—19)
    - 5. Future Destruction of Jerusalem (21:20—24)
    - 6. Heavenly Signs to Come (21:25—28)
    - 7. Parable of the Fig Tree (21:29—33)
    - 8. Believers Must Remain Watchful (21:34—38)

4. <u>Wednesday</u>—His Activities in Jerusalem (22:01—22:06)
   A. The Plot to Kill Jesus (22:01—02)
   B. Judas Agrees to Betray Jesus (22:03—06)
5. <u>Thursday</u>—The Passover & His Arrest (22:07—22:53)
   A. Disciples Prepare for Passover (22:07—13)
   B. Passover Celebrated (22:14—20)
      1. Jesus & Disciples Join Together (22:14—16)
      2. Communion Taken (22:17—20)
   C. Betrayer (Judas) Discovered at Table (22:21—23)
   D. Who Would Be the Greatest (22:24—30)
   E. Jesus Predicts Denial from Peter (22:31—38)
   F. Jesus in Garden of Gethsemane (21:39—46)
   G. Judas Brays Jesus (21:47—48)
   H. Jesus Heals Cut-off Ear (21:49—51)
   I. Jesus Arrested (21:52—53)
6. <u>Friday</u>—His Trials & Crucifixion (22:54—23:55)
   A. Peter Denies Jesus Three Times (22:54—65)
   B. Religious Leaders Condemn Jesus (22:66—71)
      1. Jesus Led Before the High Council (22:66—66)
      2. Jesus Declares He Is the Son of God (22:67—71)
   C. Jesus On Trial Before Pilate (23:01—05)
   D. Jesus On Trial Before Herod (23:06—12)
   E. Jesus Handed Over to be Crucified (23:13—25)
      1. Pilate Finds Jesus "Not Guilty" (23:13—17)
      2. Jesus Now Sentenced to Die (23:18—24)
      3. Barabbas Released (23:25—25)
   F. Jesus Sent to the Cross to be Crucified (23:26—31)
   G. Jesus Is Put Onto the Cross (23:32—43)
      1. Two Criminals Crucified with Jesus (23:32—33)
      2. Jesus Asks for Forgiveness for People (23:34a—34a)
      3. Soldiers Gamble for Jesus' Clothes (23:34b—34b)
      4. The Crowd Mocks Jesus (23:35—39)
      5. One Criminal Receives Salvation (23:40—43)
   H. Jesus Dies on the Cross (23:44—49)
   I. Jesus Buried in a Borrowed Tomb (23:50—55)
7. <u>Saturday</u>—The Sabbath Day (23:56—23:56)
   A. The People Rested on the Sabbath (23:56—56)
8. <u>Sunday</u>—Resurrection Day (24:01—24:53)
   A. Jesus Rises from the Dead (24:01—12)
      1. Women Go to Tomb for Jesus (24:01—03)
      2. Angels Appear Before the Women (24:04—07)
      3. Women Tell Apostles of Incident (24:08—12)
   B. Jesus Walks with Two Believers on Road (24:13—34)
   C. Jesus Appears to the Eleven Disciples (24:35—43)
   D. Jesus Gives the Great Commission (24:44—48)
   E. Jesus Goes to Bethany; Ascends to Heaven (24:49—53)

<u>JOHN</u>
(1:01—21:25)

1. **<u>Jesus Christ, the Son of God—His Birth & Preparation</u>** **(1:01—1:18)**

A. Jesus Prepares for His Ministry **(1:01—1:18)**

1. The Divinity of Jesus (1:01—1:02)
2. The Eternal Glory in Jesus (1:03—1:05)
3. John, the Baptist—A Witness to the Light (Jesus) (1:06—1:09)
4. Jesus Rejected by His Own Kinsman (1:10—1:11)
5. Spiritual Rebirth of Man (1:12—1:13)
6. The Embodiment of God in Jesus (1:14—1:18)

2. **<u>Jesus Christ, the Son of God—His Presentation to the World</u>** **(1:19—2:12)**

A. John, the Baptist Presents Yeshua, the Messiah **(1:19—1:34)**

1. John, the Baptist Prepares the Way for Jesus Christ (1:19—1:28)
   A. Jewish Leaders Inquire If John Is the Messiah (1:19—21)
   B. John, the Baptist Quotes Words of Isaiah 40:3 (1:22—23)
   C. John Baptizes in Jordan River (1:24—28)
2. John, the Baptist Proclaims Jesus as the Messiah (1:29—1:34)
   A. The Lamb of God Comes to John for Baptism (1:29—31)
   B. Holy Spirit Descends Upon Jesus (1:32—33)
   C. John Testifies, "Jesus **IS** the Son of God" (1:34—34)

B. John, the Baptist Presents His Disciples to Jesus **(1:35—1:51)**

1. Andrew & Phillip—The First Two to Follow Jesus (1:35—1:51)
   A. Andrew & Phillip Stay with Jesus (1:35—39)
   B. Andrew Seeks Out His Brother Simon (1:40—41)
   C. Jesus Renames Simon to Cephas (Peter) (1:42—42)
   D. Jesus Calls Phillip from Bethsaida to be Disciple (1:43—43)
   E. Nathaniel Becomes a Disciple (1:44—51)

C. Jesus' Presentation at Cana in Galilee **(2:01—2:12)**

1. Jesus Changes Water to Wine—His First Miracle (2:01—2:10)
2. Jesus' Disciples Became Believers in Him (2:11—2:11)
3. Jesus Goes to Capernaum with Mother, Brothers, Disciples (2:12—2:12)

3. **<u>Jesus Christ, the Son of God—His Message & Ministry</u>** **(2:12—12:50)**

A. The People's Belief & Unbelief **(2:12—6:71)**

1. Jesus Cleanses the Temple (2:12—2:25)
   A. Jesus Chased People from Temple (2:12—18)
   B. "Destroy This Temple, Will Make Rise in 3 Days" (2:19—19)
   C. Jesus Speaks of Temple Being Built (2:20—22)
   D. People Convinced Jesus Is the Messiah (2:23—25)
2. Jesus Receives a Night Visit from Nicodemus (3:01—3:21)
   A. Jesus Explains Being Born Again (3:01—09)
   B. Jesus Prophesies His Crucifixion (3:10—15)
   C. Salvation Explained (3:16—17)
   D. Believers Saved; Unbelievers Judged (3:18—21)
3. John, the Baptist Bears Witness of Jesus (3:22—3:36)
   A. John's Disciples Complain About Jesus Baptizing (3:22—26)

B. John, the Baptist Explains the True Messiah (3:27—36)
4. Jesus Speaks to a Woman at Jacob's Well Near Sychar (4:01—4:26)
A. Jesus' Disciples Baptized, Not Jesus (4:01—02)
B. Jesus Leaves Judea; Returns to Galilee (4:03—04)
C. Jesus Arrives to Jacob's Well (4:05—06)
D. Jesus Encounters Samaritan Woman at Well (4:07—26)
1. Jesus Asks for Drink of Water (4:07—09)
2. Jesus Tells Her About Living Water (4:10—15)
3. Jesus Reveals Her Private Life to Her (4:16—20)
4. Jesus Explains True Worshipers (4:21—26)
5. Jesus Speaks About Spiritual Harvest to His Disciples (4:27—4:38)
A. Jesus Explains Spiritual Food (4:27—34)
B. Parable of Planter & Harvester (4:35—38)
6. Many Samaritans Comes to Salvation (4:39—4:42)
7. Jesus Welcomed in Galilee (4:43—4:45)
8. Jesus Heals Officer in Herod's Service (4:46—4:54)
9. Jesus Heals Paralyzed Man at Pool in Bethesda (5:01—5:14)
10. Jesus Heals on the Sabbath (5:15—5:18)
11. Jesus Declares to be the Son of God (5:19—5:30)
12. Jesus Supports His Declaration as the Son of God (5:31—5:47)
13. Jesus Miraculously Feeds Five Thousand People (6:01—6:15)
14. Jesus Walks on Sea of Galilee (6:16—6:21)
15. Jesus' Declaration "**I AM** the Bread of Life." (6:22—6:40)
16. Religious Leaders Murmur in Disagreement (6:41—6:59)
17. Many Disciples Abandon Jesus (6:60—6:71)

B. Opposition to Jesus' Ministry in Galilee (7:01—10:42)
1. Brothers (Relatives) of Jesus Opposed Him (7:01—7:09)
2. Jesus Attends Feast at the Temple in Secret (7:10—7:31)
A. Jesus' Authority IS from God, the Father (7:10—20)
B. Healing on the Sabbath (7:21—24)
C. Jesus Speaks Out in Public (7:25—27)
D. Jesus Teaches in the Temple (7:28—31)
3. Jesus Says, "I Will Go Back to My Father" (7:32—7:36)
4. Jesus Declares He Is THE Living Water (7:37—7:39)
5. Opinion of Jesus Is Divided Because of His Declaration (7:40—7:46)
6. Pharisees Confused Over Jesus (7:47—7:49)
7. No Prophet Comes from Galilee (7:50—7:53)
8. Jesus Forgives Woman Caught in Adultery (8:01—8:11)
9. Jesus Declares, "**I AM** the Light of the World" (8:12—8:20)
10. Judgment Predicted for Unbelief in Jesus (8:21—8:27)
11. After Speaking, Many People Believed in Jesus (8:28—8:30)
12. Jesus Describes God's "True Children" (8:31—8:47)
A. True Disciples Obey His Teachings (8:31—33)
B. The Slavery of Sin (8:34—41)
C. Jesus Declares God Sent Him (8:42—43)
D. Religious Leader's Attitudes Are Satanic (8:44—47)
13. Jesus **IS** Eternal (8:48—8:59)

14. Jesus Heals Man Born Blind with Mud (9:01—9:12)
15. Healed Blind Man Questioned by Religious Leaders (9:13—9:34)
16. Jesus Declares the Pharisees Are Spiritually Blind (9:35—9:41)
17. Jesus Declares, "**I AM** The Good Shepherd" (10:01—10:21)
    A. Parable of the Good Shepherd (10:01—21)
18. Jesus Declares, "I and My Father Are One" (10:22—10:30)
19. Jewish Leaders Seek to Stone Jesus (10:31—10:33)
20. "The Father Is in Me & **I AM** in My Father," Says Jesus (10:34—10:38)
21. Religious Leaders Again Tried to Arrest Jesus (10:39—10:42)

C. Opposition to Jesus' Ministry in Jerusalem (11:01—12:50)

1. Lazarus Becomes Ill & Dies (11:01—11:16)
2. Mary & Martha Are Comforted by Jesus (11:17—11:37)
    A. Martha Meets Jesus on Road to Bethany (11:17—24)
    B. Jesus—"**I AM** THE Resurrection & THE Life" (11:25—26)
    C. Martha Confesses Jesus ***IS*** the Messiah (11:27—29)
    D. Mary Meets Jesus Outside of Bethany (11:30—32)
    E. Jesus Moved with Indignation (11:33—37)
3. Jesus Raised Lazarus from Dead After Four Days (11:38—11:44)
4. A Plot to Kill Jesus by Religious Leaders (11:45—11:57)
5. Mary Anoints the Feet of Jesus (12:01—12:11)
6. Jesus' Triumphal Entry Into Jerusalem (12:12—12:19)
7. Jesus Tells Disciples Why He Must Die (12:20—12:36)
8. Isaiah Prophecy Fulfilled (Isaiah 53:1; 6:10) (12:37—12:43)
9. Jesus Christ—Eternal Life With or Eternal Life Without (12:44—12:50)

4. <u>Jesus Christ, the Son of God His Death & Resurrection</u> (13:01—21:25)

A. Jesus Prepares His Disciples (13:01—17:26)

1. Jesus Washes the Feet of His Disciples (13:01—13:20)
2. Jesus Reveals His Betrayer, Judas Iscariot (13:21—13:30)
3. Jesus Reveals That Peter Will Deny Him Three Times (13:31—13:38)
4. Jesus **IS** THE Way, THE Truth & THE Life (14:01—14:14)
5. Jesus Promises the Gift of the Holy Spirit (14:15—14:30)
    A. To Love Jesus Is To Obey His Commandments (14:15)
    B. Love Jesus; Obey His Commandments (14:21)
    C. Love Jesus; Do What He Says (14:23)
    D. Don't Love Jesus; Don't Do What He Says (14:24)
    E. Holy Spirit Promised (14:26)
6. Parable of the Vine & the Branches (15:01—15:17)
7. The Hatred of Unbelievers Toward Believers (15:18—15:25)
8. The Spirit of Truth (15:26—16:04)
9. Jesus Teaches About the Holy Spirit (16:05—16:15)
    A. Jesus to Send the Holy Spirit (16:05—07)
    B. Holy Spirit Will Convince World Of: (16:08—11)
        1. The World's Sin (16:08)

        2. God's Righteousness (16:09)
        3. Coming Judgment (16:10)
    C. Prince of the World (Satan) Judged (16:11)
    D. Role of the Holy Spirit (16:12—15)
10. Praying in Jesus' Name (16:16—16:30)
11. Jesus Predicts His Disciples to be Scattered (16:31—16:33)
12. Jesus Prays for Himself (17:01—17:05)
13. Jesus Prays for His Disciples (17:06—17:19)
14. "Unity of Believers" Prayer (17:20—17:23)
15. Jesus Prays for All Believers (17:24—17:26)

B. The Death of Jesus Christ, the Son of God **(18:01—19:42)**

1. Jesus Is Arrested (18:01—18:09)
2. Peter Cuts Off Ear of High Priest Servant (18:10—18:11)
3. Annas Questions Jesus (18:12—18:24)
4. Peter Denies Knowing Jesus (18:25—18:27)
5. Jesus' Trial Before Pilate (18:28—18:37)
6. Jesus Handed Over to be Crucified by Pilate (18:38—19:16)
7. Jesus Led Away to be Crucified (19:17—19:18)
8. Pilate Posts a Title for the Cross (19:19—19:22)
9. Soldiers Casts Lots for Jesus' Clothing (19:23—19:24)
10. John (Apostle) Becomes Mary's Son (19:25—19:27)
11. Jesus Dies on the Cross (19:28—19:37)
12. Jesus Buried in Tomb Bought by Joseph of Arimathea (19:38—19:42)

C. The Resurrection of Jesus Christ, the Son of God **(20:01—21:25)**

1. Supernatural Resurrection of Jesus Christ from the Dead (20:01—20:10)
2. Jesus Appears to Mary Magdalene (20:11—20:18)
3. Jesus' First Appearance to Disciples; Minus Thomas (20:19—20:25)
4. Jesus' Second Appearance to Disciples; Plus Thomas (20:26—20:29)
5. Purpose of Writing the Gospels (20:30—20:31)
6. Jesus' Third Appearance to Disciples; At Sea of Galilee (21:01—21:14)
    A. Seven Disciples Go Fishing (21:01—04)
    B. Disciples Return Empty-Handed (21:05—05)
    C. Jesus Tells Them to Cast Net on Right Side (21:06—06)
    D. Jesus Appears to the Seven at the Shore (21:07—07)
    E. Peter Drags 153 Fish to Shore in a Net (21:08—09)
    F. Jesus & Disciples Ate Fried Fish for Breakfast (21:10—14)
7. Jesus Asks Peter Three Times "Do You Love Me" (21:15—21:17)
8. Prediction of Peter's Death by Crucifixion (21:18—21:19)
9. Jesus Talks with Peter About John (21:20—21:23)
10. John Identifies Himself as Writer of this Gospel (21:24—21:25)

ACTS
(1:01—28:31)

1. **The Ministry of Peter, Apostle of Jesus Christ** **(1:01—8:03)**

A. The Beginning of the Church **(1:01—2:47)**

1. Introduction to the Book of Acts (1:01—1:03)
2. The Promise of the Holy Spirit (1:04—1:08)
3. The Prayer Meeting in the Upper Room (1:09—1:14)
4. Matthias Appointed One of the Twelve (1:15—1:26)
5. The Holy Spirit Comes; Church Is Born (2:01—2:03)
6. They All Speak in Other Tongues (2:04—2:13)
7. Peter Explains Pentecost; Prophecy of Joel (2:14—2:36)
8. The Early Church Grows (2:37—2:47)

B. The Progression of the Church **(3:01—8:03)**

1. Lame Man Healed Through Peter & John (3:01—3:11)
2. Peter's Second Sermon in Solomon's Portico (3:12—3:26)
3. Peter & John Arrested (4:01—4:04)
4. Peter Addresses the Sanhedrin (4:05—4:12)
5. The Name of Jesus Forbidden (4:13—4:22)
6. The Apostle's Pray for Boldness (4:23—4:31)
7. Early Church Share in All Things (4:32—4:37)
8. Ananias Lies to Holy Spirit; Result=Death (5:01—5:06)
9. Sapphira Lies to Holy Spirit; Result=Death (5:07—5:11)
10. Apostles Perform Many Signs & Wonders (5:12—5:16)
11. Angel of the *LORD* Sets Apostles Free (5:17—5:21)
12. Apostles Go on Trial Again (5:22—5:32)
13. Gamaliel's Advice (5:33—5:42)
14. Seven Deacons Chosen to Serve (6:01—6:07)
15. Stephen Accused of Blasphemy (6:08—6:11)
16. Stephen Arrested (6:12—6:15)
17. Stephen Addresses the Council (7:01—7:53)
18. Stephen Stoned (7:54—7:60)
19. Saul Begins His Persecution of the Church (8:01—8:03)

2. **The Church Expands to Samaria & to Gaza** **(8:04—12:25)**

A. Followers of Jesus Christ Scatter to the Countryside **(8:04—11:30)**

1. Phillips Preaches in Samaria (8:04—8:08)
2. Simon, the Sorcerer Come to Faith in Christ (8:09—8:13)
3. The Sin of the Former Sorcerer Simon (8:14—8:25)
4. Philip Witnesses to an Ethiopian; He Comes to Faith (8:26—8:40)
5. Conversion of Saul on Road to Damascus (9:01—9:09)
6. Saul Baptized by Ananias (9:10—9:19)
7. Saul Escapes Death in Damascus (9:20—9:25)
8. Saul Preaches in Jerusalem (9:26—9:30)
9. The Church Grows in Strength & Numbers (9:31—9:31)
10. Peter Heals Paralyzed Man Named Aeneas (9:32—9:35)
11. Dorcas (Tabitha) Raised Back to Life (9:36—9:43)
12. Cornelia Sends for Peter in Joppa (10:01—10:09)

A. Angel Appears to Cornelius (10:01—04)
B. Angel Tells Cornelia to Send for Peter (10:05—09)

13. Peter Has Same Vision Three Times (10:10—10:16)
14. Peter Perplexed Concerning the Vision (10:17—10:17)
15. Peter Meets with Cornelius (10:18—10:33)
16. Peter Preaches the Good News to the Gentiles (10:34—10:43)
17. Holy Spirit Falls on the Gentiles (10:44—10:48)
18. Peter Defends the Grace of God (11:01—11:18)
19. The Church at Antioch (11:19—11:30)
    A. Believers from Jerusalem Preach to Jews (11:19—19)
    B. Believers from Cyprus Preach to Gentiles (11:20—21)
    C. Barnabas Sent to Antioch (11:22—24)
    D. Barnabas Goes to Taurus to Find Saul (11:25—26)
    E. Agabus Prophesied Famine to Come (11:27—28)
    F. Relief Comes to Judea (11:29—30)

B. King Herod's Persecution of the Church in Antioch **(12:01—12:25)**

1. Apostle James (John's Brother) Killed with the Sword (12:01—12:02)
2. Peter Imprisoned (12:03—12:05)
3. Angel Frees Peter from Prison (12:06—12:11)
4. Peter Goes to Home of Mary, Mother of John Mark (12:12—12:17)
5. King Herod Agrippa Orders Search for Peter (12:18—12:19)
6. King Herod Agrippa Struck with Worms Then Dies (12:20—12:23)
7. Barnabas, Saul & John Mark Return to Jerusalem (12:24—12:25)

3. <u>The Ministry of Paul, an Apostle of Jesus Christ</u> **(13:01—18:21)**

A. Paul's First Missionary Journey (A.D. 48—49) **(13:01—14:28)**

1. Paul & Barnabas Dedicated (13:01—13:03)
2. Paul & Barnabas Preach on Island of Cyprus (13:04—13:05)
3. Paul & Barnabas' Confrontation with Sorcerer Bar-Jesus (13:06—13:12)
4. Paul Preaches at Antioch of Pisidia on First Sabbath (13:13—13:43)
5. Paul Preaches at Antioch on Second Sabbath (13:44—13:52)
6. Paul's Ministry in Iconium (14:01—14:07)
7. Idolatry at Lystra (14:08—14:18)
8. Paul Stoned; Escaped to Derbe with Barnabas (14:19—14:20)
9. Paul & Barnabas Journey Back to Antioch (14:21—14:28)

B. The Council at Jerusalem **(15:01—15:35)**

1. Conflict Over Circumcision (15:01—15:05)
2. Salvation Through Grace (15:06—15:11)
3. Gentiles Are Free from the Law (15:12—15:21)
4. The Jerusalem Decree (15:22—15:29)
5. Paul Sent to Antioch (15:30—15:35)

C. Paul's Second Missionary Journey (A.D. 50—52) **(15:36—18:21)**

1. Division Over John Mark (15:36—15:41)
2. Timothy Circumcised; Joins Paul & Silas (16:01—16:05)
3. The Macedonian Call (16:06—16:10)
4. Lydia Converted & Baptized at Philippi (16:11—16:15)
5. Paul & Silas Imprisoned (16:16—16:24)
6. Philippian Jailer Converted (16:25—16:34)
7. Paul Refuses to Depart Secretly (16:35—16:40)
8. Paul Preaches at Thessalonica (17:01—17:04)
9. Christians—"Turning the World Upside Down" (17:05—17:09)
10. Ministering at Berea (17:10—17:15)
11. Philosophers—"What Does This Babbler Want to Say?" (17:16—17:21)
12. Paul Addresses the Aeropagus at Athens (17:22—17:34)
13. Paul Departs Athens & Goes to Corinth (18:01—18:17)
14. Paul Returns to Antioch (18:18—18:21)

4. <u>Paul's Third Missionary Journey (A.D. 53—57)</u> **(18:22—28:31)**

A. The Power of the Word **(18:22—21:16)**

1. Paul Goes to Caesarea (18:22—18:23)
2. The Ministry of Apollos (18:24—18:28)
3. Disciples of John (Baptist) Baptized by the Holy Spirit (19:01—19:10)
4. Miracles at Ephesus Glorify Jesus (19:11—19:20)
5. The Riot at Ephesus (19:21—19:41)
6. Missionary Journeys in Greece (20:01—20:16)
   - A. In Macedonia—Stayed There Three Months (20:01—06)
   - B. In Troas—Paul Restores Life to Eutychus (20:07—12)
   - C. Troas to Miletus—Hurrying to Jerusalem (20:13—16)
7. Ephesian Elders Exhorted (20:17—20:38)
8. Paul Warned Concerning His Trip to Jerusalem (21:01—21:16)

B. Paul's Journey to Rome **(21:17—28:31)**

1. Paul Addresses False Rumors About Him (21:17—21:25)
2. Paul Arrested in the Temple (21:26—21:36)
3. Paul Addresses the Jerusalem Mob (21:37—22:21)
4. Paul's Roman Citizenship (22:22—22:29)
5. Paul's Defense Before the Sanhedrin (22:30—23:10)
6. Jews Plot to Kill Paul (23:11—23:22)
7. Paul Sent to Felix, the Governor (23:23—23:35)
8. Paul Accused of Sedition (24:01—24:09)
9. Paul's Defense Before Felix, the Governor (24:10—24:21)
10. Felix Procrastinates in Paul's Release (24:22—24:27)
11. Paul Appeals to Caesar (25:01—25:12)
12. Paul Tried Before King Agrippa (25:13—25:27)
13. Paul Explains His Early Life (26:01—26:11)
14. Paul Recounts His Conversion (26:12—26:18)
15. Paul Explains His Life After Conversion (26:19—26:23)
16. Paul Evades King Agrippa's Challenge (26:24—26:32)
17. The Voyage to Rome Finally at Hand (27:01—27:08)

18. Paul's Warning Ignored (27:09—27:12)
19. The Ship Sets Sail to Rome (27:13—27:38)
20. Paul Shipwrecked on Island of Malta (28:01—28:02)
21. Paul Delivered from Viper Attack in Fire (28:03—28:06)
22. Paul Heals All Afflicted on Island of Malta (28:07—28:10)
23. Paul Arrives in Rome (28:11—28:16)
24. Paul's Ministry in Rome (28:17—28:31)

ROMANS
(1:01—16:27)

1. **Introduction to Romans** **(1:01—1:17)**

A. Sinfulness of Man **(1:01—1:17)**

1. Paul's Greeting (1:01—1:07)
2. Paul's Desire to Visit Rome (1:08—1:15)
3. "The Just Shall Live By Faith." (1:16—1:17)

2. **The Condemnation of Sin** **(1:18—3:20)**

A. The Sinfulness of the Gentiles **(1:18—2:16)**

1. The Wrath of God on Unregenerate Man (1:18—1:21)
    A. Perverted Thinking of Unregenerate Man (1:18—23)
    B. God's Judgment for Perverted Thinking (1:24—32)
2. The Righteous Judgment of God (2:01—2:16)

B. The Sinfulness of the Jews **(2:17—3:20)**

1. Jews and Gentiles—Equal Guilt (2:17—2:24)
2. Circumcision Has No Advantages (2:25—2:29)
3. The Judgment of God Is Defended (3:01—3:08)
4. No One Is Guiltless Before God (3:09—3:20)

3. **Justification Imputed Through Jesus Christ** **(3:21—5:21)**

A. The Revelation of Righteousness **(3:21—3:31)**

1. God's Righteousness Through Faith (3:21—3:27)
2. Boasting Is Excluded (3:28—3:31)

B. The Illustration of Righteousness **(4:01—4:25)**

1. Abraham Justified by Faith (4:01—4:08)
2. Abraham Justified Before Circumcision (4:09—4:12)
3. Abraham's Promise Granted Through Faith (4:13—4:25)

C. The Benefits of Righteousness **(5:01—5:21)**

1. Faith Triumphs in Trouble (5:01—5:05)
2. Christ Died in Our Place (5:06—5:11)
3. Death Through Adam; Life Through Christ (5:12—5:21)

4. **Sanctification Imparted Through Jesus Christ** **(6:01—8:39)**

A. The Principles of Sanctification **(6:01—6:23)**

1. Believer's Baptism Into Death (6:01—6:14)
2. Slaves of Sin to Slaves of Righteousness (6:15—6:23)

B. The Practice of Sanctification **(7:01—7:25)**

1. Set Free from the Law (7:01—7:06)
2. Sin's Advantage in the Law (7:07—7:12)
3. The Law Doesn't Save Us from Sin (7:13—7:25)

C. The Power of Sanctification **(8:01—8:39)**

1. No Condemnation in Christ (8:01—8:11)
2. Sonship Through the Holy Spirit (8:12—8:17)
3. Holy Spirit Intercedes for Us (8:18—8:30)
4. The Everlasting Love of God (8:31—8:39)

5. <u>The Vindication of Our Righteousness</u> **(9:01—11:36)**

A. Israel's Past, Present & Future **(9:01—11:36)**

1. Israel's Past (9:01—9:29)
   - A. Rejection of Christ (9:01—05)
   - B. The Purpose of God (9:06—13)
   - C. The Justice of God (9:14—29)
2. Israel's Present (9:30—10:21)
   - A. Israel's Righteousness Not by Faith (9:30—33)
   - B. Israel Needs the Gospel (10:01—13)
   - C. Israel Rejects the Gospel (10:14—21)
3. Israel's Future (11:01—11:36)
   - A. Israel's Rejection Not Total (11:01—10)
   - B. Israel's Rejection Not Final (11:11—36)

6. <u>The Application of Our Righteousness</u> **(12:01—15:13)**

A. Our Responsibilities As Christians **(12:01—15:13)**

1. To Ourselves—Being A Living Sacrifice to God (12:01—12:02)
2. To Our Church Family—Spiritual Gifts (12:03—12:08)
3. To Society—Conduct Yourself Accordingly (12:09—12:21)
4. To the Government—Submit As Unto God Himself (13:01—13:07)
5. To Our Neighbor—Love Your Neighbor (13:08—13:10)
6. To Our Walk—Put on Christ (13:11—13:14)
7. To Other Believers (14:01—15:13)
   - A. The Law of Liberty (14:01—13)
   - B. The Law of Love (14:14—23)
   - C. Bearing Other's Burdens (15:01—06)
   - D. Praise God Together (15:07—13)

7. <u>Paul's Final Greetings and Personal Notes</u> **(15:14—16:27)**

A. Benediction of Paul **(15:14—16:27)**

1. Preached from Jerusalem to Illyricum (15:14—15:21)
2. Paul's Plan to Visit Rome (15:22—15:33)
3. Paul's Praise and Greetings (16:01—16:16)
4. Avoid Divisive People (16:17—16:20)
5. Greetings from Paul's Friends (16:21—16:24)
6. Paul's Final Words (16:25—16:27)

1st CORINTHIANS
(1:01—16:24)

1. **Church Problems Addressed by Paul** **(1:01—1:09)**
   A. Expressions from Paul **(1:01—1:09)**
   1. Paul's Salutation (1:01—1:03)
   2. Paul's Expression of Thanks (1:04—1:09)

2. **Divisions Within the Church** **(1:10—4:21)**
   A. Divisions—The Fact **(1:10—1:17)**
   1. Sectarianism (1:10—1:17)

   B. Divisions—The Cause **(1:18—2:16)**
   1. Worldly Wisdom vs. Heavenly Wisdom (1:18—2:05)
   2. Lack of Spiritual Wisdom (2:06—2:16)

   C. Divisions—The Consequences **(3:01—4:05)**
   1. Our Spiritual Growth is Hindered (3:01—3:09)
   2. Loss of Rewards (3:10—4:05)
      A. By Possessing No Spiritual Wisdom (3:18—23)
      B. Being Faithless (4:01—05)

   D. The Example of Paul **(4:06—4:21)**
   1. Fools for Christ's Sake (4:06—4:13)
   2. Paul's Paternal Care (4:14—4:21)

3. **Disorder in the Church** **(5:01—6:20)**
   A. Immorality Within the Church **(5:01—6:20)**
   1. Incest Reported (5:01—5:08)
   2. Immorality Must Be Judged (5:09—5:13)
   3. Brother Suing Brother (6:01—6:11)
   4. Loose Morals (6:11—6:20)

4. **Questions Addressed from the Corinthian Church** **(7:01—16:24)**
   A. Instructions on Christian Marriage **(7:01—7:40)**
   1. Principles of Christian Marriage (7:01—7:09)
   2. Marriage and Divorce (7:10—7:24)
   3. Instructions to the Virgin and the Widow (7:25—7:38)
   4. Married and Remarriage (7:39—7:40)

   B. Instructions on Christian Freedom **(8:01—10:33)**
   1. Concerning Things Offered to Idols (8:01—8:13)
   2. A Pattern of Self-Denial (9:01—9:18)
   3. Principles for Ministry (9:19—9:27)
      A. The Imperishable Crown (9:24—9:25)
   4. Avoid Self-Indulgence (10:01—10:13)
   5. Avoid Feasts with Pagans (10:14—10:33)

   C. Instructions on Public Worship **(11:01—14:40)**
   1. Head Coverings for Women (11:01—11:16)

2. Concerning the *LORD's* Supper (11:17—11:34)
3. Concerning Spiritual Gifts (12:01—12:11)
A. Manifestations of the Holy Spirit (12:07—10)
4. Unity and Diversity (12:12—12:31)
5. Love—The Greatest Gift (13:01—13:13)
6. The Superiority of Prophecy (14:01—14:03)
7. Gift of Tongues (14:04—14:19)
8. Tongues—A Sign to Unbelievers (14:20—14:25)
9. Exercising Gifts in Public Worship (14:26—14:40)

D. Instructions on the Resurrection (15:01—15:58)
1. The Risen Christ, Faith's Reality (15:01—15:11)
2. The Risen Christ, Our Hope (15:12—15:19)
3. Death—The Last Enemy Destroyed (15:20—15:28)
4. "Evil Company Corrupts Good Morals." (15:29—15:34)
5. The Resurrection Body (15:35—15:50)
6. The Believer's Final Victory Through Christ (15:51—15:58)

E. Instructions on Personal Matters (16:01—16:24)
1. The Collection for the Jerusalem Saints (16:01—16:04)
2. Paul's Plans to Visit Corinth (16:05—16:09)
3. Paul's Final Exhortations (16:10—16:24)

2nd CORINTHIANS
(1:01—13:14)

1. Paul's Second Missionary Journey to Corinth (1:01—1:11)
A. Paul Explains Himself (1:01—1:11)
1. Paul's Greeting (1:01—1:02)
2. Comfort of God in Times of Tribulation (1:03—1:07)
3. Paul Delivered from Suffering in Asia (1:08—1:11)

2. Paul Explains His Change of Plans (1:12—2:11)
A. Constructive Criticism Necessary (1:12—2:11)
1. Paul's Original Plan (1:12—1:22)
2. Paul's Change of Plans (1:23—2:04)
3. Paul Says, "Forgive the Offender" (2:05—2:11)

3. The Ministry of Paul, an Apostle of Jesus Christ (2:12—13:14)
A. Paul Defends His Ministry (2:12—5:21)
1. Triumph in Christ (2:12—2:17)
2. Changed Lives (3:01—3:03)
3. Letter of the Law Kills; The Spirit Gives Life (3:04—3:18)
4. The Light of the Gospel of Christ (4:01—4:06)
5. Circumstances of Ministry (4:07—4:18)
6. The Assurance of Resurrection (5:01—5:08)
7. The Judgment Seat of Christ (5:09—5:11)
8. Be Reconciled to God (5:12—5:19)
9. Ambassadors for Christ (5:20—5:21)

B. Marks of the Ministry **(6:01—7:16)**

1. Today Is the Day of Salvation (6:01—6:10)
2. Be Holy (6:11—6:18)
3. The Repentance of the Corinthians (7:01—7:12)
4. Comforted in Your Comfort (7:13—7:16)

C. Paul Defends the Collection **(8:01—9:15)**

1. Principles in Giving—Excel in Giving (8:01—8:06)
2. Purposes for Giving—Christ Our Pattern (8:07—8:15)
3. Policies in Giving—Collection for the Saints (8:16—9:05)
4. Promises in Giving—The Cheerful Giver (9:06—9:15)

D. Paul Defends His Authority **(10:01—13:14)**

1. The Spiritual War (10:01—10:06)
2. Paul's Authority Is Real (10:07—10:11)
3. Limitations of Paul's Authority (10:12—10:18)
4. Paul's Concern for the Corinthian's Faithfulness (11:01—11:04)
5. False Apostles Are Workers of Satan (11:05—11:15)
6. Hesitant to Boast (11:16—11:21)
7. Paul's Vision of Paradise (12:01—12:06)
8. Paul's Thorn in the Flesh (12:07—12:10)
9. Paul's Unselfishness (12:11—12:18)
10. Paul's Appeal for Repentance (12:19—12:21)
11. Paul's Exhortation to Examine Yourselves (13:01—13:06)
12. Nothing Against the Truth, But for the Truth (13:07—13:10)
13. Final Farewells and Exhortations (13:11—13:14)

GALATIANS
(1:01—6:18)

1. **Introduction to Galatians** **(1:01—1:10)**

A. Authenticity of the Gospel **(1:01—1:10)**

1. Greetings—Grace to You (1:01—1:05)
2. Concern—Departing from Grace (1:06—1:10)

2. **Paul Defends "Justification By Faith"** **(1:11—6:18)**

A. Authenticity of the Gospel **(1:11—2:21)**

1. Paul's Call to Apostleship (1:11—1:17)
2. Paul's First Trip to Jerusalem as a Christian (1:18—1:24)
3. Paul's Authority Approved in Jerusalem (2:01—2:10)
4. Paul Rebukes Peter (2:11—2:16)
5. Crucified with Christ—Legally and Relationally (2:17—2:21)

B. Superiority of the Gospel **(3:01—3:31)**

1. Justification by Faith (3:01—3:25)
   - A. Not by the Law (3:01—09)
   - B. The Law Brings a Curse (3:10—14)
   - C. Abrahamic Covenant—Not Annulled or Voided (3:15—18)

D. Purpose of the Law (3:19—22)
E. Believers No Longer Under a Tutor (3:23—25)
2. Heirs of God Through Christ (3:26—4:07)
3. Fears for the Church (4:08—4:20)
4. The Two Covenants (4:21—4:31)
A. The One from Mount Sinai—Bondage (4:21—25)
B. The One from Jerusalem—Freedom (4:26—31)

C. Freedom of the Gospel (5:01—6:18)
1. Christian Liberty (5:01—6:10)
A. The Position—"Stand Fast" (5:01—06)
B. The Practice—"Love One Another" (5:07—15)
C. The Power—"Walk in the Spirit" (5:16—26)
D. The Performance—"Bear and Share Burdens" (6:01—10)
2. Glory Only in the Cross (6:11—6:15)
3. Final Exhortations (6:16—6:18)

EPHESIANS
(1:01—6:24)

1. **Greetings from Paul, the Apostle (1:01—1:02)**
A. Greetings from Paul to the Church of Ephesus (1:01—1:02)

2. **The Position of the Believers in Christ (1:03—3:21)**
A. Unity in Christ (1:03—3:21)
1. Redemption in Christ (1:03—1:14)
2. Prayer for Spiritual Wisdom (1:15—1:23)
3. Saved by Grace Through Faith (2:01—2:10)
4. Christians—Once Gentiles in the Flesh (2:11—2:13)
5. Christ—Our Peace (2:14—2:18)
6. Christ—Our Cornerstone (2:19—2:22)
7. The Revelation of the Church (3:01—3:15)
A. Knowledge in the Mystery (3:01—07)
B. Purpose of the Mystery (3:08—13)
C. Appreciation of the Mystery (3:14—21)

3. **The Practice of the Believers in Christ (4:01—6:24)**
A. In the Body of Christ (4:01—4:16)
1. Walking in Unity (4:01—4:06)
2. Spiritual Gifts (4:07—4:16)
A. Measure of Christ's Gift (4:07—10)
B. Leadership Gifts (4:11—11)
C. Purpose of the Gifts (4:12—16)

B. In Our Personal Life (4:17—5:21)
1. The New Man (4:17—4:24)
2. Do Not Grieve the Holy Spirit (4:25—4:32)
3. Walking in Love (5:01—5:07)
4. Walk as Children of Light (5:08—5:14)

5. Walk in Wisdom (5:15—5:21)

C. In Our Home Life (5:22—6:09)

1. Marriage (5:22—6:09)
   - A. Wives—Submit to Your Husbands (5:22—24)
   - B. Husbands—Love Your Wives (5:25—33)
   - C. Children—Obey Your Parents (6:01—04)
   - D. Employees—Obey Your Employers (6:05—09)

D. The Whole Armor of God (6:10—6:20)

1. The Armor of God (6:10—6:20)

Armor	Purpose	
A. Belt	Truth	(6:14a)
B. Breastplate	Righteousness	(6:14b)
C. Shoes	Readiness to Go	(6:15)
D. Shield	Faith	(6:16)
E. Helmet	Salvation	(6:17a)
F. Sword of Spirit	Word of God	(6:17b)

E. Final Exhortations (6:21—6:24)

PHILIPPIANS
(1:01—4:23)

1. **Introduction and Greetings (1:01—1:11)**

A. Greetings from Paul (1:01—1:11)

1. Greeting (1:01—1:02)
2. Thankfulness and Prayer (1:03—1:11)

2. **Paul's Present Circumstances (1:12—1:30)**

A. Joy in Suffering (1:12—1:30)

1. Christ Is Preached in Midst of Imprisonment (1:12—1:18)
2. To Live Is Christ, Die Is Gain (1:19—1:26)
3. Standing Fast in One Spirit (1:27—1:30)

B. Joy in Serving (2:01—2:30)

1. Humility in the Body of Christ (2:01—2:30)
   - A. Unity Through Humility (2:01—04)
   - B. Christ's Example (2:05—11)
   - C. Paul's Example (2:12—18)
   - D. Timothy's Example (2:19—24)
   - E. Epaphroditus' Example (2:25—30)

C. Joy in Believing (3:01—4:01)

1. Take No Confidence in the Flesh (3:01—3:12)
2. Pressing Toward the Goal (3:13—3:16)
3. Do Not Live for the Flesh (3:17—4:01)

D. Joy in Giving (4:02—4:19)

1. Be of Same Mind in the *LORD* (4:02—4:03)

2. Be Anxious for Nothing (4:04—4:07)
3. Things to Meditate On (4:08—4:09)
4. Peace in All Circumstances (4:10—4:19)

E. Final Exhortations **(4:21—4:23)**
1. Greetings (4:21—4:22)
2. True Secret of Joy (4:23—4:23)

COLOSSIANS
(1:01—4:18)

1. **Introduction to the Colossians** **(1:01—1:08)**
A. Greetings from Paul **(1:01—1:02)**
1. Paul Gives Thanks for the Colossians (1:03—1:08)

2. **The Preeminence of Christ in the Church** **(1:09—3:11)**
A. Supremacy of Christ **(1:09—3:11)**
1. In Creation (1:09—1:18)
2. In Redemption (1:19—1:23)
3. In the Church (1:24—1:29)

B. Our Freedom in Christ **(2:01—3:11)**
1. Not Philosophy, But Christ (2:01—2:10)
2. Not Legalism, But Christ (2:11—2:19)
3. Not Regulations, But Christ (2:20—2:23)
4. Not Carnality, But Christ (3:01—3:11)

3. **What Christians Should Do** **(3:12—4:06)**
A. Character of the New Man **(3:12—3:17)**
1. Virtues of the Spirit-Filled Believer (3:12—3:17)
2. The Christian Home (3:18—3:25)
3. The Christian Workplace (3:26—4:01)

B. Christian Graces
1. Prayer Encouraged **(4:02—4:06)**

4. **Final Exhortations** **(4:07—4:18)**
A. Final Greetings **(4:07—4:15)**
1. Closing Blessings (4:16—4:18)

1st THESSALONIANS
(1:01—5:28)

1. **Introduction to 1st Thessalonians** **(1:01—1:01)**
A. Greetings from Paul, Silvanus and Timothy **(1:01—1:01)**

2. **Paul's Commendation of the Thessalonians** **(1:02—2:12)**
A. The Thessalonians Faithfulness to the *LORD* **(1:02—2:12)**
1. Their Good Example (1:01—1:10)
2. Paul's Conduct Among the Thessalonians (2:01—2:12)

3. **Paul's Concern for the Thessalonians** (2:13—3:13)

A. Their Tribulations (2:13—3:05)

1. For Their Sufferings (2:13—2:20)
2. Concern for Their Faith (3:01—3:05)

B. Timothy Visits the Thessalonians (3:06—3:13

1. Timothy Encourages the Thessalonians (3:06—3:10)
2. Prayer for the Church (3:11—3:13)

4. **Thessalonians Receive Instructions from Paul** (4:01—5:28)

A. Watchfulness for the *LORD* (4:01—5:28)

1. Paul's Plea for Purity for the Thessalonians (4:01—4:08)
2. Mind Your Own Business (4:09—4:12)
3. The Comfort of the Coming of the *LORD* (4:13—4:18)
4. The Day of the *LORD* (5:01—5:11)
5. Final Exhortations (5:12—5:22)
   A. Recognize Those Over You in the *LORD* (5:12—13)
   B. Warn the Unruly; Be Patient With All (5:14—14)
   C. Render No Evil for Evil (5:15—15)
   D. Rejoice Always (5:16—16)
   E. Pray Without Ceasing (5:17—17)
   F. In Everything, Give Thanks (5:18—18)
   G. Do Not Quench the Spirit (5:19—19)
   H. Do Not Despise Prophecies (5:20—20)
   I. Test All Things; Hold Fast What Is Good (5:21—21)
   J. Abstain From Every Form of Evil (5:22—22)
6. Blessings and Admonition (5:23—5:28)

2nd THESSALONIANS
(1:01—3:18)

1. **Introduction to 2nd Thessalonians** (1:01—1:02)

A. Greetings from Paul, Silvanus & Timothy (1:01—1:02)

2. **Encouragement in Persecution** (1:03—1:12)

A. The Bright Hope of the Return of the *LORD* (1:03—1:12)

1. Thankfulness for Their Faith Growth (1:03—1:04)
2. Encouragement in Trials & Persecutions (1:05—1:10)
3. Prayer to be Counted Worthy (1:11—1:12)

3. **The Day of the *LORD*** (2:01—2:17)

A. Explanation of the Day of the *LORD* (2:01—2:17)

1. Relating to the Great Apostasy (2:01—2:03a)
2. Relating to the Man of Sin Revealed (2:03b—2:05)
3. The Restrainer (Holy Spirit) Taken Out of the Way (2:06—2:07)
4. The Second Coming of Christ (2:08—2:12)
5. Stand Fast (2:13—2:17)

B. Living in the Light of Christ's Return **(3:01—3:18)**
1. Confidence in the *LORD* (3:01—3:05)
2. Warning Against Idleness (3:06—3:15)
3. Benediction (3:16—3:18)

1st TIMOTHY
(1:01—6:21)

1. <u>Introduction to 1st Timothy</u> **(1:01—1:02)**
A. Paul's Greeting to Timothy **(1:01—1:02)**

2. <u>Precepts Concerning Doctrine</u> **(1:03—1:20)**
A. Paul's Exhortations Concerning Doctrine **(1:03—1:20)**
1. Warning Against False Doctrine (1:01—1:11)
2. Thankfulness for the Grace of God (1:12—1:17)
3. Paul's Charge to Timothy (1:18—1:20)

B. Paul's Exhortations to the Church **(2:01—3:16)**
1. Prayer in the Church (2:01—2:08)
2. Men and Women in the Church (2:09—2:15)
3. Qualifications for Overseers (3:01—3:07)
4. Qualifications for Deacons (3:08—3:13)
5. Mystery of Godliness (3:14—3:16)

C. Paul's Exhortations to Leaders **(4:01—4:16)**
1. The Great Apostasy (4:01—4:05)
2. A Good Minister of Jesus Christ (4:06—4:11)
3. Take Heed to Yourself and to the Doctrine (4:12—4:16)

D. Paul's Exhortations in Church Discipline **(5:01—5:25)**
1. Treatment of Church Members (5:01—5:02)
2. Treatment of True Widows (5:03—5:10)
3. Treatment of Younger Widows (5:11—5:16)
4. Treatment of the Elders of the House of God (5:17—5:20)
5. Do Nothing with Partiality (5:21—5:25)

E. Paul's Exhortations in Other Duties **(6:01—6:21)**
1. Servant's Treatment to Their Masters (6:01—6:02)
2. Godliness with Contentment Is Great Gain (6:03—6:10)
3. The Good Confession (6:11—6:16)
4. Instructions to the Rich (6:17—6:19)
5. Guard the Faith (6:20—6:21)

2nd TIMOTHY
(1:01—4:22)

1. <u>Introduction to 2nd Timothy</u> **(1:01—1:02)**
A. Greetings from Paul to Timothy **(1:01—1:02)**

2. **<u>Paul Charges Timothy to Persevere in the Present</u>** **(1:03—1:18)**

A. Foundations of Christian Service **(1:03—1:18)**

1. Paul's Expression of Thanks to Timothy (1:03—1:07)
2. Not Ashamed of the Gospel (1:08—1:12)
3. Loyalty to the Faith (1:13—1:18)

B. Characteristics of a Faithful Minister **(2:01—2:26)**

1. He Is Strong in the Grace (2:01—2:02)
2. He Is Single-Minded (2:03—2:04)
3. He Is Strict and Enduring (2:05—2:13)
4. He Is a Diligent Worker (2:14—2:19)
5. He Is a Sanctified Vessel Useful for the Master (2:20—2:23)
6. He Is a Gentle Servant (2:24—2:26)

3. **<u>Paul Charges Timothy to Persevere in the Future</u>** **(3:01—4:05)**

A. Difficult Times for Christian Service **(3:01—4:05)**

1. The Coming of Perilous Times (3:01—3:09)
2. Confronting the Perilous Times (3:10—3:15)
3. Scripture Given by Inspiration of God (3:16—3:17)
4. Charge to Preach the Word (4:01—4:05)

B. Paul's Valedictory **(4:06—4:22)**

1. Paul's Hope in Death (4:06—4:09)
   - A. Life Poured Out As an Offering (4:06—06)
   - B. Fought a Good Fight (4:07—07)
   - C. Crown of Righteousness (4:08—09)
2. Paul—The Abandoned Apostle (4:10—4:16)
3. The Faithful *LORD* (4:17—4:18)
4. Closing Exhortation (4:19—4:21)
5. Paul's Farewell (4:22—4:22)

<u>TITUS</u>
(1:01—3:15)

1. **<u>Introduction to Titus</u>** **(1:01—1:04)**

A. Greetings from Paul to Titus **(1:01—1:04)**

2. **<u>Elders in the Church</u>** **(1:05—1:16)**

A. Leadership in the Church **(1:05—1:16)**

1. Qualified Elders (1:05—1:09)
2. Rebuke False Teachers (1:10—1:16)

3. **<u>Operation of the Church</u>** **(2:01—2:15)**

A. Right Living in the Church **(2:01—2:15)**

1. Qualities of a Sound Church (2:01—2:10)
2. Trained by Saving Grace (2:11—2:15)

B. Right Living in Society **(3:01—3:15)**

1. Graces of the Heirs of Christ (3:01—3:08)
2. Avoid Dissension (3:09—3:11)

3. Final Messages (3:12—3:14)
4. Farewell (3:15—3:15)

PHILEMON
(1—25)

1. **Introduction to Philemon** **(1—3)**
   A. Greetings from Paul and Timothy **(1—3)**

2. **Praise for Philemon** **(4—7)**
   A. Paul's Appreciation of Philemon **(4—7)**
   1. Philemon's Love and Faith (4—7)

3. **Paul's Plea to Philemon** **(8—25)**
   A. Paul's Appeal for Onesimus **(8—25)**
   1. The Plea for Onesimus (8—16)
   2. Philemon's Obedience Encouraged (17—22)
   3. Farewell (23—25)

HEBREWS
(1:01—13:25)

1. **The Superiority of the Person of Jesus Christ** **(1:01—4:13)**
   A. Christ Is Greater Than the Angels **(1:01—2:18)**
   1. God's Supreme Revelation (1:01—1:04)
      A. Jesus Christ—Complete Expression of God (1:01—03)
      B. Jesus—Far Greater Than the Angels (1:04—04)
   2. The Son Exalted Above the Angels (1:05—1:14)
      A. God Says to Jesus—"You Are My Son" (1:05—05)
      B. Let All the Angels of God Worship Him (1:06—07)
      C. God's Throne Endures Forever & Ever (1:08—08)
      D. Love What Is Right, Hate What Is Wrong (1:09—09)
      E. Jesus' Authority Established Over All Creation (1:10—14)
   3. Do Not Neglect the Salvation (2:01—2:04)
      A. Listening to Christ Means Hearing & Obeying (2:01—03)
      B. God's Word Verified by Signs & Wonders (2:04—04)
   4. Son Made Lower Than the Angels for a Little While (2:05—2:09)
      A. Future World Not Controlled by Angels (2:05—05)
      B. Jesus—Given Authority Over All Things (2:06—09)
         1. Jesus Crowned With Glory & Honor (2:07)
         2. Nothing Is Left Out (2:08)
         3. Now Crowned with Glory & Honor (2:09)
   5. Bringing Many Sons to Glory (2:10—2:18)
      A. Our Suffering Makes Us Sensitive Servants (2:10—10)
      B. Jesus Calls His Holy Believers Brothers & Sisters (2:11—12)

C. Christ As Man, Died As Savior, Raised As God (2:13—14)
D. Death—Doorway to Eternal Life (2:15—15)
E. Jesus' Sacrificial Death (2:16—18)

B. Christ Is Greater Than Moses **(3:01—4:13)**
1. Jesus' Relationship to Believers (3:01—3:06)
   A. Messenger of God & High Priest to Believers (3:01—03)
   B. Ruler of Entire Household of God (3:04—06)
2. The **"<u>Catastrophe</u>"** of Unbelief (3:07—3:19)
   A. Do Not Harden Your Hearts Against Him (3:07—08)
   B. Do Not Turn Your Heart Away from the *LORD* (3:09—10)
   C. Penalty—Will **<u>NOT</u>** Enter His Rest (Heaven) (3:11—11)
   D. Have No Evil or Unbelieving Heart (3:12—19)
      1. Have No Evil or Unbelieving Heart (3:12)
      2. Warn Each Other Every Day (3:13)
      3. Be Faithful to the End (3:14)
      4. Trust God As You Did in the Beginning (3:14)
      5. Reward = Share All That Belongs to Christ (3:14)
      6. Never Forget the Warning (3:15)
      7. The People Who Rebelled (3:16—19)
3. The **"<u>Consequences</u>"** of Unbelief (4:01—4:10)
   A. God Has Prepared a Place of Rest (4:01—02)
   B. **<u>ONLY</u>** Those Who Truly Believe Enters It (4:03—09)
   C. All Who Enter Will Find Rest (4:10—10)
4. The **"<u>Cure</u>"** for Unbelief (4:11—4:13)
   A. Anyone Who Disobeys God Will Fall (4:11—11)
   B. Word of God—Living, Powerful, Sharp, Piercing & Discerner (4:12—12)
   C. All Things Are Naked & Open to Him (4:13—13)

2. <u>The Superiority of the Work of Jesus Christ</u> **(4:14—10:18)**

A. Christ Is Greater Than Old Testament Priesthood **(4:14—10:18)**
1. Our Compassionate High Priest (4:14—4:16)
2. Christ Is Superior in His Qualifications (5:01—5:11)
   A. The Aaronic Priesthood (5:01—04)
   B. The Melchizedek Priesthood (5:05—11)
3. Peril of Not Maturing (5:12—6:20)
   A. Spiritual Immaturity (5:12—14)
   B. Need for Maturity (6:01—08)
   C. Encouragement to Maturity (6:09—20)
4. Christ Is Superior in the Order of His Priesthood (7:01—7:28)
   A. Description of Melchizedek's Order (7:01—03)
   B. Superiority of Melchizedek's Order (7:04—10)
   C. Need for New Priesthood (7:11—19)
   D. Greatness of the New Priest (7:20—28)
5. Christ's Covenant Is Greater Than the Old Covenant (8:01—8:13)
   A. The New Priestly Service (8:01—06)
   B. A New Covenant (8:07—13)
6. Christ Is Superior in His Priestly Ministry (9:01—10:18)

A. Old Testament Priestly Ministry (9:01—10)
1. The Earthly Sanctuary (9:01—05)
2. Limitations of the Earthly Service (9:06—10)
B. New Testament Priestly Ministry (9:11—10:18)
1. The Heavenly Sanctuary (9:11—15)
2. The Mediator's Death Necessary (9:16—28)
3. Animal Sacrifices Insufficient (10:01—04)
4. Christ's Death Fulfills God's Will (10:05—10)
5. Christ's Death Perfects the Sanctified (10:11—18)

3. <u>The Superiority of Faith by the Christian</u> (10:19—13:25)

A. Full Assurance of Faith (10:19—11:40)

1. Hold Fast Your Confession (10:19—10:29)
2. The Just Shall Live by Faith (10:30—10:39)
A. Terrible Thing to Fall In Hands of **THE** Living God (10:30—31)
B. Remember Early Days After Salvation in Christ (10:32—34)
1. You Remained Faithful (10:32)
2. You Were Exposed to Ridicule (10:33a)
3. You Were Beaten (10:33b)
4. You Helped Others Suffering (10:33c)
5. You Suffered with Those in Jail (10:34a)
6. When All Possessions Were Taken (10:34b)
C. Confident Trust in the *LORD* (10:35)
D. Patient Endurance (10:36)
E. He Is Coming & Will Not Tarry (10:37)
F. No Pleasure in He Who Abandons the Faith (10:38)
G. True Believers (10:39)
1. Do Not Abandon the Faith (10:39a)
2. Their Souls Are Saved (10:39b)
3. The Definition of Faith (11:01—11:03)
A. Substance of Things Hoped For (11:01a)
B. Evidence of Things Not Seen (11:01b)
C. By Faith Elders Obtain Good Testimony (11:02)
D. Word of God Framed Worlds (11:03a)
E. Things Seen Not Made by Things Visible (11:03b)
4. Models of Faith (11:04—11:40)
A. Abel (11:04—04)
B. Enoch (11:05—06)
C. Noah (11:07—07)
D. Abraham and Sarah (11:08—19)
E. Isaac (11:20—20)
F. Jacob (11:21—21)
G. Joseph (11:22—22)
H. Parents of Moses (11:23—23)
I. Moses (11:24—29)
J. Joshua and the Israelites (11:30—30)
K. Rahab (11:31—31)
L. Gideon and Barak (11:32—32)
M. Samson and Jephthah (11:32—32)

N. David, Samuel and the Prophets (11:32—32)
O. Many Others (11:33—40)

B. The Endurance of Faith **(12:01—13:25)**

1. The Race of Faith (12:01—12:02)
   A. Requires Us to Give Up What Hinders Us (12:01—02)
      1. Sin Hinders Our Progress (12:01—01)
      2. We Should Run With Endurance (12:01—02)
      3. Keep Your Eyes Upon Jesus (12:02—02)
2. The Discipline of God (12:03—12:11)
   A. Suffering Is Training Ground (12:03—04)
   B. Do Not Ignore Discipline (12:05)
   C. The *LORD* Disciplines Those He Loves (12:06)
   D. Endure His Divine Discipline (12:07)
   E. No Discipline = Illegitimate Child (12:08)
   F. Submit to Discipline of the Heavenly Father (12:09)
   G. God's Discipline Is Always Right & Good (12:10)
   H. No Discipline Is Enjoyable (12:11)
3. Renew Your Spiritual Vitality (12:12—12:17)
   A. Take A New Grip & Stand Firm (12:12—13)
   B. Leave In Peace; Live A Clean & Holy Life (12:14)
   C. Do Not Miss the Special Favor of God (12:15a)
   D. Watch Out for Bitter Roots & Unbelief (12:15b)
   E. Do Not Be Immoral or Godless (12:16)
   F. You Can Be Too Late for Repentance (12:17)
4. The Drive of Life (12:18—12:24)
   A. Not Come to a Physical Mountain (12:18—21)
   B. You Have Come to the City of the Living God (12:22)
   C. You Have Come to God's Assembly (12:23a)
   D. You Have Come to God Himself (12:23b)
   E. You Have Come to Redeemed Spirits in Heaven (12:23c)
   F. You Have Come to Jesus (12:24)
5. Do Not Refuse Him Who Speaks (12:25—12:29)
   A. See To It You Obey God (12:25)
   B. God Will Shake the Earth & Heavens (12:26)
   C. Only Eternal Things Will Be Left (12:27)
   D. Worship God with Holy Fear & Awe (12:28)
   E. Our God Is a Consuming Fire (12:29)
6. Additional Moral Directives (13:01—13:06)
   A. Continue to Love with True Christian Love (13:01)
   B. Do Not Forget to Be Hospitable to Strangers (13:02a)
   C. Some Have Unknowingly Entertained Angels (13:02b)
   D. The Prisons (13:03)
      1. Do Not Forget the People There (13:03a)
      2. Be Sympathetic Concerning Them (13:03b)
      3. Be Sympathetic of the Mistreated (13:03c)
   E. Your Marriage (13:04)
      1. Give Honor to the Marriage (13:04a)
      2. God Will Judge the Immoral (13:04b)

F. Stay Away from the Love of Money (13:05—06)
7. Additional Religious Directives (13:07—13:17)
A. Remember Your Leaders (13:07)
B. Jesus Christ—The Same Today, Yesterday & Forever (13:08)
C. Spiritual Strength & God's Favor (13:09)
D. The Priests in the Temple on Earth (13:10)
E. This World Is Not Our Home (13:11—14)
F. Offer Our Sacrifice of Praise to God (13:15—16)
G. Obey Your Spiritual Leaders (13:17)
8. Requested Prayer (13:18—13:19)
9. Benediction; Final Exhortations and Farewell (13:20—13:25)

<u>JAMES</u>
(1:01—5:20)

1. <u>Introduction to James</u> (1:01—1:01)
A. Greetings from James to the Jewish Christians (1:01—1:01)

2. <u>The Test of Faith</u> (1:02—5:20)
A. Genuine Religion (1:02—1:18)
1. Profiting from Trials (1:02—1:08)
A. Faith & Endurance (1:02—08)
1. Faith Tested; Endurance Grows (1:02—04)
2. Wisdom (1:05—08)
2. Perspectives of Rich & Poor (1:09—1:11)
3. Loving God While In Trials (1:12—1:18)
A. Endure Testing—Receive Crown of Life (1:12—13)
B. Temptations (1:14—18)
1. Comes from Evil Desires (1:14)
2. Leads to Evil Actions (1:15)
3. Evil Actions Leads to Death (1:15)
4. Do Not Be Misled (1:16)
5. Good & Perfect Comes from God (1:17)
6. He Chose to Make Us His Children (1:18)

B. Genuine Faith (1:19—4:10)
1. Faith Obeys the Word (1:19—1:27)
2. Faith Overcomes Discrimination (2:01—2:13)
3. Faith Without Works Is Dead (2:14—2:26)
4. Faith is in Control of the Tongue (3:01—3:12)
5. Faith Produces Wisdom (3:13—3:18)
6. Faith Conquers Strife (4:01—4:06)
7. Faith Produces Humility (4:07—4:10)

C. The Victory of Faith (4:11—5:20)
1. Faith Produces Dependency Upon the *LORD* (4:11—5:06)
2. Faith Produces Patience and Perseverance (5:07—5:12)
3. Faith Heals the Sick (5:13—5:18)
4. Faith Brings Back the Brother in Error (5:19—5:20)

1st PETER
(1:01—5:14)

1. **<u>Introduction to 1st Peter</u>** **(1:01—1:02)**
   - **A. Greetings from Peter to the Elect Pilgrims** **(1:01—1:02)**

2. **<u>The Believer's Salvation in Jesus Christ</u>** **(1:03—1:12)**
   - **A. God's Great Blessings** **(1:03—1:12)**
     - 1. Believer's Hope for the Future (1:03—1:05)
       - A. Salvation Comes from the Mercy of God (1:03)
       - B. Our Priceless Inheritance Is In Heaven (1:04)
       - C. No Trust, No Salvation (1:05)
     - 2. Believer's Trials In This Present Age (1:06—1:09)
       - A. Endure Many Trials to Receive Wonderful Joy (1:06)
       - B. Trials Test Your Faith (1:07)
         - 1. Shows How Strong & Pure It Is (1:07a)
         - 2. Being Tested As Fire Tests (1:07b)
         - 3. If Faith Remains, It Brings You Much Praise, Glory & Honor (1:07c)
       - C. You Do Not See Jesus, But Must Trust Him (1:08)
       - D. Reward for Trusting Jesus Is Salvation (1:09)
     - 3. The Expectation of the Past Coming to the Now (1:10—1:12)

   - **B. The Believer's Sanctification in Jesus Christ** **(1:13—2:10)**
     - 1. Live Holy Before the *LORD* (1:13—1:21)
       - A. Exercise Self-Control (1:13)
       - B. As His Children, We Must Obey God (1:14a)
       - C. Do Not Revert to Old Ways (1:14b)
       - D. Be Holy In Everything You Do (1:15—16)
       - E. God Has **NO** Favorites When He Judges (1:17a)
       - F. He Judges / Rewards According to Your Actions (1:17b)
       - G. Live In Reverent Fear of Him On Earth (1:17c)
       - H. You Were Not Redeemed With Corruptible Things (1:18)
       - I. Redeemed By Precious Blood of Jesus (1:19)
       - J. Jesus Christ—Chosen from Foundation of World (1:20)
       - K. Through Christ, We Come to Trust God (1:21)
     - 2. Love the Brethren (1:22—1:25)
     - 3. Desire the Pure Milk of the *Word* (2:01—2:03)
       - A. Lay Aside All Evil Speaking & Actions (2:01)
       - B. To Grow In Fullness of Your Salvation (2:02)
       - C. Have Taste of the *LORD*'s Graciousness (2:03)
     - 4. You Are a Chosen Generation, A Royal Priesthood (2:04—2:10)

3. **<u>The Submission of the Believer</u>** **(2:11—3:12)**

A. Conduct in the Midst of Living Before the World **(2:11—3:12)**

1. Have Honorable Conduct Before the World (2:11—2:12)
2. Be Submissive to the Government As to the *LORD* (2:13—2:17)
3. Be Submissive to Employers as to the *LORD* (2:18—2:25)
4. Be Submissive to Husbands & Wives (3:01—3:07)
5. Submission to Other Believers (3:08—3:12)

2nd PETER
(1:01—3:18)

1. Introduction to 2nd Peter **(1:01—1:02)**

A. Greetings from Peter to the Faithful **(1:01—1:02)**

2. The Development of Faith **(1:03—1:21)**

A. Guidance for Growing Christians **(1:03—1:21)**

1. Fruitful Growth in the Faith (1:03—1:11)
    - A. Christ Gives What We Need to Live A Godly Life (1:03—11)
        1. Believers Called to Receive His Glory & Goodness (1:03)
        2. Believers Have Received His Rich & Wonderful Promises (1:04a)
        3. Partakers of His Divine Nature (1:04b)
        4. Knowing God Produces Life of Moral Excellence (1:05)
        5. Knowing God Leads To: (1:06—08)
            - A. Self-Control (1:06a)
            - B. Patient Endurance (1:06b)
            - C. Godliness (1:06c)
            - D. Brotherly Kindness (1:07a)
            - E. Genuine Love for Everyone (1:07b)
            - F. You Will Become Fruitful (1:08)
        6. Failure to Develop Virtues Leads to Shortsightedness (1:09)
        7. Be Diligent (1:10)
        8. Reward = Eternal Life with Christ (1:11)
2. Fruitful Grounding in the Faith (1:12—1:21)
    - A. Pay Attention to God's Word (1:12—15)
        1. Do Not Neglect Fundamentals of Our Faith (1:12)
        2. Welcome Constant Reminders (1:13)
        3. Do Not Allow Boredom / Impatience (1:14—15)
    - B. Inspiration of Scripture (1:16—21)

B. Dangers to Growing Christians **(2:01—2:22)**

1. The Destructive Doctrine of False Teachers (2:01—2:03)
    - A. They Teach Destructive Heresies (2:01)
    - B. Many Follow Their Destructive Ways (2:02)
    - C. Greed Is Their Primary Focus (2:03)

2. The Condemnation of False Teachers (2:04—2:11)

A. How It Was Done in the Past (2:04—11)

1. God Did Not Spare Angels Who Sinned (2:04)
2. God Did Not Spare the Ancient World (2:05)
3. Sodom & Gomorrah Turned to Ashes (2:06)
4. God Rescued Lot Out of Sodom (2:07)
5. Lot Was Tormented by Evil of His Day (2:08)
6. Reserves the Unjust for Punishment (2:09)
7. God Is Hard on the Evil & the Lustful (2:10)
8. Angels Don't Speak Against Fallen Angels (2:11)

3. The Depravity of False Teachers (2:12—2:17)

A. Speak Evil About What They Do Not Understand (2:12)

B. Their Destruction Is Their Reward (2:13)

C. Their Deceitfulness (2:14—17)

1. Commit Adultery with Their Eyes (2:14a)
2. Their Lust Never Satisfied (2:14b)
3. Their Lure Unstable People Into Sin (2:14c)
4. Trained to be Greedy (2:14d)
5. They Are Doomed & Cursed (2:14d)
6. They Have Wandered Off the Right Road (2:15)
7. They Are Wells Without Water (2:16)
8. They Are Doomed to Blackest Darkness (2:17)

4. The Deceptions of False Teachers (2:18—2:22)

A. They Brag About Themselves (2:18)

B. They Lure New Believers Back Into Sin (2:19)

C. They Promise Freedom (2:20)

D. Backslidden Believers Who Become Slaves to Sin Again Are Worse Off Than Before (2:21)

E. A Dog Returns to His Vomit (2:22)

C. Hope for Growing Christians **(3:01—3:18)**

1. Promises of God Are Not Slack (3:01—3:09)

2. The "Day of the *LORD*" (3:10—3:13)

A. Will Come As A Thief in the Night (3:10)

B. Heavens Will Pass Away With Terrible Noise (3:11)

C. Everything Will Disappear by Fire (3:12)

D. True Believers Look for the New Heaven (3:13)

3. Grow in the Grace and Knowledge of our *LORD* (3:14—3:18)

A. Live A Pure & Blameless Life (3:14)

B. Jesus Waits for People to be Saved (3:15)

C. Being Ignorant & Unstable Results in Disaster (3:16)

D. Don't Be Carried Away by Wicked People's Errors (3:17)

E. Grow in God's Grace (3:18)

1st JOHN
(1:01—5:21)

1. **Conditions for Fellowship** (1:01—2:27)
   - **A. God Is Light** (1:01—2:27)
     1. What We Have Heard, Seen and Touched (1:01—1:04)
     2. Walk in the Light as Christ **IS** the Light (1:05—1:07)
     3. Our Confession of Sin (1:08—2:02)
        - A. If We Say We Have No Sin, We Fool Ourselves (1:08a)
        - B. If We Refuse to Accept the Truth (1:08b)
        - C. If We Confess Our Sins to God (1:09)
          1. He Is Faithful & Just to Forgive Us (1:09a)
          2. He Cleanses Us from All Unrighteousness (1:09b)
        - D. Results If We Claim We Have Not Sinned (1:10)
          1. We Call God a Liar (1:10a)
          2. His Word Has No Place in Our Hearts (1:10b)
        - E. When We Sin, Jesus Intercedes for Us to God (2:01)
        - F. Jesus Christ Is the Sacrifice for Our Sins (2:02)
     4. The Test of Knowing Jesus as *LORD* (2:03—2:11)
     5. The State of Their Spirituality (2:12—2:14)
     6. Do Not Love the Ways of the World (2:15—2:17)
        - A. What This World System Offers You (2:15—16)
          1. Shows You Do Not Have God's Love In You (2:15)
          2. Lust for Physical Pleasure (2:16a)
          3. Lust of Things We See (2:16b)
          4. Pride In Our Possessions (2:16c)
        - B. Result of Refusing the World System (2:17—17)
          1. Do the Will of God = You Will Live Forever (2:17)
     7. The Spirit of the Anti-Christ (2:18—2:23)
     8. Let Truth Abide in You (2:24—2:27)

2. **Characteristics of Fellowship** (2:28—5:21)
   - **A. God Is Love** (2:28—4:21)
     1. The Children of God (2:28—3:03)
     2. Sin & the Child of God (3:04—3:09)
     3. The Imperative of Love (3:10—3:15)
     4. The Outworking of Love (3:16—3:23)
     5. Test Every Spirit (3:24—4:06)
     6. Knowing God Through Love (4:07—4:11)
     7. Seeing God Through Love (4:12—4:16)
     8. The Consummation of Love (4:17—4:19)
     9. Obedience by Faith (4:20—4:21)

   - **B. God Is Life** (5:01—5:21)
     1. Our Faith—Our Victory Over the World (5:01—5:05)
     2. Our Assurance of Salvation (5:06—5:13)
     3. Confidence & Guidance In Prayer (5:14—5:17)
     4. Freedom from Slavery of Sin (5:18—5:21)

2nd JOHN
(1—13)

1. **Introduction to 2nd John** **(01—03)**
   A. Greetings to the Elect Lady—The Church **(01—03)**

2. **Abiding in the Commandments of God** **(04—06)**
   A. Walking in the Love of God **(04—06)**
      1. Walk In the Truth of God's Word (04—04)
      2. Walking Loving One Another (05—06)

3. **Abiding Not With Deceivers** **(07—11)**
   A. Watch Out For False Teachers **(07—11)**
      1. Beware of Anti-Christ Deceivers (07—09)
      2. Avoid Anti-Christ Deceivers (10—11)

4. **John's Final Words** **(12—13)**
   A. John's Farewell Message **(12—13)**

3rd JOHN
(1—14)

1. **Introduction to 3rd John** **(01—01)**
   A. Greeting to Gaius **(01—01)**

2. **The Influence of Gaius** **(01—08)**
   A. Living by the Standards of the Gospel **(01—08)**
      1. Gaius' Godly Life (01—04)
      2. Gaius' Generosity (05—08)

3. **Diotrephes and Demetrius** **(09—12)**
   A. Diotrephes **(09—11)**
      1. His Selfish Ambition (09—09)
      2. His Selfish Activities (10—11)

   B. Demetrius **(12—12)**
      1. His Good Testimony (12—12)

4. **John's Final Words** **(13—14)**
   A. John's Farewell Message **(13—14)**

JUDE
(1-25)

1. **Introduction to Jude** **(01—02)**
   A. Jude's Greeting to the Called **(01—02)**

2. **The Danger of False Teachers** **(03—16)**
   A. The Exposure of the False Teachers **(03—16)**

1. Believers Are Exhorted to Contend for the Faith (03—04)
2. Judgment of Old Apostates (05—07)
3. Judgment of New Apostates (08—10)
4. Description of False teachers (11—16)

B. Defense Against False Teachers **(17—23)**
1. Apostates Predicted (17—19)
2. Maintain Your Life with God (20—23)

C. Jude's Doxology **(24—25)**
1. Glory to God (24—25)

REVELATION
(1:01—22:21)

1. <u>Introduction to Revelation</u> **(1:01—1:08)**
A. Introduction and Benediction **(1:01—1:03)**
1. Greetings from John to the Seven Churches (1:04—1:08)

2. <u>The Things Which You Have Seen</u> **(1:09—1:20)**
A. The Vision of the Son of Man **(1:09—1:20)**
1. The Circumstances of the Vision (1:09—1:11)
A. Received Vision from Jesus Christ (1:09)
B. Message from Jesus to John (1:10—11)
1. "**I AM"** the Alpha & Omega (1:11a)
2. The First & The Last (1:11b)
3. Send the Message to Seven Churches (1:11c)
2. The Content of the Vision (1:12—1:16)
A. Seven Golden Lampstands (1:12)
B. John Saw **ONE** Like the Son of Man (1:13—16)
1. Description of **ONE** Like the Son of Man (1:13—16)
A. Head & Hair White As Wool (1:14a)
B. Eyes Like a Flaming Fire (1:14b)
C. Feet Like Fine Brass (1:15a)
D. Voice Like Rushing Waters (1:15b)
E. Seven Stars in Right Hand (1:16a)
F. Two-Edged Sword from His Mouth (1:16b)
G. Countenance Like the Sun Shining (1:16b)
3. The Result of the Vision (1:17—1:19)
A. Encouragement from Jesus to John (1:17—19)
1. Do Not Be Afraid (1:17a)
2. "**I AM"** the First & The Last (1:17b)
3. "**I AM"** He Who Lives & Was Dead (1:18a)
4. Behold, "**I AM"** Alive Forevermore (1:18b)
5. I Have Keys to Death & Hades (1:18c)
6. Write Things You Have Seen (1:19a)
7. The Things Which Are (1:19b)
8. The Things Which Will Happen (1:19c)
B. Seven Stars, Seven Golden Lampstands Mystery (1:20—20)

1. Seven Stars Are the Angels of the Seven Churches (1:20a)
2. Seven Lampstands Are the Seven Churches (1:20b)

3. <u>The Things Which Are Being Seen</u> (2:01—3:22)

A. Letters to the Seven Churches (2:01—3:22)

1. Letter to Ephesus—The Loveless Church (2:01—2:07)
   A. Commendations to Church at Ephesus (2:01—03)
      1. Jesus Knew Works, Labor, Patience (2:01—02a)
      2. Being Patient (2:02b)
      3. Did Not Tolerate Sin (2:02c)
      4. False Apostles Exposed (2:02d)
      5. Endured Hardships; No Weariness (2:03)
   B. Words of Correction to Church at Ephesus (2:04—05)
      1. They Lost Their Zeal for God (2:04)
      2. Repent or Lampstand Removed (2:05)
   C. Words of Caution to Church at Ephesus (2:06—07)
      1. Continue to Hate Nicolaitan Practices (2:06)
      2. To the Overcomer—Will Eat from the Tree of Life (2:07)
2. Letter to Smyrna—The Persecuted Church (2:08—2:11)
   A. Edification to Church at Smyrna (2:08—11)
      1. Jesus Knew: (2:08—09)
         A. Works, Troubles, Poverty (2:08)
         B. The Jew's Blasphemy (2:09)
      2. Testing & Rewards (2:10—11)
         A. Some Go to Prison (2:10a)
         B. Be Faithful Unto Death (2:10b)
         C. Reward = Crown of Life (2:10c)
         D. Overcomer Not Hurt by Second Death (2:11)
3. Letter to Pergamos—The Compromising Church (2:12—2:17)
   A. Commendations to Church at Pergamos (2:12—13)
      1. Jesus Knew: (2:12—13)
         A. Their Works (2:13a)
         B. Where They Dwelled (2:13b)
         C. Where Satan's Throne Was (2:13c)
         D. They Kept the Faith (2:13d)
   B. Things Jesus Had Against Pergamos (2:14—15)
      1. They Have People Who Hold to the Doctrine of Balaam (2:14—14)
         A. Doctrine of Balaam
            1. Stumbling Block Before Israel (2:14a)
            2. Foods Sacrificed to Idols (2:14b)
            3. Commit Sexual Immorality (2:14c)
      2. They Have People Who Hold to the Nicolaitans (2:15—15)
   C. Words of Caution to Church at Pergamos (2:16—17)
      1. Repent or Jesus Will Fight Against Them with the Sword of His Mouth (2:16—16)

2. To Him Who Overcomes (2:17—17)
    A. Receive Hidden Manna (2:17a)
    B. Receive a White Stone (2:17b)
    C. Receive a New Name on the Stone (2:17c)

4. Letter to Thyatira—The Corrupt Church (2:18—2:29)
  A. These Things Says the Son of God (2:18—19)
    1. He Knows Their Works, Love, Service, Faith, Patience (2:18—19)
    2. Things Jesus Had Against Thyatira (2:20—29)
      A. Jezebel (2:20—23)
        1. Taught Servants to Commit Sexual Immorality (2:20a)
        2. Eat Things Sacrifice to Idols (2:20b)
        3. Gave Jezebel Time to Repent (2:21)
        4. Unless Repentant, Cast into Great Tribulation (2:22)
        5. Her Children Killed (2:23)
      B. To the Rest of Thyatira (2:24—29)
        1. No Other Burden (2:24)
        2. Hold Fast Until His Return (2:25)
        3. Overcomers to Receive Power Over Nations (2:26)
        4. Jesus Will Rule with Iron Rod (2:27)
        5. Will Give Him the Morning Star (2:28)
        6. Hear What Holy Spirit Says (2:29)

5. Letter to Sardis—The Dead Church (3:01—3:06)
  A. Things Says **He** Who Has the Seven Spirits of God (3:01—06)
    1. He Knows Their Works (3:01a)
    2. They Have a Name to be Alive, But Dead (3:01b—06)
      A. Be Watchful (3:02a)
      B. Strengthen What Remains (3:02b)
      C. Works Not Perfect Before God (3:02c—06)
        1. God's Response (3:02c—06)
          A. Remember How You Have Received & Heard (3:03a)
          B. Hold Fast & Repent (3:03b)
          C. Watch or I Will Come as a Thief (3:03c)
          D. You Will Not Know What Hour (3:03d)
          E. Few in Sardis Are Worthy (3:04a)
          F. He Who Overcomes Will Be Clothed in White Garments (3:05a)
          G. Name Not Blotted Out of the Book of Life (3:05b)
          H. Will Confess Him Before My Father & His Angels (3:05c)
          I. Hear What the Holy Spirit Says (3:06)

6. Letter to Philadelphia—The Faithful Church (3:07—3:13)
  A. Things Says He: (3:07—07)
    1. He Who Is Holy (3:07a)
    2. He Who Is True (3:07b)
    3. He Who Has the Key of David (3:07c)

4. He Who Opens & No One Shuts (3:07d)
5. He Who Shuts & No One Opens (3:07e)

B. Things Says He to Philadelphia (3:08—09)
1. He Knows Their Works (3:08a)
2. Open Door Set Before Them (3:08b)
3. They Have Little Strength (3:08c)
4. They Have Kept His Word (3:08d)
5. Have Not Denied His Name (3:08e)
6. Will Make Those of the Synagogue of Satan Worship Before Their Feet (3:09a)
7. That They Know, God Loves Them (3:09b)

C. God's Response (3:10—13)
1. You Have Kept Command to Persevere (3:10a)
2. Keep Them from the Hour of Trial (3:10b)
3. Will Test Those on the Earth (3:10c)
4. **"I AM"** Is Coming Quickly (3:11a)
5. Hold Fast to What You Have (3:11b)
6. No One to Take Your Crown (3:11c)
7. Overcomer to be a Pillar in the Temple of His God (3:12a)
8. Will Write on Him the Name of His God (3:12b)
9. Will Write on Him the Name of the City of His God, The New Jerusalem (3:12c)
10. Will Write on Him Jesus' New Name (3:12d)
11. Hear What the Holy Spirit is Saying (3:13)

7. Letter to Laodicea—The Lukewarm Church (3:14—3:22)

A. To the Angel of the Church at Laodicea (3:14—14)
1. These Things Says He: (3:14a—14d)
   A. The Amen (3:14b)
   B. The Faithful & True Witness (3:14c)
   C. The Beginning of the Creation of God (3:14d)

B. Things Says He to Laodicea (3:15—22)
1. I Know Your Works (3:15a)
2. Neither Cold Nor Hot (3:15b)
3. Results of Lukewarmness (3:16—19)
4. The *LORD*'s Response (3:20—22)
   A. I Stand at the Door & Knock (3:20a)
   B. Open the Door & Let Me In (3:20b)
   C. Must Be an Overcomer (3:21)
   D. Hear What the *LORD* Says (3:22)

4. <u>The Things Which Are to be Seen After This</u> (4:01—22:21)

A. Message for the Seven Churches (4:01—5:14)
1. The Throne Room of Heaven (4:01—4:11)
2. The Lamb of God Takes the Sealed Book (5:01—5:07)
3. The Lamb of God Is Worthy (5:08—5:14)

B. The Opening of the Seven Seals (6:01—8:05)
1. First Seal: The White Horse—The Conqueror (6:01—6:02)
2. Second Seal: The Red Horse—Conflict on Earth (6:03—6:04)
3. Third Seal: The Black Horse—Famine on Earth (6:05—6:06)

4. Fourth Seal: The Pale Horse—Death on Earth (6:07—6:08)
5. Fifth Seal: The Cry of the Martyrs (6:09—6:11)
6. Sixth Seal: Cosmic Disturbances (6:12—6:17)
7. 144,000 Sealed of Israel (7:01—7:08)
8. A Multitude of the Great Tribulation (7:09—7:17)
9. Seventh Seal: Silence in Heaven For 30 Minutes; Ushers in Seven Trumpet Judgments (8:01—8:05)

C. The Seven Trumpets of Judgment **(8:06—11:19)**

1. First Trumpet: Hail & Fire—Vegetation Struck (8:06—8:07)
2. Second Trumpet: Volcanic Eruptions—The Seas Struck (8:08—8:09)
3. Third Trumpet: Asteroid—The Waters Struck (8:10—8:11)
4. Fourth Trumpet: Nuclear Explosions—The Heavens Struck (8:12—8:13)
5. Fifth Trumpet: Locusts from Bottomless Pit—Unbelievers Tortured for Five Months (9:01—9:12)
    A. Locust's King Is in Hebrew-***Abaddon,*** Greek-***Apollyon*** (9:11)
6. Sixth Trumpet: The Angels from the Euphrates (9:13—9:21)
    A. Loosed to Kill One-Third of All People on Earth (9:15)
    B. Two-Hundred Millions Troops Used (9:16)
    C. Characteristics of the Troops & Horses (9:17-19)
        1. Armor—Fiery Red, Sky Blue & Yellow (3 Plagues) (9:17a)
        2. Description of Horse's Heads (9:17b)
            A. Heads of Lions
            B. Mouths Billowed Fire, Smoke, Burning Sulfur (9:17c)
            C. Three Plagues Kills One-Third of Inhabitants (9:18)
            D. Horse's Tails Had Heads Like Snakes (9:19a)
            E. Had Power to Injure People (9:19b)
7. Mighty Angel with the Little Book (10:01—10:07)
8. John Eats the Little Book (10:08—10:11)
9. The Two Witnesses—Enoch & Elijah (11:01—11:06)
10. The Two Witnesses Killed (11:07—11:10)
11. The Two Witnesses Resurrected (11:11—11:14)
12. Seventh Trumpet: Ushers in the Seven Bowl Judgments (11:15—11:19)

D. Observing of the Great Tribulation **(12:01—14:20)**

1. The Signs in the Heaven (12:01—12:06)
    A. First Sign: The Woman (Israel) (12:01-02)
        1. Clothed with the Sun (12:01a)
        2. The Moon Under Her Feet (12:01b)
        3. Garland of Twelve Stars on Her Head (12:01c)
        4. In Painful Labor Ready to Give Birth (12:02)
    B. Second Sign: Satan—The Fiery Red Dragon (12:03-06)
        1. Having Seven Heads, Ten Horns & Seven Diadems (Crowns) on His Head (12:03a)

2. Actions of the Great Red Dragon (12:04—04)
A. Cast a Third of Stars (Demons) to Earth (12:04a)
B. Stood Before the Pregnant Woman (12:04b)
C. Ready to Devour Child Born (Jesus) (12:04c)
3. Actions of the Pregnant Woman (12:05—06)
A. She Bore a Child to Rule All Nations with an Iron Rod (12:05)
B. Child Caught Up to God & His Throne (12:05b)
C. Woman (Israel) Fled (12:06—06)
1. Into the Wilderness (12:06a)
2. Has a Place Prepared by God (12:06b)
3. Should Be Fed for 1260 Days (12:06c)
2. Satan Thrown Out of Heaven (12:07—12:12)
A. War in Heaven (12:07—09)
1. Archangel Michael & Angels Under Him (12:07—09)
A. Fought Satan & His Fallen Angels (12:07)
B. Satan Lost Battle; Cast Out of Heaven (12:08)
C. Thrown Down to Earth with Fallen Angels (12:09)
2. It Has Finally Happened (12:10—12)
A. The Salvation, Power, Kingdom of Our God, Authority of His Christ Have Come (12:10a)
B. Accuser of the Brethren Cast to Earth (12:10b)
C. Satan's Critical Defeat (12:11—12)
1. By the Blood of the Lamb (12:11a)
2. By the Word of Their Testimony (12:11b)
3. Terror Comes to Earth & Sea (12:12a)
4. Satan Has Great Anger Now (12:12b)
5. Has a Short Time Left (12:12)
3. The Woman (Israel) Persecuted (12:13—12:17)
A. Satan Steps-Up Persecution (12:13—17)
1. Satan Pursues the Woman (Israel) (12:13)
2. Israelites Flee to Petra; Protected for Forty-two Months (12:14)
3. Satan Tries to Drown Israelites with Flood (12:15)
4. Earthquake Stopped Flooding Waters (12:16)
5. Satan Enraged with Anger (12:17a)
A. Declares War on Rest of Israelites (12:17b)
B. All Who Keep God's Commandments—Remaining Jews (12:17c)
C. Have the Testimony of Jesus Christ—Christians Left on Earth (12:17d)
4. The Beast from the Sea—The Anti-Christ (13:01—13:10)
A. Beginning of the Great Tribulation Period (13:01—10)
1. The End-Time Anti-Christ (13:01—02c)
A. Description (13:01—02c)
1. Has Seven Heads & Ten Horns (13:01a)
2. Has Ten Crowns on Its Horns (13:01b)
3. Heads Had Blasphemous Names (13:01c)
4. Looked Like a Leopard (13:02a)

5. Had Bear's Feet, Lion's Mouth (13:02b)
6. Satan Gave Him His Power, Throne & Great Authority (13:02c)

2. Anti-Christ Killed & Resurrected (13:03—04)
   A. One Head Wounded Beyond Recovery (13:03a)
   B. The Fatal Wound Was Healed (13:03b)
   C. The World Marveled at the Miracle (13:03c)
   D. The World Followed the Anti-Christ (13:03d)
   E. The World Worshiped Satan (13:04—04)
      1. Satan Gave Anti-Christ Great Power (13:04a)
      2. Who Can Fight Against Anti-Christ (13:04b)
3. The Anti-Christ Begins His Reign (13:05—13:10)
   A. Activities of the End-Time Anti-Christ (13:05—10)
      1. Give Authority for Forty-two Months (13:05)
      2. Spoke Blasphemies Against God (13:06a)
      3. Slandered God's Name (13:06b)
      4. Waged War Against the True Believers (13:07a)
      5. Given Authority Over Every Tribe, Tongue & Nation (13:07b)
      6. Worldly People Worshiped the Beast (13:08a)
      7. Unbelievers Had Not Their Name in the Lamb's Book of Life (13:08b)
      8. He Who Has an Ear Let Him Hear (13:09)
      9. Those Destined for Prison, Go to Prison (13:10a)
      10. Those Destined for Death, Will Be Killed (13:10b)
      11. Opportunity for Endurance & Faith AvailaBIBLE (13:10c)

5. The Beast from the Earth (False Prophet) (13:11—13:18)
   A. His Description (13:11—11)
      1. Had Two Horns Like a Lamb (13:11a)
      2. Spoke with the Voice of a Dragon (Satan) (13:11b)
   B. Activities of False Prophet (Religious Leader) (13:12—18)
      1. Exercised All Authority of Anti-Christ (13:12a)
      2. Christians & People Who Belonged to the World Required to Worship Anti-Christ (13:12b)
      3. Called Fire from Heaven in Men's Sight (13:13)
      4. He Deceived People to Who Belonged to the World (13:14a)
      5. Ordered People of the World to Make Image of the Resurrected Beast (Anti-Christ) (13:14b)
      6. Life Was Given to the Image (Anti-Christ) to Speak (13:15a)
      7. Caused All Non-Worshipers to be Killed (13:15b)
      8. Caused Everyone to Receive His Mark on Their Right Hand or Forehead (13:16)
      9. Without His Mark No One Could Buy Things (13:17)
      10. The Number of the Beast Is 666 (13:18)

6. The Lamb and the 144,000 (14:01—14:05)
  A. Characteristics of the 144,000 (14:01—05)
    1. God's Name Written on Forehead (14:01)
    2. Redeemed from the Earth (14:03)
    3. They Are Virgins (14:04a)
    4. They Follow the Lamb Everywhere (14:04b)
    5. Being First to God & the Lamb (14:04c)
    6. Spoke No Deceptive Words (14:05a)
    7. Without Fault Before Throne of God (14:05b)
7. The Announcement of the Three Angels (14:06—14:13)
  A. Proclamation of First Angel (14:06—07)
    1. Carried the Gospel to the Unbelievers (14:06)
    2. Angel Shouts "Fear God" (14:07a)
    3. Angel Shouts "Give Glory to Him" (14:07b)
    4. Judgment Time Has Come (14:07c)
    5. Worship Him Who Made All Things (14:07d)
  B. Proclamation of Second Angel (14:08—08)
    1. Babylon Is Fallen (14:08—08)
  C. Proclamation of Third Angel (14:09—13)
    1. Proclaims If Anyone Takes the Mark Will Encounter God's Wrath (14:09—10a)
    2. Wrath Poured Out Undiluted (14:10b)
    3. God's Wrath Includes Tormenting with Fire & Burning Sulfur (14:10c)
    4. Smoke of Torment Rises Forever & Ever (14:11)
    5. True Believers Encouraged to Endure Persecution Patiently (14:12)
    6. Voice from Heaven Proclaims "Blessed Are Those Who Die Beginning at That Time" (14:13)
8. Reaping the Harvest of the Earth (14:14—14:16)
  A. Son of Man Reaps His Believers (14:14—16)
9. Reaping the Grapes of Wrath (14:17—14:20)
  A. Unbelievers Reaped for Judgment (14:17—20)

E. The Seven Bowls of Judgment (15:01—16:21)

1. Prelude to the Bowl Judgments (15:01—15:08)
  A. The Song of Moses & of the Lamb (Jesus) (15:01—04)
  B. The Seven Bowls of the Seven Plagues (15:05—08)
2. First Bowl Judgment: Loathsome Soars (Boils) (16:01—16:02)
3. Second Bowl Judgment: Sea Turns to Blood (16:03—16:03)
4. Third Bowl Judgment: Waters Turn to Blood (16:04—16:07)
5. Fourth Bowl Judgment: Men Are Scorched (16:08—16:09)
6. Fifth Bowl Judgment: Darkness & Pain (16:10—16:11)
7. Sixth Bowl Judgment: Euphrates River Dries Up (16:12—16:16)
8. Seventh Bowl Judgment: "It Is Done!" (16:17—16:21)

F. Seizing the Final Victory (17:01—19:05)

1. Judgment of the Great Harlot (17:01—17:18)
  A. Description of the Great Harlot (17:01—06)
  B. Destruction of the Great Harlot (17:07—18)
2. The Fall of Babylon the Great (18:01—19:05)

A. Destruction of Babylon the Great (18:01—08)
B. Mourning of the Fall of Babylon the Great (18:09—19)
C. Finality of Babylon's Fall (18:20—24)
D. Heaven Rejoices Over the Fall of Babylon (19:01—05)

G. The Second Coming of Jesus Christ (19:06—19:21)

1. Marriage Supper of the Lamb (19:06—19:10)
2. The Second Coming of Jesus Christ (19:11—19:16)
   A. Description of Christ at His Coming (19:11—16)
      1. He Is Called Faithful & True (19:11a)
      2. He Judges & Makes War (19:11b)
      3. His Eyes Like Flaming Fire (19:12a)
      4. Many Crowns on His Head (19:12b)
      5. He Has a Name Nobody Else Knew (19:12c)
      6. Clothed with a Blood-Dipped Robe (19:13a)
      7. His Name Is Called "The *WORD* of God" (19:13b)
      8. Saints of God Followed on White Horses (19:14)
      9. Sharp Sword Proceeds from His Mouth (19:15a)
      10. He Will Rule with an Iron Rod (19:15b)
      11. He Treads the Winepress of the Fierceness of Almighty God (19:15c)
      13. *KING* of Kings & *LORD* of Lords (19:16)
3. The Beast and His Armies Defeated (19:17—19:21)
   A. The Great Supper of God Called (19:17—18)
   B. The Battle of Armageddon (Location—Megiddo) (19:19—21)
      1. Anti-Christ Makes War Against Christ (19:19)
      2. Anti-Christ & False Prophet Captured (19:20a)
      3. They Were Cast Alive Into Lake of Burning Fire: The Final Destination of All Unbelievers (19:20b)
      4. The Rest Were Killed with the Sword of Christ (19:21a)
      5. The Birds Had Their Great Supper (19:21b)

H. The Beginning of the Millennium (20:01—20:15)

1. Satan Bound for 1000 Years in Bottomless Pit (20:01—20:03)
2. The Saints Reign 1000 Years with Christ on Earth (20:04—20:06)
   A. Description of the Saints of God (20:04—04)
      1. Tribulation Period Martyrs (20:04—04)
         A. Beheaded for Their Witness to Jesus (20:04a)
         B. Had Not Worshiped the Anti-Christ (20:04b)
         C. Had Not Received His Mark (20:04c)
         D. Reigns with Christ 1000 Years (20:04d)
      2. The First Resurrection (20:05—06)
         A. Dead Unbelievers Remained Dead for a 1000 Years (Second Death) (20:05)
         B. Blessed Are Believers of the First Resurrection (20:06a)
         C. Second Death Has No Power Over It (20:06b)
         D. Believers Reign with Christ 1000 Years (20:06c)

3. Results of Satan's Release from Bottomless Pit (20:07—20:10)

A. Satan Released After the 1000 Years (20:07)

B. Goes to Deceive Tribulation Saints (20:08)

C. Armies of Satan Surround Tribulation Saints in Jerusalem (20:09a)

D. God Sends Fire from Heaven; Devours Them (20:09b)

E. Satan Cast Into Lake of Fire with Anti-Christ & False Prophet (20:10a)

F. They Are Tormented Forever & Ever Day & Night (20:10b)

4. The Great White Throne Judgment (20:11—20:15)

A. Events of the Great White Throne Judgment (20:11—13)

1. Jesus Christ Sits on the Throne (20:11)

2. The Dead Unbelievers from the Tribulation Period Stood Before God (20:12a)

3. The Book of Life Was Opened (20:12b)

4. Works of the Unbelieving Dead from Tribulation Period Judged (20:12c)

5. The Sea Gave Up the Dead (20:13a)

6. Death & the Grave (Hades) Gave Up the Dead (20:13b)

7. Results of the Judgment (20:14—15)

A. Spiritually Dead from Tribulation Period Were Cast Into the Lake of Fire (20:14a)

B. Spiritually Dead from the Grave Were Cast Into the Lake of Fire (20:14b)

C. The Lake of Fire Is the Second Death and the Final Destination for ALL Unbelievers (20:15)

I. All Things Made New **(21:01—22:21)**

1. A New Heaven and a New Earth (21:01—21:05)

A. First Heaven & Earth Disappeared (21:01)

B. New Jerusalem Comes from Heaven (21:02)

C. Loud Voice from Heaven Speaks Saying: (21:03—04)

1. "Tabernacle (Jesus) of God Is with Men" (21:03a)

2. He Will Dwell with Them (21:03b)

3. They Shall Be His People (21:03c)

4. God Himself Will Be There with Them & Be Their God (21:03d)

5. Every Tear Wiped Away (21:04a)

6. No More Death, Sorrow or Crying (21:04b)

7. "Behold, I Make All Things New" (21:05)

2. The Alpha and the Omega, The Beginning & the End (21:06—21:08)

A. Fountain of Water of Life (21:06)

B. Overcomers Shall Inherit All Things (21:07a)

C. He Will Be His God (21:07b)

D. People to Inherit the Lake of Fire—**Second Death:** (21:08—08)

1. The Cowardly Who Turned Away from God (Backsliders)
2. The Unbelieving of God (The Unsaved)
3. The Abominable (Corrupt People)
4. All Unrepentant Murderers (Physical & of the Heart)
5. All the Sexual Immoral (Adulterers & Fornicators)
6. Those Who Practice Witchcraft or Magic Arts (Sorcerers, Witches, Magicians)
7. Idolaters (Worshiped False Idols as God)
8. All Liars (Habitual & Unrepentant)

3. The Bride—The Wife of the ***LAMB*** (21:09—21:09)

4. The New Jerusalem (21:10—21:21)

A. Description of The New Jerusalem (21:10—21)

1. Descended Out of Heaven from God (21:10)
2. Filled with the Glory of God (21:11a)
3. Sparkled Like a Precious Gem (21:11b)
4. Crystal Clear Like Jasper (21:11c)
5. Walls Were Broad & High (21:12a)
6. Twelve Gates Guarded by Twelve Angels—Names of Twelve Sons of Israel on the Gates (21:12b)
7. New Jerusalem Had Three Gates on Each Side (21:13)
8. Wall of City Had Twelve Foundation Stones—Names of Twelve Apostles Written on Stones (21:14)
9. Gold Measuring Stick Measured the City; The Walls & the Gates (21:15)
10. Description of the New Jerusalem Wall (21:16—21)
    - A. Wall Was 1400 Miles High, Wide & High (21:16)
    - B. Wall Was 216 Feet Thick (Human Measure) (21:17)
    - C. Wall Made of Jasper (21:18a)
    - D. City Made of Pure Gold, Clear as Glass (21:18b)
    - E. Built on Foundation Stones Inlaid with Twelve Gems (21:19—20)
11. Description of the Twelve Gates (21:21)
    - A. Gates Made of Pearls (21:21a)
    - B. Streets Made of Transparent Gold (21:21b)

5. The Glory of the New Jerusalem (21:22—21:27)

6. The River of Life (22:01—22:05)

7. The Time Is Near (22:06—22:11)

8. "Behold, **I AM** Coming Quickly; My Reward Is with Me" (22:12—22:13)

9. Blessed Are Those Who Do His Commandments (22:14—22:15)

10. Jesus Testifies to the Churches (22:16—22:17)

11. Word of Warning (22:18—22:19)

12. "**I AM** Coming Quickly!" (22:20—22:21)

The Parables of Jesus Christ in the Four Gospels

1. **Parables Concerning The Teachings of Jesus**
   - A. **Parable Concerning Humility**
     1. The Wedding Feast
        - A. Luke 14:7-11
     2. The Proud Pharisee & The Corrupt Tax Collector
        - A. Luke 18:9-14

   - B. **Parable Concerning The Kingdom of God**
     1. The Soils
        - A. Matthew 13:3-8
        - B. Mark 4:4-8
        - C. Luke 8:5-8
     2. The Weeds
        - A. Matthew 13:24-30
     3. The Mustard Seed
        - A. Matthew 13:31-32
        - B. Mark 4:30-32
        - C. Luke 13:18-19
     4. The Yeast
        - A. Matthew 13:33
        - B. Mark 13:20-21
     5. The Treasure
        - A. Matthew 13:44
     6. The Pearl
        - A. Matthew 13:45-46
     7. The Fishing Net
        - A. Matthew 13:47-50
     8. The Growing Seed
        - A. Mark 4:26-29

   - C. **Parables Concerning Neighbors**
     1. The Good Samaritan
        - A. Luke 10:30-37

   - D. **Parables Concerning Prayer**
     1. The Friend at Midnight
        - A. Luke 11:5-8
     2. The Unjust Judge
        - A. Luke 18:1-8

   - E. **Parables Concerning Obedience & Service**
     1. The Workers of the Vineyard
        - A. Matthew 20:1-16
     2. The Loaned Money
        - A. Matthew 25:14-30
     3. The Nobleman's Servants
        - A. Luke 19:11-27
     4. The Servant's Role
        - A. Luke 17:7-10

   - F. **Parables Concerning Wealth**
     1. The Rich Fool
        - A. Luke 12:16-21
     2. The Great Feast
        - A. Luke 14:16-24

3. The Shrewd Manager
A. Luke 16:1-9

7. **Parables Concerning The Goodness of God**
A. **Parables Concerning God's Love**
1. The Lost Sheep
A. Matthew 18:12-14
B. Luke 15:3-7
2. The Lost Coin
A. Luke 15:8-10
3. The Lost Son
A. Luke 15:11-32
B. **Parables Concerning Thankfulness**
1. The Forgiven Debts
A. Luke 7:41-43

3. **Parables Concerning The Future of The Coming Judgments**
A. **The Return of the *LORD***
1. The Ten Bridesmaids
A. Matthew 25:1-3
2. The Faithful, Sensible Servants
A. Matthew 24:45-51
B. Luke 12:42-48
3. The Traveling Homeowner
A. Mark 13:34-37

2. **Parables Concerning the Values of God**
A. **The Values of God**
1. The Two Sons
A. Matthew 21:28-32
2. The Evil Farmer
A. Matthew 21:33-34
B. Mark 12:1-9
C. Luke 20:9-16
3. The Unproductive Fig Tree
A. Luke 13:6-9
4. The Wedding Feast
A. Matthew 22:1-14
5. The Unforgiving Debtor
A. Matthew 18:23-35

Topical Concordance for the New Testament

3 ½ Years – **49-**4d3a2
216 Feet Thick (Human Measure) – **54-**4i4a10b
666 – **50-**4d5b10
1000 Years – **52-**4h1,2;4h2a1d;4h2a2a,d;4h2a3a
1260 Days – **48-**4d1b3c3
1400 Miles High, Wide & High – **54-**4i4a10a
144,000 Sealed of Israel – **47-**4b7; **50-**4d6;4d6a

A

A Child to Rule – **49-**4d1b3a
A Chosen Generation – **39-**2b4
A Clean & Holy Life – **36-**3b3b
A Consuming Fire – **37-**3b5e
A Dog Returns – **40-**2b4e
A Flaming Fire – **44-**2a2b1b
A Flood – **49-**4d3a3
A Gentle Servant – **32-**2b6
A Good Fight – **32-**3b1b
A Good Minister – **31-**2c2
A Liar – **41-**1a3d1
A Lion's Mouth – **49-**4d4a1a5
A Multitude – **48-**4b8
A Name – **46-**3a5a2
A New Covenant – **35-**2a5b
A New Grip – **36-**3b3a
A New Heaven & A New Earth – **53-**4i1
A New Name – **45-**3a3c2b
A Placed Prepared by God – **49-**4d1b3c2
A Precious Gem – **54-**4i4a3
A Pure & Blameless Life – **41-**2c3a
A Royal Priesthood – **39-**2b4
A Short Time Left – **49-**4d2a2c5
A Third of Stars – **48-**4d1b2a
A White Stone – **45-**3a3c2b
Aaronic Priesthood – **34-**2a2a
Abaddon – **48-**4c5a
Abandon – **16-**3a17
Abandoned Apostle – **32-**3b2
Abandons the Faith – **35-**3a2f;3a2g1
Abel – **35-**3a4a
Abide – **41-**1a8
Abiding – **42-**#2;#3
Abominable (Corrupt People) – **53-**4i2d3
About – **9-**2c1; **13-**5a3c,d,f; **15-**3a3a;3a4d2;3a5; **17-**4a9; **18-**4c9; **21-**4b1; **40-**2b3a;2b4a
About the Angels – **33-**1a2
Abraham – **36-**3a4d
Abraham Covenant – **26-**2b1c
Abraham Justified Before Circumcision – **22-**3b2
Abraham Justified by Faith – **22-**3b1
Abraham's Promise Granted Through Faith – **22-**3b3
Abstain From Every Form of Evil – **30-**4a5j
Abused – **7-**3a6d
Accept the Truth – **41-**1a3b
According – **39-**2b1f
Accordingly – **23-**6a3
Account – **8-**1a
Account of the Ten Servants – **12-**4b28b
Accused – **2-**3b5; **11-**4a9a
Accused of Sedition – **21-**4b8
Accuser of the Brethren – **49-**4d2a2b
Actions – **37-**2a3b2,3; **39-**2b1f;2b3a
Actions of the Great Red Dragon – **48-**4d1b2
Actions of the Pregnant Woman – **49-**4d1b3
Activities – **6-**3a1; **7-**3a2,4
Activities of End-time Anti-Christ – **49-**4d4a3a
Activities of False Prophet – **50-**4d5b
Activities of the Other People – **7-**3a4
Activities—Passover to Arrest – **7-**3a5
Activities in Jerusalem – **13-**5a4
Adam – **9-**1c6
Additional – **37-**3b6;3b7
Addressed – **24-**#4
Addressed by Paul – **23-**#1
Addresses False Rumor – **21-**4b1
Addresses the Aeropagus – **20-**3c12
Addresses the Council – **18-**1b17
Addresses the Jerusalem Mob – **21-**4b3
Addresses the Sanhedrin – **18-**1b4
Admonition – **30-**4a6
Adulterers & Fornicators – **53-**4i2d5
Adultery – **1-**2c4; **16-**3b8; **40-**2b3c1
Advanced Leprosy – **9-**2b5
Advantage in the Law – **22-**4b2
Advantages – **22-**2b2
Advice – **18-**1b13
Aeneas – **19-**2a10
Afflicted – **21-**4b22
Afraid – **44-**2a3a1
After – **5-**6b21; **17-**3c3
After Conversion – **21-**4b15
After Salvation – **35-**3a2b
After Speaking – **16-**3b11
After the 1000 Years – **52-**4h3a
After This – **47-**#4
Agabus Prophesied Famine – **19-**2a19e
Again – **4-**5a2,5c7;6b6; **13-**5a2a; **16-**3b21; **18-**1b12; **40-**2b4d
Against – **3-**4c2; **10-**3c23; **11-**4a10;4b1-3; **26-**3d12; **34-**1b2a; **45-**3a3b
Against Anti-Christ – **50-**4d4a2e2
Against Christ – **52-**4g3b1
Against Fallen Angels – **40-**2b2a8
Against False Doctrine – **31-**2a1
Against False Teachers – **43-**2b
Against God – **49-**4d4a3a2
Against Him (Jesus) – **34-**1b2a
Against Idleness – **31-**3b2
Against Pergamos – **45-**3a3b
Against Thyatira – **46-**3a4a2
Against the True Believers – **49-**4d4a3a4

Against the Truth – **26**-3d12
Against Them – **45**-3a3c1
Age (Years) – **8**-1c2
Age (Dispensation) – **4**-6a2; **38**-2a2
Age of Dispensation – **4**-6a2
Agonizes – **4**-6b7
Agonizing – **7**-3a5e
Agrees – **13**-5a4b
Alert – **7**-3a3j5
Alive – **13**-5a; **44**-2a3a4
Alive, But Dead – **46**-3a5a2
Alive Into Lake of Burning Fire – **52**-4g3b3
Almighty God – **52**-4g2a11
Always Right & Good – **36**-3b2g
All – **18**-1a6; **30**-4a5b; **33**-1a2e
All Afflicted – **21**-4b22
All Authority of the Anti-Christ – **50**-4d5b1
All Believers – **17**-4a15
All Circumstances – **28**-2d4
All Evil Speaking / Actions – **39**-2b3a
All Liars (Unrepentant Liars) – **53**-4i2d8
All Nations – **49**-4d1b3a
All People – **48**-4c6a
All Possessions – **35**-3a2b6
All That Belongs to Christ – **34**-1b2d5
All the Sexual Immoral (Adulterers & Fornicators) – **53**-4i2d5
All Things – **18**-1b7; **30**-4a5i; **34**-1a4b; **50**-4d7a5; **53**-4i2b
All Things New – **53**-4i1c7
All Things Are Naked & Open to Him – **34**-1b4c
All Things Made New – **53**-4i
All Unbelievers – **52**-4g3b3; **53**-4h4a7c
All Unrepentant Murderers (Physical & of the Heart) – **53**-4i2d4
All Who Enter Will Find Rest – **34**-1b3c
All Who Keep God's Commandments – **49**-4d3a5b
All Non-Worshipers to be Killed – **50**-4d5b7
Alpha & Omega – **44**-2a1b1
Already – **9**-3a2f
Always – **30**-4a5d
Ambassadors for Christ – **25**-3a9
Amen – **47**-3a7a1a
Among the Thessalonians – **29**-2a2
An Overcomer – **47**-3a7b4c
Ananias – **18**-1b8; **19**-2a6
Ancient World – **40**-2b2a2
Andrew – **15**-2b1;2b1a,b
Angel – **50**-4d7a;4d7a2,3; **51**-4d7c
Angel Appears to Cornelius – **19**-2a12a
Angel Frees Peter from Prison – **19**-2b3
Angel Gabriel – **8**-1b1b;1b2a
Angel of the Laodicean Church – **47**-3a7a
Angel of the *LORD* – **8**-1b5c; **18**-1b11
Angel Shouts – **50**-4d7a2,3
Angel Tells Cornelius to Send for Peter – **19**-2a12b
Angel with the Little Book – **48**-4c7
Angels – **14**-5a8a2; **33**-1a;1a1b;1a2,4;1a2b;1a4a; **40**-2b2a8; **46**-3a5a2c1h; **49**-4d2a1a,c; **50**-4d7; **54**-4i4a6
Angels from the Euphrates – **48**-4c6
Angels of God Worship Him – **33**-1a2b
Angels of the Seven Churches – **44**-2a3b1
Angels Under Him – **49**-4d2a1
Angels Who Sinned – **40**-2b2a1
Anger – **1**-2c2; **9**-2a2d; **49**-4d2a2c4;4d3a5
Angered – **9**-2a2c
Animal Sacrifices Insufficient – **35**-2a6b3
Anna – **8**-1c1c
Annas (High Priest) – **17**-4b3
Announcement – **1**-1a2; **50**-4d7
Annulled or Voided – **26**-2b1c
Anointed – **2**-3b; **10**-3c4
Anointing – **2**-3a12
Anoints – **4**-6b2; **7**-3a4b; **17**-3c5
Another – **42**-2a2
Answered – **4**-5c4
Answers – **4**-5c1-3
Anti-Christ – **41**-1a7; **49**-4d4a1; **49**-4d4a2;4d4a2d;4d4a2e1,2; **50**-4d5b1,2,5,6; **52**-4h2a1b
Anti-Christ & False Prophet – **52**-4g3b2;4h3e
Anti-Christ Begins His Reign – **49**-4d4a3
Anti-Christ Deceivers – **42**-3a1,2
Anti-Christ Killed & Resurrected – **49**-4d4a2
Anti-Christ Makes War Against Christ – **52**-4g3b1
Antioch – **19**-2a19;2a19c;2b; **20**-3a5,9;3b5;3c14
Antioch of Pisidia – **20**-3a4
Anxious – **28**-2d2
Anxious for Nothing – **28**-2d2
Anyone – **10**-3c23
Anyone Who Takes the Mark – **51**-4d7c1
Anyone Who Disobeys God – **34**-1b4a
Apollos – **20**-4a2
Apollyon – **48**-4c5a
Apostates – **43**-2a2,3;2b1
Apostates Predicted – **43**-2b1
Apostle – **18**-#1; **19**-2b; **20**-#3; **25**-#3; **27**-#1; **32**-3b2
Apostle of Jesus Christ – **25**-#3
Apostles – **14**-5a8a3; **18**-1b6,10,11,12; **26**-3d5
Apostles Pray for Boldness – **18**-1b6
Apostles Written on Stones – **54**-4i4a8
Apostleship – **26**-2a1
Appeal for Onesimus – **33**-3a
Appear – **14**-5a8a2
Appears – **5**-6c2; **14**-5a8c; **18**-4c2;4c6d; **19**-2a12a
Appearance – **18**-4c6
Appearances – **7**-4a7b; **18**-4c3,4,6
Application of Our Righteousness – **23**-#6
Appointed – **18**-1a4
Appreciation for Philemon – **33**-2a
Apostasy – **30**-3a1; **31**-2c1
Appeals to Caesar – **21**-4b11
Appreciation of the Mystery – **27**-2a7c
Approved in Jerusalem – **26**-2a3
Archangel Michael – **49**-4d2a1
Are Being Seen – **44**-#3
Are Naked – **34**-1b4c
Are Not Slack – **41**-2c1

Are Saved – **35**-3a2g2
Are Those Who Do His Commandments – **54**-4i9
Are Tormented Forever & Ever – **52**-4h3f
Are Worse Off – **40**-2b4d
Are Worthy – **46**-3a5a2c1e
Armageddon – **52**-4g3b
Armies Defeated – **52**-4g3
Armies of Satan Surround – **52**-4h3c
Armor – **28**-3d;3d1; **48**-4c6c1
Armor of God – **28**-3d;3d1
Arrest – **4**-6b8; **7**-3a5; **13**-5a5; **16**-3b21
Arrested – **7**-3a5f; **13**-5a5i; **17**-4b1; **18**-1b3,16; **21**-4b2
Arrives – **15**-3a4c
Arrives in Rome – **21**-4b23
As a Thief – **41**-2c2a; **46**-3a5a2c1c
As an Offering – **32**-3b1a
As Fire Tests – **38**-2a2b2
As His Children – **38**-2b1b
As in the Days of Lot – **12**-4b21d
As in the Days of Noah – **12**-4b21c
As to the *LORD* – **39**-3a2,3
As Unto God Himself – **23**-6a4
As You Did in the Beginning – **34**-1b2d4
Ascends – **14**-5a8de
Ascension – **7**-4a7c
Ashamed – **32**-2a2
Ashes – **40**-2b2a3
Asia – **25**-1a3
Aside – **39**-2b3a
Ask – **9**-2c1; **11**-4a7c; **15**-3a4d1
Ask, Seek, Knock – **11**-4a7c
Asks – **2**-3b6; **3**-4c1; **6**-2c14; **14**-5a6g2; **18**-4c7
Assembly – **36**-3b4c
Assurance of Faith – **35**-3a
Assurance of Resurrection – **25**-3a6
Assurance of Salvation – **42**-2b2
Asteroid – **48**-4c3
At Ephesus – **44**-3a1a; **45**-3a1b,c
At That Time – **51**-4d7c6
Ate Fried Fish – **18**-4c6f
Athens – **20**-3c12,13
Attack – **21**-4b21
Attention – **40**-2a2a
Attitude – **6**-2d4a; **11**-4a6
Attitudes – **16**-3b12d
Authentic – **2**-3b7
Authenticity of the Gospel – **26**-1a;2a
Authority – **2**-#3; **4**-5a4; **7**-3a3b; **26**-3d3; **49**-4d4a1a6
Authority Approved – **26**-2a3
Authority Established Over All Creation – **33**-1a2e
Authority for Forty-two Months – **49**-4d4a3a1
Authority **IS** from God – **16**-3b2a
Authority Is Real – **26**-3d2
Authority of His Christ – **49**-4d2a2a
Authority of Anti-Christ – **50**-4d5b1
Authority Over Every Tribe – **49**-4d4a3a5
Authority Over All Things – **33**-1a4b
Authority Over Condemnation – **5**-2a11
Authority Over Demons – **5**-2a3
Authority Over Diseases – **5**-2a4
Authority Over Religiosity – **5**-2a8
Authority Presented – **9**-2b
Authority Questioned – **13**-5a3a
Availabible – **50**-4d4a3a11
Avoid Anti-Christ Deceivers – **42**-3a1
Avoid Dissensions – **33**-3b2
Avoid Divisive People – **23**-7a4
Avoid Feasts with Pagans – **24**-4b5
Avoid Self-Indulgence – **24**-4b4
Awaits – **10**-3a2g
Away – **5**-6b16; **34**-1b2b; **37**-3b6f; **41**-2c2b;2c3d; **53**-4i1c5
Away from God (Backsliders) – **53**-4i2d1
Awe – **36**-3b5d

B

Babbler – **20**-3c11
Babel – **3**-3c,3c1
Babylon Has Fallen – **50**-4d7b1
Babylon the Great – **51**-4f2;4f2a,b
Babylon's Fall – **51**-4f2c
Back – **38**-2c4
Back Into Sin – **40**-2b4b
Back to Antioch – **20**-3a9
Back to Life – **19**-2a11
Backslidden Believers – **40**-2b4d
Backsliders – **53**-4i2d1
Bad Fruit – **10**-3b1d
Balaam – **45**-3a3b1;3a3b1a
Baptism – **15**-2a2a
Baptism Into Death – **22**-4a1
Baptized – **1**-1a7; **5**-1a2; **8**-1c5; **15**-3a4a; **19**-2a6; **20**-4a3
Baptized at Philippi – **20**-3c4
Baptizes – **15**-2a1c
Baptizing – **15**-3a3a
Barabbas – **14**-5a6e3
Barnabas Escapes to Derbe – **20**-3a8
Barnabas Goes to Taurus – **19**-2a19d
Barnabas Returns to Jerusalem – **20**-2b7
Barnabas Sent to Antioch – **19**-2a19c
Barrenness – **8**-1b1a
Bartimaeus – **6**-2d5
Battle – **49**-4d2a1b
Battle of Armageddon – **52**-4g3b
Be A Pillar – **47**-3a6c7
Be Alive, But Dead – **46**-3a5a2
Be An Overcomer – **47**-3a7b4c
Be Anxious for Nothing – **28**-2d2
Be Clothed – **46**-3a5a2c1f
Be Diligent – **40**-2a1a7
Be Faithful – **34**-1b2d3; **45**-3a2a2b
Be Fed 1260 Days – **49**-4d1b3c3
Be His God – **53**-4i2c
Be Holy – **25**-3b2; **38**-2b1d
Be Hospitable – **37**-3b6b
Be Killed – **50**-4d4a3a10;4d5b7
Be Left – **36**-3b5c

Be Misled – **37**-2a3b4
Be Patient with All – **30**-4a5b
Be Reconciled to God – **25**-3a8
Be Submissive – **39**-3a2-4
Be Sympathetic – **37**-3b6d2,3
Be Their God – **53**-4i1c4
Be There – **53**-4i1c4
Be Watchful – **46**-3a5a2a
Be of Same Mind in Christ – **28**-2d1
Be Too Late for Repentance – **36**-3b3f
Bear & Share Burdens – **27**-2c1d
Bears a Son – **8**-1b1c
Bears Witness – **15**-3a3
Bear's Feet – **50**-4d4a1a5
Bearing Other's Burdens – **23**-6a7c
Beast – **49**-4d4; **50**-4d4a3a6;4d5b5; **50**-4d5b10
Beast & His Armies Defeated – **52**-4g3
Beaten – **7**-3a6d; **35**-3a2b3
Beatitudes – **1**-2b1; **9**-3a
Became – **15**-2c2
Because of – **16**-3b5
Become Fruitful – **39**-2a1a5f
Become Slaves – **40**-2b4d
Becomes – **8**-1b1e; **15**-2b1e; **16**-3c1; **18**-4b10
Before – **4**-6b13; **7**-3a6a,c; **8**-1b4e; **14**-5a6b1;5a6c,d; **14**-5a8a2; **18**-4b5; **21**-4b5,9,12; **40**-2b4d; **48**-4d1b7b; **53**-4h4a2
Before Circumcision – **22**-3b2
Before God – **22**-2b4; **46**-3a5a2c
Before Israel – **45**-3a3b1a1
Before My Father – **46**-3a5a2c1h
Before the *LORD* – **38**-2b1
Before Throne of God – **50**-4d6a7
Before the World – **39**-3a;3a1
Before Their Feet – **47**-3a6b6
Before Them – **47**-3a6b2
Beggars – **3**-4d18
Begins – **1**-#2;2a,2a1; **5**-2a,2a1; **9**-2a; **18**-1b19
Begins His Reign – **49**-4d4a3
Beginning – **18**-1a; **34**-1b2d4; **53**-4i2
Beginning at That Time – **51**-4d7c6
Beginning of the Church – **18**-1a
Beginning of the Great Tribulation – **48**-4d; **49**-4d4a
Beginning of the Millennium – **52**-4h
Beheaded – **3**-4a2
Beheaded for Their Witness – **52**-4h2a1a
Behind – **8**-1c2a
Behold – **44**-2a3a4
"Behold, **I AM** Coming Quickly; My Reward Is with Me" – **54**-4i8
"Behold, I Make All Things New" – **53**-4i1c7
Being – **2**-2d7;3b5; **10**-3c18; **11**-4a9a; **15**-3a1c;3a2a
Being A Living Sacrifice to God – **23**-6a1
Being Faithless – **24**-2c2b
Being First to God – **50**-4d6a5
Being Ignorant – **41**-2c3b
Being Patient – **44**-3a1a2
Being Seen – **44**-#3
Being Tested – **38**-2a2b2
Belief – **15**-3a
Believed – **16**-3b11
Believer – **29**-3a1; **39**-#3
Believers – **17**-4a7,15; **23**-6a7; **26**-2b1e; **34**-1b1; **35**-3a2g; **39**-3a5;2a1a1,2; **40**-2b4b;2b4d; **41**-2c2d; **49**-4d4a3a4; **51**-4d8
Believers Are Exhorted – **43**-2a1
Believers Encouraged to Endure – **51**-4d7c5
Believers from Cyprus – **19**-2a19b
Believers from Jerusalem – **19**-2a19a
Believers in Christ – **27**-#2; #3
Believers in Him (Jesus) – **15**-2c2
Believers of the First Resurrection – **52**-4h2a2b
Believers on Road – **14**-5a8b
Believers Saved – **15**-3a2d
Believers Reigns with Christ 1000 Years – **52**-4h2a2d
Believers Remain Watchful – **13**-5a3g8
Believer's Baptism Into Death – **22**-4a
Believer's Final Victory Through Christ – **24**-4d6
Believer's Hope for the Future – **38**-2a1
Believer's Sanctification – **38**-2b
Believer's Salvation – **38**-#2
Believer's Trials in This Present Age – **38**-2a2
Believing – **28**-2c
Belong to the World – **50**-4d5b2,4
Belongs to Christ – **34**-1b2d5
Belt – **28**-3d1a
Benediction – **23**-7a; **31**-3b3; **37**-3b8; **44**-1a
Berea – **20**-3c10
Bethany – **4**-6b2; **7**-3a4b; **14**-5a8e; **17**-3c2a,d
Bethesda – **16**-3a9
Bethlehem – **8**-1b5
Bethsaida – **15**-2b1d
Betrayal – **4**-6b8
Betray – **7**-3a4c; **13**-5a4b
Betrayal – **4**-6b8
Betrayer – **13**-5a5c; **17**-4a2
Betrays – **4**-6b3; **13**-5a5g
Between – **4**-5c; **11**-4a6
Beware – **42**-3a1
Beyond Recovery – **49**-4d4a2a
Billowed – **48**-4c6c2b
Birds Had Their Great Supper – **52**-4g3b5
Birth – **1**-#1;1a; **5**-#1; **8**-#1;1b,1b1,2,4; **14**-#1; **48**-4d1a4
Bitter Roots & Unbelief – **36**-3b3d
Black Horse – **48**-4b3
Blackest Darkness – **40**-2b3c8
Blameless Life – **41**-2c3a
Blasphemies Against God – **49**-4d4a3a2
Blasphemous Names – **49**-4d4a1a3
Blasphemy – **18**-1b15; **45**-3a2a1b
Blessed – **9**-3a2a-d
Blessed Are Believers of the First Resurrection – **52**-4h2a2b
Blessed Are Those Who Do His Commandments – **54**-4i9
"Blessed Are Those Who Die Beginning at That Time" – **51**-4d7c6
Blesses – **12**-4b23
Blessings – **1**-2b1; **30**-4a6; **38**-2a

Blind – **10**-3b1c; **16**-3b14-16
Blind Man – **6**-2c16
Blind Beggar – **3**-4d18; **6**-2d5; **12**-4b26
Blindness – **2**-3a11
Blood – **51**-4e3,4
Blood-Dipped Robe – **52**-4g2a6
Blood of Jesus – **39**-2b1i
Blood of the Lamb – **49**-4d2a2c1
Blotted Out – **46**-3a5a2c1g
Blue – **48**-4c6c1
Boast – **26**-3d6
Boasting Is Excluded – **22**-3a2
Body – **24**-4d5
Body of Christ – **27**-3a; **28**-2b1
Boils – **51**-4e2
Boldness – **18**-1b6
Bondage – **26**-2b4a
Book – **47**-4a2; **48**-4c7,8
Book of Life – **46**-3a5a2c1g; **50**-4d4a3a7; **53**-4h4a3

NEW TESTAMENT BOOKS OF THE BIBLE

Book of Matthew – Pg**1**
Book of Mark – Pg**5**
Book of Luke – Pg**8**
Book of John – Pg**14**
Book of Acts – Pg**18**
Book of Romans – Pg**21**
Book of 1st Corinthians – Pg**23**
Book of 2nd Corinthians – Pg**25**
Book of Galatians – Pg**26**
Book of Ephesians – Pg**27**
Book of Philippians – Pg**28**
Book of Colossians – Pg**29**
Book of 1st Thessalonians – Pg**29**
Book of 2nd Thessalonians – Pg**30**
Book of 1st Timothy – Pg**31**
Book of 2nd Timothy – Pg**32**
Book of Titus – Pg**32**
Book of Philemon – Pg**33**
Book of Hebrews – Pg**33**
Book of James – Pg**37**
Book of 1st Peter – Pg**38**
Book of 2nd Peter – Pg**39**
Book of 1st John – Pg**41**
Book of 2nd John – Pg**42**
Book of 3rd John – Pg**42**
Book of Jude – Pg**43**
Book of Revelation – Pg**44**

Bore a Child – **49**-4d133a
Boredom – **40**-2a2a3
Born – **8**-1b4a;1b5;1b5b; **16**-3b14; **18**-1a5; **49**-4d1b2c
Borrowed – **5**-6b22
Borrowed Tomb – **14**-5a6i
Bottomless Pit – **48**-4c5; **52**-4h1; **52**-4h3
Bought – **18**-4b12
Bound for 1000 Years in Bottomless Pit – **52**-4h1
Bowl Judgments – **48**-4c12; **51**-4e1;e4e2-8
Bowls – **51**-4e1b
Bowls of Judgment – **51**-4e
Boy – **3**-4d5; **6**-2d2; **10**-3c20
Branches – **13**-5a1a2
Brag – **40**-2b4a
Brass – **44**-2a2b1c
Bread – **1**-1a8a; **12**-4b9b
Bread of Life – **16**-3a15
Breakfast – **18**-4c6f
Breastplate – **28**-3d1b
Brethren – **39**-2b2; **49**-4d2a2b
Bribe – **5**-6c3
Bride – **54**-4i3
Bright Hope – **30**-2a
Bringing Many Sons to Glory – **34**-1a5
Brings – **38**-2a2b3
Brings a Curse – **26**-2b1b
Brings Back – **38**-2c4
Broad & High – **54**-4i4a5
Brother – **15**-2b1b
Brother In Error – **38**-2c4
Brother Suing Brother – **24**-3a3
Brotherly Kindness – **39**-2a1a5d
Brothers (Relatives) – **15**-2c3; **16**-3b1
Brothers & Sisters – **34**-1a5b
Builder – **8**-3b24
Built – **15**-3a1c
Built on Foundation Stones – **54**-4i4a10e
Burden – **46**-3a4a2b1
Burdens – **23**-6a7c; **27**-2c1d
Burial – **7**-3a6g; **13**-#5
Buried – **5**-6b22; **14**-5a6i; **18**-4b12
Burning Fire – **52**-4g3b3
Burning Sulfur – **48**-4c6c2b; **51**-4d7c3
Business – **30**-4a2
But Christ – **29**-2b1-4
But Dead – **46**-3a5a2
But For the Truth – **26**-3d12
Buy Things – **50**-4d5b9
By Faith – **35**-3a3c
By Fire – **41**-2c2c
By Second Death – **45**-3a2a2d
By Things Visible – **35**-3a3e
By Wicked People's Errors – **41**-2c3d

C

Caesar – **21**-4b11
Caesarea – **20**-4a

Caiaphas – **4**-6b9
Call God a Liar – **41**-1a3d1
Call to Apostleship – **26**-2a1
Called – **9**-2b4; **39**-2a1a1; **43**-1a; **52**-4g3a
Called Faithful & True – **51**-4g2a1
Called Fire from Heaven – **50**-4d5b3
Called "The *WORD* of God" – **52**-4g2a7
Calls – **5**-2a2; **11**-4b7; **15**-2b1d; **34**-1a5b
Calms – **6**-2c1; **10**-3c9
Can Be Too Late – **36**-3b3f
Can Fight Against Anti-Christ – **50**-4d4a2e2
Cana – **15**-2c
Capernaum – **15**-2c3
Captured – **52**-4g3b2
Care – **24**-2d2
Careless – **10**-3a2h
Carried Away – **41**-2c3d
Carried the Gospel – 50-4d7a1
Cast a Third of Stars – **48**-4d1b2a
Cast Alive Into Lake of Burning Fire – **52**-4g3b3
Cast Into Great Tribulation – **46**-3a4a2a4
Cast Into the Lake of Fire – **53**-4h4a7a
Cast Into Lake of Fire with Anti-Christ & False Prophet – **52**-4h3e
Cast Lots – **18**-4b9
Cast Out – **11**-4a8
Cast Out of Heaven – **49**-4d2a1b
Cast to Earth – **49**-4d2a2b
Catastrophe of Unbelief – **34**-1b2
Caught – **16**-3b8
Caught Up to God – **49**-4d1b3b
Cause – **23**-2b
Caused All Non-Worshipers to be Killed – **50**-4d5b7
Caused Everyone to Receive His Mark – **50**-4d5b8
Caution to Ephesus Church – **45**-3a1b
Caution to Pergamos Church – **45**-3a3c
Ceasing – **30**-4a5e
Celebrated – **7**-3a5b; **13**-5a5b
Census – **8**-1b5a
Centurion – **10**-3c1
Cephas (Peter) – **15**-2b1c
Ceremony – **8**-1b4b;1c1a
Challenge – **21**-4b16
Challenges – **4**-5a4
Change of Plans – **25**-#2;2a2
Changed Lives – **25**-3a2
Changes – **15**-2c1
Character – **29**-3a
Character of the New Man – **29**-3a
Characteristics of Fellowship – **42**-#2
Characteristics of a Faithful Minister – **32**-2b
Characteristics of the 144,000 – **50**-4d6a
Characteristics of the Troops & Horses – **48**-4c6c
Charge to Preach the Word – **32**-3a4
Charge to Timothy – **31**-2a3
Charges Timothy – **32**-#2;#3
Charges Timothy to Persevere – **32**-#2;#3
Chased – **15**-3a1a
Cheerful – **25**-3c4
Child – **8**-1b2b; **36**-3b2e; **49**-4d1b3a
Child Born – **49**-4d1bc2
Child Caught Up to God – **49**-4d1b3b
Child of God – **42**-2a2
Child to Rule All Nations – **49**-4d1b3a
Children – **3**-4d13; **6**-2d4d; **12**-4b23; **16**-3b12; **27**-3b4;3c1c; **38**-2a3b6;2b1b
Children Killed – **46**-3a4a2a5
Children of God – **42**-2a1
Children of Light – **27**-3b4
Chooses – **1**-2a2; **11**-4a3
Chose – **38**-2a3b6
Chosen – **9**-3a; **18**-1b14; **39**-2b1j;2b4
Chosen from Foundation of World – **39**-2b1j
Christ – **1**-1a2,3; **8**-1b2; **19**-2a2; **22**-4c1;5a1a; **23**-6a6; **24**-4d1,2,6; **25**-#3;3a1,4,7,9; **26**-2a5;2b2; **27**-#2;2a; 2a1,5,5;#3;3a; **28**-2a1,2;2b1; **29**-#2;2a,b;2b1-4; **30**-3a4; **31**-3b; **33**-3b1; **34**-1b;1b2d5;2a;2a2,4; **35**-2a6; 3a2b; **39**-2b1k; **40**-2a1a8; **49**-4d2a2a; **52**-4g3b1,4; **52**-4h2
Christ Child – **1**-1a3
Christ as Man – **34**-1a5c
Christ at His Coming – **51**-4g2a
Christ Is Greater Than Angels – **33**-1a
Christ Is Greater Than Moses – **34**-1b
Christ Is Greater Than the Old Testament Priesthood – **34**-2a
Christ Is Preached – **28**-2a1
Christ Is Superior – **34**-2a2,4; **35**-2a6
Christ Is the Light – **41**-1a2
Christ on Earth – **52**-4h2
Christ Our Pattern – **25**-3c1
Christ's – **2**-3b; **3**-4d3; **27**-3a2a; **28**-2b1b
Christ's Covenant Is Greater – **35**-2a5
Christ's Death Fulfills God's Will – **35**-2a6b4
Christ's Death Perfects the Sanctified – **35**-2a6b5
Christ's Example – **28**-2b1b
Christ's Gift – **27**-3a2a
Christ Gives Us – **39**-2a1a
Christ's Return – **31**-3b
Christ's Sake – **24**-2d1
Christian – **26**-2a2; **29**-3a1,2;3b; **35**-#3
Christian Graces – **29**-3b
Christian Liberty – **26**-2c1
Christian Freedom – **24**-4b
Christian Home – **29**-3a2
Christian Marriage – **24**-4a;4a1
Christian Service – **32**-2a;3a
Christian Workplace – **29**-3a3
Christians – **20**-3c9; **23**-6a; **27**-2a4; **29**-#3; **37**-1a; **39**-2a; **40**-2b; **41**-2c
Christians & People Who Belong to the World – **50**-4d5b2
Christians Left on Earth – **49**-4d3a5c
Christians Should Do – **29**-#2
Church – **18**-1a;1a5,8;1a8;1b;1b7,19; **19**-#2;2a9; **23**-#1;#2; **24**-#3;3a;#4; **26**-2b3; **27**-2a7; **29**-#2; 2a3; **30**-3b2; **31**-2b;2b1,2; **32**-#2;2a; **33**-#3;3a;3a1; **42**-1a; **44**-3a1;3a1a; **45**-3a1b,c;3a2;3a2a;3a3;

3a3a; **45**-3a4; **46**-3a5;3a6; **47**-3a7
Church at Antioch – **19**-2a19
Church at Ephesus – **27**-1a; **44**-3a1a; **45**-3a1b,c
Church at Laodicea – **47**-3a7a
Church at Pergamos – **45**-3a3a;3a3c
Church Family – **23**-6a2
Church Is Born – **18**-1a5
Church Members – **31**-2d1
Church Problems – **23**-#1
Churches – **44**-2a3b1,2;3a; **47**-#4
Circumcised – **20**-3c2
Circumcision – **8**-1b4b;1c1a; **20**-3b1; **22**-2b2;3b2
Circumstances – **25**-3a5; **28**-#2;2d4; **44**-2a1
Circumstances of Ministry – **25**-3a5
Circumstances of the Vision – **44**-2a1
Citizens – **3**-4a1
Citizenship – **21**-4b4
City – **54**-4i4a9
City Had Twelve Foundation Stones – **54**-4i4a8
City of the Living God – **36**-3b4b
"City Who Kills the Prophets" – **12**-4b11b
City Made of Pure Gold, Clear as Glass – **54**-4i4a10d
Claim – **41**-1a3d
Clean & Holy Life – **36**-3b3b
Cleansed – **7**-3a2b
Cleanses – **4**-5a2; **15**-3a1
Clear as Glass – **54**-4i4a10d
Clear Like Jasper – **54**-4i4a4
Cleared – **13**-5a2a
Closing – **29**-4a1
Closing Blessings – **29**-4a1
Closing Exhortation – **32**-3b4
Clothed – **46**-3a5a2c1f; **48**-4d1a1
Clothed with a Blood-Dipped Robe – **52**-4g2a6
Clothes – **14**-5a6g3
Coin – **3**-4d7
Collection – **25**-4e1;3c;3c3
Collection for Jerusalem Saints – **25**-4e1
Collection for the Saints – **25**-3c3
Cold or Hot – **47**-3a7b2
Colossians – **29**-#1;1a1
Come – **13**-5a3g2,3,4,6; **15**-3a6; **19**-2a19e; **36**-3b4a-f; **39**-2b1k; **41**-2c2a; **49**-4d2a2a; **50**-4d7a4
Comes – **3**-4a; **12**-4b27; **15**-2a2a; **16**-3b7; **18**-1a5; **19**-2a2,4;2a19f; **37**-2a3b1,5; **38**-2a1a
Comes from Heaven – **53**-4i1b
Comes to Earth & Sea – **49**-4d2a2c3
Comes to Faith – **19**-2a2,4
Comfort – **25**-3b4
Comfort of God – **25**-1a2
Comfort of the Coming of the *LORD* – **30**-4a3
Comforted – **17**-3c2
Comforted in Your Comfort – **25**-3b4
Coming – **35**-3a2e; **38**-2a3
Coming of Christ – **30**-3a4
Coming of Perilous Times – **32**-3a1,2
Coming – **1**-1a2; **37**-3b5e
Coming Division – **11**-4b5
Coming Future Crisis – **11**-4b6
Coming of the *LORD* – **30**-4a3
Coming Judgment – **17**-4a9b3
Coming Quickly – **47**-3a6c4; **54**-4i8,12
Command to Persevere – **47**-3a6c1
Commanded – **4**-6a5
Commandment – **4**-5c3
Commandments – **17**-4a5a,b; **49**-4d3a5b; **54**-4i9
Commandments of God – **42**-#2
Commendation – **29**-#2
Commendations – **44**-3a1a; **45**-3a3a
Commission – **5**-6c,6c4
Commit Adultery – **40**-2b3c1
Commit Sexual Immorality – **45**-3a3b1a3; **46**-3a4a2a1
Communion – **13**-5a5b2
Compassion – **11**-4a12b2
Compassionate High Priest – **34**-2a1
Complain – **15**-3a3a
Complete Expression of God – **33**-1a1a
Concern – **26**-3d4;1a2; **30**-#3
Concerning Being Prudent – **2**-2d7
Concerning Christ's Kingdom – **2**-3b
Concerning Doctrine – **31**-#2;2a
Concerning His Return – **11**-4b4
Concerning Death of Jesus – **3**-4d2,6,16
Concerning Destruction of Future Temple – **4**-6a1
Concerning Faith – **7**-3a3a
Concerning False Teaching – **6**-2c15
Concerning Fasting – **2**-2d3;3a9; **5**-2a8a
Concerning Forgiving Fellow Believers – **3**-4d11
Concerning Fruitful Lives – **2**-2e2
Concerning Giving – **7**-3a3i
Concerning Giving to the Needy – **2**-2d1
Concerning Going to Heaven – **2**-2e1
Concerning His Authority – **7**-3a3b
Concerning His *LORDship* – **7**-3a3g
Concerning His Second Coming – **12**-4b21
Concerning Israel's Leaders – **7**-3a3c
Concerning Jesus – **2**-3b1
Concerning Judging Others – **2**-2d6
Concerning Kingdom Living – **9**-3b2
Concerning Looking Down on People – **3**-4d10
Concerning Marriage & Divorce – **3**-4d12
Concerning Money – **2**-2d4
Concerning Obedience to God's Word – **2**-2e3
Concerning Paul's Trip to Jerusalem – **21**-4a8
Concerning Prayer – **2**-2d1,8
Concerning Pride – **7**-3a3h
Concerning Religious Leaders – **4**-5c5
Concerning Taxes – **7**-3a3d
Concerning Temptations – **3**-4d9
Concerning the Coming Division – **11**-4b5
Concerning the Coming Future Crisis – **11**-4b6
Concerning the End-Times – **4**-6a
Concerning the Future – **7**-3a3j
Concerning the Great Commission – **7**-3a3f
Concerning the *LORD's* Supper – **24**-4c2
Concerning the Resurrection – **7**-3a3e
Concerning the Sabbath – **2**-3b3
Concerning Them – **37**-3b6d2

Concerning Spiritual Gifts – **24**-4c3
Concerning the Vision – **19**-2a14
Concerning Things Offered to Idols – **24**-4b1
Concerning Wealth – **3**-4d14; **6**-2d4e
Concerning Worrying – **2**-2d5
Condemn – **13**-5a6b
Condemnation – **5**-2a11; **21**-#2; **40**-2b2
Condemnation of Sin – **21**-#2
Condemns – **4**-5c6;6b11
Conditions for Fellowship – **41**-#1
Conduct – **39**-3a1
Conduct Yourself Accordingly – **23**-6a3
Conduct Before the World – **39**-3a;3a1
Confess – **41**-1a3c
Confession – **31**-2e3; **35**-3a1; **41**-1a3
Confidence – **28**-2c1; **31**-3b1; **42**-2b3
Confidence in the *LORD* – **31**-3b1
Confident Trust in the *LORD* – **35**-3a2c
Conflict – **4**-5c
Conflict on Earth – **47**-4b2
Conflict Over Circumcision – **20**-3b1
Confrontation – **20**-3a3
Confronting the Perilous Times – **32**-3a2
Confused – **16**-3b6
Conqueror – **47**-4b1
Conquers – **38**-2b6
Consequences – **23**-2c
Consequences of Unbelief – **34**-1b3
Consolation – **9**-3a2f
Constant Reminders – **40**-2a2a2
Constructive Criticism Necessary – **25**-2a
Consummation of Love – **42**-2a8
Contend for the Faith – **43**-2a1
Content of the Vision – **44**-2a2
Contentment – **31**-2e2
Continue to Hate – **45**-3a1c1
Continue to Love – **37**-3b6a
Control – **38**-2b4
Controlled – **33**-1a4a
Controversies – **2**-3b3
Conversion – **21**-4b14,15
Converted – **20**-3c4,6
Conversion of Saul – **19**-2a5
Converted – **20**-3c6
Convince – **17**-4a9b
Convinced – **15**-3a1d
Corinth – **20**-3c13; **25**-4e2; **25**-#1
Corinthian Church – **24**-#4
Corinthian's Faithfulness – **26**-3d4
Cornelius – **19**-2a12,15;2a12a-b
Cornerstone – **27**-2a6
Correction to Ephesus Church – **45**-3a1b
Corrupt Church – **45**-3a4
Corrupt People – **53**-4i2d3
Corruptible Things – **39**-2b1h
Corrupts Good Habits – **24**-4d4
Cosmic Disturbances – **48**-4b6
Cost – **10**-3c18; **10**-4a2
Cost of Being a Disciple – **10**-3c18; **12**-4b13
Cost of Discipleship – **10**-4a2
Could Buy Things – **50**-4d5b9
Council – **18**-1b17
Council at Jerusalem – **20**-3b
Counted Worthy – **30**-2a3
Countenance – **44**-2a2b1g
Countryside – **19**-2a
Covenant – **26**-2b1c; **35**-2a5;2a5b
Covenants – **26**-2b4
Coverings – **24**-4c1
Covetousness – **11**-4b2
Cowardly Who Turned Away from God (Backsliders) – **53**-4i2d1
Creation – **29**-2a1; **33**-1a2e
Creation of God – **47**-3a7a1c
Criminal – **14**-5a6g5
Criminals – **5**-6b18; **14**-5a6g1
Crippled Woman – **11**-4b8
Crisis – **11**-4b6
Critical Defeat – **49**-4d2a2c
Criticism – **25**-2a
Criticize – **10**-3b1b
Criticized – **12**-4b8b
Cross – **5**-6b17,20; **14**-5a6f,g; **18**-4b8,11; **27**-2c2
Crowd – **14**-5a6g4
Crowds – **2**-3b4
Crown – **47**-3a6c6
Crown of Life – **37**-2a3a; **45**-3a2a2c
Crown of Rejoicing – **12**-4b15a
Crown of Righteousness – **32**-3b1c
Crown (Imperishable) – **24**-4b3a
Crowns – **48**-4d1b1; **49**-4d4a1a2
Crowns on His Head – **51**-4g2a4
Crucified – **4**-6b14; **5**-6b16,18; **14**-5a6e,f;5a6g1; **18**-4b6,7
Crucified With Christ – **26**-2a5
Crucifixion – **7**-3a6,3a6e; **13**-5a6; **15**-3a2b; **18**-4c8
Cry of the Martyrs – **47**-4b5
Crying – **53**-4i1c6
Crystal Clear Like Jasper – **54**-4i4a4
Cure – **34**-1b4
Curse – **26**-2b1b
Cursed – **7**-3a2a; **9**-3a2d; **40**-2b3c5
Curses – **4**-5a3
Cut-off Ear – **13**-5a5h; **17**-4b2
Cyprus – **20**-3a2

D

Damascus – **19**-2a5,7
Dance – **3**-4a2; **6**-2c6
Danger of False Teachers – **43**-#2
Dangers to Growing Christians – **40**-2b
Dares – **1**-1a8a-b
Darkness – **40**-2b3c8
Darkness & Pain – **51**-4e6
Daughter – **3**-4b5; **10**-3c12
David – **36**-3a4n; **46**-3a6a3
David, Samuel & the Prophets – **36**-3a4n

Day – **14**-5a8; **34**-1b2d2; **40**-2b2a5
Day & Night – **52**-4h3f
Day of Salvation – **25**-3b1
Day of the *LORD* – **30**-4a4;2nd Thess-**30**-#3;3a; **41**-2c2
Days – **17**-3c3
Days After Salvation – **35**-3a2b
Deacons – **18**-1b14; **31**-2b4
Dead – **5**-6c1; **7**-4a7a; **10**-3c2,12; **14**-5a8a; **18**-4c1; **38**-2b3; **44**-2a3a3; **46**-3a5a2; **53**-4h4a5;4h4a7a,b
Dead Church – **46**-3a5
Dead for a 1000 Years – **52**-4h2a2a
Dead from Tribulation Period Judged – **53**-4h4a4
Dead Unbelievers from the Tribulation Period – **53**-4h4a2
Dead Unbelievers Remained Dead – **52**-4h2a2a
Deaf – **6**-2c12
Deafness – **2**-3a11
Death – **2**-3a10; **6**-2c3; **11**-4a12b5; **18**-4c8;1b7,8; **19**-2a7; **22**-4a1; **32**-3b1; **34**-1a5d; **37**-2a3b3; **45**-3a2a2b,d; **48**-4b4; **50**-4d4a3a10; **52**-4h2a2a,c; **53**-4h4a7c; **53**-4i2d
Death (of Jesus) – **3**-4d2,6,16; **6**-2c18;2d3;2d4f; **7**-3a6f; **10**-3c17,21; **12**-4b25; **13**-#5; **17**-#4;4b; **35**-2a6b2,4,5
Death—The Last Enemy Destroyed – **24**-4d3
Death & Hades – **44**-2a3a5; **53**-4h4a6
Death, Sorrow or Crying – **53**-4i1c6
Deceitfulness – **40**-2b3c
Deceive Tribulation Saints – **52**-4h3b
Deceived People – **50**-4d5b4
Deceivers – **42**-#3;3a1,2
Deceptions – **40**-2b4
Deceptive Words – **50**-4d6a6
Deciding – **11**-4b6b
Declaration – **16**-3a12,15
Declares – **6**-2c17; **14**-5a6b2; **16**-3a11;3b4,9;3b12c;3b16-18
Declares War – **49**-4d3a5a
Decree – **20**-3b4
Decreed – **8**-1b5a
Dedicated – **20**-3a1
Defeat – **49**-4d2a2c
Defeated – **52**-4g3
Defended – **22**-2b3
Defends – **19**-2a18; **25**-3a
Defends His Authority – **25**-3d
Defends the Collection – **25**-3c;3d
Defense Against False Teachers – **43**-2b
Defense Before the Sanhedrin – **21**-4b5
Defense Before Felix the Governor – **21**-4b5
Defile – **6**-2c10d
Defiles – **6**-2c10e
Defined – **2**-3c2; **10**-3c8
Definition – **5**-2a12
Definition of Faith – **35**-3a3
Delivered – **3**-4b5;4d5; **6**-2d2; **10**-3c10e;3c20
Delivered from Viper Attack – **21**-4b21
Delivers – **6**-2c11
Demetrius – **43**-3b
Demon – **3**-4b5; **6**-2c11; **9**-2b1
Demons – **5**-2a3,9; **6**-2c2; **9**-2b1a; **10**-3c10c,d
Demon-Possessed – **3**-4d5; **6**-2d2; **9**-2b1a; **10**-3c10;3c10b,e;3c20
Demonic Forces – **2**-3a6
Demonstrates – **5**-2a3,4
Denial – **4**-6b6; **13**-5a5e
Denied His Name – **47**-3a6b5
Denies – **4**-6b10; **7**-3a6b; **13**-5a6a; **18**-4b4
Deny – **7**-3a5d; **17**-4a3
Depart Secretly – **20**-3c7
Departing from Grace – **26**-1a2
Departs – **20**-3c13
Dependency – **38**-2c1
Depravity – **40**-2b3
Derbe – **20**-3a8
Descended Out of Heaven from God – **54**-4i4a1
Descends – **15**-2a2b
Describes – **2**-3b7; **16**-3b12
Description – **49**-4d4a1a; **50**-4d5a
Description of Christ at His Coming – **51**-4g2a
Description of False Teachers – **43**-2a4
Description of Horse's Head – **48**-4c6c2
Description of Melchizedek's Order – **35**-2a4a
Description of the Great Harlot – **51**-4f1a
Description of the New Jerusalem – **53**-4i4a
Description of the New Jerusalem Wall – **54**-4i4a10
Description of the **ONE** – **44**-2a2b1
Description of the Saints of God – **52**-4h2a
Description of the Twelve Gates – **54**-4i4a11
Desire Pure Milk of the Word – **39**-2b3
Desires – **37**-2a3b1
Destination of All Unbelievers – **52**-4g3b3; **53**-4h4a7c
Destined to Death – **50**-4d4a3a10
Destined to Prison – **50**-4d4a3a9
Destroyed – **24**-4d3
"Destroy This Temple, I Will Make It Rise in Three Days" – **15**-3a1b
Destruction – **4**-6a1; **13**-5a3g5; **40**-2b3b
Destruction of Babylon the Great – **51**-4f2a
Destruction of the Great Harlot – **51**-4f1b
Destructive Doctrine – **40**-2b1
Destructive Heresies – **40**-2b1a
Destructive Ways – **40**-2b1b
Develop Virtues – **40**-2a1a6
Development of Faith – **39**-#2
Devour – **49**-4d1b2c
Devours Them – **52**-4h3d
Diadems – **48**-4d1b1
Did Not Spare – **40**-2b2a1,2
Did Not Tolerate Sin – **45**-3a1a3
Die – **14**-5a6e2; **17**-3c7; **28**-2a2; **51**-4d7c6
Die Is Gain – **28**-2a2
Died As Savior – **34**-1a5c
Dies – **5**-6b20,21; **16**-3c1; **18**-4b11; **19**-2b6
Difference – **11**-4a6
Different – **3**-#4
Difficult Times – **32**-3a
Diligent – **40**-2a1a7
Diligent Worker – **32**-2b4

Dines – **11**-4a12a
Diotrephes – **43**-#3;3a
Directives – **37**-3b6;3b7
Disagreement – **16**-3a16
Disappear – **41**-2c2c
Disappeared – **53**-4i1a
Disaster – **41**-2c
Disasters – **5**-6b21; **13**-5a3g3
Discerner – **34**-1b4b
Discerning – **11**-4b6a
Disciple – **10**-3c18; **12**-4b13; **15**-2b1d,e
Disciples – **2**-3b3a; **4**-6b4; **5**-2a2,10; **6**-2c5;2d4,2d4a; **7**-3a3j1; **9**-2c3;3a; **10**-3c13; **11**-4a3; **13**-5a1a1;5a5a; 5a5b1; **14**-5a8c; **15**-2b;2c3;3a3a;3a4a;3a5; **16**-3a17;3b12a; **17**-3c7;4a;4a1;4a11; **18**-4c3,4,6; 4c6a,b,f.
Disciples of John (Baptist) – **20**-4a3
Discipleship – **2**-3a4; **10**-4a2
Discipline – **36**-3b2;3b2a,d-h
Discipline of God – **36**-3b2
Disciplines – **36**-3b2c
Discourse – **13**-5a3g
Discovered – **13**-5a5c
Discrimination – **38**-2b2
Diseases – **2**-3a3
Disobeys God – **34**-1b4a
Disorder in the Church – **24**-#3
Dispensation – **4**-6a2
Dissension – **33**-3b2
Distance – **2**-3a2
Disturbances – **48**-4b6
Diversity – **24**-4c4
Divided – **11**-4a9b; **16**-3b5
Divisions – **23**-2a-c
Divisions Within the Church – **23**-#2
Divine Discipline – **36**-3b2d
Divine Nature – **39**-2a1a3
Divinity – **14**-1a1
Division – **11**-4b5; **20**-3c1
Divisive – **23**-7a4
Divorce – **1**-2c5; **3**-4d12; **6**-2d4c; **24**-4a2
Do His Commandments – **54**-4i9
Do Not Abandon the Faith – **35**-3a2g1
Do Not Allow Boredom / Impatience – **40**-2a2a3
Do Not Be Afraid – **44**-2a3a1
Do Not Be Carried Away – **41**-2c3d
Do Not Be Immoral or Godless – **36**-3b3e
Do Not Be Misled – **37**-2a3b4
Do Not Despise Prophesies – **30**-4a5h
Do Not Hinder – **3**-4d13
Do Not Forget – **37**-3b6b;3b6d1
Do Not Grieve the Holy Spirit – **27**-3b2
Do Not Harden Your Hearts Against Him – **34**-1b2b
Do Not Ignore Discipline – **36**-3b2b
Do Not Live for the Flesh – **28**-2c3
Do Not Love Ways of the World – **41**-1a6
Do Not Miss the Special Favor of God – **36**-3b3c
Do Not Neglect Fundamentals of Our Faith – **40**-2a2a1
Do Not Neglect Salvation – **33**-1a3
Do Not Quench the Spirit – **30**-4a5g
Do Not Refuse Him Who Speaks – **36**-3b5
Do Not Revert to Old Ways – **38**-2b1c
Do Not See Jesus – **38**-2a2c
Do Not Speak Out Against Fallen Angels – **40**-2b2a8
Do Not Turn Your Heart Away from the *LORD* – **34**-1b2a
Do Not Understand – **40**-2b3a
Do Nothing With Partiality – **31**-2d5
Do What He Says – **17**-4a5c
"Do You Love Me?" – **18**-4c7
Doctrine – **31**-#2;2a;2a1;2c3; **40**-2b1
Doctrine of Balaam – **45**-3a3b1;3a3b1a;
Doesn't Do What He Says – **17**-4a5d
Dog Returns to His Vomit – **40**-2b4e
Done – **51**-4e8
Done in the Past – **40**-2b2a
Donkey – **13**-5a1a;5a1a1
Don't – **6**-2c10d; **10**-3b1b; **17**-4a5d
Don't Love Jesus – **17**-4a5d
Doomed – **11**-4a9b; **40**-2b3c5,8
Door & Knock – **47**-3a6b2
Door & Let Me In – **47**-3a7b4b
Doorway to Eternal Life – **34**-1a5d
Dorcas – **19**-2a11
Doubt – **2**-3b1; **10**-3c3
Down to Earth – **49**-4d2a1c
Doxology – **43**-2c
Dragon – **48**-4d1b;4d1b2; **50**-4d5a2
Drags Fish to Shore – **18**-4c6e
Dries Up – **51**-4e7
Drink of Water – **15**-3a4d1
Drive of Life – **36**-3b4
Drives – **6**-2c2
Drown Israelites – **49**-4d3a3
Duty – **12**-4b19c
Dwell with Them – **53**-4i1ac2
Dwelled – **45**-3a3a1b

E

Each Head -- **49**-4d4a1a3
Each Other – **34**-1b2d2
Each Side – **54**-4i4a7
Ear – **13**-5a5h; **50**-4d4a3a8
Early Church – **18**-1a8;1b7
Early Days After Salvation – **35**-3a2b
Early Life – **21**-4b13
Earth – **36**-3b5b; **37**-3b7d; **39**-2b1g; **47**-3a6c3;4b2; **48**-4b3; **48**-4c6a;4d1b2a; **49**-4d2a1c;4d2a2b;4d3a5c; **50**-4d6a2; **52**-4h2; **53**-4i1
Earth & Sea – **49**-4d2a2c3
Earth Disappeared – **53**-4i1a
Earthly Sanctuary – **35**-2a6a1
Earthly Service – **35**-2a6a2
Earthquake – **49**-4d3a4
Eases – **10**-3c3
Eat Foods – **45**-3a3b1a2
Eat From – **45**-3a1c2
Eat Things – **46**-3a4a2a2

Eats – **5**-2a7; **9**-2b7
Eats the Little Book – **48**-4c8
Edification to Smyrna Church – **45**-3a2a
Elders of the House of God – **31**-2d4
Egypt – **1**-1a4
Elders – **32**-Titus-2a1; **35**-3a3c
Elders Exhorted – **21**-4a7
Elders in the Church – **32**-#2
Elect Lady – **42**-1a
Elect Pilgrims – **38**-1a
Eleven Disciples – **14**-5a8c
Elijah – **48**-4c9
Elizabeth – **8**-1b1a,c;1b3,1b3a-c
Embodiment of God – **14**-1a6
Employees – **27**-3c1d
Employers – **27**-3c1d; **39**-3a3
Empty-Handed – **18**-4c6b
Encounter God's Wrath – **51**-4d7c1
Encounters – **10**-3c10; **15**-3a4d
Encouraged – **29**-3b1; **33**-3a2
Encouraged to Endure – **51**-4d7c5
Encourages the Thessalonians – **30**-3b1
Encouragement – **30**-#2;2a2; **44**-2a3a
Encouragement from Jesus to John – **44**-2a3a
Encouragement in Persecution – **30**-#2
Encouragements in Trials & Persecutions – **30**-2a2
Encouragement to Maturity – **34**-2a3c
End – **4**-6a2; **34**-1b2d3; **53**-4i2
End-time – **4**-#6;6a,6a8
End-time Anti-Christ – **49**-4d4a1
Endurance – **35**-3a2d; **36**-3b1a2; **37**-2a1a;2a1a1; **39**-2a1a5b
Endurance Grows – **37**-2a1a1
Endurance & Faith Availabible – **50**-4d4a3a11
Endurance of Faith – **36**-3b
Endure His Divine Discipline – **36**-3b2d
Endure Many Trials – **38**-2a2a
Endure Persecution Patiently – **51**-4d7c5
Endure Testing – **37**-2a3a
Endured Hardships – **45**-3a1a5
Endures Forever – **33**-1a2c
Enduring – **32**-2b3
Enemies – **10**-3b1a; **13**-4b28b5
Enemy – **24**-4d3
Enjoyable – **36**-3b2h
Enoch – **35**-3a4b
Enoch & Elijah – **48**-4c9
Enraged with Anger – **49**-4d3a5
Enter – **10**-3c10d; **34**-1b3c
Enter His Rest – **34**-1b2c
Enters – **13**-5a1a; **34**-1b3b
Entertained – **37**-3b6c
Entire Household – **34**-1b1b
Entry – **4**-5a1; **6**-3a1a; **13**-5a1; **17**-3c6
Epaphroditus' Example – **28**-2b1e
Ephesian Elders Exhorted – **21**-4a7
Ephesus – **20**-4a4,5; **44**-3a1;3a1a; **45**-3a1b,c
Equal Guilt – **22**-2b1
Error – **38**-2c4
Errors – **41**-2c3d
Eruptions – **48**-4c2
Escaped to Derbe – **20**-3a8
Escapes – **19**-2a7
Establish – **33**-1a2e
Eternal – **16**-3b13; **36**-3b5c
Eternal Glory – **14**-1a2
Eternal Life – **34**-1a5d
Eternal Life With – **17**-3c9; **40**-1a2a8
Eternal Life Without – **17**-3c9
Eternal Things – **36**-3b5c
Ethiopian – **19**-2a4
Euphrates – **48**-4c6
Euphrates River Dries Up – **51**-4e7
Eutychus – **20**-4a6b
Evades – **21**-4b16
Events – **8**-1b;1c
Events of the Great White Throne Judgment – **53**-4h4a
Everlasting Love of God – **22**-4c3
Ever – **33**-1a2c
Every Day – **34**-1b2d2
Every Form of Evil – **30**-4a5j
Every Spirit – **42**-2a5
Every Tear Wiped Away – **53**-4i1c5
Every Tribe – **49**-4d4a3a5
Everyone – **39**-2a1a5e
Everyone to Receive His Mark – **50**-4d5b8
Everything – **30**-4a5f; **38**-2b1d; **41**-2c2c
Everywhere – **50**-4d6a4
Evidence of Things Not Seen – **35**-3a3b
Evil – **12**-4b22b; **30**-4a5c,j; **34**-1b2d;1b2d1; **40**-2b3a
Evil & the Lustful – **40**-2b2a7
Evil Actions – **37**-2a3b3
"Evil Company Corrupts Good Habits" – **24**-4d4
Evil Desires – **37**-2a3b1
Evil for Evil – **30**-4a5c
Evil Judge – **12**-4b22b
Evil of His Day – **40**-2b2a5
Evil Speaking – **39**-2b3a
Exalted Above the Angels – **33**-1a2
Examine Yourself – **26**-3d11
Example – **11**-4b4a-b; **28**-2b1b-4; **29**-2a1
Example of Paul – **24**-2d
Exceedingly – **1**-2b1j
Excel in Giving – **25**-3c1
Excellence – **39**-2a1a4
Excluded – **22**-3a2
Executed – **12**-4b28b5
Exercise – **38**-2b1
Exercised All Authority – **50**-4d5b1
Exercising Gifts – **24**-4c9
Exhortation – **7**-3a3j5; **25**-4e3; **26**-3d11; **32**-3b4
Exhortations – **26**-3d13; **27**-2c3; **28**-3e;Phil.2e; **29**-#4; **30**-4a5; **31**-2a-e; **37**-3b9
Exhortations Concerning Doctrine – **31**-2a
Exhortations in Church Leadership – **31**-2d
Exhortations in Other Duties – **31**-2e
Exhortations to Leaders – **31**-2c
Exhortations to the Church – **31**-2b

Exhorted – **21**-4a7; **43**-2a1
Expands – **9**-#3; **19**-#2
Explained – **10**-3c7; **15**-3a2c
Explains – **15**-3a2a,b;3a4d3;3a5a; **18**-1a7; **21**-4b13,15;
25-1a;#2
Explains His Change of Plans – **25**-#2
Explanation of the Day of the *LORD* – 2nd Thess-**30**-3a
Explosions – **48**-4c4
Exposed – **11**-4a12b3-4; **35**-3a2b2; **45**-3a1a4
Exposes – **11**-4a12b
Exposure of the False Teachers – **43**-2a
Expresses – **5**-2a8
Expression of God – **33**-1a1a
Expression of Thanks – **23**-1a2; **32**-2a1
Expressions from Paul – **23**-1a
Eyes – **36**-3b1a3; **40**-2b3c1; **51**-4g2a3
Eyes Like a Flaming Fire – **44**-2a2b1b; **51**-4g2a3

F

Fact – **23**-2a
Failure to Develop Virtues – **40**-2a1a6
Faith – **2**-3a2; **7**-3a3a; **12**-4b19,4b19c; **19**-2a2,4; **21**-1a3;
22-3a1;3b1,3; **26**-2b1; **27**-2a3; **28**-3d1d; **31**-2e5;
32-2a3; **33**-2a1; **35**-#3;3a;3a2;3a2f;3ag1;3a2f;3a2
g1;3a3;3a3c;3a4; **36**-3b;3b1; **37**-#2; 2a1a;2a1a1;
38-2b;2b1-7;2c;2c1-4; **39**-#2;2a1; **42**-2a9;2b1; **43**-
2a1; **45**-3a3a1d; **46**-3a4a1.
Faith & Endurance – **37**-2a1a
Faith Availabible – **50**-4d4a3a11
Faith by the Christian – **35**-#3
Faith Tested – **37**-2a1a1
Faith Without Works – **38**-2b3
Faith's Reality – **24**-4d1
Faithful – **34**-1b2d3; **35**-3a2b1; **45**-3a2a2b; **47**-3a7a1b
Faithful & Just – **41**-1a3c1
Faithful & True – **51**-4g2a1
Faithful Church – **46**-3a6
Faithful Minister – **32**-2b
Faithfulness – **12**-4b28b4; **26**-3d4
Faithfulness to the *LORD* – **29**-2a
Faithless – **24**-2c2b
Fall – **34**-1b4a; **51**-4f2;4f2b-d
Fall of Babylon—**51**-4f2;4f2b,d
Fallen – **40**-2b2a8; **49**-4d2a1a; **50**-4d7b1
Fallen Angels – **40**-2b2a8; **49**-4d2a1a
Falls – **19**-2a17
False Apostles – **26**-3d5; **45**-3a1a4
False Christ – **12**-4b21b; **13**-5a3g2
False Comings – **12**-4b21b
False Doctrine – **31**-2a1
False Idols as God – **53**-4i2d7
False Prophet – **50**-4d5;4d5b; **52**-4h3e
False Prophet Captured – **52**-4g3b2
False Prophet Deceived People – **50**-4d5b4
False Rumor – **21**-4b1
False Teachers – **32**-Titus-2a2; **40**-2b1-4; **42**-3a;
43-#2;2a;2a4;2b
False Teaching – **3**-4c2
Family – **1**-1a4-5; **2**-3b7; **5**-2a12**10**-3c8
Famine to Come – **19**-2a19e
Famine on Earth – **48**-4b3
Far Greater Than the Angels – **33**-1a1b
Farewell – **32**-3b5; **33**-3b4;3a3; **37**-3b9
Farewell Message – **42**-4a; **43**-4a
Farewells & Exhortations – **26**-3d13
Farmers – **4**-5b2; **13**-5a3b
Fast (To Stand) – **26**-2c1b; **28**-2a3; **30**-4a5i; **31**-3a5;
46-3a4a2b2;3a5a2c1b; **47**-3a6c5
Fasted – **1**-1a8b
Fasting – **2**-2d3,3a9; **5**-2a8a; **9**-2c1
Fatal Wound – **49**-4d4a2b
Father (God) – **11**-4a7d; **16**-3b2a;3b3;3b18,20; **36**-3b2f
Father & His Angels – **46**-3a5a2c1h
Fault – **50**-4d6a7
Favor – **37**-3b7c
Favor of God – **36**-3b3c
Fear of Him (Jesus) – **39**-2b1g
Fear & Awe – **36**-3b5d
"Fear God" – **50**-4d7a2
Fears of the Church – **26**-2b3
Feast – **11**-4b4a; **16**-3b2
Feasts with Pagans – **24**-4b5
Fed – **49**-4d1b3c3
Feeds – **3**-4b1,7; **6**-2c7,13; **10**-3c15; **16**-3a13
Feet – **10**-3c4; **17**-4a1; **47**-3a6b6; **48**-4d1a2; **49**-4d4a1a5
Feet of Jesus – **17**-3c5
Feet Thick (Human Measure) – **54**-4i4a10b
Felix Procrastinates in Paul's Release – **21**-4b10
Felix the Governor – **21**-4b7,9
Fellow Believers – **3**-4d11
Fellowship – **41**-#1;#2
Few in Sardis Are Worthy – **46**-3a5a2c1e
Fierceness of Almighty God – **52**-4g2a11
Fiery Red – **48**-4c6c1
Fiery Red Dragon – **48**-4d1b
Fifth Bowl Judgment – **51**-4e6
Fifth Seal – **48**-4b5
Fifth Trumpet – **48**-4c5
Fig Tree – **4**-5a3; **7**-3a2a,3a374; **13**-5a3g7
Fight – **32**-3b1b
Fight Against Anti-Christ – **49**-4d4a2e2
Filled – **8**-1b3b;1b4c; **10**-3c10c
Filled with The Glory of God – **54**-4i4a2
Final – **23**-5a3b
Final Destination of All Unbelievers – **52**-4g3b3;
53-4h4a7c
Final Exhortations – **25**-4e3; **27**-2c3; **28**-3e;Phil.2e; **29**-
#4; **30**-4a5; **37**-3b9
Final Farewells & Exhortations – **26**-3d13
Final Greetings – **23**-#7; **29**-4a
Final Messages – **33**-3b3
Final Victory – **51**-4f
Final Victory Through Christ – **24**-4d6
Final Words – **23**-7a6; **42**-#4; **43**-#4
Finality of Babylon's Fall – **51**-4f2c
Finally at Hand – **21**-4b17
Finally Happened – **49**-4d2a2

Finance – **10**-3c5
Find Rest – **34**-1b3c
Find Saul – **19**-2a19d
Finds – **14**-5a6e1
Fine Brass – **44**-2a2b1c
Fire – **21**-4b21; **37**-3b5e; **38**-2a2b2; **41**-2c2c; **44**-2a2b1b; **48**-4c1;4c6c2b; **51**-4g2a3; **52**-4g3b3; **53**-4i2d
Fire & Burning Sulfur – **51**-4d7c3
Fire from Heaven – **50**-4d5b3; **52**-4h3d
Fire with Anti-Christ & False Prophet – **52**-4h3e
Firm – **36**-3b3a
First – **3**-4d2; **5**-2a2; **6**-2c18; **9**-2b4; **15**-2b1;2c1
First Angel – **50**-4d7a
First Bowl Judgment – **51**-4e2
First Disciples – **9**-2b4
First Heaven & Earth Disappeared – **53**-4i1a
First Miracle – **15**-2c1
First Resurrection – **52**-4h2a2;4h2a2b
First Seal – **47**-4b1
First Sign – **48**-4d1a
First to God – **50**-4d6a5
First Trumpet – **48**-4c1
Five-fold – **12**-4b28b2
First Sabbath – **20**-3a4
First Servant – **12**-4b28b1
First Time – **10**-3c17
First Trip to Jerusalem – **26**-2a2
Fish – **3**-4d7; **18**-4c6e,f; **18**-4c6e,f
Fishermen – **1**-2a2
Fishing – **9**-2b4a; **18**-4c6a
Five Months – **48**-4c5
Five Thousand – **3**-4b1; **6**-2c7; **10**-3c15; **16**-3a13
Flaming Fire – **44**-2a2b1b; **51**-4g2a3
Fled – **49**-4d1b3c
Flee – **1**-1a4
Flee to Petra – **49**-4d3a2
Flesh (Human spirit) – **26**-3d8; **27**-2a4; **28**-2c1,3
Flood – **49**-4d3a3
Flooding Waters – **49**-4d3a4
Focus – **40**-2b1c
Follow – **2**-3b4;**15**-2b1
Follow the Lamb – **50**-4d6a4
Followed – **49**-4d4a2d; **52**-4g2a8
Follower – **6**-2c20
Followers – **4**-6a5; **13**-5a1a2; **19**-2a
Food – **15**-3a5a
Foods Sacrificed to Idols – **45**-3a2b1a2
Fool for Christ's Sake – **24**-2d1
Fool Ourselves – **41**-1a3a
Foods – **6**-2c10d
For a 1000 Years – **52**-4h2a2a
For Forty-two Months – **49**-4d4a3a1
For God – **45**-3a1b1
For Judgment – **51**-4d9
For Maturity – **34**-2a3c
For Our Sins – **41**-1a3f
For Punishment – **40**-2b2a6
For the Faith – **43**-2a1
For the *LORD* – 30-**4a**
For the Thessalonians – **30**-4a1
For the Future – **38**-2a1
For the Grace of God – **31**-2a2
For the Master – **32**-2b5
For Their Faith – **30**-3a2
For Their Sufferings – **29**-3a1
For Their Witness – **52**-4h2a1a
For Unbelief – **34**-1b4
For Us to God – **41**-1a3e
Forbidden – **18**-1b5
Forces – **2**-3a6
Forehead – **50**-4d6a1
Foretold – **8**-1b1,2
Forever – **33**-1a2c; **37**-3b7b
Forever & Ever – **51**-4d7c4; **52**-4h3f
Forevermore – **44**-2a3a4
Forget – **34**-1b2d6; **37**-3b6b;3b6d1
Forgive – **10**-3b1b; **12**-4b19b; **25**-2a3; **41**-1a3c1
"Forgive the Offender" – **25**-2a3
Forgiven – **2**-3a7,8
Forgiveness – **12**-4b19; **14**-5a6g2
Forgiving – **3**-4d11
Forgives – **16**-3b8
Forehead – **50**-4d5b8
Form of Evil – **30**-4a5j
Former – **19**-2a3
Fornicators – **53**-4i2d5
Forsake – **9**-2b4b
Forty Days – **7**-4a7b
Forty Nights – **1**-1a8b
Forty-two Months – **49**-4d3a2
Forty Years – **1**-1a8b
Fought a Good Fight – **32**-3b1b
Fought Satan – **49**-4d2a1a
Found – **3**-4d7
Foundation – **10**-3b1e
Foundation of World – **39**-2b1j
Foundation Stones – **54**-4i4a8;4i4a10e
Foundations of Christian Service – **32**-2a
Fountain of Water of Life – **53**-4i2a
Four – **1**-2a2; **5**-2a2
Four Days – **17**-3c3
Four Thousand – **3**-4b7; **6**-2c13
Fourth Bowl Judgment – **51**-4e5
Fourth Seal – **48**-4b4
Fourth Trumpet – **48**-4c4
Fox – **12**-4b11a
Framed Worlds – **35**-3a3d
Free – **18**-1b11
Free from the Law – **20**-3b3; **22**-4b1
Freedom – **24**-4b; **26**-2b4b;2c; **29**-2b; **40**-2b4c
Freedom from Slavery of Sin – **42**-2b4
Freedom in Christ – **29**-2b
Friday – **7**-3a6; **13**-5a6
Fried Fish – **18**-4c6f
Friends – **23**-7a5
From All Unrighteousness – **41**-1a3c3
From Bottomless Pit – **52**-4h3
From Every Form of Evil – **30**-4a5j

From Evil Desires – **37**-2a3b1
From God – **37**-2a3b5; **53**-4i2d1
From Heaven – **52**-4h3d
From His Mouth – **44**-2a2b1f
From the Earth – **50**-4d6a2
From the Grave – **53**-4h4a7a
From the *LORD* – **34**-1b2b
Fruitful – **2**-2e2; **39**-2a1; **39**-2a1a5f
Fruitful Grounding – **40**-2a2
Full Assurance of Faith – **35**-3a
Fulfilled – **9**-2a2b; **17**-3c8
Fulfills God's Will – **35**-2a6b4
Fullness – **39**-2b3b
Fundamentals – **40**-2a2a1
Furious – **11**-4a12b7
Future – **4**-6a1; **7**-3a3j; **22**-5a3; **38**-2a1
Future Crisis – **11**-4b6
Future Destruction – **13**-5a3g5
Future World – **33**-1a4a

G

Gabriel (Angel) – **8**-1b1b,1b2a
Gadarenes – **10**-3c10f
Gain – **28**-2a2; **31**-2e2
Gaius – **42**-1a; **43**-#2;2a1,2
Galilee – **1**-2a,2a2-3; **5**-2a; **9**-2a,2a1; **15**-2c;3a4b; **16**-3a7,14
Gamaliel – **18**-1b13
Gambles – **14**-5a6g3
Garden of Gethsemane – **4**-6b7; **13**-5a5f
Garland of Twelve Stars – **48**-4d1a3
Garments – **46**-3a5a2c1f
Gates – **54**-4i4a6,7,9,11,11a
Gates Guarded by Twelve Angels – **54**-4i4a6
Gates Made of Pearls – **54**-4i4a11a
Gates on Each Side – **54**-4i4a7
Gave Anti-Christ Great Power – **49**-4d4a2e1
Gave Him His Power – **49**-4d4a1a6
Gave Jezebel – **46**-3a4a2a3
Gave Up the Dead – **53**-4h4a5,6
Gaza – **19**-#2
Gem – **54**-4i4a3
Gems – **54**-4i4a10e
Genealogy – **9**-1c6
Genealogy of Christ – **1**-#1;1a1
Generosity – **43**-2a2
Gentiles – **19**-2a16,17;2a19b; **20**-3b3; **22**-2a;2b
Gentiles in the Flesh – **27**-2a4
Gentle Servant – **32**-2b6
Genuine Faith – **38**-2b
Genuine Love – **39**-2a1a5e
Genuine Religion – **37**-2a
Gethsemane – **7**-3a5e-f
Gideon & Barak – **36**-3a4l
Gift – **24**-4c3,5,7
Gifts – **23**-6a2; **24**-4c3,7; **27**-3a2;3a2a-c
Gift of the Holy Spirit – **17**-4a5
Gift of Tongues – **24**-4c7
Girl – **6**-2c11
Give Authority – **49**-4d4a3a1
Give Birth – **48**-4d1a4
Give Him (Jesus) – **46**-3a4a2b5
"Give Glory to Him" – **50**-4d7a2
Give Honor – **37**-3b6e1
Given – **9**-3a; **11**-4b4d; **12**-4b12; **50**-4d5b6
Given Authority – **34**-1a4b; **49**-4d4a3a5
Given by Inspiration of Holy Spirit – **32**-3a3
Giver – **25**-3c4
Gives – **1**-2b1; **8**-1b3d; **9**-3a2; **11**-4b4; **14**-5a8d; **25**-3a3; **29**-1a1; **39**-2a1a
Gives Thanks – **29**-1a1; **30**-4a5f
Giving – **2**-2d1; **7**-3a3i; **25**-3c1-4; **28**-2d
Glad – **1**-2b1j
Glass – **54**-4i4a10d
Glory – **34**-1a4b2;1a5; **39**-2a1a1
Glory of God – **54**-4i4a2
Glory of the New Jerusalem – **54**-4i5
Glory to God – **43**-2c1
Glory to Him – **50**-4d7a3
Glorify Jesus – **20**-4a4
Glorified – **11**-4b8a
Glory – **14**-1a2; **38**-2a2b3
Glory Only in the Cross – **27**-2c2
Go – **13**-5a1a1; **14**-5a8a1; **18**-1b12
Go Fishing – **18**-4c6a
Go to Prison – **45**-3a2a2a; **50**-4d4a3a9
Goal – **28**-2c2
God – **1**-1a8b; **8**-1c1c; **13**-5a1a3; **14**-5a6b2;1a6; **16**-3b12;3b12c; **19**-2a18; **21**-2a1,2; **22**-2b3,4;4c4; **23**-6a1,4;6a7d; **25**-1a2;3a8; **26**-2b2; **28**-3d;3d1;3d1f; **31**-2a2; **32**-3a3; **33**-1a1a;1a2a,c;1a3b; **34**-1a5c;1b1a,b;1b2d4;1b4b; **35**-3a2a;3a3d; **36**-3b2;3b3c;3b4b-d;3b5a,b,d; **37**-3b5e; 3b6e2; 3b7f; **37**-2a3b5; **38**-2a1a;2b1b,e; **39**-2b1k;2a1a4,5; **41**-2c1;1a;1a3c,e;1a3d1; **42**-2a1,2,6,7;#2; 2a;2a1; **43**-2b2;2c1; **45**-3a1b1; **46**-3a5a;3a5a2c;3a5a2c1; **47**-3a6c7-9;3a7a1c;4a2,3; **49**-4d1b3c2; 4d2a2a;4d4a3a2; **50**-4d6a5,7;4d7a2; **52**-4g2a8;4g2a11; **52**-4g3a;4h2a; **53**-4h4a2;4i1c4;4i2c; 4i2d1,2,7; **53**-4i4a1,2.
God & His Throne – **49**-4d1b3b
God Called – **52**-4g3a
God Did Not Spare – **40**-2b2a1,2
God Has **NO** Favorites – **39**-2b1e
God Has Prepared – **34**-1b3a
God Himself – **23**-6a4; **36**-3b4d
God Himself Will Be There – **53**-4i1c4
God Is Hard on Evil – **40**-2b2a7
God Is Life – **42**-1a
God Is Light – **41**-1a
God Is Love – **42**-1a
God Is with Men – **53**-4i1c1
God Loves Them – **47**-3a6b7
God Rescued Lot – **40**-2b2a4
God Says to Jesus – **33**-1a2a
God Sends Fire from Heaven – **52**-4h3d

God Will Judge – **37**-3b6e3
God Will Shake – **36**-3b5b
God the Father – **16**-3b2a
God's Assembly —**36**-3b4c
God's Commandments – **49**-4d3a5b
God's Grace – **41**-2c3e
God's Great Blessings – **38**-2a
God's Discipline – **36**-3b2g
God's Favor – **37**-3b7c
God's Judgment – **21**-2a1b;2a2
God's Justice – **22**-5a1c
God's Kingdom – **12**-4b24b
God's Love – **41**-1a6a1
God's Name – **49**-4d4a3a2; **50**-4d6a1
God's Response – **46**-3a5a2c1; **47**-3a6c
God's Righteousness – **17**-4a9b2; **22**-3a1
God's Supreme Revelation – **33**-1a1
God's Throne Endures Forever – **33**-1a2c
God's "True Children" – **16**-3b12
God's Will – **35**-2a6b4
God's Word – **2**-2e3; **33**-1a3b; **40**-2a2a
God's Wrath – **51**-4d7c1,3
God's Wrath Includes Tormenting – **51**-4d7c2
Godly Life – **39**-2a1a; **43**-2a1
Godless – **36**-3b3e
Godliness – **31**-2b5; **39**-2a1a5c
Godliness With Contentment Is Great Gain – **31**-2e2
Goes Fishing – **9**-2b4a
Goes to Bethany – **14**-5a8e
Goes to Capernaum – **15**-2c3
Goes to Caesarea – **20**-4a1
Goes to Corinth – **20**-3c13
Goes to Deceive Tribulation Saints – **52**-4h3b
Goes to Mary's Home – **19**-2b4
Gold – **54**-4i4a11b
Gold, Clear as Glass – **54**-4i4a10d
Gold Measuring Stick Measured the City – **54**-4i4a9
Golden Lampstands – **44**-2a2a; **44**-2a3b
Good – **2**-2d7; **30**-4a5i; **36**-3b2g
Good & Perfect – **37**-2a3b5
Good Confession – **31**-2e3
Good Fight – **32**-3b1b
Good Minister – **31**-2c2
Goodness – **39**-2a1a1
Good Example – **29**-2a1
Good Father – **11**-4a7d
Good Fruit – **10**-3b1d
Good Habits – **24**-4d4
Good News – **19**-2a16
Good Shepherd – **16**-3b17;3b17a
Good Testimony – **35**-3a3c; **43**-3a3a
Gospel – **18**-4c10; **22**-5a2b,c; **26**-1a;2a-c; **32**-2a2; **50**-4d7a1
Gospel of Christ – **25**-3a4
Gospels – **8**-1a; **18**-4c5
Government – **23**-6a4; **39**-3a2
Governor – **21**-4b7,9
Grace – **20**-3b2; **26**-1a2; **27**-2a3; **32**-2b1; **33**-3a2; **41**-2c3;2c3e
Grace & Knowledge of Our *LORD* – **41**-2b3
Grace of God – **19**-2a18; **31**-2a2
Grace to You – **26**-1a1
Graces – **29**-3b
Graces of the Heirs of Christ – **33**-3b1
Graciousness – **39**-2b3c
Granted Through Faith – **22**-3b3
Grapes of Wrath – **51**-4d9
Grave – **53**-4h4a7a
Great – **51**-4f2;4f2a,b
Great Anger – **49**-4d2a2c4
Great Apostasy – **30**-3a1; **31**-2c1
Great Authority – **50**-4d4a1a6
Great Blessings – **38**-2a
Great Commission – **5**-6c,6c4; **7**-3a3f; **14**-5a8d
Great Gain – **31**-2e2
Great Persecution – **13**-5a3g4
Great Power – **49**-4d4a2e1
Great Red Dragon – **48**-4d1b2
Great Supper of God – **52**-4g3a;4g3b5
Great Tribulation – **46**-3a4a2a4; **48**-4b8
Greater Than the Angels – **33**-1a;1a1b
Greater Than Moses – **34**-1b
Greater Than Old Testament Priesthood – **34**-2a
Greater Than the Old – **35**-2a5
Great White Throne Judgment – **53**-4h4; **53**-4h4a
Greatest – **4**-5c3; **10**-3c22; **13**-5a5d
Greatest Commandment – **4**-5c3
Greatest Gift – **24**-4c5
Greatness of the New Priest – **35**-2a4d
Greed – **40**-2b1c
Greedy – **40**-2b3c4
Greek – *Apollyon* – **48**-4c5a
Greeting – **25**-1a1; **28**-1a1
Greeting to Gaius – **42**-1a
Greeting to the Called – **43**-1a
Greetings – **23**-#7;7a3,5; **26**-1a1; **27**-#1;1a; **28**-#1;1a;2e; **29**-#1;4a; **37**-1a; **42**-1a
Greetings from John – **44**-1a1
Greetings from Paul – **27**-#1;1a; **28**-1a; **29**-#1;1a; **30**-1a; **32**-1a;Titus-1a
Greetings from Paul & Timothy – **33**-1a
Greetings from Peter – **38**-1a; **39**-1a
Grieve – **27**-3b2
Grieves – **4**-5c7
Grip – **36**-3b3a
Ground – **36**-3b2a
Grounding – **40**-2a2
Grow – **39**-2b3b
Grow in God's Grace – **41**-2c3e
Grow in the Grace – **41**-2c3
Growing Christians – **39**-2a; **40**-2b; **41**-2c
Grows – **18**-1a8; **19**-2a9; **37**-2a1a1
Growth – **30**-2a1; **39**-2a1
Growth Hindered – **23**-2c1
Guard the Faith – **31**-2e5
Guarded by Twelve Angels – **54**-4i4a6
Guards – **5**-6b23;6c3
Guidance – **39**-2a; **42**-2b3

Guilt – **22**-2b1
Guiltless – **21**-2b4; **22**-2b4

H

Habits – **24**-4d4
Habitual & Unrepentant Liars – **53**-4i2d8
Had Against – **45**-3a3b
Had Bear's Feet – **49**-4d4a1a5
Had Blasphemous Names – **49**-4d4a1a3
Had Heads – **48**-4c6c2d
Had Not Received His Mark – **52**-4h2a1c
Had Not Worshiped – **52**-4h2a1b
Had Power – **48**-4c6c2e
Had Their Great Supper – **52**-4g3b5
Had Three Gates on Each Side – **54**-4i4a7
Had Twelve Foundation Stones – **54**-4i4a8
Had Two Horns – **50**-4d5a1
Hades – **44**-2a3a5; **53**-4h4a6
Hail & Fire – **48**-4c1
Hair – **44**-2a2b1a
Hand – **2**-3b3b; **21**-4b17; **44**-2a2b1e; **50**-4d5b8
Hands of the Living God – **35**-3a2a
Handed – **4**-6b14
Handed Over – **14**-5a6e; **18**-4b6
Hangs – **4**-6b12
Happen – **44**-2a3a8
Happened – **49**-4d2a2
Hard on the Evil – **40**-2b2a7
Harden Your Hearts – **34**-1a2a
Hardships – **45**-3a1a5
Harvest – **15**-3a5
Harvest of the Earth – **51**-4d8
Harvester – **15**-3a5b
Has a Name Nobody Else Knew – **51**-4g2a5
Has A Place Prepared by God – **49**-4d1b3c2
Has Come – **50**-4d7a4
Has Finally Happened – **49**-4d2a2
Has No Place in Our Hearts – **41**-1a3d2
Has Seven Heads & Ten Horns – **49**-4d4a1a1
Has the Key of David – **46**-3a6a3
Has the Seven Spirits of God – **46**-3a5a
Hate – **33**-1a2d; **45**-3a1c1
Hated – **9**-3a2d
Hatred of Unbelievers Toward Believers – **17**-4a7
Have – **47**-3a6c5
Have a Name – **46**-3a5a2
Have Come – **49**-4d2a2a
Have God's Love in You – **41**-1a6a1
Have Heard – **41**-1a1
Have Honorable Conduct – **39**-3a1
Have Kept Command – **47**-3a6c1
Have Kept His Word – **47**-3a6b4
Have Keys to Death & Hades – **44**-2a3a5
Have Little Strength – **47**-3a6b3
Have No Evil or Unbelieving Heart – **34**-1b2d;1b2d1
Have No Sin – **41**-1a3a
Have Not Denied His Name – **47**-3a6b5
Have People Who Hold – **45**-3a3b1,2
Have Seen – **44**-2a3a6
Have Received – **39**-2a1a2
Have Taste of *LORD*'s Graciousness – **39**-2b3c
Have the Testimony of Jesus Christ – **49**-4d3a5c
Have Wandered – **40**-2b3c6
Having Seven Heads – **48**-4d1b1
He (God/Jesus) – **17**-3c7; **38**-2a3b6; **46**-3a6a;
47-3a7a1;3a7b
He (False Prophet) Deceived People – **50**-4d5b4
He Has a Name Nobody Else Knew – **51**-4g2a5
He (Jesus) Is – **14**-5a6b2; **16**-3b4
He (Jesus) Judges – **39**-2b1e,f; **51**-4g2a2
He (Jesus) Knows – **45**-3a4a1
He (Jesus) Loves – **36**-3b2c
He (Jesus) Rewards – **39**-2b1f
He (Jesus) Says – **17**-4a5d
He Is Coming – **35**-3a2e
He Is Faithful – **41**-1a3c1
He Is Single-Minded – **32**-2b2
He is Strict & Enduring – **32**-2b3
He Is Strong in Grace – **32**-2b1
He Is a Diligent Worker – **32**-2b4
He Is a Gentile Servant – **32**-2b6
He Is a Sanctified Vessel Useful for the Master – **32**-2b5
He Is Called Faithful & True – **51**-4g2a1
He Knows – **46**-3a5a1; **47**-3a6b1
He Treads the Winepress – **52**-4g2a11
He Who Abandons the Faith – **35**-3a2f
He Who Has an Ear – **50**-4d4a3a8
He Who Has the Key of David – **46**-3a6a3
He Who Has the Seven Spirits of God – **46**-3a5a
He Who Is True – **46**-3a6a2
He Who Lives – **44**-2a3a3
He Who Opens – **46**-3a6a4
He Who Overcomes – **46**-3a5a2c1f
He Will Be His God – **53**-4i2c
He Will Dwell with Them – **53**-4i1ac2
He Will Give Him – **46**-3a4a2b5
He Will Rule – **52**-4g2a10
Head & Hair – **44**-2a2b1a
Head – **4**-6b2; **7**-3a4b; **48**-4d1a3;4d1b1; **49**-4d4a1a3;
51-4g2a4
Head Coverings – **24**-4c1
Head Wounded – **50**-4d4a2a
Heads – **48**-4c6c2;4d1b1; **49**-4d4a1a1
Heads of Lions – **48**-4c6c2a
Heads Like Snakes – **48**-4c6c2d
Healed – **2**-3a7; **5**-2a6; **6**-2c9;2d2; **10**-3c5; **12**-4b20,26;
16-3b15; **18**-1b1; **49**-4d4a2b
Healing – **3**-4b6; **5**-2a8c; **11**-4b8; **16**-3b2b
Heals – **2**-3b3b; **3**-4b3; **5**-2a5; **6**-2c12,16;2d5;
9-2b2,5,6;2c4; **10**-3c1; **12**-4b12a; **13**-5a5h;
16-3a8;3b14 **19**-2a10; **21**-4b22.
Heals the Sick – **38**-2c3
Hearing & Obeying – **33**-1a3a
Hear – **50**-4d4a3a8
Hear What the Holy Spirit Is Saying – **47**-3a6c11
Hear What the Holy Spirit Says – **46**-3a5a2c1i
Hear What the *LORD* Says – **47**-3a7b4d

Heard – **41**-1a1
Heart – **1**-2b1f; **34**-1b2b;1b2d;1b2d1; **53**-4i2d4
Heart Purity – **11**-4a12b1
Hearts – **34**-1b2a; **41**-1a3d2
Heaven – **2**-2e1; **6**-2c14; **7**-4a7c; **9**-3a2e; **14**-5a8e; **36**-3b4e; **38**-2a1b; **41**-2c2d; **47**-4a1; **48**-4b9; **49**-4d2; 4d2a; **50**-4d5b3; **51**-4d7c6; **52**-4h3d; **53**-4i1;4i1b; **54**-4i4a1
Heaven & Earth Disappeared – **53**-4i1a
Heaven Rejoices – **51**-4f2d
Heaven Speaks Saying – **53**-4i1c
Heavenly Father – **36**-3b2f
Heavenly Sanctuary – **35**-2a6b1
Heavenly Sign – **3**-4c1
Heavenly Signs – **13**-5a3g6
Heavenly Wisdom – **23**-2b1
Heavens – **36**-3b5b
Heavens Struck – **48**-4c4
Heavens Will Pass Away – **41**-2c2b
Hebrew - *Abaddon* – **48**-4c5a
Heed – **31**-2c3
Heirs of Christ – **33**-3b1
Heirs of God – **26**-2b2
Helmet – **28**-3d1e
Helped Others – **35**-3a2b4
Her Children Killed – **46**-3a4a2a5
Her (Female) – **15**-3a4d2,3
Her Head – **48**-4d1a3
Her Feet – **48**-4d1a2
Herd – **6**-2c2
Herd of Pigs – **10**-3c10d
Heresies – **40**-2b1a
Herod – **14**-5a6d
Hesitant to Boast – **26**-3d6
Hid Money – **12**-4b28b3
Hidden Manna – **45**-3a3c2a
Hide – **11**-4a12b6
High – **54**-4i4a5
High Council – **14**-5a6b1
High Priest – **4**-6b9; **17**-4b2,3; **34**-1b1a;2a1
High Priest Servant – **17**-4b2
Hills of Judea – **8**-1b3a
Him (God Related) – **3**-4b3;4d14b; **7**-3a5d; **16**-3b1;3b12c; **17**-4a3; **33**-1a2b **34**-1b2a; **36**-3b5; **38**-2a2c; **39**-2b1g; **46**-3a4a2b5; **47**-3a6c8-10; **50**-4d7a3
Him (Person) – **12**-4b19b; **21**-4b1; **49**-4d2a1
Him Before My Father – **46**-3a5a2c1h
Him Who Made All Things – **50**-4d7a5
Him Who Overcomes – **45**-3a3c2
Himself (Non-God Related) – **4**-6b12; **6**-2c19; **18**-4c10; **25**-1a
Himself (God Related) – **6**-3a; **15**-3a4a; **17**-4a12; **23**-6a4; **35**-3b4d
Himself Will Be There – **53**-4i1c4
Hindered – **23**-2c1
Hinders – **36**-3b1a;3a1a1
His (God Related) – **1**-#1,#2,2a1,2b; **2**-#3;3b7; **4**-6a5; **5**-#1;#2;2a,2a1-4,10,12; **6**-2c5,18;2d3-4,2d4a,2d4f; **6**-#3;3a1,3a1a; **7**-3a2-3;3a3b,g;3a3j3;#4;4a7; **8**-#1;1a;1c2c; **9**-2a1;2b1;#3;3a2; **10**-3c13,17,21;#4; **11**-4b4; **12**-4b21;4b25; **13**-#5;5a;5a1;5a2;5a3;5a4;5a5;5a6; **14**-#1;1a;1a4;#2; **15**-2b;2c1,2;#3; 3a2b; **16**-3b5; **17**-4a13.
His (Non-God Related) – **8**-1a; **12**-4b21b; **15**-2b1b; **18**-1b19; **21**-4b13-15; **40**-2b2a5; **43**-3a1,2;3b1
His Angels – **46**-3a5a2c1h
His (Anti-Christ) Armies Defeated – **52**-4g3
His Authority (Paul) – **25**-3d
His Believers – **51**-4d8
His Betrayer – **17**-4a2
His Children – **38**-2a3b6;2b1b
His Christ Have Come – **49**-4d2a2a
His Coming – **51**-4g2a
His Commandments – **17**-4a5a,b; **54**-4i9
His Crucifixion – **15**-3a2b
His Death – **17**-#4
His Declaration – **16**-3a12
His Description – **50**-4d5a
His Divine Discipline – **36**-3b2d
His Divine Nature – **39**-2a1a3
His Eyes Like Flaming Fire – **51**-4g2a3
His (Satan) Fallen Angels – **49**-4d2a1a
His Glory & Goodness – **39**-2a1a1
His God – **47**-3a6c7-9; **53**-4i2c
His Head – **48**-4d1b1; **51**-4g2a4
His Holy Believers – **34**-1a5b
His Mark – **50**-4d5b8,9; **52**-4h2a1c
His Ministry (Jesus) – **1**-#2;2a1; **3**-#4; **15**-#3
His Ministry (Paul) – **25**-3a
His Mouth – **44**-2a2b1f; **45**-3a3c1; **52**-4g2a9
His (Jesus) Name – **47**-3a6b5
His Name Is Called "The *WORD* of God" – **52**-4g2a7
His Own – **14**-1a4
His (Satan) Power – **49**-4d4a1a6
His Priesthood – **34**-2a4
His Priestly Ministry – **35**-2a6
His Qualifications – **34**-2a2
His (Satan) Reign – **49**-4d4a3
His Rest (God) – **34**-1b2c
His Resurrection – **17**-#4
His Return – **46**-3a4a2b2
His Rich & Wonderful Promises – **39**-2a1a2
His Right Hand – **50**-4d5b8
His Teachings – **16**-3b12a
His Throne – **49**-4d1b3b
His (Dog) Vomit – **40**-2b4e
His (God's) Word – **41**-1a3d2; **47**-3a6b4
Hold Fast – **30**-4a5i; **35**-3a1; **46**-3a4a2b2;3a5a2c1b; **47**-3a6c5
Hold Fast Your Confession – **35**-3a1
Hold To – **45**-3a3b1,2
Holy – **25**-3b2; **34**-1a5b; **38**-2b1d; **46**-3a6a1
Holy Fear & Awe – **36**-3b5d
Holy Life – **36**-3b3b
Holy Spirit – **1**-1a8a; **8**-1b2c;1b3b;1b4c; **15**-2a2b; **17**-4a5;4a5e;4a9;4a9a-c; **18**-1a2,5;1b8,9; **19**-2a17;

20-4a3; **22**-4c2,3; **24**-4c3a; **27**-3b2; **32**-3a3; **46**-3a4a2b6;3a5a2c1i; **47**-3a6c11.
Holy Spirit Intercedes for Us – **22**-4c2
Home – **5**-2a7; **11**-4a12a; **12**-4b27; **27**-3c; **29**-3a2; **37**-3b7e
Home Life – **27**-3c
Home of Mary – **19**-2b4
Homeowner – **11**-4b4b
Hometown—**9**-2a2
Honor – **34**-1a4b2; **37**-3b6e1; **38**-2a2b3
Honorable Conduct – **39**-3a1
Hope – **24**-4d2; **30**-2a; **41**-2c
Hope For the Future – **38**-2a1
Hope in Death – **32**-3b1
Hoped For – **35**-3a3a
Horns – **48**-4d1b1; **49**-4d4a1a1,2; **50**-4d5a1
Horse – **47**-4b1,2
Horse's Heads – **48**-4c6c2
Horses – **48**-4c6c;4c6c2c; **52**-4g2a8
Horse's Tails – **48**-4c6c2d
Hospitable – **37**-3b6b
Hot – **47**-3a7b2
Hour – **46**-3a5a2c1d
Hour of Trial – **47**-3a6c2
House of God – **31**-2d4
Household – **34**-1b1b
How It Was Done in the Past – **40**-2b2a
How You Have Received & Heard – **46**-3a5a2c1a
Human Measure – **54**-4i4a10b
Humility – **3**-4d8; **28**-2b1;2b1a; **38**-2b7
Humility in the Body of Christ – **28**-2b1
Hunger – **1**-2b1d; **9**-3a2b; **10**-3a2g
Hurrying to Jerusalem – **21**-4a6c
Husbands – **27**-3c1a,b; **39**-3a4
Hypocrisy – **6**-2c10b; **11**-4b1
Hypocritical – **11**-4a12b

I

"I AM" Alive Forevermore – **44**-2a3a4
"I AM" Coming Quickly – **47**-3a6c4; **54**-4i8,12
"I AM" He Who Lives, Was Dead – **44**-2a3a3
"I AM" the Alpha & Omega – **44**-2a1b1
"I AM" the Bread of Life – **16**-3a15
"I AM" the First & the Last – **44**-2a3a2
"I AM" the Good Shepherd – **16**-3b17
"I AM" the Light of the World – **16**-3b9
"I AM" the Resurrection & the Life – **17**-3c2b
"I and My Father Are One" – **16**-3b18
"I Will Go Back to My Father" – **16**-3b3
"I Know Your Works" – **47**-3a7b1
"I Make All Things New" – **53**-4i1c7
"I Stand at the Door & Knock" – **47**-3a7b4a
"I Will Come" – **46**-3a5a2c1c
Iconium – **20**-3a6
Identifies – **18**-4c10
Idleness – **31**-3b2
Idols – **24**-4b1; **45**-3a3b1a2; **46**-3a4a2a2
Idolaters (Worshiped Objects as God) – **53**-4i2d7
Idolatry – **6**-2c10c
Idolatry at Lystra – **20**-3a7
Idols – **45**-3a3b1a2
Idols as God – **53**-4i2d7
If Faith Remains – **38**-2a2b3
If Anyone Takes the Mark – **51**-4d7c1
If We Claim – **41**-1a3d
If We Confess – **41**-1a3c
Ignorant – **41**-2c3c
Ignore Discipline – **36**-3b2b
Ignored – **21**-4b18
Ill (ill) – **16**-3c1
Illegitimate Child – **36**-3b2e
Illustration – **22**-3b
Illyricum – **23**-7a1
Image – **50**-4d5b5,6
Immaturity – **34**-2a3a
Immoral – **37**-3b6e3
Immoral (Adulterers & Fornicators) – **53**-4i2d5
Immoral Woman – **10**-3c4
Immoral or Godless – **36**-3b3e
Immorality – **24**-3a;3a2; **45**-3a3b1a3; **46**-3a4a2a1
Immorality Must Be Judged – **24**-3a2
Immorality Within the Church – **24**-3a
Impatience – **40**-2a2a3
Imperative of Love – **42**-2a3
Imperishable Crown – **24**-4b3a
Imprisoned – **8**-1c4; **19**-2b2; **20**-3c5
Imprisonment – **28**-2a1
Imputed – **22**-#3
In Bottomless Pit – **52**-4h1
In Christ – **35**-3a2b
In Church Discipline – **31**-2d
In Control – **38**-2b4
In Creation – **29**-2a1
In Death – **32**-3b1
In Disaster – **41**-2c3c
In Error – **38**-2c4
In Everything, Give Thanks – **30**-4a5f
In Everything You Do – **38**-2b1d
In Fullness – **39**-2b3b
In Grace – **32**-2b1
In Hands of **THE** Living God – **35**-3a2a
In Heaven – **36**-3b4e; **38**-2a1b; **49**-4d2a
In Jail – **35**-3a2b5
In Jerusalem – **52**-4h3c
In Jesus Christ – **38**-#2;2b
In Light of – **11**-4b
In Men's Sight – **50**-4d5b3
In Midst of Living Before the World – **39**-3a
In Other Duties – **31**-2e
In Our Hearts – **41**-1a3d2
In Painful Labor – **48**-4d1a4
In Peace – **36**-3b3b
In Prayer – **42**-2b3
In Redemption – **29**-2a2
In Reverent Fear – **39**-2b1g
In Right Hand – **44**-2a2b1e
In Sardis – **46**-3a5a2c1e

In Society – **33**-3b
In His Qualifications – **34**-2a2
In His Priestly Ministry – **35**-2a6
In Length, Width & Height – **54**-4i4a10a
In the Beginning – **34**-1b2d4
In the Church – **29**-#2;2a3; **31**-2b1,2; **32**-#2;2a; **33**-3a
In the Commandments of God – **42**-#2
In the Faith – **39**-2a1; **40**-2a2
In the Future – **32**-#3
In the *LORD* – **35**-3a2c
In the Love of God – **42**-2a
In the Order of His Priesthood – **34**-2a4
In the Past – **40**-2b2a
In the Present – **32**-#2
In the Truth of God's Word – **42**-2a1
In This Present Age – **38**-2a2
In White Garments – **46**-3a5a2c1f
Incest Reported – **24**-3a1
Incident – **14**-5a8a3
Includes Tormenting – **51**-4d7c3
Indignation – **17**-3c2e
Influence – **43**-#2
Inhabitants – **48**-4c6c2c
Inherit All Things – **53**-4i2b
Inherit the Lake of Fire – **53**-4i2d
Inheritance – **38**-2a1b
Injure People – **48**-4c6c2e
Inlaid with Twelve Gems – **54**-4i4a10e
Inner Purity – **3**-4b4
Inquire – **14**-2a1a
Inspiration of Scripture – **40**-2a2b
Inspirational of the God – **32**-3a3
Instead – **10**-3b1b
Instituted – **7**-3a5c
Instructions – **11**-4b; **12**-4b12; **24**-4a-d;4a3;4d; **25**-4e; **30**-#4
Instructions on Christian Freedom – **24**-4b
Instructions on Christian Marriage – **24**-4a
Instructions on Personal Matters – **25**-4e
Instructions on Public Worship – **24**-4c
Instructions on the Resurrection – **24**-4d
Instructions to the Rich – **31**-2e4
Instructs – **9**-2c
Insufficient – **35**-2a6b3
Intercedes for Us – **22**-4b3; **41**-1a3e
Into Great Tribulation – **46**-3a4a2a4
Into Heaven – **7**-4a7c
Into Herd of Pigs – **6**-2c2
Into Lake of Burning Fire – **52**-4g3b3
Into Lake of Fire with Anti-Christ & False Prophet – **52**-4h3e
Into Jerusalem – **4**-5a1; **6**-3a1a; **17**-3c6
Into Sin – **40**-2b3c3;2b4b
Into the Lake of Fire – **53**-4h4a7a
Into the Wilderness – **49**-4d1b3c1
Into Wilderness – **1**-1a8a
Introduction – **18**-1a1; **21**-#3; **26**-#1; **28**-#1; **29**-#1
Introduction & Benediction – **44**-1a
Introduction to 1st Thessalonians – **29**-#1
Introduction to 2nd Thessalonians – **30**-#1
Introduction to 1st Timothy – **31**-#1
Introduction to 2nd Timothy – **32**-#1
Introduction to Acts – **18**-1a1
Introduction to Galatians – **26**-#1
Introduction to Philippians – **28**-#1
Introduction to Philemon – **33**-#1
Introduction to Romans – **21**-#3
Introduction to Titus – **32**-#1
Introduction to James – **33**-#1
Introduction to 1st Peter – **38**-#1
Introduction to 2nd Peter – **39**-#1
Introduction to 2nd John – **42**-#1
Introduction to 3rd John – **42**-#1
Introduction to Jude – **43**-#1
Introduction to Revelation – **44**-#1
Inward Purity – **6**-2c10
Iron Rod – **46**-3a4a2b4; **49**-4d1b3a; **52**-4g2a10
Is Dead – **38**-2b3
Is Done – **51**-4e8
Is Fallen – **50**-4d7b
Is Holy – **46**-3a6a1
Is Near – **54**-4i7
Is Saying – **47**-3a6c11
Is True – **47**-3a6a1
Is with Me – **54**-4i8
Is Worthy – **47**-4a3
Is In Control – **38**-2b4
Isaac – **36**-3a4e
Isaiah – **9**-2a2a; **14**-2a1b
Isaiah Prophecy Fulfilled – **17**-3c8
Isaiah 6:10 – **17**-3c8
Isaiah 40:3 – **14**-2a1b
Isaiah 53:1 – **17**-3c8
Island of Cyprus – **20**-3a2
Island of Malta – **21**-4b20,22
Israel – **45**-3a3b1a1; **48**-4b7; **49**-4d1b3c;4d3a1
Israel Needs the Gospel – **22**-5a2b
Israel on the Gates – **54**-4i4a6
Israel Rejects the Gospel – **22**-5a2c
Israel's Future – **23**-5a3
Israel's Leaders (Nation) – **7**-3a3c
Israel's Past – **22**-5a1
Israel's Present – **22**-5a2
Israel's Rejection – **23**-5a3a,b
Israel's Righteousness – **22**-5a2a
Israelites – **49**-4d3a2,3,5a
"It Is Done!" – **51**-4e8

J

Jacob – **36**-3a4f
Jacob's Well – **15**-3a4;3a4c
Jail – **35**-3a2b5
Jailer Converted – **20**-3c6
Jairus – **10**-3c12
James (Son of Zebedee) **9**-2b4b
James (John's Brother) – **19**-2b1; **37**-#1;1a
Jasper – **54**-4i4a4;4i4a10c

Jericho – **12**-4b26
Jerusalem – **4**-5a,5a1,5c7; **5**-6b21; **6**-3a1a; **10**-4a; **12**-4b11,11b; **13**-5a1a;5a3g5;5a4; **16**-3c; **17**-3c6; **19**-2a7; **20**-3b;3b4;4a6c;4a8; **26**-2a2,3;2b4b; **47**-3a6c9; **52**-4h3c; **54**-4i4,5,10;4i5.
Jerusalem Decree – **20**-3b4
Jerusalem Mob – **21**-4b3
Jerusalem Saints – **25**-4e1
Jerusalem to Illyricum – **23**-7a1
Jesus – **1**-1a4,5,7,8;1a8a-e;2a,2a1-3;2b,2b1,2; **2**-3a12; **3**-4a,4a1;4b1-7;4c,4c2;4d1-2,4-6,8,13-14,16,18; **4**-5a1-4;5c,5c1-7;6a,6a5;6b1-3,6-11,13-14; **5**-6b15-23;6c1-2;Mark-1a2,3;2a2-5,7-12;2b; **6**-2c, 2c1-5,7-20;2d,2d1,3-5;3a; **7**-3a4b-c;3a5d,f;3a6b,d;4a7a-c; **8**-1b2b;1b5b,d;1c1;1c1a,d;1c2;1c2a-c 1c3,5; **9**-1c6,7; **9**-2a,2a2;2a2a-d;2b;2b1a;2b2-6;2c;2c1,4;3a1,2; **10**-3b1; 3c1,3-5,8-11,13,15-18, 20-21,23;4a,4a1; **11**-4a3,4,7-9,12;4a12a-b;4b1-4,7,8a; **12**-4b8b;4b10-12;4b21-25; **13**-5a1a;5a2a; 5a3a,c,d,f,g;5a3g1;5a4a-b;5a5b1;5a5e-l;5a6a,b; **14**-5a6b1-2;5a6c-g;5a6h,i;5a6h,l;5a8a;5a8a1; 5a8b-e;1a;1a1-6; **15**-2a2;2a2b,c;2b;2b1a-d;2c;2c1-3;3a1;3a1a,c,d;3a2;3a2a,b;3a3;3a4;3a4a-d; 3a4d1-4;3a5;3a5a; **16**-3a7-17;3b;3b1-21; **17**-3c2;3c2b-e;3c3-9;4a9-15;4b1,3; **18**-4b4-7,9,11,12; **18**-4c2-4,6,7,9; **20**-4a4; **33**-1a1b;1a2a;1a2e; **34**-1a4b;1a5b,e; **36**-3b1a3; **36**-3b4f; **38**-2a2c,d; **39**-2b1i; **41**-2c3b;1a4; **52**-4h2a1a.
Jesus Christ – **1**-#1; #2; **2**-#3,3a;3b1-2,4-7;3b3b; **3**-#4;4b;4d; **4**-6b; **5**-6c;#1;#2; **6**-2c20;#3; **7**-3a6e-g; **7**-#4; **8**-#1;1b,1b5;1c; **9**-#2;#3; **10**-3c;#4; **11**-4b; **13**-#5; **14**-#1;#2;2a1; **15**-#3; **17**-3c9;#4;4b; **18**-4c; 4c1;#1; **19**-2a; **20**-#3; **22**-#3; **25**-#3; **31**-2c2; **33**-#1;1a1a; **34**-#2; **37**-3b7b; **38**-#2;2b; **39**-2b1j; **41**-1a3f; **44**-2a1a; **49**-4d3a5c; **51**-4e1a;4g;4g2.
Jesus & Disciples – **18**-4c6f
Jesus Arrested – **17**-4b1
Jesus As *LORD* – **41**-1a4
Jesus Asks Peter Three Times – **18**-4c7
Jesus Attends Feast – **16**-3b2
Jesus Buried – **14**-5a6i; **18**-4b12
Jesus Declares – **16**-3b4,9;3b12c;3b16-18
Jesus Describes – **16**-3b12
Jesus Dies – **14**-5a6h; **18**-4b11
Jesus: Far Greater Than the Angels – **33**-1a1b
Jesus Forgives – **16**-3b8
Jesus Had Against Pergamos – **45**-3a3b
Jesus Had Against Thyatira – **46**-3a4a2
Jesus Handed Over – **18**-4b6
Jesus Heals – **16**-3b14
"Jesus **IS** the Messiah" – **17**-3c2c
Jesus **"IS" THE** Way, **THE** Truth & **THE** Life – **17**-4a4
Jesus Intercedes for Us to God – **41**-1a3e
Jesus Knew – **44**-3a1a1; **45**-3a2a1; **45**-3a2a2;3a3a1
Jesus Led Away – **18**-4b7
Jesus Moved with Indignation – **17**-3c2e
Jesus Prays – **17**-4a12,13,15
Jesus Predicts – **17**-4a11
Jesus Prepares Disciples – **17**-4a
Jesus Promises the Holy Spirit – **17**-4a5
Jesus Questioned by Annas, the High Priest – **17**-4b3
Jesus Raised Lazarus from the Dead – **17**-3c3
Jesus Reveals His Betrayer – **17**-4a2
Jesus Reveals Peter's Denial – **17**-4a3
Jesus Rises from the Dead – **14**-5a8a
Jesus Says – **9**-2a2b; **16**-3b3;3b20; **17**-3c2c
Jesus Speaks Out – **16**-3b2c
Jesus Talks with Peter – **18**-4c9
Jesus Teaches – **16**-3b2c; **17**-4a9
Jesus Tells Disciples – **17**-3c7
Jesus Testifies to the Churches – **54**-4i10
Jesus Will Fight Against Them – **45**-3a3c1
Jesus Will Rule – **46**-3a4a2b4
Jesus to John – **44**-2a1b;2a3a
Jesus Washes Disciple's Feet – **17**-4a1
Jesus' Authority – **16**-3b2a; **33**-1a2e
Jesus' Clothes – **14**-5a6g3
Jesus' Clothing – **18**-4b9
Jesus' First Appearance – **18**-4c3
Jesus' Ministry – **16**-3b;3c
Jesus' Name – **17**-4a10
Jesus' New Name – **47**-3a6c10
Jesus' Relationship to Believers – **34**-1b1
Jesus' Sacrificial Death – **34**-1a5e
Jesus' Second Appearance – **18**-4c4
Jesus' Third Appearance – **18**-4c6
Jesus' Trial – **18**-4b5
Jesus' Triumphal Entry – **17**-3c6
Jesus Christ Sits on the Throne – **53**-4h4a1
Jew's Blasphemy – **45**-3a2a1b
Jewish – **6**-2c10a
Jewish Christians – **37**-1a
Jewish Leaders – **13**-5a1a5; **14**-2a1a; **16**-3b19
Jews – **19**-2a19a; **21**-2b;2b1; **49**-4d3a5b
Jews & Gentiles – **22**-2b1
Jews Plot to Kill Paul – **21**-4b6
Jezebel – **46**-3a4a2a;3a4a2a3
Joel – **18**-1a7
John (Apostle) – **18**-4b10;4c9,10;1b1-3; **42**-#4;4a; **43**-#4;4a; **44**-1a1;2a1b;2a2b;2a3a
John (Apostle) Eats the Little Book – **48**-4c8
John (Baptist) – **8**-1c4,5
John (the Baptist) – **1**-1a6-7; **2**-3b1; **3**-4a2; **5**-1a1,2; **6**-2c6; **8**-1b1;1b1c-d;1b4,1b4a-b;1bd-e;1c3; **10**-3c3; **10**-3c14; **14**-1a3;2a;2a1;2a1a,b; **15**-2a1c;2a2;2a2a,c;2b;3a3;3a3a,b.
John (Son of Zebedee) – **9**-2b4b
John Mark – **19**-2b4; **20**-3c1
John Mark Returns to Jerusalem – **20**-2b7
Join – **13**-5a5b1
Joins – **20**-3c2
Jonah – **11**-4a10a
Joppa – **19**-2a12
Jordan River – **8**-1c5; **15**-2a1c
Joseph (Son of Jacob) – **36**-3a4g
Joseph of Arimathea – **18**-4b12
Joshua & the Israelites – **36**-3a4j

Journey – **10**-4a; **20**-3a;3c;#4; **25**-#1
Journey Back to Antioch – **20**-3a9
Journey to Rome – **21**-4b
Journeys to Greece – **20**-4a6
Joy – **28**-2a-d;2e2; **38**-2a2a
Joy in Believing – **28**-2c
Joy in Giving – **28**-2d
Joy in Serving – **28**-2b
Joy in Suffering – **28**-2a
Judas (Iscariot) – **4**-6b3,12; **7**-3a4c; **13**-5a4b;5a5g; **17**-4a2
Jude's Doxology – **43**-2c
Jude's Greeting to the Called – **43**-1a
Judea – **8**-1b3;1b3a; **9**-2b3; **15**-3a4b; **19**-2a19f
Judean Wilderness – **1**-1a6
Judge – **10**-3b1b; **12**-4b22b; **37**-3b6e3
Judged – **15**-3a2d; **24**-3a2; **53**-4h4a4
Judges – **39**-2b1e
Judges & Makes War – **51**-4g2a2
Judges / Rewards – **39**-2b1f
Judging – **2**-2d6
Judgment – **2**-2d7; **4**-6a8; **16**-3b10; **17**-4a9b3; **48**-4c; **51**-4d9;4e;4e2-8; **53**-4h4;4h4a;4h4a7
Judgment of God – **21**-2a2; **22**-2b3
Judgment of God Defended – **22**-2b3
Judgment of New Apostates – **43**-2a3
Judgment of Old Apostates – **43**-2a2
Judgment of the Great Harlot – **51**-4f1
Judgment Seat of Christ – **25**-3a7
Judgment Time Has Come – **50**-4d7a4
Judgments – **48**-4c12; **51**-4e1
Just (Righteous) – **41**-1a3c1
Justified – **22**-3b1,2
"Justification By Faith" – **26**-#2;2b1
Justification Imputed Through Christ – **22**-#3
Justice of God – **22**-5a1c

K

Keep God's Commandments – **49**-4d3a5b
Keep Them From the Hour of Trial – **47**-3a6c2
Kept Command – **47**-3a6c1
Kept His Word – **47**-3a6b4
Kept the Faith – **45**-3a3a1d
Key of David – **46**-3a6a3
"Key to Knowledge" – **11**-4a12b6
Keys to Death & Hades – **44**-2a3a5
Kill – **4**-6b1; **9**-2a2d; **13**-5a4a; **48**-4c6a
Killed & Resurrected – **49**-4d4a2
Killed – **6**-2c6; **10**-3c14; **46**-3a4a2a5; **48**-4c10; **50**-4d4a3a10;4d5b7
Killed with the Sword – **19**-2b1
Killed with the Sword of Christ – **52**-4g3b4
Kills – **25**-3a3
Kills One-Third – **48**-4c6c2c
Kindness – **39**-2a1a5d
King – **1**-#1;1a,1a1; **2**-#2;#3; **3**-#4; **6**-#3; **7**-#4; **12**-4b28; **13**-4b28b5; **48**-4c5a
King Agrippa – **21**-4b12,16
King Herod – **19**-2b;2b5,6
King Herod Agrippa – **19**-2b5-6
King Herod Antipas – **8**-1c4; **10**-3c14; **12**-4b11a
KING of Kings – **52**-4g2a13
King Jesus – **4**-#5;5a
Kings – **1**-1a3
Kings of the East – **1**-1a3
Kingdom – **1**-2c; **2**-3b; **11**-4a9b; **12**-4b24b
Kingdom of God – **6**-2d4d; **12**-4b9
Kingdom Living – **2**-2d,2e; **10**-3b,3b1
Kingdom of Our God – **49**-4d2a2a
Kinsman – **6**-2c4; **14**-1a4
Knew – **44**-3a1a1; **45**-3a2a1a;3a3a1; **51**-4g2a5
Knock – **11**-4a7c; **47**-3a7b4a
Know God Loves Them – **47**-3a6b7
Know Their Works – **47**-3a6b1
Know Your Works – **47**-3a7b1
Know What Hour – **46**-3a5a2c1d
Knowing – **18**-4b4
Knowing God – **39**-2a1a4,5; **42**-2a6
Knowledge of Our *LORD* – **41**-2c3
Knowledge in the Mystery – **27**-2a7a
Knows – **45**-3a4a1; **46**-3a5a1

L

Labor – **44**-3a1a1; **48**-4d1a4
Lack of Spiritual Wisdom – **23**-2b2
Lake – **6**-2c1
Lake of Fire – **53**-4h4a7a
Lake of Burning Fire – **52**-4g3b3
Lake of Fire with Anti-Christ & False Prophet – **52**-4h3e
Lamb – **49**-4d2a2c1; **50**-4d5a1,4,5; **51**-4e1a;4g1; **54**-4i3
Lamb of God – **15**-2a2a; **47**-4a2,3
Lamb's Book of Life – **50**-4d4a3a7
Lame Man – **18**-1b1
Lampstand Removed – **45**-3a1b2
Lampstands – **44**-2a2a;2a3b
Land of the Gadarenes – **10**-3c10f
Laodicea – **47**-3a7;3a7a;3a7b
Large – **2**-3b4
Last – **7**-4a7b
Last Enemy Destroyed – **24**-4d3
Last Supper – **4**-6b5
Last Week – **4**-6b
Laughter – **10**-3a2h
Law – **1**-2c1-7; **2**-2c8;2d8; **20**-3b3; **22**-4b1-3; **23**-6a7a,b; **25**-3a3; **26**-2b1a,b,d
Law Brings a Curse – **26**-2b1b
Law Doesn't Save Us from Sin – **22**-4b3
Law Kills – **25**-3a3
Law of Liberty – **23**-6a7a
Law of Love – **23**-6a7b
Lay Aside – **39**-2b3a
Lazarus – **16**-3c1; **17**-3c3
Lead – **9**-1c7
Leaders – **2**-3b6; **3**-4c,4c1; **4**-5a4,5c,5c4-6; **5**-6b19;6c3; **6**-2c14; **7**-3a3c,3a4a; **13**-5a1a5;5a3e;5a6b; **14**-2a1a; **16**-3a16;3b12d;3b15,19,21; **17**-3c4; **37**-3b7a,g.

Leadership in the Church – **32**-Titus-2a
Leadership Gifts – **27**-3a2b
Leading – **8**-1b;1c; **10**-3b1c
Leads – **37**-2a3b2,3
Leads To – **39**-2a1a5; **40**-2a1a6
Least – **10**-3c22
Leaves – **10**-3c10f; **15**-3a4b
Led – **1**-1a8a; **5**-6b16; **14**-5a6b1
Led Away – **18**-4b7
Left – **8**-1c2a; **36**-3b5c; **49**-4d2a2c5
Left on Earth – **49**-4d3a5c
Left Out – **34**-1a4b1
Legally & Relationally – **26**-2a5
Legion – **10**-3c10c,d
Legion of Demons – **10**-3c10c,d
Length, Width & Height – **54**-4i4a10a
Leopard – **49**-4d4a1a4
Leprosy – **5**-2a5; **9**-2b5
Lesson – **12**-4b24a
Lesson from the Evil Judge – **12**-4b22b
Lessons from the Rich Young Ruler – **12**-4b24a
Lesson on Gratitude – **12**-4b20
Let All the Angels Worship Him – **33**-1a2b
Let Him Hear – **50**-4d4a3a8
Let Me In – **47**-3a7b4a
Let the Truth Abide in You – **41**-1a8
Letter of the Law Kills – **25**-3a3
Letter to Ephesus – **44**-3a1
Letter to Laodicea – **47**-3a7
Letter to Pergamos – **45**-3a3
Letter to Philadelphia – **46**-3a6
Letter to Sardis – **46**-3a5
Letter to Smyrna – **45**-3a2
Letter to Thyatira – **45**-3a4
Letters to the Seven Churches – **44**-3a
Levi – **9**-2b7
Liberty – **26**-2c1
Liars (Habitual & Unrepentant) – **53**-4i2d8
Lie (Not True) – **5**-6c3
Lies (Not True) – **18**-1b8,9
Life – **4**-6b; **15**-3a4d3; **16**-3a15; **17**-3c2b; **19**-2a11; **21**-4b13,15; **25**-3a3; **27**-3b;3c; **34**-1a5d; **36**-3b3b;3b4; **37**-2a3a; **39**-2a1a; **41**-2c3a; **43**-2a1; **46**-3a5a2c1g; **53**-4h4a3;4i2a.
Life (Crown of) – **45**-3a2a2c
Life (River of) – **54**-4i6
Life (Tree of) – **45**-3a1c
Life (Jesus) – **17**-4a4
Life Poured Out – **32**-3b1a
Life Was Given – **50**-4d5b6
Life with Christ – **40**-2a1a8
Life with God – **43**-2b2
Life's Foundations – **10**-3b1e
Light – **1**-2b2; **11**-4b; **14**-1a3; **16**-3b9; **25**-3a4; **27**-3b4; **41**-1a;1a2
Light of Christ's Return – **31**-3b
Light of the Gospel of Christ – **25**-3a4
Light of the World – **16**-3b9
Like Jasper – **54**-4i4a4
Like a Flaming Fire – **44**-2a2b1b; **51**-4g2a3
Like a Lamb – **50**-4d5a1
Like a Leopard – **49**-4d4a1a4
Like a Precious Gem – **54**-4i4a3
Like Fine Brass – **44**-2a2b1c
Like Rushing Waters – **44**-2a2b1d
Like Snakes – **48**-4c6c2d
Like the Son of Man – **44**-2a2b;2a2b1
Like the Son Shining – **44**-2a2b1g
Limitations – **26**-3d3; **35**-2a6a2
Lions – **48**-4c6c2a
Lion's Mouth – **49**-4d4a1a5
Listening to Christ Means Hearing & Obeying – **33**-1a3
Little Book – **48**-4c7,8
Little Children – **12**-4b23
Little Strength – **47**-3a6b3
Little While – **33**-1a4
Live – **21**-1a3; **28**-2a2; **35**-3a2
Live A Clean & Holy Life – **36**-3b3b
Live A Pure & Blameless Life – **41**-2c3a
Live by Faith – **21**-1a3; **35**-3a2
Live Godly Life – **39**-2a1a
Live Holy – **38**-2b1
Live In Peace – **36**-3b3b
Live In Reverent Fear – **39**-2b1g
Lives (People) – **25**-3a2
Lives (Life) – **2**-2e2; **8**-1b4e; **44**-2a3a3
Living – **1**-2c; **10**-3b,3b1; **34**-1b4b
Living Before the World – **39**-3a
Living by the Standards – **43**-2a
Living God – **35**-3a2a; **36**-3b4b
Living in Society – **33**-3b
Living in the Church – **33**-3a
Living in the Light of Christ's Return – **31**-3b
Living Sacrifice to God – **23**-6a1
Living Water – **15**-3a4d2; **16**-3b4
Locust from Bottomless Pit – **48**-4c5
Locust's King – **48**-4c5a
Look for the New Heaven – **41**-2c2d
Looked Like a Leopard – **49**-4d4a1a4
Looking Down on People – **3**-4d10
Loose Morals – **24**-3a4
Loosed – **48**-4c6a
LORD – **4**-6b; **8**-1b1d,1b3c-d; **28**-2d1; **29**-2a; **30**-4a;4a3,4;4a5a;2a; **30**-4a;4a3,4;4a5a;2Thess-2a;#3;3a; **31**-3b1; **32**-3b3; **34**-1b2b; **35**-3a2c; **36**-3b2c; **38**-2c1;2b1; **39**-3a2,3; **41**-2c2-4.
LORD of Lords – **52**-4g2a11
LORD Says – **47**-3a7b4d
LORD's – **4**-6a3; **7**-3a5c; **11**-4a7a
LORDSHIP – **7**-3a3g
LORD's Graciousness – **39**-2b3c
LORD's Response – **47**-3a7b4
LORD's Return – **4**-6a3
LORD's Supper – **7**-3a5c; **24**-4c2
Loss of Rewards – **23**-2c2
Lost Battle – **49**-4d2a1b
Lost Their Zeal – **45**-3a1b1
Lot (Person) – **12**-4b21d; **40**-2b2a4,5

Lot Was Tormented – **40**-2b2a5
Loathsome Soars – **51**-4e2
Lots – **18**-4b9
Loud Voice from Heaven Speaks Saying – **53**-4i1c
Love – **2**-2c8; **10**-3b1a; **17**-4a5a-d; **18**-4c7; **22**-4c4; **23**-6a5;6a7b; **24**-4c5; **26**-2c1b; **27**-3b3;3c1b; **37**-3b6f; **39**-2a1a5e; **42**-2a;2a3-8; **45**-3a4a1.
Love & Faith – **33**-2a1
Love of God – **22**-4c4; **42**-2a
Love of Money – **37**-3b6f
Love the Brethren (Believers) – **39**-2b2
Love What Is Right – **33**-1a2d
Love Ways of the World – **41**-1a6
Love Your Neighbor – **23**-6a5
Love Your Wives – **27**-3c1b
Loves – **36**-3b2c
Loves Them – **47**-3a6b7
Loveless Church – **44**-3a1
Loving One Another – **42**-2a2
Loving God in Trials – **37**-2a3
Lower Than the Angels – **33**-1a4
Loyalty to the Faith – **32**-2a3
Luke – **8**-1a
Lukewarm Church – **47**-3a7
Lukewarmness – **47**-3a7b3
Lure – **40**-2b4b
Lust – **1**-2c4
Lust for Physical Pleasure – **41**-1a6a2
Lust for Things We See – **41**-1a6a3
Lustful – **40**-2b2a7
Lydia Converted & Baptized – **20**-3c4
Lystra – **20**-3a7

M

Macedonia – **20**-4a6a
Macedonian Call – **20**-3c3
Made – **35**-3a3e
Made All Things – **50**-4d7a5
Made of Jasper – **54**-4i4a10c
Made of Pearls – **54**-4i4a11a
Made of Pure Gold, Clear as Glass – **54**-4i4a10d
Made of Transparent Gold – **54**-4i4a11b
Made Lower Than the Angels – **33**-1a4
Made New – **53**-4i
Magic Arts – **53**-4i2d6
Magicians – **53**-4i2d6
Maintain Your Life with God – **43**-2b2
Make – **1**-1a8a
Make All Things New – **53**-4i1c7
Make Image – **50**-4d5b5
Make Those – **47**-3a6b6
Make Us – **38**-2a3b6
Makes – **34**-1a5a
Makes War – **51**-4g2a2; **52**-4g3b1
Makes War Against Christ – **52**-4g3b1
Makers – **1**-2b1g
Malta – **21**-4b20,22
Man – **5**-2a5,6; **6**-2c2,12,16; **9**-2b1a;2b5,6;2c4; **10**-3c10,3c10b,c,e; **12**-4b12a; **14**-1a4; **16**-3b14,15; **18**-1b1; **19**-2a10; **21**-1a;2a1;2a1a; **27**-3b1; **29**-3a; **34**-1a5c.
Man of Sin – **30**-3a2
Manifestations of the Holy Spirit – **24**-4c3a
Man's Hand – **2**-3b3b
Manna – **45**-3a3c2a
Many Crowns on His Head – **51**-4g2a4
Many Disciples – **16**-3a17
Many Others – **36**-3a4o
Many People – **16**-3b11
Many Samaritans – **15**-3a6
Many Signs & Wonders – **18**-1b10
Many Sons to Glory – **34**-1b5
Many Trials – **38**-2a2a
Many Will Follow – **40**-2b1b
Mark – **50**-4d5b; **52**-4h2a1c
Mark on His Right Hand – **50**-4d5b8
Marks of the Ministry – **25**-3b
Marriage – **3**-4d12; **6**-2d4c; **24**-4a;4a1-2; **27**-3c1; **37**-3b6e;3b6e1
Marriage & Divorce – **24**-4a2
Marriage Supper of the Lamb – **51**-4g1
Married – **24**-4a4
Martha Confesses "Jesus Is the Messiah" – **17**-3c2c
Martha (Mary of Bethany's Sister) – **17**-3c2a,c;3c2a
Martha (Sister of Mary of Bethany) – **11**-4a6
Martha Meets Jesus – **17**-3c2a
Martyrs – **48**-4b5; **52**-4h2a1
Marveled – **3**-4b6; **50**-4d4a2c
Mary (of Bethany) Anoints Jesus' Feet – **17**-3c5
Mary (of Bethany) – **4**-6b2; **7**-3a4b; **17**-3c;3c5
Mary (the Virgin) – **8**-1b2a-c;1b3;1b3a,d; **18**-4b10
Mary (Bethany) & Martha (Mary's Sister) – **11**-4a6; **17**-3c2
Mary (Magdalene) – **18**-4c2
Mary (Mother of John Mark) – **19**-2b4
Mary Meets Jesus – **17**-3c2d
Mat – **9**-2b6
Matthias – **18**-1a4
Matthew – **5**-2a7
Maturing – **34**-2a3;2a3b,c
Maturity – **34**-2a3b
Me (Jesus) – **54**-4i8
Me (Jesus) In – **47**-3a7b4a
Means – **33**-1a3a
Measure – **54**-4i4a10b
Measure of Christ's Gift – **27**-3a2a
Measured the City – **54**-4i4a9
Measuring Stick Measured the City – **54**-4i4a9
Meditate – **28**-2d3
Mediator's Death Necessary – **35**-2a6b2
Meek – **1**-2b1c
Meets – **17**-3c2a,d
Megiddo – **52**-g3b
Melchizedek's Order – **35**-2a4a,b
Melchizedek Priesthood – **34**-2a2b
Men – **53**-4i1c1

Men & Women – **31**-2b2
Men Are Scorched – **51**-4e5
Men's Sight – **50**-4d5b3
Mercy of God – **38**-2a1a
Merciful – **1**-2b1e
Message – **5**-#2; **42**-4a; **43**-4a
Message & Ministry – **15**-#3
Message from Jesus to John – **44**-2a1b
Message for the Seven Churches – **47**-4a
Message to the Seven Churches – **44**-2a1b3
Messages – **4**-#6;6a,6a1; **33**-3b3
Messenger of God – **34**-1b1a
Messiah – **3**-4d1; **4**-6b1; **5**-1a1; **6**-2c17; **10**-3c16; **14**-2a;2a1a; **15**-2a2;3a1d;3a3b; **17**-3c2c
Meeting – **18**-1a3
Midst – **28**-2a1
Midst of Imprisonment – **28**-2a1
Midst of Living Before the World – **39**-3a
Mighty Angel – **48**-4c7
Mighty Works – **3**-4b
Miles In Length, Width & Height – **54**-4i4a10a
Miletus – **21**-4a6c
Milk – **39**-2b3
Millennium – **52**-4h
Mind – **28**-2d1
Mind Your Own Business – **30**-4a2
Minister – **32**-2b
Ministering at Berea – **20**-3c10
Ministry – **1**-2a; **3**-4a; **5**-#1;#2;2a; **8**-#1;1b4e;1c; **9**-#2;#3; **10**-3c,3c5;4a; **13**-5a3; **14**-1a; **15**-#3; **16**-3b;3c; **20**-#3;3a6; **24**-4b3; **25**-3a;3a5;3b.
Ministry in Rome – **21**-4b24
Ministry of Apollos – **20**-4a2
Ministry of Paul – **20**-#3; **25**-#3
Ministry of Peter – **18**-#1
Minus Thomas – **18**-4c3
Minutes of Silence – **48**-4b9
Miracle – **2**-3b6; **15**-2c1; **49**-4d4a2c
Miracles at Ephesus – **20**-4a4
Miraculous – **3**-4b1,7
Miraculously – **6**-2c7,13; **10**-3c15; **16**-3a13
Misled – **37**-2a3b4
Missionary Journey – **20**-3a;3c;#4;4a6; **25**-#1
Mistreated – **37**-3b6d3
Mob – **9**-2a2d; **21**-4b3
Mocked – **5**-6b15,19; **9**-3a2d
Mocks – **14**-5a6g4
Models of Faith – **35**-3a4
Monday – **7**-3a2; **13**-5a1a5
Money – **2**-2d4; **12**-4b28b3; **37**-3b6f
Months – **48**-4c5; **49**-4d4a3a1
Moon Under Her Feet – **48**-4d1a2
Moral Directives – **37**-3b6
Moral Excellence – **39**-2a1a4
Morals – **24**-3a4
Morning Star – **46**-3a4a2b5
Moses – **1**-2c1; **34**-1b; **36**-3a4i; **51**-4e1a
Mother (Jesus') – **8**-1c2c; **15**-2c3
Mother-in-law – **9**-2b2
Mother of John Mark – **19**-2b4
Mother of the *LORD* – **8**-1b3c
Mount Sinai – **26**-2b4a
Mount of Olives – **4**-#6; **13**-5a3g
Mountain – **3**-4d4; **10**-3c19; **36**-3b4a
Mountaintop – **6**-2d1
Mourn – **1**-2b1b
Mourning of the Fall of the Babylon the Great – **51**-f2b
Mourns – **12**-4b11
Mouth – **3**-4d7; **44**-2a2b1f; **45**-3a3c1; **49**-4d4a1a5; **52**-4g2a9
Mouths Billowed – **48**-4c6c2b
Moved – **17**-3c2d
Much – **11**-4b4d; **38**-2a2b3
Much Is Required – **11**-4b4d
Mud – **16**-3b14
Multitude – **48**-4b8
Murder – **1**-2c2
Murderers (Physical & of the Heart) – **53**-4i2d4
Murmur – **16**-3a16
Must – **13**-5a3g8; **17**-3c7
Must Be an Overcomer – **47**-3a7b4c
Must Obey – **38**-2a1b
Must Trust – **38**-2a2c
Mustard Seed – **12**-4b9a;4b19c
Mute – **8**-1b1e; **11**-4a8
My Father & His Angels – **46**-3a5a2c1h
My Reward Is with Me – **54**-4i8
My Son (Jesus) – **33**-1a2a
Mystery – **27**-2a7a-c; **31**-2b5; **44**-2a3b
Mystery of Godliness – **31**-2b5

N

Nailed – **5**-6b17
Naked – **34**-1b4c
Name – **45**-3a3c2c; **46**-3a5a2; **47**-3a6b5;3a6c10; **49**-4d4a3a2; **50**-4d6a1
Name Is Called "The *WORD* of God" – **52**-4g2a7
Name Nobody Else Knew – **51**-4g2a5
Name Not Blotted Out – **46**-3a5a2c1g
Name of His God – **47**-3a6c8-10
Name of the City – **47**-3a6c9
Name of Jesus Forbidden – **18**-1b5
Named – **8**-1b2b; **19**-2a10
Names of Twelve Apostles Written on Stones – **54**-4i4a8
Names of Twelve Sons of Israel on the Gates – **54**-4i4a6
Nathaniel – **15**-2b1e
Nation – **50**-4d4a3a5
Nations – **46**-3a4a2b3; **49**-4d4a1a3
Nations with an Iron Rod – **49**-4d1b3a
Nature – **2**-3a5; **39**-2a1a3
Nazareth – **3**-4a1; **6**-2c4; **8**-1c1d;1c2c; **9**-2a2
Near – **15**-3a4; **54**-4i7
Necessary – **25**-2a; **35**-2a6b2
Need – **39**-2a1a
Need for Maturity – **34**-2a3b
Need for New Priesthood – **35**-2a4c
Needs the Gospel – **22**-5a2b

Needy – **2**-2d1
Neglect Fundamentals – **40**-2a2a1
Neglect Salvation – **33**-1a3
Neighbor – **23**-6a5
Neither Hot or Cold – **47**-3a7b2
Net – **18**-4c6c,e
Never Forget the Warning – **34**-1b2d6
Never Satisfied – **40**-2b3c2
New – **53**-4i; **54**-4i1c7
New Apostates – **43**-2a3
New Believers – **40**-2b4b
New Covenant – **35**-2a5b
New Grip – **36**-3b3a
New Earth – **53**-4i1
New Heaven – **41**-2c2d; **53**-4i1
New Jerusalem – **47**-3a6c9; **53**-4i4,5,10;4i5
New Jerusalem Comes from Heaven – **53**-4i1b
New Jerusalem Had Three Gates on Each Side – **54**-4i4a7
New Jerusalem Wall – **54**-4i4a10
New Man – **27**-3b1; **29**-3a
New Name – **47**-3a6c10
New Priest – **35**-2a4d
New Priesthood – **35**-2a4c
New Priestly Service – **35**-2a5a
New Testament – **35**-2a6b
Nicodemus – **15**-3a2
Nicolaitan Practices – **45**-3a1c1
Nicolaitans – **45**-3a3b1a3
Night – **41**-2c2a
Night Vision – **15**-3a2
Nineveh – **11**-4a10c
No Advantages – **22**-2b2
No Condemnation in Christ – **22**-4c1
No Confidence in the Flesh – **28**-2c1
No Deceptive Words – **50**-4d6a5
No Discipline=Illegitimate Child – **36**-3b2e
No Discipline Is Enjoyable – **36**-3b2h
No Evil or Unbelieving Heart – **34**-1b2d
No Evil for Evil – **30**-4a5c
NO Favorites – **39**-2b1e
No Gain – **12**-4b28b3
No One Could Buy Things – **50**-4d5b9
No One Guiltless – **22**-2b4
No One Opens – **46**-3a6a5
No One Shuts – **46**-3a6a4
No One to Takes – **47**-3a6c6
No Other Burden – **46**-3a4a2b1
No Longer Under a Tudor – **26**-2b1e
No More Death, Sorrow or Crying – **53**-4i1c6
No Place – **41**-1a3d2
No Pleasure in He Who Abandons the Faith – **35**-3a2f
No Prophet – **16**-3b7
No Salvation – **38**-2a1c
No Sin – **41**-1a3a
No Spiritual Wisdom – **24**-2c2a
No Trust – **38**-2a1c
No Visible Signs – **12**-4b21a
No Weariness – **45**-3a1a5
Noah – **12**-4b21c; **35**-3a4c
Nobody Else Knew – **51**-4g2a5
Non-Worshipers to be Killed – **50**-4d5b7
Not Annulled or Voided – **26**-2b1c
Not Ashamed of the Gospel – **32**-2a2
Not Blotted Out – **46**-3a5a2c1g
Not by Faith – **22**-5a2a
Not by the Law – **26**-2b1
Not Carnality – **29**-2b4
Not Come to a Physical Mountain – **36**-3b4a
Not Controlled by Angels – **33**-1a4a
Not Denied His Name – **47**-3a6b5
Not Final – **23**-5a3a
"Not Guilty" – **14**-5a6e1
Not Hurt – **45**-3a2a2d
Not Legalism – **29**-2b2
Not Live for the Flesh – **28**-2c3
Not Made by Things Visible – **35**-3a3e
Not Maturing – **34**-2a3
Not Our Home – **37**-3b7e
Not Perfect – **46**-3a5a2c
Not Philosophy – **29**-2b1
Not Received His Mark – **52**-4h2a1c
Not Redeemed – **39**-2b1g
Not Regulations – **29**-2b3
Not Seen – **35**-3a3b
Not Slack – **41**-2c1
Not Tarry – **35**-3a2e
Not Total – **23**-5a3a
Not With Deceivers – **42**-#3
Not Worshiped the Anti-Christ – **52**-4h2a1b
Notes – **23**-#7
Nothing – **26**-3d12; **28**-2d2
Nothing Against the Truth – **26**-3d12
Nothing Is Left Out – **34**-1a4b1
Notorious Sinner – **12**-4b27
Now – **14**-5a6e2
Now Crowned – **34**-1a4b2
Nuclear Explosions – **48**-4c4
Number of His Name Is 666 – **50**-4d5b10
Numbers – Pg**10**; **12**-4b1,2; **19**-2a9
Nun (Pronounced: noon) – **36**-#14

O

Oaths – **1**-2c6
Obedience – **2**-2e3; **12**-4b10d; **42**-2a9
Obedience Encouraged – **33**-3a2
Obey – **16**-3b12a; **17**-4a5a,b; **27**-3c1c
Obey God – **36**-3b5a
Obey Your Employer – **27**-3c1d
Obey Your Parents – **27**-3c1c
Obey Your Spiritual Leaders – **37**-3b7g
Obeys the Word – **38**-2b1
Obeying – **33**-1a3a
Obtain – **35**-3a3c
Off the Right Road – **40**-2b3c6
Offender – **25**-2a3
Offer Our Sacrifice of Praise to God – **37**-3b7f
Offered – **24**-4b1

Offering – **32**-3b1a
Offers You – **41**-1a6a
Officer – **16**-3a8,9
Oil – **4**-6b2
Old – **34**-2a1; **35**-2a5;2a6a
Old Apostates – **43**-2a2
Old Testament – **34**-2a1; **35**-2a6a
Old Testament Priesthood – **34**-2a1
Old Testament Priestly Ministry – **35**-2a6a
Omega – **44**-2a1b1
On the Earth – **47**-3a6c3; **52**-4h2
On the Gates – **54**-4i4a6
On the Stone – **45**-3a3c2c
One – **14**-5a6g5; **16**-3b18; **18**-1a4; **28**-2a3; **46**-3a6a4
One Another – **42**-2a2
One from Jerusalem – **26**-2b4b
One from Mount Sinai – **26**-2b4a
ONE Like the Son of Man – **44**-2a2b;2a2b1
One Head Wounded – **49**-4d4a2a
One-Third – **48**-4c6a;4c6c2c
Onesimus – **33**-3a;3a1
Once Gentiles in the Flesh – **27**-2a4
Only Eternal Things – **36**-3b5c
Only in the Cross – **27**-2c2
Only We Who Truly Believes Enters – **34**-1b3b
Open – **10**-3a2i
Open Door – **47**-3a6b2
Open to Him (Jesus) – **34**-1b4c
Open the Door & Let Me In - **47**-3a7b4b
Opened – **53**-4h4a3
Opens – **46**-3a6a4,5
Operation of the Church – **33**-#3
Opinion – **16**-3b5
Opposed – **16**-3b1
Opposition – **16**-3b; **16**-3c
Opportunity for Endurance & Faith Availabible – **50**-4d4a3a11
Order of His Priesthood – **34**-2a4
Ordered People of the World – **50**-4d5b5
Orders – **19**-2b5
Original Plan – **25**-2a1
Other – **11**-4a3
Other Believers – **23**-6a7; **39**-3a5
Other Burden – **46**-3a4a2b1
Other Duties – **31**-2e
Other Tongues – **18**-1a6
Others – **9**-2b2; **35**-3a2b4
Our – **12**-4b19c
Our Assurance – **42**-2b2
Our Church Family – **23**-6a2
Our Compassionate High Priest – **34**-2a1
Our Confession of Sin – **41**-1a3
Our Cornerstone – **27**-2a6
Our Faith – **40**-2a2a1; **42**-2b1
Our Freedom – **29**-2b
Our God – **49**-4d2a2a
Our God Is a Consuming Fire – **37**-3b5e
Our Hearts – **41**-1a3d2
Our Home – **37**-3b7e
Our Home Life – **27**-3c
Our Hope – **24**-4d2
Our *LORD* – **41**-2c3
Our Neighbor – **23**-6a5
Our Pattern – **25**-3c2
Our Peace – **27**-2a5
Our Personal Life – **27**-3b
Our Possessions – **41**-1a6a4
Our Priceless Inheritance – **38**-2a1b
Our Progress – **36**-3b1a1
Our Responsibilities – **23**-6a
Our Righteousness – **22**-#5; **23**-#6
Our Sacrifice – **37**-3b7f
Our Sins – **41**-1a3c,f
Our Spiritual Growth – **23**-2c1
Our Suffering – **34**-1a5a
Our Victory – **42**-2b1
Our Walk – **23**-6a6
Ourselves – **23**-6a1; **41**-1a3a
Out – **9**-2b1a; **15**-2b1b; **16**-3b2c; **30**-3a3; **32**-3b1a; **34**-1a4b1; **40**-2b2a8; **42**-3a; **46**-3a5a2c1g
Out of Heaven – **49**-4d2;4d2a1b; **54**-4i4a1
Out of Sodom – **40**-2b2a4
Outside of Bethany – **17**-3c2d
Outworking of Love – **42**-2a4
Over – **9**-2b1; **10**-3c11; **12**-4b11; **16**-3b6; **30**-4a5a
Over All Creation – **33**-1a2e
Over Every Tribe – **49**-4d4a3a5
Over Nations – **46**-3a4a2b3
Over the Fall – **51**-4f2d
Over the World – **42**-2b1
Overcomer – **45**-3a1c2;3a2a2d; **47**-3a6c7;3a7b4c
Overcomers – **46**-3a4a2b3
Overcomers Shall Inherit All Things – **53**-4i2b
Overcomes – **38**-2b2; **45**-3a3c2; **46**-3a5a2c1f
Overseers – **31**-2b3
Own Business – **30**-4a2

P

Pain – **51**-4e6
Painful Labor – **48**-4d1a4
Pagans – **24**-4b5
Pale Horse – **48**-4b4
Palm Branches – **13**-5a1a2
Parable of the Dragnet (Fishing Net) – **3**-3c9
Parable of the Expensive Pearl – **3**-3c8
Parable of the Faithful & Unfaithful Servant – **11**-4b4c
Parable of the Fig Tree – **4**-6a4; **7**-3a3j4; **11**-4b7b; **13**-5a3g7
Parable of the Four Soils – **2**-3c1-2; **5**-2b1; **10**-3c6,7
Parable of the Friend – **11**-4a7b
Parable of the Good Samaritan – **11**-4a5
Parable of the Good Shepherd – **16**-3b17a
Parable of the Great Feast – **12**-4b12c
Parable of the Guest – **12**-4b12b
Parable of the Hidden Treasure – **3**-3c7
Parable of the King with Ten Servants – **12**-4b28
Parable of the Leaven – **3**-3c5

Parable of the Lighted Lamp – **11**-4a11
Parable of the Loaned Money – **4**-6a7
Parable of the Lost Coin – **12**-4b15
Parable of the Lost Sheep – **12**-4b14
Parable of the Lost Son – **12**-4b16
Parable of the Mustard Seed – **3**-3c4; **6**-2b3
Parable of the Persistent Widow – **12**-4b22a
Parable of the Planter & Harvester – **15**-3a5b
Parable of the Praying Pharisee & Tax
Collector – **12**-4b22c
Parable of the Shrewd Manager – **12**-4b17
Parable of the Rich Man & Beggar – **12**-4b18
Parable of the Ten Virgins – **4**-6a6
Parable of the Two Sons – **4**-5b1
Parable of the Vine & the Branches – **17**-4a6
Parable of the Vineyard Workers – **3**-4d15
Parable of the Wedding Feasts – **4**-5b3
Parable of the Wheat & the Tares – **3**-3c3; **5**-2b2
Parable of the Wheat & Tares Defined – **3**-3c6
Parable of the Wicked Farmers – **4**-5b2; **13**-5a3b
Parable of the Wineskins – **9**-2c2
Parables – **4**-5b; **5**-2b
Paradise – **26**-3d7
Paralyzed Man – **2**-3a7; **5**-2a6; **9**-2b5; **16**-3a9; **19**-2a10
Parents – **27**-3c1c
Parents of Moses – **36**-3a4h
Partakers – **39**-2a1a3
Partiality – **31**-2d5
Pass Away – **41**-2c2b
Passion Week – **13**-5a
Passover – **4**-6b4; **7**-3a5,3a5a-b; **13**-5a5;5a5a,b;5a5a,b
Past – **22**-5a1; **38**-2a2d
Paternal Care – **24**-2d2
Patience – **44**-3a1a1; **46**-3a4a1
Patience & Perseverance – **38**-2c2
Patient – **30**-4a5b; **44**-3a1a2
Patient Endurance – **35**-3a2c; **39**-2a1a5b
Patient With All – **30**-4a5b
Patiently – **51**-4d7c5
Pattern – **25**-3c2
Pattern of Self-Denial – **24**-4b2
Paul (Apostle) – **20**-#3;3a;3a1-9; **21**-4b6; **23**-#1;1a1-2;
24-2d;2d2; **25**-#1;1a;1a1,3;#2;2a1-3;#3;3a; #3;3a;
26-3d2-4,7-11;#2;2a1-4; **27**-#1;1a; **28**-1a;#2;
29-1a;1a1;1st Thess.1a;#2;2a2;#3; **30**-#4;4a1;
32-3b2.
Paul & Barnabas' Confrontation – **20**-3a3
Paul & Barnabas Dedicated – **20**-3a1
Paul & Barnabas Journey to Antioch – **20**-3a9
Paul & Barnabas Preach – **20**-3a2
Paul & Silas – **20**-3c2,5
Paul & Silas Imprisoned – **20**-3c5
Paul & Timothy – **33**-1a
Paul Accused of Sedition – **21**-4b8
Paul Addresses False Rumor – **21**-4b1
Paul Addresses the Aeropagus – **20**-3c12
Paul Addresses the Jerusalem Mob – **21**-4b3
Paul an Apostle of Jesus Christ – **25**-#3
Paul Appeals to Caesar – **21**-4b11
Paul Arrested – **21**-4b2
Paul Arrives in Rome – **21**-4b23
Paul Charges Timothy – **32**-#2;#3
Paul Defends – **25**-3a;3c;3d; **26**-#2
Paul Defends His Authority – **25**-3d
Paul Defends His Ministry – **25**-3a
Paul Defends the Collection – **25**-3c
Paul Delivered – **21**-4b21; **25**-1a3
Paul Delivered from Viper Attack – **21**-4b21
Paul Departs Athens – **20**-3c13
Paul Evades King Agrippa's Challenge – **21**-4b16
Paul Explains Himself – **25**-1a
Paul Explains His Change of Plans – **25**-#2
Paul Explains His Early Life – **21**-4b13,15
Paul Explains Life After Conversion – **21**-4b15
Paul Gives Thanks for the Colossians – **29**-1a1
Paul Goes to Caesarea – **20**-4a1
Paul Goes to Corinth – **20**-3c13
Paul Heals All Afflicted – **21**-4b22
Paul Preaches at Antioch – **20**-3a4,5
Paul Preaches at Thessalonica – **20**-3c8
Paul Rebukes Peter – **26**-2a4
Paul Recounts His Conversion – **21**-4b14
Paul Refuses to Depart Secretly – **20**-3c7
Paul Restores Life to Eutychus – **20**-4a6b
Paul Returns to Antioch – **20**-3c14
Paul Says, "Forgive the Offender" – **25**-2a3
Paul Sent to Felix – **21**-4b7
Paul Sent to Antioch – **20**-3b5
Paul Shipwrecked – **21**-4b20
Paul Stoned – **20**-3a8
Paul Tried Before King Agrippa – **21**-4b12
Paul Warned – **21**-4a8
Paul's Appeal for Repentance – **26**-3d10
Paul's Appeal for Onesimus – **33**-3a
Paul's Appreciation of Philemon – **33**-2a
Paul's Authority – **26**-3d2,3;2a3
Paul's Authority Approved – **26**-2a3
Paul's Call to Apostleship – **26**-2a1
Paul's Change of Plans – **25**-2a2
Paul's Charge to Timothy – **31**-2a3
Paul's Commendation – **29**-#2
Paul's Concern – **26**-3d4; **30**-#2
Paul's Conduct – **29**-2a2
Paul's Defense Before Felix – **21**-4b9
Paul's Defense Before Sanhedrin – **21**-4b5
Paul's Desire to Visit Rome – **21**-1a2
Paul's Example – **28**-2b1c
Paul's Exhortation – **26**-3d11
Paul's Exhortations Concerning Doctrine – **31**-2a
Paul's Exhortations for Other Duties – **31**-2e
Paul's Exhortations in Church Discipline – **31**-2d
Paul's Exhortations to the Church – **31**-2b
Paul's Exhortations to Leaders – **31**-2c
Paul's Expression of Thanks – **23**-1a2; **32**-2a1
Paul's Farewell – **32**-3b5
Paul's Final Exhortations – **25**-4e3
Paul's Final Greetings – **23**-#7
Paul's Final Words – **23**-7a6

Paul's First Missionary Journey – **20**-3a
Paul's First Trip to Jerusalem as a Christian – **26**-2a2
Paul's Friends – **23**-7a5
Paul's Greeting – **25**-1a1
Paul's Greetings to Timothy – **31**-1a
Paul's Greetings to Romans – **21**-1a1
Paul's Hope in Death – **32**-3b1
Paul's Journey to Rome – **21**-4b
Paul's Ministry in Iconium – **20**-3a6
Paul's Ministry in Rome – **21**-4b24
Paul's Original Plan – **25**-2a1
Paul's Paternal Care – **24**-2d1
Paul's Plans to Visit Corinth – **25**-4e2
Paul's Plans to Visit Rome – **23**-7a2
Paul's Plea for Purity – **30**-4a1
Paul's Plea to Philemon – **33**-#3
Paul's Praise & Greetings – **23**-7a3
Paul's Present Circumstances – **28**-#2
Paul's Release – **21**-4b10
Paul's Roman Citizenship – **21**-4b4
Paul's Salutation – **23**-1a1
Paul's Second Missionary Journey – **20**-3c; **25**-#1
Paul's Thorn in the Flesh – **26**-3d8
Paul's Unselfishness – **26**-3d9
Paul's Valedictory – **32**-3b
Paul's Vision of Paradise – **26**-3d7
Paul's Warning Ignored – **21**-4b18
Pay – **3**-4d7
Pay Attention – **40**-2a2a
Paying Taxes – **13**-5a3c
Peace – **1**-2b1g; **27**-2a5; **28**-2d4; **36**-3b3b
Peace in All Circumstances – **28**-2d4
Pearls – **54**-4i4a11a
Penalty – **34**-1b2c
Pentecost – **18**-1a7
People – **1**-2b1i; **3**-4b6; **4**-5c5; **6**-2c7,13,15; **7**-3a4; **9**-2a2c; **10**-3c15; **11**-4a10c;4b7; **12**-4b10; **13**-5a1a3-4; **14**-5a6g2;5a7a; **15**-3a;3a1a;3a1d; **16**-3a13;3b11; **23**-7a4; **37**-3b6d1; **40**-2b3c3; **41**-2c3b; **48**-4c6c2e; **50**-4d4a3a6;4d5b4; **53**-4i2d3.
People of the World – **50**-4d5b5
People on Earth – **48**-4c6a
People to Inherit the Lake of Fire – **53**-4i2d
People Who Belong to the World – **50**-4d5b2
People Who Rebelled – **34**-1b2d7
People Who Hold – **45**-3a3b1,2
People's Errors – **41**-2c3d
Perfect – **37**-2a3b5
Perfect Before God – **46**-3a5a2c
Perfects the Sanctified – **35**-2a6b5
Perform – **18**-1b10
Performance – **27**-2c1d
Perfumed Oil – **4**-6b2
Pergamos – **45**-3a3;3a3a-c
Peril of Not Maturing – **34**-2a3
Perilous Times – **32**-3a1,2
Period – **49**-4d4a; **53**-4h4a2,4;4h4a7a
Perish – **11**-4b7a
Persecute – **1**-2b1i
Persecuted – **1**-2b1h; **45**-3a2
Persecution – **13**-5a3g4; **30**-#2; **49**-4d2a
Persecutions – **30**-2a2
Persecution of the Church – **19**-1b19;2b
Persecution Patiently – **51**-4d7c5
Perseverance – **38**-2c2
Persevere – **47**-3a6c1
Persevere in the Future – **32**-#3
Persevere in the Present – **32**-#2
Persistent Prayer – **12**-4b22
Person – **6**-2c10d,e **33**-#1
Personal Notes – **23**-#7
Personal Life – **27**-3b
Perspectives – **37**-2a2
Perverted Thinking – **21**-2a1a,b
Peter – **3**-4d1; **4**-6b6,10; **6**-2c17,19; **7**-3a5d;3a6b; **10**-3c16; **13**-5a5e;5a6a; **15**-2b1c; **17**-4a3;4b2; **18**-4c6e; 4c7-9; **18**-#1;1a7;1b1-4; **19**-2a12-16,18;2a12b;2b2-5; **26**-2a4.
Peter & John – **18**-1b1,3
Peter Cuts Off Ear of High Priest – **17**-4b1
Peter's Death by Crucifixion – **18**-4c8
Peter Defends God's Grace – **19**-2a18
Peter Denies Jesus – **18**-4b4
Peter Drags Fish to Shore – **18**-4c6e
Peter Freed from Prison – **19**-2b3
Peter Imprisoned – **19**-2b2
Peter Meets Cornelius – **19**-2a15
Peter Perplexed – **19**-2a14
Peter Preaches Good News – **19**-2a16
Peter Searched For – **19**-2b5
Peter's Second Sermon – **18**-1b2
Petra – **49**-4d3a2
Pharisee – **11**-4a12a
Pharisees – **9**-2c,2c1; **11**-4a12b;4a12b1-4,6; **13**-5a1a4; **16**-3b6,16
Philadelphia – **46**-3a6; **47**-3a6a
Philemon – **33**-#1-3
Philemon's Love & Faith – **33**-2a1
Philemon's Obedience Encouraged – **33**-3a2
Philippi – **20**-3c4
Philippian Jailer Converted – **20**-3c6
Philosophers – **20**-3c11
Phillip – **15**-2b1;2b1a,d; **19**-2a1,4
Phillip Preaches – **19**-2a1
Phillip Witnesses – **19**-2a4
Physical & of the Heart – **53**-4i2d4
Physical Mountain – **36**-3b4b
Physical Pleasure – **41**-1a6a2
Pick Wheat – **2**-3b3a; **9**-2c3
Picking Wheat – **5**-2a8b
Piercing – **34**-1b4b
Pigs – **6**-2c2; **10**-3c10d
Pilate – **4**-6b13; **7**-3a6c; **14**-5a6c;5a6e1; **18**-4b5,6,8
Pilgrims – **38**-1a
Pillar in the Temple – **47**-3a6c7
Pisidia – **20**-3a4
Pit – **48**-4c5; **52**-4h1,3
Place of Rest – **34**-1b3a

Place Prepared by God – **49**-4d1b3c2
Plagues – **48**-4c6c1;4c6c2c; **51**-4e1b
Plan – **23**-7a2; **25**-2a1
Plans – **7**-3a4c; **25**-#2;2a2
Plans to Visit Corinth – **25**-4e2
Planters – **15**-3a5b
Plea for Onesimus – **33**-3a1
Plea to Philemon – **33**-#3
Pleasure – **41**-1a6a2
Plot –**7**-3a4a
Plot to Kill Jesus – **4**-6b1; **13**-5a4a; **17**-3c4
Plot to Kill Paul – **21**-4b6
Plus Thomas – **18**-4c4
Policies in Giving – **25**-3c3
Pool in Bethesda – **16**-3a9
Poor – **1**-2b1a; **9**-3a2a; **37**-2a2
Position – **26**-2c1a
Position of Believers in Christ – **27**-#2
Possessed – **11**-4a9a
Possessing No Spiritual Wisdom – **24**-2c2a
Possessions – **35**-3a2b6; **41**-1a6a4
Posts a Title for Cross – **18**-4b8
Posted – **5**-6b23
Poured – **32**-3b1a
Poured Out – **51**-4d7c2
Poverty – **45**-3a2a1a
Power – **2**-3a,3a1-6;3a10-11;3b5; **6**-2c,2c3; **9**-2b,2b1; **10**-3c11; **27**-2c1c; **46**-3a4a2b3; **48**-4c6c2e; **50**-4d2a2a;4d4a2e1.
Power of Sanctification – **22**-4c
Power of the Word – **20**-4a
Powerful – **34**-1b4b
Practice – **26**-2c1b
Practice of the Believers in Christ – **27**-#3
Practice of Sanctification – **22**-4b
Practice Witchcraft or Magic Arts (Sorcerers, Witches, Magicians) – **53**-4i2d6
Practices – **2**-2d; **45**-3a1c1
Praise – **8**-1b3d; **10**-3a2i; **23**-7a3
Praise, Glory & Honor – **38**-2a2b3
Praise for Philemon – **33**-#2
Praise God Together – **23**-6a7d
Praise to God – **37**-3b7f
Praises – **13**-5a1a3
Praising – **8**-1c1c
Pray – **18**-1b6; **30**-4a5e
Pray for Boldness – **18**-1b6
Pray Without Ceasing – **30**-4a5e
Prayer – **2**-2d2,8; **7**-3a5e; **11**-4a7,4a7a; **12**-4b22; **17**-4a14; **28**-1a2; **37**-3b8; **42**-2b3
Prayer Encouraged – **29**-3b1
Prayer for Spiritual Wisdom – **27**-2a2
Prayer for the Church – **30**-3b2
Prayer in the Church – **31**-2b1
Prayer to be Counted Worthy – **30**-2a3
Prayer Meeting – **18**-1a3
Prays – **17**-4a12,13,15
Praying – **12**-4b22c
Praying in Jesus' Name – **17**-4a10
Preach on Cyprus – **20**-3a2
Preach the Word – **32**-3a4
Preach to Gentiles – **19**-2a19b
Preach to Jews – **19**-2a19a
Preached – **23**-7a1; **28**-2a1
Preaches – **1**-1a6,2b; **9**-2b3; **19**-2a1,8
Preaching – **1**-2a; **5**-2a1; **9**-2a1
Precepts Concerning Doctrine – **31**-#2
Precepts of Jesus – **6**-2d
Precious Blood of Jesus – **39**-2b1i
Precious Gem – **54**-4i4a3
Predicted – **43**-2b1
Prediction – **3**-4d2,6,16; **18**-4c8
Predicts – **4**-6b6; **7**-3a5d; **10**-3c17; **12**-4b25; **13**-5a5e; **17**-4a11
Preeminence of Christ – **29**-#2
Pregnant Woman – **48**-4d1b2b; **49**-4d1b3
Prelude to the Bowls Judgments – **51**-4e1
Prepared – **34**-1b3a
Prepared by God – **49**-4d1b3c2
Prepares – **17**-4a
Preparation – **8**-#1
Preparation – **5**-#1;1a; **14**-#1
Prepare – **4**-6b4; **13**-5a5a
Prepared – **7**-3a5a
Prepares – **5**-1a1; **6**-2d4; **8**-1b1d;1c3; **14**-1a;2a1
Present Circumstances – **28**-#2
Present (Time) – **22**-5a2
Present Age – **38**-2a2
Presents – **6**-3a; **14**-2a; **15**-2b
Presented – **4**-5a; **8**-1c; **9**-2b
Presentation – **4**-#5; **14**-#2; **15**-2c
Press Toward the Goal – **28**-2c2
Priceless – **38**-2a1b
Pride – **7**-3a3h; **41**-1a6a4
Priests – **35**-2a4d; **37**-3b7d
Priesthood – **34**-2a;2a2a;2a4; **35**-2a4c; **39**-2b4
Priestly – **35**-2a5a;2a6;2a6a;2a6b
Priestly Ministry – **35**-2a6;2a6a;2a6b
Priestly Service – **35**-2a5a
Primary Focus – **40**-2b1c
Prince of the World – **17**-4a9b1
Principles – **1**-2c; **10**-3b
Principles for Ministry – **24**-4b3
Principles of Christian Marriage – **24**-4a1
Principles of Sanctification – **22**-4a
Principles in Giving – **25**-3c1
Prison – **19**-2b3; **45**-3a2a2a; **50**-4d4a3a9
Prisons – **37**-3b6d
Private – **15**-3a4d3
Private Life – **15**-3a4d3
Problems – **23**-#1
Proceeds from His Mouth – **52**-4g2a9
Proclaimed – **48**-4c12
Proclaims – **3**-4d1; **10**-3c16; **15**-2a2; **51**-4d7c1,6
Proclamation of First Angel – **50**-4d7a
Proclamation of Second Angel – **50**-4d7b
Proclamation of Third Angel – **51**-4d7c
Procrastinates – **21**-4b10

Produces – **38**-2b5; **38**-2b7;2c1,2
Produces Life – **39**-2a1a4
Profiting from Trials – **37**-2a1
Progress – **36**-3b1a1
Progression of the Church – **18**-1b
Promise – **18**-1a2; **40**-2b4c
Promise Granted Through Faith – **22**-3b3
Promises – **2**-3b2; **17**-4a5; **39**-2a1a2
Promises of God – **41**-2c1
Promises in Giving – **25**-3c4
Promised – **17**-4a5e
Proof – **2**-2e,#3
Prophesied – **6**-2c18;2d3;2d4f; **8**-1b4d; **19**-2a19e
Prophecies (Proclaims) – **8**-1b4d; **15**-3a2b
Prophecies (Prophecy) – **30**-4a5h
Prophecy – **17**-3c8; **24**-4c6
Prophecy of Joel – **18**-1a7
Prophet – **8**-1c1c; **50**-4d5b
Prophet's – **11**-4a12b5
Prosperous – **10**-3a2g
Protected – **49**-4d3a2
Proudness – **11**-4a12b3
Prudent – **2**-2d7
Public – **16**-3b2c
Publicly – **4**-5a
Public Worship – **24**-4c;4c9
Punishment – **40**-2b2a6
Pure – **1**-2b1f; **38**-2a2b1
Pure Gold, Clear as Glass – **54**-4i4a10d
Pure Milk of the Word – **39**-2b3
Purification – **8**-1c1a
Purity – **6**-2c10; **11**-4a12b1
Purpose – **8**-1a; **18**-4c5; **28**-3d1
Purpose of God – **22**-5a1b
Purpose of the Gifts – **27**-3a2c
Purpose of the Law – **26**-2b1d
Purposes in Giving – **25**-3c2
Purpose of the Mystery – **27**-2a7b
Pursues the Woman (Israel) – **49**-4d3a1
Put – **14**-5a6g
Put on Christ – **23**-6a6

Q

Qualifications – **34**-2a2
Qualifications for Deacons – **31**-2b4
Qualifications for Overseers – **31**-2b3
Qualified Elders – **32**-Titus-2a1
Queen of Sheba – **11**-4a10b
Quench the Spirit – **30**-4a5g
Question – **4**-5c4
Questioned – **4**-6b9; **13**-5a3a,c,d,e; **16**-3b15
Questions – **4**-5c1-3; **7**-3a3j1; **17**-4b3
Questions Addressed – **24**-#4
Quickly – **47**-3a6c4; **54**-4i8,12
Quotes – **14**-2a1b

R

Race of Faith – **36**-3b1
Rahab – **36**-3a4k
Raised – **10**-3c2,12; **17**-3c2; **19**-2a11
Raised As God – **34**-1a5c
Reactions – **3**-#4
Readiness – **28**-3d1c
Reads – **9**-2a2a
Ready to Devour – **49**-4d1b2c
Ready to Give Birth – **48**-4d1a4
Real – **26**-3d2
Reality – **24**-4d1
Reaped for Judgment – **51**-4d9
Reaping the Grapes – **51**-4d9
Reaping the Harvest – **51**-4d8
Reaps His Believers – **51**-4d8
Rebelled – **34**-1b2d7
Rebirth – **14**-1a5
Rebuke – **13**-5a1a4
Rebuke False Teachers – **32**-Titus-2a2
Rebukes – **6**-2c19
Rebukes Peter – **26**-2a4
Receive – **10**-3a2i; **30**-#4; **37**-2a3a; **38**-2a2a; **39**-2a1a1
Receive A New Name – **45**-3a3c2c
Receive A White Stone – **45**-3a3c2b
Receive Hidden Manna – **45**-3a3c2a
Receive His Mark to be Killed – **50**-4d5b8
Receive Power – **46**-3a4a2b3
Received – **9**-3a2f; **39**-2a1a2
Received & Heard – **46**-3a5a2c1a
Received His Mark – **52**-4h2a1c
Received Vision from Jesus Christ – **44**-2a1a
Receives – **14**-5a6g5; **15**-3a2
Reciprocation – **2**-2d9
Recognize Those Over You in the *LORD* – **30**-4a5a
Reconciled to God – **25**-3a8
Reconciliation – **1**-2c3
Recounts Conversion – **21**-4b14
Red – **48**-4c6c1
Red Dragon – **48**-4d1b;4d1b2
Red Horse – **47**-4b2
Redeemed by the Precious Blood of Christ – 39-2b1i
Redeemed from the Earth – **50**-4d6a2
Redemption in Christ – **27**-2a1
Redeemed Spirits in Heaven – **36**-3b4e
Redeemed with Corruptible Things – **39**-2b1h
Refers – **12**-4b11a
Refuse – **36**-3b5; **41**-1a3b
Refuses – **20**-3c7
Reign – **49**-4d4a3
Reign 1000 Years with Christ on Earth – **52**-4h2
Reigns with Christ 1000 Years – **52**-4h2a2d
Reject – **3**-4a1; **10**-4a1,9
Rejected – **3**-4c; **6**-2c4; **9**-2a2; **13**-5a1a5; **14**-1a4
Rejects – **22**-5a2c
Reigns with Christ 1000 Years – **52**-4h2a1d
Rejection – **10**-#4; **11**-4b

Rejection of Christ – **22**-5a1a
Rejects – **11**-4a12
Rejoice – **1**-2b1j
Rejoice Always – **30**-4a5d
Rejoices Over the Fall of Babylon – **51**-4f2d
Relating to the Great Apostasy – **30**-3a1
Relating to the Man of Sin Revealed – **31**-3a2
Relationally – **26**-2a5
Release from Bottomless Pit – **52**-4h3
Released – **14**-5a6e3
Released After the 1000 Years – **52**-4h3a
Release – **21**-4b10
Relief Comes – **19**-2a19f
Religion – **37**-2a
Religiosity – **5**-2a8; **11**-4a12b4
Religious Directives – **37**-3b7
Religious Leader – **50**-4d5b
Religious Leaders – **2**-3b6; **3**-4c,4c1; **4**-5a4,5c,5c4-6; **5**-6b19;6c3; **6**-2c14; **7**-3a4a; **8**-1c2;1c2b; **11**-4a9,12 **13**-5a3e;5a6b; **16**-3a16;3b12d;3b15,21; **17**-3c4.
Remain – **13**-5a3g8
Remained Dead for a 1000 Years – **52**-4h2a2a
Remained Faithful – **35**-3a2b1
Remaining Jews – **49**-4d3a5b
Remains – **38**-2a2b3; **46**-3a5a2b
Remarks – **9**-2a2c
Remarriage – **24**-4a4
Remember Early Days After Salvation in Christ – **35**-3a2b
Remember How You Have – **46**-3a5a2c1a
Remember Your Leaders – **37**-3b7a
Reminders – **40**-2a2a2
Removed – **45**-3a1b2
Renames – **15**-2b1c
Render No Evil for Evil – **30**-4a5c
Renew – **36**-3b3
Repent – **11**-4b7;4b7a; **45**-3a1b2;3a3c1; **46**-3a4a2a3;3a5a2c1b
Repent or Perish – **11**-4b7a
Repents – **12**-4b19b
Repentance – **25**-3b3; **26**-3d10
Repentance of the Corinthians – **25**-3b3
Repentant – **46**-3a4a2a4
Reported – **24**-3a1
Requested Prayer – **37**-3b8
Required – **11**-4b4d
Required to Worship Anti-Christ – **50**-4d5b2
Requires – **36**-3b1a
Rescue – **1**-1a8b
Rescued – **40**-2b2a4
Reserves – **40**-2b2a6
Response – **46**-3a5a2c1; **47**-3a6c;3a7b4
Responsible – **11**-4a12b5
Responsibilities – **23**-6a
Rest (Physical) – **2**-3b2; **34**-1b3c
Rest (Heaven) – **34**-1b2c;1b3a,c
Rest of Israelites – **49**-4d3a5a
Rest of Thyatira – **46**-3a4a2b
Rest Were Killed – **52**-4g3b4
Rested – **14**-5a7a
Restores Life – **20**-4a6b
Restrainer – **30**-3a3
Results of Satan's Release – **52**-4h3
Results of Lukewarmness – **47**-3a7b3
Resurrected – **48**-4c11; **49**-4d4a2
Resurrected Beast – **50**-4d5b5
Resurrection – **4**-5c2; **5**-6c; **7**-3a3e;4a7,4a7a; **13**-#5;5a3d; **17**-3c2b; **18**-4c;4c1; **24**-4d;4d5; **25**-3a6; **52**-4h2a2;4h2a2b.
Resurrection Body – **24**-4d5
Resurrection Day – **14**-5a8
Result – **18**-1b8,9
Result of the Vision – **44**-2a3
Results – **41**-1a3d
Results of the Judgment – **53**-4h4a7
Results in Disaster – **41**-2c3c
Retaliation – **1**-2c7
Retrieve – **13**-5a1a1
Return – **1**-1a5; **4**-6a3,5; **11**-4a4;4b4; **12**-4b28b1-2; **13**-5a3g1; **18**-4c6b; **31**-3b; **46**-3a4a2b2
Return of the *LORD* – **30**-2a
Returns – **8**-1c1d;1c2c; **15**-3a4b; **20**-3c14; **40**-2b4e
Revealed – **30**-3a2
Reveals – **15**-3a4d3; **17**-4a2,3
Revelation – **3**-4d3; **33**-1a1; **43**-#1
Revelation of Righteousness – **22**-3a
Revelation of the Church – **27**-2a7
Revelations – **3**-4d
Reverent Fear – **39**-2b1g
Revert – **38**-2b1c
Revile – **1**-2b1i
Reward – **9**-3a2e; **34**-1b2d5; **38**-2a2d; **40**-2a1a8; **45**-3a2a2c; **54**-4i8
Rewards – **3**-4d14b; **12**-4b24b; **23**-2c2; **45**-3a2a2
Rich – **9**-3a2f; **31**-2e4
Rich & Poor – **37**-2a2
Rich & Wonderful Promises – **39**-2a1a2
Rich Young Ruler – **3**-4d14a; **12**-4b24a
Ridicule – **35**-3a2b2
Right (Choice) – **33**-1a2d
Right & Good – **36**-3b2g
Right & Wrong – **11**-4b6b
Right Hand – **44**-2a2b1e
Right Hand or Forehead – **50**-4d5b8
Right Living in the Church – **33**-3a
Right Living in Society – **33**-3b
Right Road – **40**-2b3c6
Right Side – **18**-4c6c
Righteousness – **1**-2b1d,h; **17**-4a9b2; **22**-3a;3a1;3b;4a2;#5;5a2a; **28**-3d1b; **32**-3b1c
Righteous Judgment of God – **21**-2a2
Riot at Ephesus – **20**-4a5
Risen Christ – **24**-4d1-2
Rises – **5**-6c1; **14**-5a8a
Rises Forever – **51**-4d7c4
Rituals – **6**-2c10a
River Dries Up – **51**-4e7
River of Life – **54**-4i6
Road – **14**-5a8b; **40**-2b3c6

Road to Bethany – **17**-3c2a
Road to Jericho – **12**-4b26
Road to Damascus – **19**-2a5
Robe – **52**-4g2a6
Rod – **46**-3a4a2b4; **49**-4d1b3a; **52**-4g2a10
Role of the Holy Spirit – **17**-4a9c
Roman – **21**-4b4
Romans – **21**-#1
Rome – **21**-4b;4b17,19,23,24;1a2; **23**-7a2
Roman Centurion – **10**-3c1
Roman Citizenship – **21**-4b4
Roman Guards – **5**-6b23
Roman Soldiers – **5**-6b15
Room – **47**-4a1
Royal Priesthood – **39**-2b4
Rule – **46**-3a4a2b4; **52**-4g2a10
Rule All Nations – **49**-4d1b3a
Ruler of Entire Household – **34**-1b1b
Rumor – **21**-4b1
Run – **36**-3b1a2
Rushing Waters – **44**-2a2b1d

S

Sabbath – **2**-3b3,3b3a-b; **5**-2a8b,c; **9**-2c3,4; **12**-4b12a; **14**-5a7;5a7a; **16**-3a10;3b2b; **20**-3a4,5
Sabbath Day – **14**-5a7
Sacrifice – **6**-#3; **12**-4b24; **41**-1a3f
Sacrifice of Praise – **37**-3b7f
Sacrificed to Idols – **45**-3a3b1a2; **46**-3a4a2a2
Sacrificial Death – **34**-1a5e
Sacrificing – **12**-4b24b
Sacrifices – **35**-2a6b3
Sail – **21**-4b19
Saints – **25**-4e1;3c3; **52**-4h3b,c
Saints in Jerusalem – **52**-4h3c
Saints of God – **52**-4g2a8;4h2a
Saints Reign 1000 Years – **52**-4h2
Sake – **1**-2b1h; **24**-2d1
Salutation – **23**-1a1
Salvation – **12**-4b27; **13**-5a1a5; **14**-5a6g5; **15**-3a6; **25**-3b1; **28**-3d1e; **33**-1a3; **35**-3a2b; **38**-#2;2a1a;2a1c; 2a2d; **39**-2b3b; **42**-2b2; **49**-4d2a2a.
Salvation Comes from – **38**-2a1a
Salvation Explained – **15**-3a2c
Salvation Through Grace – **20**-3b2
Salt & the Light – **1**-2b2
Samaria – **19**-#2;2a1
Samaritan Woman – **15**-3a4d
Samaritans – **10**-4a1; **15**-3a6
Same Today – **37**-3b7b
Same Mind in the *LORD* – **28**-2d1
Same Vision Three Times – **19**-2a13
Samson & Jephthah – **36**-3a4m
Samuel – **36**-3a4n
Sanctified – **35**-2a6b5
Sanctified Vessel – **32**-2b5
Sanctification – **22**-#4;4a-c; **38**-2b
Sanctification Imparted Through Christ – **22**-#4
Sanctuary – **35**-2a6a1;2a6b1
Sanhedrin – **4**-6b11; **7**-3a6a; **18**-1b4; **21**-4b5
Sarah (Abraham) – **36**-3a4d
Sardis – **46**-3a5;3a5a2c1e
Satan (Lucifer, Great Red Dragon) – **1**-1a8; **9**-1c7; **11**-4a9a; **26**-3d5; **49**-4d4a2e; **50**-4d5a2
Satan & His Fallen Angels – **49**-4d2a1a
Satan Bound for 1000 Years – **52**-4h1
Satan Cast Into Lake of Fire with Anti-Christ & False Prophet – **52**-4h3e
Satan Dares God – **1**-1a8d
Satan Dares Jesus – **1**-1a8c
Satan Desires Worship – **1**-1a8e
Satan Enraged with Anger – **49**-4d3a5
Satan Gave Anti-Christ Great Power – **49**-4d4a2e1
Satan Gave Him His Power – **49**-4d4a1a6
Satan Has Great Anger – **49**-4d2a2c4
Satan in the Wilderness – **5**-1a3
Satan Lost Battle – **49**-4d2a1b
Satan Pursues the Woman – **49**-4d3a1
Satan's Release – **52**-4h3
Satan Released After the 1000 Years – **52**-4h3a
Satan Spoke Through Him – **6**-2c19
Satan Steps-up Persecution – **49**-4d3a
Satan Surround Tribulation Saints – **52**-4h3c
Satan—The Fiery Red Dragon – **48**-4d1b
Satan Thrown Out of Heaven – **49**-4d2
Satan Tries to Drown Israelites – **49**-4d3a3
Satan Worship – **47**-3a6b6
Satan's Critical Defeat – **49**-4d2a2c
Satan's Power – **2**-3b5
Satan's Throne – **45**-3a3a1c
Satanic – **16**-3b12d
Satisfied – **40**-2b3c2
Saturday – **14**-5a7
Saul – **19**-2a19d
Saul Baptized – **19**-2a6
Saul Escapes Death – **19**-2a7
Saul Persecutes the Church – **18**-1b19
Saul Preaches – **19**-2a8
Saul Returns to Jerusalem – **20**-2b7
Saved – **12**-4b10; **15**-3a2d; **35**-3a2g2; **41**-2c3b
Saved by Grace Through Faith – **27**-2a3
Save Us from Sin – **22**-4b3
Saving Grace – **33**-3a2
Savior – **8**-#1; **9**-#2;#3; **10**-#4; **13**-#5; **34**-1a5c
Saw – **44**-2a2b
Say We Have No Sin – **41**-1a3a
Saying – **47**-3a6c11; **53**-4i1c
Says – **46**-3a4a2b6;3a5a2c1i; **47**-3a6b;3a7a1;3a7b4d
Says He (Jesus) – **46**-3a5a;3a6a; **47**-3a6b;3a7a1;3a7a1b
Says Jesus – **10**-3c23; **16**-3b20
Says the Son of God – **45**-3a4a
Scatter – **19**-2a
Scattered – **17**-4a11
Scorched – **51**-4e5
Scripture – **9**-2a2b; **40**-2a2b
Scripture Given by Inspiration of God – **32**-3a3
Scroll – **9**-2a2a

Sea – **10**-3c9; **49**-4d2a2c3
Sea of Galilee – **3**-4b2; **10**-3c9; **16**-3a14; **18**-4c6
Sea Gave Up the Dead – **53**-4h4a5
Sea Turns to Blood – **51**-4e3
Sealed Book – **47**-4a2
Sealed of Israel – **48**-4b7
Seal – **47**-4b1,2; **48**-4b3-6,9
Seals – **47**-4b
Search for Peter – **19**-2b5
Seas Struck – **48**-4c2
Seat of Christ – **25**-3a7
Second – **3**-4d6; **20**-3c
Second Angel – **50**-4d7b
Second Bowl Judgment – **51**-4e3
Second Sign – **48**-4d1b
Second Coming – **3**-4d3; **7**-3a3j3; **12**-4b25; **30**-3a4; **51**-4g;4g2
Second Death – **45**-3a2a2d; **52**-4h2a2a,c;4h4a7c; **53**-4i2d
Second Missionary Journey – **20**-3c; **25**-#1
Second Seal – **47**-4b2
Second Servant – **12**-4b28b2
Second Sabbath – **20**-3a5
Second Sermon – **18**-1b2
Second Time – **6**-2d3; **10**-3c20
Secret – **16**-3b2; **28**-2e2
Secret of Joy – **28**-2e2
Secretly – **20**-3c7
Sectarianism – **23**-2a1
Sedition – **21**-4b8
See – **41**-1a6a3
See to It – **36**-3b5a
Seeing God Through Love – **42**-2a7
Seek – **11**-4a7c; **16**-3b19
Seeks – **15**-2b1b
Seen – **35**-3a3b,d; **41**-1a1; **44**-#2;2a3a6;#3
Seen After This – **47**-#4
Seizing the Final Victory – **51**-4f
Selects – **5**-2a10; **9**-3a1
Self-Control – **38**-2b1a; **39**-2a1a5a
Self-Denial – **24**-4b2
Self-Indulgence – **24**-4b4
Selfish Activities – **43**-3a2
Selfish Ambition – **43**-3b1
Send – **17**-4a9a; **19**-2a12b
Send for Peter – **19**-2a12b
Send the Message – **44**-2a1b3
Sends – **6**-2c5; **10**-3c13; **19**-2a12
Sends Fire from Heaven – **52**-4h3d
Sensitive Servants – **34**-1a5a
Sent – **14**-5a6f; **16**-3b12c; **19**-2a19c; **21**-4b7
Sent Out – **2**-3a12; **10**-3c13
Sent – **20**-3b5
Sentenced – **14**-5a6e2
Sermon – **18**-1b2
Sermon on the Mount – **1**-2b; **9**-3a2
Servant – **5**-#1;1a;#2; **6**-3a; **12**-4b28b1-3; **17**-4b2; **32**-2b6
Servants – **34**-1a5a
Servant's Treatment to Their Masters – **31**-2e
Servanthood – **6**-2d4g
Servants – **12**-4b28; **46**-3a4a2a1
Serve – **18**-1b14
Service – **16**-3a8; **32**-3a; **35**-2a5a;2a6b; **45**-3a4a1
Serving – **3**-4d14b; **28**-2b
Serving Others – **3**-4d17
Set Before Them – **47**-3a6b2
Set Free from the Law – **22**-4b1
Sets – **18**-1b11; **21**-4b19
Seven – **18**-4c6a,d
Seven Bowls – **51**-4e1b
Seven Bowl Judgments – **48**-4c12; **51**-4e
Seven Churches – **44**-2a1b3;2a3b1,2; **47**-4a
Seven Deacons – **18**-1b14
Seven Diadems – **48**-4d1b1
Seven Disciples – **18**-4c6a
Seven Golden Lampstands – **44**-2a2a;2a3b
Seven Heads – **48**-4d1b1; **49**-4d4a1a1
Seven Plagues – **51**-4e1b
Seven Seals – **47**-4b
Seven Spirits of God – **46**-3a5a
Seven Stars – **44**-2a2b1e;2a3b;2a3b1,2
Seven Trumpets – **48**-4c
Seven-Year Tribulation – **7**-3a3j2
Seventh Bowl – **51**-4e8
Seventh Seal – **48**-4b9
Seventh Bowl Judgment – **51**-4e8
Seventh Trumpet – **48**-4c12
Seventy-two – **11**-4a3,4
Sexual Immoral (Adulterers & Fornicators) – **53**-4i2d5
Sexual Immorality – **45**-3a3b1a3; **46**-3a4a2a1
Shall Inherit All Things – **53**-4i2b
Shall Live by Faith – **21**-1a3; **35**-3a2
Shake – **36**-3b5b
Share – **18**-1b7
Share All That Belongs to Christ – **34**-1b2d5
Share Burdens – **27**-2c1d
Sharp Sword Proceeds from His Mouth – **52**-4g2a9
She Bore a Child – **49**-4d1ba
Shepherd – **16**-3b17;3b17a
Shepherds – **8**-1b5c,d
Shield – **28**-3d1d
Shining – **44**-2a2b1g
Ship Sets Sail – **21**-4b19
Shipwrecked – **21**-4b20
Shod – **28**-3d1c
Shore – **18**-4c6d,e
Short Time Left – **49**-4d2a2c5
Shortsightedness – **40**-2a1a6
Should – **29**-#3; **36**-3b1a2
Should Be Fed 1260 Days – **49**-4d1b3c3
Should Do – **29**-#3
Shout – **13**-5a1a3
Shows How Strong – **38**-2a2b1
Shows You – **41**-1a6a1
Shuts – **46**-3a6a4,5
Sickness – **6**-2c3; **10**-3c11
Sick – **38**-2c3

Side – **54**-4i4a7
Sight – **50**-4d5b3
Sign – **4**-6a3; **6**-2c14; **11**-4a10a-c; **13**-5a3g1; **48**-4d1a,b
Signs – **4**-6a2; **12**-4b21a; **13**-5a3g6
Signs & Wonders – **18**-1b10; **33**-1a3b
Signs in the Heaven – **48**-4d1
Signs of the Times – **11**-4b4a
Sign to Unbelievers – **24**-4c8
Silence in Heaven – **48**-4b9
Silvanus – **29**-1st Thess.1a; **30**-1a
Simon (Sorcerer) – **19**-2a2,3
Simon (Peter) – **9**-2b2;2b4a,b; **15**-2b1b,c
Simeon – **8**-1c1b
Sin – **16**-3b12b; **17**-4a9b1; **19**-2a3; **21**-#2; **22**-4a2;4b3; **30**-3a2; **40**-2b3c3;2b4b,d; **41**-1a3;1a3a,e; **42**-2a2; 2b4; **44**-3a1a3.
Sin to Slaves – **22**-4a2
Sin Hinders – **36**-3b1a1
Sins – **41**-1a3c,f
Sin's Advantage in the Law – **22**-4b2
Sinfulness of the Gentiles – **21**-2a
Sinfulness of the Jew – **22**-2b
Sinfulness of Man – **21**-1a
Single-Minded – **32**-2b2
Sinned – **40**-2b2a1; **41**-1a3d
Sinner – **12**-4b19b
Sinners – **5**-2a7
Sisters – **34**-1a5b
Sits on the Throne – **53**-4h4a1
Sixth Bowl – **51**-4e7
Sixth Seal – **48**-4b6
Sixth Trumpet – **48**-4c6
Sky Blue – **48**-4c6c1
Slandered God's Name – **49**-4d4a3a3
Slaves of Righteousness – **22**-4a2
Slaves to Sin – **22**-4a2; **40**-2b4d
Slavery of Sin – **16**-3b12; **42**-2b4
Sleeping Mat – **9**-2b6
Smoke – **48**-4c6c2b
Smoke of Torment – **51**-4d7c4
Smyrna – **45**-3a2;3a2a
Snakes – **48**-4c6c2d
Soars – **51**-4e2
Society – **23**-6a3; **33**-3b
Sodom – **40**-2b2a4
Sodom & Gomorrah – **40**-2b2a3
Soldiers – **5**-6b15; **7**-3a6d; **14**-5a6g3; **18**-4b9
Solomon's Portico – **18**-1b1
Some Go to Prison – **45**-3a2a2a
Some Have Entertained Strangers – **37**-3b6c
Son of God – **14**-5a6b1;#1;#2; **15**-2a2c;#3; **16**-3a11,12; **17**-#4;4b; **18**-4c; **45**-3a4a
Son of Man – **44**-2a;2a2b;2a2b1; **51**-4d8
Son (God) – **33**-1a2a;1a4
Son (Human) – **8**-1b1c; **10**-3c2; **18**-4b10
Son Made Lower Than the Angels for a While – **33**-1a4
Song of Moses – **51**-4e1a
Song of Simeon – **8**-1c1b
Sons of Israel on the Gates – **54**-4i4a6
Sons to Glory – **34**-1a5
Sonship Through the Holy Spirit – **22**-4c2
Sorcerer Bar-Jesus – **20**-3a3
Sorcerer Simon – **19**-2a2,3
Sorcerers, Witches, Magicians – **53**-4i2d6
Sorrow – **10**-3a2h
Sorrow or Crying – **53**-4i1c6
Soul – **2**-3b2
Souls Are Saved – **35**-3a2g2
Sovereign – **6**-2c
Spare the Ancient World – **40**-2b2a2
Spare the Angels – **40**-2b2a1
Sparkled Like a Precious Gem – **54**-4i4a3
Speak – **18**-1a6; **50**-4d5b6
Speak Evil About – **40**-2b3a
Speak Out – **40**-2b2a8
Speaking – **16**-3b11; **39**-2b3a
Speaks – **3**-4d14a; **8**-1c2;1c2b; **9**-2b1a; **15**-3a1c;3a4;3a5;3a5; **16**-3b2c; **36**-3b5; **53**-4i1c
Speaks Out – **9**-2b1a; **16**-3b2c
Special Favor of God – **36**-3b3c
Spirit of Anti-Christ – **41**-1a7
Spirit of Truth (Jesus) – **17**-4a8
Spirit (Holy) – **1**-1a8a; **8**-1b2c;1b3b;1b4c; **15**-2a2b; **17**-4a5;4a5e;4a9;4a9a-c; **18**-1a2,5;1b8,9; **19**-2a17; **20**-4a3; **22**-4c2,3; **24**-4c3a; **25**-3a3; **27**-2c1c;3b2; **28**-2a3; **30**-4a5g.
Spirit (Body/Flesh) – **1**-2b1a; **42**-2a5
Spirit (Demonic) – **11**-4a8
Spirit-Filled Believer – **29**-3a1
Spirits of God – **46**-3a5a
Spirits in Heaven – **36**-3b4e
Spiritual – **14**-1a5; **34**-2a3a
Spiritual Food – **15**-3a5a
Spiritual Gifts – **23**-6a2; **24**-4c3; **27**-3a2
Spiritual Growth – **23**-2c1
Spiritual Harvest – **15**-3a5
Spiritual Immaturity – **34**-2a3a
Spiritual Leaders – **37**-3b7g
Spiritual Strength – **37**-3b7c
Spiritual Vitality – **36**-3b3
Spiritual War – **25**-3d1
Spiritual Wisdom – **23**-2b2; **24**-2c2a; **27**-2a2
Spirituality – **41**-1a5
Spiritually Dead – **53**-4h4a7a,b
Spoke – **6**-2c19
Spoke Blasphemies – **49**-4d4a3a2
Spoke No Deceptive Words – **50**-4d6a6
Spoke with the Voice – **50**-4d5a2
Standards of the Gospel – **43**-2a
Stands – **4**-6b13
Stand Fast – **26**-2c1a; **31**-3a5
Stand Firm – **36**-3b3a
Standing Fast – **28**-2a3
Stars – **44**-2a2b1e;2a3b;2a3b1,2; **48**-4d1b2a
Stars on Her Head – **48**-4d1a3
State of Their Spirituality – **41**-1a5
Stay – **15**-2b1a
Stay Away – **37**-3b6f

Stayed There Three Months – **20**-4a6a
Stephen Accused – **18**-1b15
Stephen Arrested – **18**-1b16
Stephen Stoned – **18**-1b18
Steps-up Persecution – **49**-4d3a
Stick Measured the City – **54**-4i4a9
Stone – **16**-3b19; **45**-3a3c2b,c
Stoned – **19**-1b18; **20**-3a8
Stones – **54**-4i4a8; 4i4a10e
Stood Before – **48**-4d1b2b; **53**-4h4a2
Stopped Flooding Waters – **49**-4d3a4
Storm – **6**-2c1
Stormy Sea – **10**-3c9
Strangers – **37**-3b6b,c
Streets Made of Transparent Gold – **54**-4i4a11b
Strength – **37**-3b7c; **47**-3a6b3
Strength & Numbers – **19**-2a9
Strengthen What Remains – **46**-3a5a2b
Strict & Enduring – **32**-2b3
Strife – **38**-2b6
Strong – **38**-2a2b1
Strong in Grace – **32**-2b1
Struck – **48**-4c1-4
Struck with Worms – **19**-2b6
Stumbling Block – **45**-3a3b1a1
Submission of the Believer – **39**-#3
Submission to Other Believers – **39**-3a5
Submissive – **39**-3a2-4
Submit As Unto God Himself – **23**-6a4
Submit to Discipline – **36**-3b2f
Submit to Your Husbands – **27**-3c1a
Substance of Things Hoped For – **35**-3a3a
Suffering – **25**-1a3; **28**-2a; **34**-1a5a; **35**-3a2b4
Sufferings – **29**-3a1
Suffering in Asia – **25**-1a33
Suffering Is Training Ground – **36**-3b2a
Suing Brother – **24**-3a3
Sulfur – **48**-4c6c2b; **51**-4d7c
Sun – **48**-4d1a1
Sun Shining – **44**-2a2b1g
Sunday – **6**-3a1; **7**-4a7; **13**-5a1; **14**-5a8
Superior – **34**-2a2,4; **35**-2a6
Superiority of Faith by the Christian – **35**-#3
Superiority of Melchizedek's Order – **35**-2a4b
Superiority of Prophecy – **24**-4c6
Superiority of the Gospel – **26**-2b
Superiority of the Person of Jesus Christ – **33**-#1
Superiority of the Work of Jesus Christ – **34**-#2
Supernatural – **18**-4c1
Supper – **9**-2b7; **24**-4c2; **52**-4g3a;4g3b5
Supper of God Called – **52**-4g3a
Supports – **16**-3a12
Supremacy of Christ – **29**-2a
Supreme Revelation – **33**-1a1
Surround Tribulation Saints in Jerusalem – **52**-4h3c
Sword – **19**-2b1; **28**-3d1f; **44**-2a2b1f
Sword of Christ – **52**-4g3b4
Sword of His Mouth – **45**-3a3c1
Sword Proceeds from His Mouth – **52**-4g2a9
Sychar – **15**-3a4
Synagogue of Satan – **47**-3a6b6

T

"Tabernacle (Jesus) of God Is with Men" – **53**-4i1c1
Tabitha – **19**-2a11
Table – **13**-5a5c
Tails – **48**-4c6c2d
Take A New Grip – **36**-3b3a
Take Heed to Yourself – **31**-2c3
Take No Confidence in the Flesh – **28**-2c1
Take Your Crown – **47**-3a6c6
Taken – **13**-5a5b2; **30**-3a3; **35**-3a2b6
Takes the Mark – **51**-4d7c1
Takes the Sealed Book – **47**-4a2
Talks – **18**-4c9
Tarry – **35**-3a2e
Taste – **39**-2b3c
Taught – **6**-2c10
Taught Servants – **46**-3a4a2a1
Tax – **3**-4d7
Taxes – **4**-5c1; **7**-3a3d; **13**-5a3c
Tax Collector – **2**-3a8; **9**-2b7; **12**-4b22c
Teach – **40**-2b1a
Teachers – **32**-Titus-2a2
Teaches – **1**-2b2; **3**-4b4;4d8,4d14b; **10**-3b1; **11**-4a7; **12**-4b10;4b21,22,24; **13**-5a3f; **16**-3b2d; **17**-4a9
Teaching – **2**-3b; **3**-4d12,14; **6**-2c15
Teachings – **3**-4a1;4d; **7**-3a3; **16**-3b12a
Tear Wiped Away – **53**-4i1c5
Tells – **14**-5a8a2; **15**-3a4d2; **17**-3c7; **18**-4c6c; **19**-2a12b
Temple – **4**-5a2;6a1; **7**-3a2b; **8**-1c1;1c1c;1c2a-b; **13**-5a2;5a2a; **15**-3a1;3a1a-c; **16**-3b2;3b2d; **21**-4b2; **37**-3b7d; **47**-3a6c7.
Temptation – **6**-2d4b
Temptations – **1**-1a8; **3**-4d9; **37**-2a3b
Tempted – **5**-1a3; **9**-1c7
Tempter – **12**-4b19a
Ten-Fold – **12**-4b28b1
Ten Crowns – **49**-4d4a1a2
Ten Horns – **48**-4d1b1
Ten Lepers – **12**-4b20
Ten Servants – **12**-4b28;4b28b
Terrible Thing – **35**-3a2a
Terror Comes to Earth & Sea – **49**-4d2a2c3
Test All Things – **30**-4a5i
Test Every Spirit – **42**-2a5
Test of Faith – **37**-#2
Test Those – **47**-3a6c3
Test Your Faith – **38**-2a2b
Tested – **37**-2a1a1
Testifies – **15**-2a2c
Testifies to the Churches – **54**-4i10
Testing – **37**-2a3a; **45**-3a2a2
Testimony – **35**-3a3c; **49**-4d2a2c2
Testimony of Jesus Christ – **49**-4d3a5c
Than Before – **40**-2b4d
Thankfulness – **30**-2a1

Thankfulness & Prayer – **28**-1a2
Thankfulness for the Grace of God – **31**-2a2
Thanks – **23**-1a2; **29**-1a1; **30**-4a5f
Thanks for the Colossians – **29**-1a1
That They Know God – **47**-3a6b7
That Time – **51**-4d7c6
The 1000 Years – **52**-4h3a
The 144,000 – **50**-4d6;4d6a
The Aaronic Priesthood – **34**-2a2a
The Abandoned Apostle – **32**-3b2
The Abominable (Corrupt People) – **53**-4i2d3
The Alpha & Omega – **44**-2a1b1; **53**-4i2
The Amen – **47**-3a7a1a
The Angel – **47**-3a7a
The Announcement – **50**-4d7
The Angels from the Euphrates – **48**-4c6
The Anti-Christ – **49**-4d4; **52**-4h2a1b
The Anti-Christ Begins His Reign – **49**-4d4a3
The Battle of Armageddon – **52**-4g3b
The Beast – **50**-4d4a3a6; **52**-4g3
The Beast from the Earth – **50**-4d5
The Beast from the Sea – **49**-4d4
The Beginning – **47**-3a7a1c; **53**-4i2
The Beginning of the Millennium – **52**-4h
The Believer – **39**-#3
The Birds Had Their Great Supper – **52**-4g3b5
The Black Horse – **48**-4b3
The Blood of the Lamb – **49**-4d2a2c1
The Book of Life – **53**-4h4a3
The Bowl Judgments – **51**-4e1
The Bride – **53**-4i3
The Bright Hope – **30**-2a
The Called – **43**-1a
The Cause – **23**-2b
The Christian – **35**-#3
The Church – **42**-1a; **47**-3a7a
The Churches – **54**-4i10
The City – **47**-3a6c9; **54**-4i4a9
The Compromising Church – **45**-3a3
The Conqueror – **47**-4b1
The Consequences – **23**-2c
The Corrupt Church – **45**-3a4
The Cowardly Who Turned Away from God (Backsliders) – **53**-4i2d1
The Creation – **47**-3a7a1c
The Cry – **48**-4b5
The Day of the *LORD* – **30**-#3;3a
The Dead – **53**-4h4a5,6
The Dead Church – **46**-3a5
The Dead Unbelievers – **53**-4h4a2
The Depravity of False Teachers – **40**-2b3
The Doctrine – **45**-3a3b1
The Door – **47**-3a7b4a
The Drive of Life – **36**-3b4
The Earth – **36**-3b5b; **47**-3a6c3; **50**-4d5;4d6a2; **51**-4d8
The Earthly Sanctuary – **35**-2a6a1
The Elect Lady – **42**-1a
The End – **44**-2a1b1; **53**-4i2
The End-Time Anti-Christ – **49**-4d4a1
The Euphrates – **48**-4c6
The Evil of His Day – **40**-2b2a5
The Expectation – **38**-2a2d
The Fact – **23**-2a
The Faith – **31**-2e5; **32**-2a3; **35**-3a2g1; **39**-2a1; **40**-2a2;2a2a1; **43**-2a1; **45**-3a3a1d
The Faithful – **32**-3b3; **39**-1a; **47**-3a7a1b
The Faithful Church – **46**-3a5
The Faithful *LORD* – **32**-3b3
The Fall of Babylon – **51**-4f2;4f2b,d
The False Teachers – **43**-2a
The Fatal Wound – **49**-4d4a2b
THE Father Is in Me & "**I AM**" in My Father – **16**-3b20
The Fiery Red Dragon – **48**-4d2
The Fierceness – **52**-4g2a11
The Final Destination of All Unbelievers – **52**-4g3b3; **53**-4h4a7c
The Final Victory – **51**-4f
The First & the Last – **44**-2a1b2;2a3a2
The First Resurrection – **52**-4h2a2;4h2a2b
The Gates – **54**-4i4a6,9
The Glory of God – **54**-4i4a2
The Glory of the New Jerusalem – **54**-4i5
The Good Confession – **31**-2e3
The Gospel – **32**-2a2; **43**-2a; **50**-4d7a1
The Grapes – **51**-4d9
The Grave – **53**-4h4a6;4h4a7a
The Great – **51**-4f2;4f2a,b
The Great Apostasy – **31**-2c1
The Great Harlot – **51**-4f1;4f1a,b
The Great Red Dragon – **48**-4db2
The Great Supper of God – **52**-4g3
The Great Tribulation – **48**-4b8;4d; **49**-4d4a
The Great White Throne Judgment – **53**-4h4; **53**-4h4a
The Harvest – **51**-4d8
The Heart – **53**-4i2d4
The Heavenly Father – **36**-3b2f
The Heavenly Sanctuary – **35**-2a6b1
The Heaven – **48**-4d1
The Heavens – **36**-3b5b
The Heavens Struck – **48**-4c4
The Holy Spirit – **46**-3a4a2b6;3a5a2c1i; **47**-3a6c11
The Hour of Trial – **47**-3a6c2
The Image – **50**-4d5b6
The Immoral – **37**-3b6e3
The Jew's Blasphemy – **45**-3a2a1b
The Judgment – **53**-4h4a7
The Just Will Live by Faith – **21**-1a3; **35**-3a2
The Key of David – **46**-3a6a3
The Lake of Fire – **53**-4h4a7a-c;4i2d
The Lamb – **50**-4d6;4d6a4,5; **51**-4e1a;4g1; **53**-4i3
The Lamb & the 144,000 – **50**-4d6
The Lamb's Book of Life – **50**-4d4a3a7
THE Life – **17**-3c2b;4a4
The Little Book – **48**-4c7,8
THE Living God – **35**-3a2a; **36**-3b4b
The *LORD* – **38**-2c1; **39**-3a2,3
The *LORD* Disciplines – **36**-3b2c
The *LORD*'s Response – **47**-3a7b3

The *LORD* Says – **47**-3a7b4d
The Love of Money – **37**-3b6f
The Lukewarm Church – **47**-3a7
The Lustful – **40**-2b2a7
The Macedonian Call – **20**-3c3
The Mark – **51**-4d7c1
The Marriage – **37**-3b6e1
The Martyrs – **48**-4b5
THE Master (Jesus) – **32**-2b5
The Mediator's Death Necessary – **35**-2a6b2
The Melchizedek Priesthood – **34**-2a2b
The Message to Seven Churches – **44**-2a1b3
The Millennium – **52**-4h
The Miracle – **49**-4d4a2c
The Mistreated – **37**-3b6d3
The Moon Under Her Feet – **48**-4d1a2
The Morning Star – **46**-3a4a2b5
The Name of **His** God – **47**-3a6c8-10
The New Heaven – **41**-2c2d
The New Jerusalem – **47**-3a6c9; **54**-4i4,5,10;4i5
The New Man – **27**-3b1
The New Priestly Service – **35**-2a5a
The Nicolaitans – **45**-3a3b2
The Now – **38**-2a2d
The Number of the Beast Is 666 – **50**-4d5b10
The Omega – **44**-2a1b1; **53**-4i2
The Opening – **47**-4b
The Overcomer – **45**-3a1c2
The Pale Horse – **48**-4b4
The Past – **38**-2a2d
The People – **37**-3b6d1
The Persecuted Church – **45**-3a2
The Performance – **27**-2c1d
The Plea for Onesimus – **33**-3a1
The Position – **26**-2c1a
The Power – **27**-2c1c
The Practice – **26**-2c1b
The Pregnant Woman – **48**-4d1b2b; **49**-4d1b3
The Prisons – **37**-3b6d
The Prophets – **36**-3a4n
The Red Horse – **47**-4b2
The Resurrection Body – **24**-4d5
The Restrainer (Holy Spirit) – **30**-3a3
The Result of the Vision – **44**-2a3
The Resurrected Beast – **50**-4d5b5
The Rest Were Killed – **52**-4g3b4
The Rich – **31**-2e4
The Risen Christ – **24**-4d1,2
The River of Life – **54**-4i6
The Saints Reign 1000 Years – **52**-4h2
The Salvation – **49**-4d2a2a
The Same Today, Yesterday & Forever – **37**-3b7b
The Sanctified – **35**-2a6b5
The Sea – **49**-4d4
The Sealed Book – **47**-4a2
The Sea Gave Up the Dead – **53**-4h4a5
The Seas Struck – **48**-4c2
The Second Coming of Jesus Christ – **51**-4g
The Second Death – **53**-4h4a7c
The Seven Bowls – **51**-4e1b
The Seven Bowl Judgments – **48**-4c12; **51**-4e
The Seven Churches – **44**-1a1;2a1b3;3a; **47**-4a
The Seven Plagues – **51**-4e1b
The Seven Seals – **47**-4b
The Seven Spirits of God – **46**-3a5a
The Seven Trumpets of Judgment – **48**-4c
The Sexual Immoral (Adulterers & Fornicators) – **53**-4i2d5
The Sick – **38**-2c3
The Signs in Heaven – **48**-4d1
The Son Exalted Above the Angels – **33**-1a2
The Son of God – **45**-3a4a
The Son of Man – **44**-2a2b;2a2b1
The Song of Moses – **51**-4e1a
The Special Favor of God – **36**-3b3c
The Sun – **48**-4d1
The Sword of Christ – **52**-4g3b4
The Synagogue of Satan – **47**-3a6b6
The Temple of His God – **47**-3a6c7
The Temple on Earth – **37**-3b7d
The Test of Knowing Jesus – **41**-1a4
The Testimony of Jesus Christ – **49**-4d3a5c
The Things Which Are – **44**-2a3a7,8; **47**-#4
The Three Angels – **50**-4d7
The Throne – **53**-4h4a1
The Throne Room – **47**-4a1
The Time Is Near – **54**-4i7
The Tongue – **38**-2b4
The Tree of Life – **45**-3a1c2
The Tribulation Period – **53**-4h4a2;4h4a7a
The Troops & Horses – **48**-4c6c
The True Believers – **49**-4d4a3a4
THE (Jesus) Truth – **17**-4a4
The Truth – **41**-1a3b
The Two Witnesses – **48**-4c9-11
The Unbelievers – **50**-4d7a1
The Unbelieving Dead – **53**-4h4a4
The Unbelieving of God – **53**-4i2d2
The Unjust – **40**-2b2a6
The Unsaved – **53**-4i2d2
The Vision – **44**-2a;2a1-3
The Voice – **50**-4d5a2
The Walls & the Gates – **54**-4i4a9
The Warning – **34**-1b2d6
The Waters Struck – **48**-4c3
THE Way – **17**-4a4
The White Horse – **47**-4b1
The Wife of the *LAMB* – **53**-4i3
The Wilderness – **49**-4d1b3c1
The Winepress – **52**-4g2a11
The Woman (Israel) – **48**-4d1a; **49**-4d3a1
The Woman Persecuted – **49**-4d3
The *Word* – **39**-2b3
"The *WORD* of God" – **52**-4g2a7
The World – **39**-3a;3a1; **50**-4d5b2,4,5
The World Followed – **49**-4d4a2d
The World Marveled – **49**-4d4a2c
The World Worshiped Satan – **49**-4d4a2e

Their Deceitfulness – **40**-2b3c
Their Destruction – **40**-2b3b
Their Destructive Ways – **40**-2b1b
Their Eyes – **40**-2b3c1
Their Faith – **30**-3a2
Their Faith Growth – **30**-2a1
Their Feet – **47**-3a6b6
Their God – **53**-4i1c4
Their Good Example – **29**-2a1
Their Great Supper – **52**-4g3b5
Their Lure – **40**-2b3c3
Their Lust – **40**-2b3c2
Their Name – **50**-4d4a3a
Their Primary Focus – **40**-2b1c
Their Reward – **40**-2b3b
Their Souls Are Saved – **35**-3a2g2
Their Sufferings – **29**-3a1
Their Testimony – **49**-4d2a2c2
Their Tribulations – **30**-3a
Their Witness – **52**-4h2a1a
Their Works – **45**-3a3a1a;3a4a1; **46**-3a5a1; **47**-3a6b1
Their Zeal – **45**-3a1b1
Them – **18**-4c6c; **45**-3a3c1; **47**-3a6b2;3a6c2; **52**-4h3d
Themselves – **40**-2b4a
These Things Says He – **47**-3a7a1
These Things Says the Son of God – **45**-3a4a
Thessalonians – **29**-1st Thess-#1;#2;2a;2a2;
 30-#3;#4;4a1
Thessalonians Faithfulness to the *LORD* – **29**-2a;
Thessalonians Receive Instructions from Paul – **30**-#4
Thessalonica – **20**-3c8
They – **40**-2b3a
They All Speak – **18**-1a6
They Are Doomed & Cursed – **40**-2b3c5
They Are Doomed to Blackest Darkness – **40**-2b3c8
They Are Tormented Forever & Ever – **52**-4h3f
They Are Virgins – **50**-4d6a3
They Are Wells – **40**-2b3c7
They Brag – **40**-2b4a
They Dwelled – **45**-3a3a1b
They Follow the Lamb Everywhere – **50**-4d6a4
They Have Kept His Word – **47**-3a6b4
They Have Little Strength – **47**-3a6b3
They Have People – **45**-3a3b1,2
They Have Wandered – **40**-2b3c6
They Kept the Faith – **45**-3a3a1c
They Know God Loves Them – **47**-3a6b7
They Lost Their Zeal for God – **45**-3a1b1
They Lure – **40**-2b4b
They Promise – **40**-2b4c
They Teach – **40**-2b1a
They Were Cast Alive – **52**-4g3b3
Thief – **41**-2c2a; **46**-3a5a2c1c
Time Left – **49**-4d2a2c5
Time to Repent – **46**-3a4a2a3
Thing – **35**-3a2a
Things – **18**-1b7; **24**-4b1; **28**-2d3; **30**-4a5i; **34**-1a4b; **39**-
 2b1h; **41**-1a6a3; **44**-#2; **45**-3a3b;3a4a; **50**-4d5b9;
 4d7a5; **53**-4i2b
Things Hoped For – **35**-3a3a
Things Jesus Had Against – **45**-3a3b; **46**-3a4a2
Things Made New – **53**-4i
Things New – **53**-4i1c7
Things Not Seen – **35**-3a3b
Things Offered to Idols – **24**-4b1
Things Sacrificed to Idols – **46**-3a4a2a2
Things Says He – **46**-3a5a;3a6a; **47**-3a6b;3a7a1;3a7a1b
Things Seen – **35**-3a3e
Things to Meditate On – **28**-2d3
Things Visible – **35**-3a3e
Things Which Are – **44**-2a3a7;#3; **47**-#4
Things You Have Seen – **44**-2a3a6
Thinking – **21**-2a1a,b
Third – **3**-4d16; **18**-4c6; **48**-4b3;4c3
Third Angel – **51**-4d7c
Third Appearance – **18**-4c6
Third Bowl Judgment – **51**-4e4
Third Seal – **48**-4b3
Third Time – **6**-2d4f; **12**-4b25
Third Servant – **12**-4b28b3
Third Trumpet – **48**-4c3
Third of Stars – **48**-4d1b2a
Thirst – **1**-2b1d
Thirty Minutes of Silence – **48**-4b9
This – **47**-#4
This Present Age – **38**-2a2
This World – **37**-3b7e
Thomas – **18**-4c3,4
Thorn in the Flesh – **26**-3d8
Those – **1**-2b1b,h; **9**-3a2a-c; **35**-3a2b5; **47**-3a6b6;3a6c3
Those Destined to Death – **50**-4d4a3a10
Those Destined to Prison – **50**-4d4a3a9
Those He (Jesus) Loves – **36**-3b2c
Those Over You in the *LORD* – 4a5a
Those Who Do His Commandments – **54**-4i9
Those Who Die – **51**-4d7c6
Those Who Practice Witchcraft or Magic Arts (Sorcerers,
 Witches, Magicians) – **53**-4i2d6
Three – **4**-6b10
Three Gates on Each Side – **54**-4i4a7
Three Months – **20**-4a6a
Three Plagues – **48**-4c6c2c
Three Things – **17**-4a9b
Three Times – **13**-5a6a; **17**-4a3; **18**-4c7; **19**-2a13
Throne – **33**-1a2c; **45**-3a3a1c; **49**-4d1b3b; **49**-4d4a1a6;
 53-4h4;4h4a;4h4a1
Throne of God – **50**-4d6a7
Throne Room of Heaven – **47**-4a1
Through – **6**-2c19; **18**-1b1; **20**-3b2
Through Christ – **26**-2b2; **39**-2b1k
Through Faith – **22**-3a1;3b3; **27**-2a3
Through Humility – **28**-2b1a
Through Jesus Christ – **22**-#3; **24**-4d6
Through Love – **42**-2a6,7
Through Peter & John – **18**-1b1
Through the Holy Spirit – **22**-4c2
Throughout – **1**-2a3; **9**-2b3
Thrown Down to Earth – **49**-4d2a1c

Thrown Out of Heaven – **49**-4d2
Thursday – **7**-3a5; **13**-5a5
Thyatira – **45**-3a4; **46**-3a4a2;3a4a2b
Time – **6**-2c18;2d3,2d4f; **11**-4b6a; **12**-4b25; **51**-4d7c6
Time Has Come – **50**-4d7a4
Time Is Near – **54**-4i7
Times – **4**-6b10; **13**-5a6a **32**-3a;3a1,2
Times of Tribulation – **25**-1a2
Timothy – **20**-3c2; **28**-2b1c; **29**-1a;3b;3b1; **30**-1a; **31**-1a;2a3; **32**-1a;#2;2a1; **33**-1a
Timothy Circumcised – **20**-3c2
Timothy Encourages Thessalonians – **30**-3b1
Timothy Visit Thessalonians – **30**-3b
Timothy's Example – **28**-2b1c
Title – **18**-4b8
Titus – Pg**32**; **32**-#1;1a
To Believers – **34**-1b1;1b1a
To Christ – **34**-1b2d5
To Church at Pergamos – **45**-3a3a
To Church at Ephesus – **44**-3a1a
To Church at Smyrna – **45**-3a2a
To Commit Sexual Immorality – **46**-3a4a2a1
To Contend for the Faith – **43**-2a1
To Death & Hades – **44**-2a3a5
To Deceive Tribulation Saints – **52**-4h3b
To Discipline – **36**-3b2f
To Employers – **39**-3a3
To Ephesus – **44**-3a1
To Eternal Life – **34**-1a5d
To Fall in the Hands of **THE** Living God – **35**-3a2a
To Forgive Us – **41**-1a3c1
To Give Birth – **48**-4d1a4
To Give Up – **36**-3b1a
To Glory – **34**-1a5
To God – **41**-1a3c,e; **43**-2c1
To God & His Throne – **49**-4d1b3b
To God Himself – **36**-3b4d
To God's Assembly – **36**-3b4c
To Grow – **39**-2b3b
To Him (Jesus) – **34**-1b4c
To Husbands & Wives – **39**-3a4
To Inherit the Lake of Fire – **53**-4i2d
To Injure People – **48**-4c6c2e
To Kill – **48**-4c6a
To Jesus – **36**-3b4f; **52**-4h2a1a
To Live Godly Life – **39**-2a1a
To Live Is Christ – **28**-2a2
To Obey – **17**-4a5a
To Old Ways – **38**-2b1c
To Our Church Family – **23**-6a2
To Our Neighbor – **23**-6a5
To Our Walk – **23**-6a6
To Ourselves – **23**-6a1
To Leaders – **31**-2c
To Love – **17**-4a5a; **37**-3b6a
To Make Image – **50**-4d5b5
To Much Is Given – **11**-4b4d
To Other Believers – **23**-6a7
To Persevere – **47**-3a6c1
To Philemon – **33**-#3
To Receive Power – **46**-3a4a2b3
To Redeemed Spirits in Heaven – **36**-3b4e
To Repent – **46**-3a4a2a2
To Ridicule – **35**-3a2b2
To Seven Golden Lampstands – **44**-2a2b3
To Society – **23**-6a3
To Strangers – **37**-3b6b
To Maturity – **34**-2a3c
To Persevere – **32**-#2
To Preach the Word – **32**-3a4
To Receive – **38**-2a2a; **50**-4d5b8
To Rule All Nations – **49**-4d1b3a
To Speak – **50**-4d5b6
To Take – **47**-3a6c6
To Timothy – **31**-2a3; **32**-1a;2a1
To Titus – **32**-#1;1a; **45**-3a1c2
To Trust God – **39**-2b1k
To Yourself – **31**-2c3
To the Angel – **47**-3a7a
To the Called – **43**-1a
To the Church – **31**-2b
To the Churches – **54**-4i10
To the City of the Living God – **36**-3b4b
To the Doctrine – **31**-2c3
To the End – **34**-1b2d3
To the Faith – **32**-2a3
To the Government – **23**-6a4; **39**-3a2
To the *LORD* – **39**-3a2
To the Rest of Thyatira – **46**-3a4a2b
To the Rich – **31**-2e4
To the Seven Churches – **44**-3a
To Their Masters – **31**-2e
To Your Actions – **39**-2b1f
Today – **9**-2a2b; **25**-3b1; **37**-3b7b
Today Is the Day of Salvation – **25**-3b1
Together – **13**-5a5b1; **23**-6a7d
Tolerate Sin – **45**-3a1a3
Tomb – **5**-6b22,23; **14**-5a6i;5a8a1; **18**-4b12
Tongue – **38**-2b4; **50**-4d4a3a5
Tongues – **18**-1a6; **24**-4c7,8
Too Late for Repentance – **36**-3fb3
Torment Rises Forever – **51**-4d7c4
Tormented – **40**-2b2a5
Tormented Forever & Ever – **52**-4h3f
Tormenting with Fire – **51**-4d7c3
Tortured – **48**-4c5
Total – **23**-5a3a
Touched – **3**-4b3; **6**-2c9; **41**-1a1
Toward – **17**-4a7; **28**-2c2
Toward Believers – **17**-4a7
Toward the Goal – **28**-2c2
Trained – **40**-2b3c4
Trained by Saving Grace – **33**-3a2
Training Ground – **36**-3b2a
Transfigured – **6**-2d1
Transfiguration of Jesus – **3**-4d4
Transfiguration on the Mountain – **10**-3c19
Transparent Gold – **54**-4i4a11b

Travels – **1**-2a3; **8**-1b3a
Treads the Winepress – **52**-4g2a11
Treatment of Church Members – **31**-2d1
Treatment of True Widows – **31**-2d2
Treatment of Younger Widows – **31**-2d3
Treatment of the Elders of the House of God – **31**-2d4
Tree of Life – **45**-3a1c2
Trial – **4**-6b13; **7**-3a6a,c; **14**-5a6c,d; **18**-4b5;1b12; **47**-3a6c2
Trials – **7**-3a6; **13**-5a6; **37**-2a1,3; **38**-2a2;2a2a,b
Trials & Persecutions – **30**-2a2
Tribe – **49**-4d4a3a5
Tribulation – **7**-3a3j2; **25**-1a2; **46**-3a4a2a4; **48**-4b8;4d; **49**-4d4a
Tribulation Period – **52**-4h2a1; **53**-4h4a2,4;4h4a7a
Tribulation Saints – **52**-4h3b,c
Tribulations – **30**-3a
Tried – **9**-2a2d; **16**-3b21
Tried Before King Agrippa – **21**-4b12
Tries to Drown Israelites – **49**-4d3a3
Trip to Jerusalem – **21**-4a8
Triumph – **25**-3a1
Triumph in Christ – **25**-3a1
Triumphal – **4**-5a1; **6**-3a1a
Triumphal Entry – **13**-5a1; **17**-3c6
Troas – **20**-4a6b
Troas to Miletus – **21**-4a6c
Troops – **48**-4c6b,c
Troubles – **45**-3a2a1a
True – **46**-3a6a2; **51**-4g2a1
True Believers – **35**-3a2g; **41**-2c2d; **49**-4d4a3a4; **51**-4d7c5
True Children – **16**-3b12
True Christian Love – **37**-3b6a
True Disciples – **16**-3b12a
True Cost of Discipleship – **10**-4a2
True Family – **5**-2a12; **10**-3c8
True Follower – **6**-2c20
True Messiah – **15**-3a3b
True Secrets of Joy – **28**-2e2
True Widows – **31**-2d2
True Witness (Jesus) – **47**-3a7a1b
True Worship – **3**-4d17
True Worshipers – **15**-3a4d4
Truly Believes – **34**-1b3b
Trumpets – **48**-4c1-6,12
Trumpets of Judgments – **48**-4c
Trust – **38**-2a1c;2a2c
Trust God – **39**-2b1k
Trust God As You Did in the Beginning – **34**-1b2d4
Trust in the *LORD* – **35**-3a2c
Trusting – **38**-2a2d
Trusting Jesus – **38**-2a2d
Truth (Jesus) – **17**-4a4;4a8
Truth – **26**-3d12; **28**-3d1a; **41**-1a3b;1a8
Truth of God's Word – **42**-2a1
Try – **13**-5a1a3
Tudor – **26**-2b1e
Tuesday – **7**-3a3; **13**-5a3
Turned to Ashes – **40**-2b2a3
"Turning the World Upside Down" – **20**-3c9
Turn Your Heart Away – **34**-1b2b
Turned Away from God (Backsliders) – **53**-4i2d1
Turns – **10**-3a2h
Turns to Blood – **51**-4e3,4
Twelve – **9**-3a1; **18**-1a4
Twelve Angels – **54**-4i4a6
Twelve Apostles Written on Stones – **54**-4i4a8
Twelve Disciples – **5**-2a10; **6**-2c5; **10**-3c13
Twelve Foundation Stones – **54**-4i4a8
Twelve Gates Guarded by Twelve Angels – **54**-4i4a6
Twelve Gates – **54**-4i4a11
Twelve Gems – **54**-4i4a10e
Twelve Sons of Israel on the Gates – **54**-4i4a6
Twelve Stars – **48**-4d1a3
Two – **5**-6b18; **15**-2b1
Two Believers – **14**-5a8b
Two Covenants – **26**-2b4
Two Criminals – **14**-5a6g1
Two Disciples – **13**-5a1a1
Two-Edged Sword – **44**-2a2b1f
Two Horns – **50**-4d5a1
Two-Hundred Million – **48**-4c6b
Two Witnesses – **48**-4c9-11

U

Unbelief – **11**-4a10; **15**-3a; **16**-3b10; **34**-1b2-4; **36**-3b3d
Unbelievers – **4**-6a8; **15**-3a2d; **17**-4a7; **24**-4c8; **50**-4d7a1; **52**-4g3b3; **53**-4h4a7c
Unbelievers from the Tribulation Period – **53**-4h4a2
Unbelievers Had Not Their Name – **50**-4d4a3a7
Unbelievers Remained Dead – **52**-4h2a2a
Unbelievers Reaped for Judgment – **51**-4d9
Unbelievers Tortured – **48**-4c5
Unbelieving – **34**-1b2d;1b2d1
Unbelieving Dead from Tribulation Period Judged – **53**-4h4a4
Unbelieving of God (The Unsaved) – **53**-4i2d2
Uncleanness – **2**-3a1
Under Satan's Power – **2**-3b5
Under a Tudor – **26**-2b1e
Under Her Feet – **48**-4d1a2
Under Him – **49**-4d2a1
Under Fire – **3**-4a
Understand – **40**-2b3a
Undiluted – **51**-4d7c2
Unfaithfulness – **12**-4b28b4
Unity – **27**-3a1
Unity & Diversity – **24**-4c4
Unity in Christ – **27**-2a
Unity of Believers – **17**-4a14
Unity Through Humility – **28**-2b1a
Unless Repentant – **46**-3a4a2a4
Unregenerate Man – **21**-2a1;2a1a
Unrepentant Liars – **53**-4i2d8
Unrepentant Murderers (Physical & of the Heart) – **53**-4i2d4

Unruly – **30-**4a5b
Unsaved – **53-**4i2d2
Unselfishness – **26-**3d9
Unstable – **40-**2b3c3; **41-**2c3c
Until His Return – **46-**3a4a2b2
Unto Death – **45-**3a2a2b
Unto God Himself – **23-**6a4
Unwanted King – **12-**4b28a
Up – **36-**3b1a; **51-**4e7
Up the Dead – **53-**4h4a5,6
Up to God – **49-**4d1b3b
Upon – **15-**2a2b; **36-**3a1a3
Upon the *LORD* – **38-**2c1
Upon Jesus – **36-**3b1a3
Upper Room – **18-**1a3
Upside Down – **20-**3c9
Us from All Unrighteousness – **41-**1a3c2
Us His (God) Children – **38-**2a3b6
Us to Give Up – **36-**3b1a
Used – **48-**4c6b
Useful for the Master – **32-**2b5
Ushers In – **48-**4c12

V

Valedictory – **32-**3b
Valley of Megiddo – **52-**g3b
Vegetation Struck – **48-**4c1
Verified – **33-**1a3b
Vessel – **32-**2b5
Victory – **51-**4f
Victory of Faith – **38-**2c
Victory Over the World – **42-**2b1
Victory Through Christ – **24-**4d6
Vindication of Our Righteousness – **22-#**5
Viper – **21-**4b21
Virgin – **24-**4a3
Virgins – **50-**4d6a3
Virtues – **29-**3a1; **39-**2a1a6
Virtues of the Spirit-Filled Believer – **29-**3a1
Visible – **35-**3a3e
Visible Signs – **12-**4b21a
Vision – **19-**2a13,14; **44-**2a;2a1-3;2a1a
Vision from Jesus Christ – **44-**2a1a
Vision of Paradise – **26-**3d7
Vision of the Son of Man – **44-**2a
Visit – **1-**1a3; **21-**1a2
Visit Corinth – **25-**4e2
Visit Rome – **23-**7a2
Visited – **8-**1b5d
Visits –**8-**1b1b;1b2a;1b3;1b3a,c;1b5c; **30-**3b
Visits the Thessalonians – **30-**3b
Vitality – **36-**3b3
Voice – **44-**2a2b1d
Voice from Heaven Proclaims – **51-**4d7c6
Loud Voice from Heaven Speaks Saying – **53-**4i1c
Voice of a Dragon – **50-**4d5a2
Voided – **26-**2b1c
Volcanic Eruptions – **48-**4c2
Vomit – **40-**2b4e
Vow(s)(Pledge) – **1-**2c6
Voyage to Rome – **21-**4b17

W

Waged War – **49-**4d4a3a4
Waits – **41-**2c3b
Waiting – **9-**3a2e
Walk in the Light – **41-**1a2
Walk in the Spirit – **27-**2c1c
Walk in the Truth of God's Word – **42-**2a1
Walk as Children of Light – **27-**3b4
Walk in Wisdom – **27-**3b5
Walking in Love – **27-**3b3
Walking in the Love of God – **42-**2a
Walking in Unity – **27-**3a1
Walking Loving One Another – **42-**2a2
Walks – **3-**4b2; **6-**2c8;5a8b; **16-**3a14
Wall – **54-**4i4a10a-c
Wall of City Had Twelve Foundation Stones – **54-**4i4a8
Wall Made of Jasper – **54-**4i4a10c
Wall Was 216 Feet Thick (Human Measure) – **54-**4i4a10b
Wall Was 1400 Miles In Length, Width & Height – **54-**4i4a10a
Walls & the Gates – **54-**4i4a9
Walls Were Broad & High – **54-**4i4a5
Wandered – **40-**2b3c6
Want – **20-**3c11
War – **25-**3d1; **49-**4d3a5a;4d4a3a4; **51-**4g2a2
War Against Christ – **52-**4g3b1
War in Heaven – **49-**4d2a
Warn Each Other Everyday – **34-**1b2d2
Warn the Unruly – **30-**4a5b
Warned – **6-**2c15
Warning – **3-**4d9-11; **6-**2d4b; **11-**4a10;4b4; **11-**4b4-6; **34-**1b2d6; **54-**4i11
Warning Against False Doctrine – **31-**2a1
Warning Against Idleness – **31-**3b2
Warning Ignored – **21-**4b18
Warns – **3-**4c2; **4-**5c5; **11-**4b1-3
Was Dead – **44-**2a3a3
Was Healed – **49-**4d4a2b
Was Opened – **53-**4h4a3
Washes – **17-**4a1
Watch or I Will Come – **46-**3a5a2c1c
Watch Out – 3b3d; **42-**3a
Watchful – **4-**6a5; **13-**5a3g8; **46-**3a5a2a
Watchfulness for the *LORD* – 30-**4a**
Water – **6-**2c8; **15-**3a4d1,2; **16-**3b4; **40-**2b3c7
Water of Life – **53-**4i2a
Waters – **44-**2a2b1d; **49-**4a3a4
Waters Struck – **48-**4c3
Waters Turn to Blood – **51-**4e4
Water to Wine – **15-**2c1
Wave – **13-**5a1a2
Way – **5-**1a1; **8-**1b1d; **9-**1c3; **14-**2a1; **30-**3a3
Way (Jesus) – **17-**4a4
Ways – **11-**4a12b; **40-**2b1b

Ways of the World – **41**-1a6
We Call God a Liar – **41**-1a3d1
We Claim –**41**-1a3d
We Come to Trust God – **39**-2b1k
We Confess Our Sins – **41**-1a3c
We Fool Ourselves – **41**-1a3a
We Have Heard – **41**-1a1
We Have No Sin – **41**-1a3a
We Have Not Sinned – **41**-1a3d
We Must Obey God – **38**-2a1b
We Refuse to Accept the Truth – **41**-1a3b
We See – **41**-1a6a3
We Should Run With Endurance – **36**-3b1a2
We Sin – **41**-1a3e
Wealth – **3**-4d14; **6**-2d4e
Weariness – **45**-3a1a5
Wedding – **11**-4b4a
Wednesday – **7**-3a4; **13**-5a4
Week – **4**-6b; **13**-5a
Weep – **9**-3a2c
Welcome – **40**-2a2a2
Welcomed –**16**-3a7
Well – **15**-3a4;3a4c,d
Wells Without Water – **40**-2b3c7
Were Beaten – **35**-3a2b3
Were Broad & High – **54**-4i4a5
Were Cast Alive – **52**-4g3b3
Were Cast Into the Lake of Fire – **53**-4h4a7a
Were Exposed – **35**-3a2b2
Were Killed – **52**-4g3b4
Were Taken – **35**-3a2b6
What Christians Should Do – **29**-#3
"What Does This Babbler Want to Say" – **20**-3c11
What Hinders Us – **36**-3b1a
What Hour – **46**-3a5a2c1d
What Is Good – **30**-4a5i
What Is Right – **33**-1a2d
What Is the Kingdom of God Like – **12**-4b9
What Is Wrong – **33**-1a2d
What Remains – **46**-3a5a2b
What the Holy Spirit Is Saying – **47**-3a6c11
What the Holy Spirit Says – **46**-3a4a2b6;3a5a2c1i
What the *LORD* Says – **47**-3a7b4d
What They Do Not Understand – **40**-2b3a
What We Have Heard – **41**-1a1
What We Need – **39**-2a1a
What You Have – **47**-3a6c5
Wheat – **5**-2a8b; **9**-2c3
When All Possessions Were Taken – **35**-3a2b6
When He (God) Judges – **39**-2b1e
When We Sin – **41**-1a3e
Where Satan's Throne Was – **45**-3a3a1
Where They Dwelled – **45**-3a3a1b
Which Are – **44**-2a3a7;#3; **47**-#4
Which Will Happen – **44**-2a3a8
Which You Have Seen – **44**-#2
While – **33**-1a4
While In Trials – **37**-2a3
White As Wool – **44**-2a2b1a
White Garments – **46**-3a5a2c1f
White Horse – **47**-4b1
White Horses – **52**-4g2a8
White Stone – **45**-3a3c2b
White Throne Judgment – **53**-4h4
Who – **1**-2b1b,d;2b2; **3**-4b3; **6**-2c9; **10**-3a2i; **10**-3c23; **13**-5a5d
Who Abandons the Faith – **35**-3a2f
Who Become Slaves to Sin Again – **40**-2b4d
Who Belong to the World – **50**-4d5b2,4
Who Can Fight Against Anti-Christ – **49**-4d4a2e2
Who Do His Commandments – **54**-4i9
Who Die Beginning at That Time – **51**-4d7c6
Who Disobeys God Will Fall – **34**-1b4a
Who Has an Ear – **50**-4d4a3a8
Who Has the Key of David – **46**-3a6a3
Who Has the Seven Spirits of God – **46**-3a5a
Who Hold To – **45**-3a3b1,2
Who Is Holy – **46**-3a6a1
Who Is True – **46**-3a6a2
Who Keep God's Commandments – **49**-4d3a5b
Who Lives – **44**-2a3a3
Who Made All Things – **50**-4d7a5
Who Opens – **46**-3a6a4
Who Overcomes – **45**-3a3c2
Who Practice Witchcraft or Magic Arts (Sorcerers, Witches, Magicians) – **53**-4i2d6
Who Rebelled – **34**-1b2d7
Who Speaks – **36**-3b5
Who Truly Believes Enters – **34**-1b3b
Who Turned Away from God (Backsliders) – **53**-4i2d1
Whole Armor of God – **28**-3d
Wicked – **4**-5b2; **13**-5a3b; **41**-2c3d
Widow – **24**-4a3
Widows – **31**-2d2,3
Widow's Mite – **13**-5a3f
Widow's Son – **10**-3c2
Wife of the *LAMB* – **53**-4i3
Wilderness – **1**-1a8a; **5**-1a3; **8**-1b4e;1c7; **49**-4d1b3c1
Will (Verb) – **17**-4a3;4a9b
Will Be Clothed – **46**-3a5a2c1f
Will Be His God – **53**-4i2c
Will Be Killed – **50**-4d4a3a10
Will Be Left – **36**-3b5c
Will Be There – **53**-4i1c4
Will Confess Him – **46**-3a5a2c1h
Will Come – **41**-2c2a; **46**-3a5a2c1c
Will Disappear – **41**-2c2c
Will Dwell with Them – **53**-4i1ac2
Will Eat From – **45**-3a1c2
Will Encounter – **51**-4d7c1
Will Fall – **34**-1b4a
Will Fight Against Them – **45**-3a3c1
Will Follow – **40**-2b1b
Will Give Him – **46**-3a4a2b5
Will Judge – **37**-3b6e3
Will Make Those – **47**-3a6b6
Will Not Enter His Rest – **34**-1b2c
Will Not Know – **46**-3a5a2c1d

Will Not Tarry – **35**-3a2e
Will Pass Away – **41**-2c2b
Will Rule – **46**-3a4a2b4; **52**-4g2a10
Will Shake – **36**-3b5b
Will Test Those – **47**-3a6c3
Will Write on Him – **47**-3a6c8-10
Wine – **15**-2c1
Winepress of the Fierceness – **52**-4g2a11
Wisdom – **23**-2b1-2; **24**-2c2a; **27**-2a2;3b5; **37**-2a1a2; **38**-2b5
Wiped Away – **53**-4i1c5
Witchcraft or Magic Arts (Sorcerers, Witches, Magicians) – **53**-4i2d6
Witches – **53**-4i2d6
With – **17**-3c9; **40**-2b3c1
With Anti-Christ & False Prophet – **52**-4h3e
With a Flood – **49**-4d3a3
With All – **30**-4a5b
With an Iron Rod – **52**-4g2a10
With Angels – **49**-4d2a1c
With Anger – **49**-4d3a5
With Christ – **40**-2a1a8; **52**-4h2
With Christ 1000 Years – **52**-4h2a1d
With Corruptible Things – **39**-2b1h
With Deceivers – **42**-#3
With Endurance – **36**-3b1a2
With God – **43**-2b2
With Iron Rod – **46**-3a4a2b4
With Me (Jesus) – **54**-4i8
With Men – **53**-4i1c1
With the Sun – **48**-4d1a1
With the Sword – **45**-3a3c1
With Them – **53**-4i1ac2,3
With Those in Jail – **35**-3a2b5
Within the Church – **23**-#2; **24**-3a
Without – **17**-3c9; **40**-2b3c7
Without Ceasing – **30**-5a5e
Without Fault – **50**-4d6a7
Without His Mark – **50**-4d5b9
Without Works – **38**-2b3
Witness to Jesus – **52**-4h2a1a
Witness to the Light – **14**-1a3
Witness (Jesus) – **47**-3a7a1b
Witnesses – **19**-2a4; **48**-4c9-11
Witnesses Killed – **48**-4c10
Witnesses Resurrected – **48**-4c11
Wives – **27**-3c1a,b; **39**-3a4
Woe – **9**-3a2f; **10**-3a2g-l; **12**-4b19a
Wool – **44**-2a2b1a
Woman – **10**-3c4; **11**-4b8; **15**-3a4;3a4d; **16**-3b8; **48**-4d1a;4d1b2b; **49**-4d1b3;4d1b3c
Woman's – **3**-4b5; **10**-3c11
Women – **5**-6c2; **10**-3c5; **14**-5a8a1-3; **24**-4c1; **31**-2b2
Wonderful – **39**-2a1a2
Wonderful Joy – **38**-2a2a
Wonders – **18**-1b10; **33**-1a3b
Word (God's) – **20**-4a; **38**-2b1; **40**-2a2a; **41**-1a3d2; **42**-2a1
Word of God – **28**-3d1f; **34**-1b4b; **35**-3a3d
"WORD of God" – **52**-4g2a7
Word of Their Testimony – **49**-4d2a2c2
Word of Warning – **54**-4i11
Words – **14**-2a1b; **23**-7a6; **42**-#4; **43**-#4; **47**-3a6b4; **50**-4d6a5
Words of Caution – **45**-3a1c;3a3c
Words of Correction – **45**-3a1b
Work – **13**-5a2,3
Worker – **32**-2b4
Workers of Satan – **26**-3d5
Workplace – **29**-3a3
Works – **38**-2b3; **44**-3a1a1; **45**-3a2a1a;3a3a1a;3a4a1; **46**-3a5a1; **47**-3a6b1;3a7b1
Works from the Unbelieving Dead – **53**-4h4a4
Work of Jesus Christ – **34**-#2
Works Not Perfect Before God – **46**-3a5a2c
World – **14**-#2; **16**-3b9; **17**-4a9b; **20**-3c9; **33**-1a4a; **37**-3b7e; **39**-2b1j;3a;3a1; **40**-2b2a2; **41**-1a6; **42**-2b1; **50**-4d5b2,4,5
World Followed – **49**-4d4a2d
World Marveled – **49**-4d4a2c
World System – **41**-1a6a
World Worshipped Satan – **49**-4d4a2e
Worlds – **35**-3a3d
World's Sin – **17**-4a9b1
Worldly People – **50**-4d4a3a6
Worldly Wisdom – **23**-2b1
Worms – **19**-2b6
Worry – **11**-4b3
Worrying – **2**-2d5
Worse Off – **40**-2b4d
Worship – **1**-1a8c; **3**-4d17; **24**-4c;4c9; **47**-3a6b6
Worship Anti-Christ – **50**-4d5b2
Worshiped False Idols as God – **53**-4i2d7
Worshiped Satan – **49**-4d4a2e
Worshiped the Anti-Christ – **52**-4h2a1b
Worshiped the Beast – **50**-4d4a3a6
Worshipers – **15**-3a4d4
Worship God – **36**-3b5d
Worship Him (Jesus) – **33**-1a2b; **50**-4d7a5
Worthy – **30**-2a3; **46**-3a5a2c1e; **47**-4a3
Would Be – **10**-3c22; **13**-5a5d
Wound – **49**-4d4a2b
Wounded – **49**-4d4a2a
Wrath – **51**-4d7c1-3;4d9
Wrath of God – **21**-2a1
Wrath Poured Out Undiluted – **51**-4d7c2
Write on Him – **47**-3a6c8-10
Write Things You Have Seen – **44**-2a3a6
Written on Forehead – **50**-4d6a1
Written on Stones – **54**-4i4a8
Writer of this Gospel – **18**-4c10
Writing – **8**-1a; **18**-4c5
Writing the Gospels – **18**-4c5
Wrong – **11**-4b6b; **33**-1a2d
Wrong Teaching – **6**-2c15

X

Y

Years – **49-**4d3a2; **52-**4h1,2;4h2a1d;4h2a2a,d;4h2a3 a;4h3a
Yeast – **12-**4b9b
Yellow – **48-**4c6c1
Yeshua – **14-**2a
Yesterday – **37-**3b7b
Younger Widows – **31-**2d3
You – **1-**2b1i; **9-**3a2e; **10-**3g,l; **10-**3c23; **26-**1a1; **30-**4a5a; **38-**2a2b3;2a2bc;2b1d; **41-**1a6a;1a6a1;1a8
You Are A Chosen Generation – **39-**2b4
"You Are My Son" – **33-**1a2a
You Can Be Too Late for Repentance – **36-**3b3f
You Have – **47-**3a6c5
You Have Come – **36-**3b4b-f
You Have Kept Command – **47-**3a6c1
You Have Received & Heard – **46-**3a5a2c1a
You Have Seen – **44-**#2;2a3a6
You Helped Others Suffering – **35-**3a2b4
You Obey God – **36-**3b5a
You Remained Faithful – **35-**3a2b1
You Suffered with Those in Jail – **35-**3a2b5
You Were Beaten – **35-**3a2b3
You Were Exposed to Ridicule – **35-**3a2b2
You Were Not Redeemed – **39-**2b1h
You Will Not Know – **46-**3a5a2c1d
You Will Become Fruitful – **39-**2a1a5f
Your – **10-**3b1a; **23-**6a5; **27-**3c1a-d; **34-**1b2a,b
Your Actions – **39-**2b1f
Your Confession – **35-**3a1
Your Crown – **47-**3a6c6
Your Employers – **27-**3c1d
Your Eyes – **36-**3b1a3
Your Faith – **38-**2a2b
Your Husbands – **27-**3c1a
Your Life with God – **43-**2b2
Your Marriage – **37-**3b6e
Your Own Business – **30-**4a2
Your Leaders – **37-**3b7a
Your Neighbor – **23-**6a5
Your Parents – **27-**3c1c
Your Salvation – **39-**2b3b
Your Spiritual Leaders – **37-**3b7f
Your Spiritual Vitality – **36-**3b3
Your Wives – **27-**3c1b
Your Works – **47-**3a7a1
Yourself – **23-**6a3; **31-**2c3
Yourselves – **26-**3d11

Z

Zacchaeus – **12-**4b27
Zechariah – **8-**1b1;1b1b,e;1b4c-d
Zeal – **45-**3a1b1

Printed in the United States
By Bookmasters